Anatole Abragam

Time Reversal
An Autobiography

ANATOLE ABRAGAM

CLARENDON PRESS · OXFORD
1989

Oxford University Press, Walton Street, Oxford OX2 6DP
Oxford New York Toronto
Delhi Bombay Calcutta Madras Karachi
Petaling Jaya Singapore Hong Kong Tokyo
Nairobi Dar es Salaam Cape Town
Melbourne Auckland
and associated companies in
Berlin Ibadan

Oxford is a trade mark of Oxford University Press

Published in the United States
by Oxford University Press, New York

British Library Cataloguing in Publication Data
Abragam, A. (Anatole), 1914–
Time reversal.
1. Physics. Biographies
I. Title
530'.0924
ISBN 0–19–853926–6

Library of Congress Cataloging in Publication Data
Abragam, A.
Time reversal, an autobiography.
Translation of: De la physique avant toute chose.
1. Abragam, A. 2. Physicists—Biography.
3. Physicists—France—Biography. I. Title.
QC16.A29A3 1989 530'.092'4 [B] 88–33013
ISBN 0–19–853926–6

Set by CentraCet, Cambridge
Printed in Great Britain by
Bookcraft Ltd.
Midsomer Norton, Bath

Preface

I hasten to laugh at everything . . .
Beaumarchais

Gallicisms will stay dear to me
Pushkin

This book is an autobiography which has appeared in French with the title *De la physique avant toute chose*. My reasons for writing it are given in the Introduction. An additional encouragement was provided by the illustrious British physicist, Sir Nevill Mott, who said about one of my former books (*Réflexions d'un Physicien*): "His French is a joy to read". Will some illustrious Frenchman say it about my English?

Beside circumstances of my life, one will find here portraits of physicists I have known and numerous anecdotes about them. One will also find, marked with an asterisk, some passages about physics, mine and that of others, that I tried to make accessible to as many as possible. Two asterisks mark those passages where I believe I have reached, although not exceeded, the limits of what can be explained without figures and formulae.

In recounting in this book, facts, ideas, and anecdotes from my past, I have, with very few exceptions, relied on my memory alone. It used to be fairly good but must, like the rest of me, have deteriorated with age. Therefore I beg of my fellow physicists not to take the index at the end for the Citation Index and not to limit their perusal of the book to the looking up of their own entry.

I would like to thank my Oxford friends Brebis Bleaney, John Griffith, and Nicholas Kurti for making the chapters dealing with Oxford palatable to the Oxonian community (at least I hope so). Nicholas most of all for his very conscientious and thorough weeding out of the most shocking blunders.

A special mention is due to my old friend Lydia Cassin whose constant interest, pertinent suggestions, and assistance with both the French and English version are gratefully acknowledged.

Paris   A.A.
January 1989

Contents

The plates fall between pp 200 and 201

Introduction	1

I A RUSSIAN CHILDHOOD

A Russian childhood	4

II FRANCE, CHILDHOOD, ADOLESCENCE, YOUTH

Mademoiselle Bertin	23
Les Cinq Glorieuses	28
A false start	35
Masters and examinations	41
In search of research	49

II MAN'S ESTATE

Armageddon, or the gaieties of the squadron	69
The verdigris years	79
Second service	96
The Three Musketeers	101
Physicists' stories	115
A year of transition	121
Oxford	127
Between Oxford and Cambridge	147
America, America!	156
Accelerators and resonances	170
Nuclear magnetism and I	186
Looking back	201
Going up	212
Collège de France	220
Director of Physics	248

Nuclear magnetic order   267
East and West   294
The groves of Academe   342

Epilogue   363

Index   364

Introduction

Even false modesty is a very good thing
Jules Renard

I am going to tell a few stories here, some from my own life and some which are just stories. Why? Who could they interest? Myself, I would like to think, but nothing could be further from the truth. Whenever I find it difficult to fall asleep (more and more often, unfortunately) and I try to call to mind some incident from my past to kill the time, the result is always disappointing: boring, but, alas, never enough to put me to sleep. Besides sleeping pills, the only remedy which works sometimes is to recite to myself passages from *Eugene Onegin* a poem by Pushkin, which is over five thousand lines long, and which I forced myself to memorize, under circumstances that I shall perhaps recount.

In fact, this narrative, is 'motivated', as they say nowadays, by several things.

The first, and the most urgently 'motivating', is access to the 'Instrument of Liberation' known as a word-processor. In a film by Frank Capra in the thirties, a housewife became a writer because a few years earlier a typewriter had been delivered to her house by mistake.

A second reason for this preposterous venture: some of the little stories that I would like to tell have in the past amused my friends, the faithful 'auditeurs' of my lectures at the Collège de France, and my young coworkers. At least they made me believe so by laughing heartily. Alas, they have ended up knowing them all. When I was carrying the exalted duties of Director of Physics at the Commisssariat à l'Energie Atomique, I had as administrative assistant a young man of great charm and diplomacy, named Jean Pellerin. Whenever I asked him: 'Monsieur Pellerin, had you heard that story before?', he answered with an enchanting smile 'Not completely, Monsieur'.

A new audience then? Is that what I am looking for? Perhaps. I have been told that in riding-schools, beginners cannot help sliding little by little toward the crupper of the horse, and that one of the novices, reaching in spite of his efforts the tail of the animal cried out to the instructor: 'Could I have another horse, this one is finished?'

Another horse then to replace the one that is finished? Let us be a little circumspect about it. Monsieur André François-Poncet, who represented France in Berlin before the last war with great lucidity, used, so I am told, to gather his immediate coworkers for a briefing every morning and to comment on the events of the previous day in front of them with all the finesse and wit of a great professional diplomat. His listeners never failed to appreciate the true value of the Ambassador's wit. Yet one morning one of his younger colleagues, among the most appreciative of the master's humour, remains ice-cold. 'Well, Dutheillet de la Mothe!' (I do not know where I heard that name but it seems to me highly suitable for a young Secretary of an Embassy of the Republic), exclaims the Ambassador, accustomed to greater receptivity, 'don't you see the point?' 'I do indeed, Sir, but I am being transferred to Copenhagen.'

Would a new public laugh as heartily as my young coworkers, carried by their affection for me? Maybe not! Not just *any* horse will do then!

No, my true reason lies elsewhere. Admiral Strauss (far more Strauss than admiral if truth be told) who presided in the fifties over the destinies of the American Atomic Energy Commission and who counts among his claims to fame the disgrace of Robert Oppenheimer, used to say that one should never 'declassify', that is bring into the open, a 'classified' document, that has hitherto been kept secret. 'Once declassified', he used to say with great pertinence, 'it cannot be reclassified again.' What guides me today is a feeling, in some way symmetrical to the one which moved the good admiral. Let me explain.

I have passed what the Bible calls *three score years and ten*, the age assigned to Adam, and as for those referred to in these stories, as Pushkin says: 'Some are no more and others are far away'. What I will not tell today will never be told by anyone. Like our admiral I am moved by a feeling of the irreversible, of the irreparable.

It is better to say straight away that *my* declassification, just like that advocated by the good admiral, will be prudent and even reticent. My old Judeo-Christian self (more Judeo than Christian, my last point in common with our admiral), will see to it. But it will leave me free to chat, to ramble back and forth across the chronology, to change the subject when the mood takes me. Jean-Luc Godard, the film director, was once asked by a journalist: 'But don't you agree that every film should have a beginning, a middle, and an end?' 'Oh yes', said Godard, 'but not necessarily in that order.'

And now cut the cackle and come to business.

I

A RUSSIAN CHILDHOOD

A Russian childhood

Ce vice impuni, la lecture

The parents—The hero—The books—The school

I spent the first ten years of my life in Moscow, the city of the *forty times forty churches*. It must be said however that after 1918 the new masters of Russia did not do things by halves in reducing this exorbitant square to a value more compatible with their principles and with the requirements of modernity. It is not generally known that in the late twenties there were plans to knock down Saint Basil's Church, the jewel of the Red Square, destined later to become a 'must' for the Intourist flocks in order to ease the flow of the motor vehicles that the Socialist State would not fail to equip itself with. The Socialist State *was* looking far ahead . . . At any rate, in June 1925, when a horse-drawn cab took us to the railway station where my western fate was awaiting me, I can assert that no congestion of motorcars slowed down our course. I was shedding bitter tears, not at the idea of leaving my fatherland, but because I had been refused permission to ride to the station in one of the first buses which were beginning to run in Moscow and on which I had not yet ridden. The fact that part of the family, including my sister, went to the station by bus because there was no room for all of us in the cab, did nothing to soothe my feelings. Our slow progress was further hindered by our cabby's insistence on taking off his bonnet and crossing himself at the sight of every church, of which there were still quite a few left, that we encountered on our way. My vexation at the thought of my sister riding regally in her bus, my annoyance at seeing the bald pate of the coachman each time he crossed himself, and above all my fear, that fear which still haunts me whenever I travel, of missing the train through his fault—such were my feelings at the time of leaving my native country.

As to the journey itself, my memories are blurred. I remember only that we were travelling 'hard class', that is on wooden seats, that our main occupation was to unpack or repack all our viands and to consume them, and, while we were still in Russia, to run to the station buffet with a large kettle whenever we stopped, to get some *kipyatok* or boiling water for our tea. We had with us our pillows and our quilts and so must have had the possibility of lying down on the benches. Our journey involved three stages: Moscow–Riga (capital of the then independent Latvia), Riga–Berlin, Berlin–Paris. I remember my curiosity at the sight of the policemen's headgear: Latvian, Lithuanian, (we had crossed Lithuania without stopping), then German and French, all so different from the pointed cloth helmets of the Red Guards to which I was accustomed. We did not go through Poland. My parents had spoken a lot of the 'Polish Corridor' and I am ashamed to admit now that in my mind the 'Polish Corridor' was that of the first railway carriage with a corridor that I saw on leaving Riga.

We stayed two weeks in Riga with my aunt Tatyana, a sister of my father (butchered by the Germans in 1941), and two weeks in Berlin where we were met by a brother of my father, my uncle Joseph or, as he preferred to be called, Joe, for he was a British citizen of long standing. In Berlin we were waiting for a French visa for the three of us: my mother, my sister, two years older than I, and myself, before proceeding to Paris. My father was supposed to join us in a few months; I shall tell later what became of him. Meanwhile let us return to Moscow and to my parents.

My father was a small manufacturer whose plant made buttons; my mother was a doctor. I honestly believe that each of them, in their own way, for they were very different from each other, was an interesting person.

My father had created his small business himself, and it employed some twenty people. He had no university degree of any kind but he had great respect for culture. The most tangible evidence of this respect was the incredible quantity of books that filled our apartment. I do not think that my father had been a great reader himself for he was very busy and preferred to spend his rare moments of leisure with his family, brothers and sisters, cousins, or just friends, chatting around the table adorned by the traditional samovar; but he had a religious respect for books. Besides complete works of all the great Russian writers (my father bought complete works only), his library contained translations of many classics of foreign literature. Among those I remember: Goethe, Schiller, Heine, Byron, Shakespeare in two or three editions, Dante's 'Divine Comedy' (where the illustrations of the Inferno so frightened me), and in a minor vein: Dickens, Fenimore Cooper, Jules Verne, Mayne Reid etc. To these one should add a large number of encyclopaedias. Some evenings, I remember him sitting down to a large volume from one of his encyclopaedias with the laudable aim of improving his culture. More often than not, he was interrupted in his reading by some more or less urgent task.

Besides his talents as a manufacturer, he had three great qualities that I have always admired: a physical courage verging on temerity, remarkable manual skill, and great generosity; he owed to these three qualities the respect and affection of the workers and employees of his firm, where he spent the greater part of his time. His little factory was within walking distance of our house and I liked to go there from time to time. It was pervaded by the smell of machine oil and even today whenever I smell it

(Proust's madeleine, here we are!) I can see again the presses driven by large belts, making innumerable round holes in large metal sheets, and the flow of small metal disks falling into large buckets. I never left without a provision of those in my pockets. I remember the old foreman, Sergey Romanovich, with his grey walrus moustache, always engaged in a hushed discussion with my father. He came sometimes to our house and I can still see him, emptying in a gulp the glass of vodka which was always offered to him, and taking a sniff at a crust of black bread as a chaser.

I must admit that I never understood what the status of my father's enterprise was under the regime called NEP or New Economic Policy, which had replaced around 1922 what was then known as war communism. Was he the owner or the manager? As a child I never asked myself the question and there is no one to answer it now.

My mother was a very different person from my father and, I think, quite a remarkable one. Born in a small town in Bielorussia, she refused to tread the path marked for her by the family: to marry an honest tradesman and to assist him in his business. A gentle and respectful daughter, she was the opposite of a rebel, but on decisions she considered important she was steadfast. This was already apparent in the way she arranged her secondary education. With the assistance of the wife of the pope, or Orthodox priest, who plied his trade in that small town (the pope's wife is called *popadya*) she undertook to prepare, as what was then called an 'external' candidate, that is one who did not attend a secondary school regularly, the 'Attestation of Maturity', testifying to a successful completion of secondary studies.

From the pope, a *Grand* Russian who had strayed to Bielorussia, and from his *popadya* (who seems to have been a remarkable woman in her own right) she received the marvellous gift of the Russian language in all its purity and beauty. It was not quite, one must admit, the language spoken in the family of my grand-parents on my mother's side, and her dealings with the pope and the *popadya* had the smell of brimstone. The Russian language was my mother's most beautiful gift to me in my childhood and during the years of 'exile'.

Once her 'maturity' was duly 'attested', she wanted to go to university, something that was practically impossible for a woman in Russia before 1900. And that is how my mother, who had hardly ever ventured outside the confines of her little native town, embarked (figuratively speaking) for Switzerland in order to study medicine at the University of Bern. She was not yet twenty when she launched herself in that venture, and if my grand-parents resigned themselves to it in the end it was in the hope that she would be quickly discouraged and would come back home to get married.

She did come back home to get married, but eight years later, after passing her thesis examination in Bern and practising for two years in a hospital in Berlin. She was fond of telling how she covered herself with glory during a second stay in a Berlin hospital after practising for some time in Russia. During the daily visit of the professor, a patient who had come from Russia was produced, whose complaint no one, including the *Herr Professor*, could identify. My mother easily recognized an infection, which, I believe, is called the 'Siberian Ulcer' in Russia, of which she had seen several cases but which was unknown in aseptic Germany.

She practised medicine till the beginning of the First World War, when my parents came to Moscow with my elder brother (who died in 1922) and my sister (I was not born yet although expected). She took it up again in 1918 as a military doctor in the Red Army. There was a terrible winter when we survived thanks to the supplementary rations she received in that capacity.

She liked to tell me about her time in Bern, when she shared a tiny flat with two other Russian student girls, and where she seems to have fed mainly on bread, butter, salami, and tea for six years. Bern was then, almost as much as Geneva, filled with revolutionaries of all kinds, who did their best to mould the revolutionary conscience of the numerous students who had come from Russia. Thus my mother had many opportunities to hear talks given by gurus of marxism like Plekhanov, Lenin and Trotsky. She knew Zinoviev well, that other star of Russian communism, who was shot by Stalin after the Moscow trials of the thirties. He was about the same age as my mother. I had an uncle on my father's side named Raphael, a great admirer of Zinoviev. This Raphael had emigrated to America before the 1914 war but came back in 1918, persuaded that the Revolution needed him. Since then he had never stopped 'biting his elbow' (the Russian equivalent of kicking himself) but he had kept his admiration for Zinoviev. I remember heated discussions between him and my mother about his hero. (He lived very near to us and came so frequently that my mother once asked him: 'why do you leave so often?'.) Whenever he announced 'Zinoviev made another thundering speech today' my mother quietly replied: 'Your Zinoviev is a moron' and my poor uncle shouted: 'Zinoviev's greatest misfortune is that you knew him in Bern!'

About her medical studies in Bern, her favourite story, but which for obvious reasons she told me only years later, was the following: the professor in charge of the course on venereal diseases, a fat Swiss German began his first lecture in these terms: '*Meine Damen und Herren, wer vor uns hat nicht einmal einen kleinen Tripper gehabt?*' (Ladies and gentlemen, who among us has never once had a tiny gonorrhoea?)

It sounds silly, but it is only recently that I have realized that my mother had been beautiful. The few photographs from her youth in my possession leave no doubt about it. She had slightly prominent cheekbones, a small slant to her eyes, a tiny upturned nose, dazzling teeth, and magnificent black hair. On all the family photographs, next to my father, in the midst of aunts and cousins, she seems a stranger come from a remote country. What great-grandmother had the primrose path of dalliance trod?

In Moscow we lived in a district called Zamoskvorechiye which means 'beyond the Moskva river', that is in relation to the Kremlin, in a small street with a name too long to be transcribed here. Our house was a two-storey stone building. I think it must have been good-looking in its prime, but even in my childhood it was considerably dilapidated. I saw it again for the first time in 1956 at the time of my first return to Russia, and then in 1961, each time more run down. It was torn down with the whole district in the late sixties. Behind the house there was a yard, separated from the street by a large iron gate, where stood two other houses similar to ours. The yard, vast in my memories, had shrunk considerably in 1961. It had always been full of kids, boys and girls. In the middle of it stood a tall wild cherry tree, a challenge for the boldest to climb, which too had shrunk considerably in my mind's eye over thirty-five years.

I believe that at the beginning, that is before the revolution of 1917, the whole house had belonged to us, but after that date we were only tenants, in a space which also kept shrinking over the years, but not in my mind's eye. At first we gave up the ground floor, and then room after room on the first floor, as new lodgers were brought in. This operation was called; *uplotneniye*, literally 'increase in density'. At a certain time we had three 'invalids', soldiers discharged after having been wounded, installed in our kitchen. One of them, Aleksey, was an invalid of the 'imperialistic', that is the war against Germany; the second, Stepan from the 'civil', the war against the White army; (the third has left no trace in my memory). They were colourful personalities with whom I hit it off immediately; I cele-brated their arrival in a quatrain that my father typed up for posterity and of which two verses only remain in my memory: 'Arrived three invalids, they look like three intrepids' (imperfect translation from the Russian). In spite of their evident willingness to chop wood or shovel snow, I think I was the only one to lament their departure when after some time (weeks, months?) they disappeared as suddenly as they had arrived. I must have been six or seven at the time.

The other lodgers of the first floor, 'intellectuals', a dentist and an accountant, were far less interesting. I shall say a few words about the dwellers on the ground floor a little later. In 1925, when my mother, my sister and I left Russia, our apartment was composed of four rooms: the bedroom (of the parents), the children's room where our maid also slept, the dining room and a room called *salon* or *cabinet* and which in fact was the library where all our books were crammed. (I remember my amazement when around my seventh or eighth year, I read in a novel the description of a lodging with three bedrooms. 'They are mad' I thought, 'Do they sleep each night in a different bed?')

The bathroom was shared by the inhabitants of the first floor. Taking a bath was a large scale operation that had to be planned in advance like moving house. The hot water was produced in a vast vertical cylinder of red copper called the 'column' under which a wood fire had to be started at least two hours before the bath, or rather the baths, for it was out of the question to waste hot water that cost such efforts. For the heating we had two large Dutch stoves with white wall tiles, against which I loved to warm myself. On the whole, considering what was rapidly becoming the Soviet standard of comfort, we were rather well housed.

And I, what was I? Rather small, with a health, which, looking back, I believe to have been much less fragile than was admitted in the family. Apart from a few digestive troubles, whose gravity my poor mother, who had lost my elder brother through an appendicitis diagnosed too late, was inclined to exaggerate, and which occasionally earned me a diet based on lumpy semolina cooked in water, which makes me shudder even today, I was reasonably well and was growing up (slowly) without special problems. I was not very keen on physical exercise (I never skated and did not cycle before coming to France), and like Panurge 'had a natural aversion to blows'. To be fair, it must be said that being very advanced in school for my age and, what is more, rather small, I was surrounded with children much bigger than I, which explains, at least in part, my tendency to keep away from fights. In fact when I had an opponent of my size I faced up, but this seldom happened.

There was at least one boy, smaller and weaker than myself, whom I treated with patronizing contempt and who was my usual companion. He shared the Christian name Kolka with a good many boys in our yard and he lived on our ground floor. His main attraction for me resided in the marvellous collection of toys of which he was the happy owner, and with which he let me play when his parents were away. The origins of this abundance of toys gave rise to various comments in the yard: the generally accepted explanation was that his father, a telephone repairman by trade, had free access to toy shops and took advantage of it to help himself. Why he was operating especially in toy shops was not clear. In any case he was an unpleasant fellow, although less so than his wife, a fat slut whom he beat whenever he was drunk, which happened at least once a week. In contrast to the bourgeois inhabitants of the first floor he was an authentic representative of the proletarian class and, whenever drunk, liked to mention the desirability of slitting the bellies of all the bourgeois or, to pronounce it *à la russe*, 'the boorjuy'. He made an exception for my parents whom he always treated with respect: my father because he recognized in him a 'manual worker' like himself and appreciated his courage and physical strength; my mother because she was an ever-available doctor, but also, as I realize only today, because he was far from indifferent to her beauty. This interpretation is confirmed by his wife's hatred for my mother.

Kolka was the most perverted boy I ever met. Protected by an impenetrable armour of innocence, not to say stupidity, it was only in my adolescence that I finally understood some of the horrors he had been telling me; there was no risk of my asking for an explanation: it would have meant losing face in front of someone I considered an inferior in age, physical strength, and intelligence.

Apart from Kolka, when I was not in school I was alone most of the time, but not altogether alone. I had my early favourite companions, books.

Like many people, I do not remember when and how I learned to read. I have one reference point, though: the arrival from Leningrad of the family of the aforementioned uncle Raphael with a newborn baby, my cousin Simon. I remember very well that I was reading a fairy tale story by the brothers Grimm, when they arrived, coming straight from the station. Since Simon is four years younger than I, here is a well established point of chronology: I could read fluently at four. My mother claimed that I knew the alphabet at two and had taught myself to read before I was three, but a mother's testimony is sometimes unreliable. It is certain that from the moment I could read, the world changed. I did not depend on others to read or tell me stories; I had become my own master.

What was I reading then? Well, everything! The Russian classics to begin with, at least their prose, as poetry was then for me something one learned by heart. Before I was ten I had read the whole prose of Pushkin, Lermontov and Gogol. I have no doubts about it because, having undertaken to reread them systematically at thirteen, I discovered that I had read everything and remembered everything. Of Tolstoy I had naturally read *Childhood, Adolescence, Youth*, but also *War and Peace* in spite of my annoyance at the interminable French dialogues, and *Anna Karenina*; of Turgenev: *Tales of a Hunter* and *Fathers and Sons*. I had read *Oblomov* by Goncharov and *Crime and Punishment* by Dostoevsky (yes I had), and plenty of other novelists of the nineteenth century whom only Slavists know in the West: Leskov, Pisemski, Grigorovich, Saltykov-Shchedrin, and my favourite, Aleksey Tolstoy, not the Soviet novelist but the playwright and novelist of the last century, implacable portrayer of the crimes of Ivan the Terrible, and my first guide to Russian History. As a child I had never been tempted to read Chekhov; I am glad of it: reading it then would have spoilt him for me. Among translations, apart from children's books such as Jules Verne, Mayne Reid and my favourite, Fenimore Cooper, I liked Alexandre Dumas. After devouring his *Joseph Balsamo*, Louis Quinze, La Pompadour, La du Barry, the Duke of Choiseul and the Chancellor Maupeou held no secrets for me; nor did Sherlock Holmes, Conan Doyle's immortal hero, although he raised problems that I shall mention a little later.

But above all there was Shakespeare, of whom we had two or three

Russian translations. I did not become strongly attached to Hamlet because I could not fathom whether he was mad or only feigned to be (it seems that I was not the only one). But *Othello, Macbeth, the Merchant of Venice* (because of Shylock?), and some historical plays, the two parts of *Henry IV* and *Richard III*, enchanted me. Later the French translations including André Gide's highly praised *Hamlet* repelled me, and it was only in my late thirties that my English had sufficiently improved to make reading Shakespeare in the original pleasurable. An even greater pleasure is to hear him recited by Shakespearian actors. Bernard Shaw is right when he says that Shakespeare's lines are a music which must be heard. I think that if Tolstoy had had that opportunity he would not have written his long and absurd diatribe against Shakespeare in his pamphlet *What is Art?* (admirably analysed by George Orwell). Over a few years I have built up a collection of cassettes recorded by the best Shakespearian actors, and I enjoy listening to them on a Walkman, while walking in the woods. A music lover of a peculiar kind, I amuse myself by comparing versions by Laurence Olivier, Paul Scofield, and John Gielgud, or Peggy Ashcroft and Claire Bloom.

Did I understand everything I was reading in those days? Yes, in my own way, which is not the generally accepted one. I will give two examples, both again taken from Shakespeare. To me, the great hero, the valiant knight of the chronicles of the kings Henry, well, it was Falstaff, the fat knight. I took at their face value all the declamations of this flamboyant character who dwarfed all his companions, and perhaps I was not so far wrong. The same with 'honest Iago'. More obstinate than Othello, I kept my trust in him to the end, and Desdemona's death appeared to me as a deplorable misunderstanding for which she was the first to blame.

Another word about my reading. I had very strong onomastic prejudices. Before accusing me of pedantry allow me this digression: while a 'young', (forty-five-year-old), professor at the Collège de France, during one of my first meetings ('*assemblées*'), the President ('*Administrateur*') of the Collège de France announced that the Collège de France had received a request to send a representative to a conference on onomastics. I raised my hand: 'I do not mind going if someone explains to me what it is', giving rise among my colleagues to the indignation of the '*littéraires*' and the joy of the '*scientifiques*'. Onomastics, I was told, is the science of proper names. I had violent prejudices about the names of the various characters, or rather about the letters they were made of. Letters like L, M, A, R, F, G, were noble, O, P, K, Sh (a single letter in Russian), B, were ignoble, others neutral. This may have been partly responsible for my liking of Falstaff. Sometimes there was a conflict with my favourite authors who were forcing names I disliked on characters whom I liked. When the character had two names, like Sherlock Holmes, my way out was to consider them as two different persons. To avoid this schizophrenia I used to spin interminable yarns for myself, based or not on my readings, where I tailored names made to measure for my characters. For a long time one of my heroes was called Gar. These stories that I told myself all had one feature in common, which I encountered later among many tellers of adventure stories, Jules Verne most of all. In the midst of hostile and dangerous environments, biting cold, ferocious beasts, bloodthirsty savages, or arrant villains, the heroes of the story always managed to recreate for themselves an atmosphere of comfort and security, which the external dangers and wintry winds made even more delectable, to the extent of appearing their only *raison d'être*.

Another window on the world was an enormous bound collection of various illustrated periodicals, going, I believe, from 1880 to 1910, of which I was an assiduous reader. One of these periodicals, called *News and Mosaics* (whatever the meaning of this title, it was unconnected with the Jewish religion), aimed to entertain and to educate at the same time. There was in particular a division called *Army and Navy*, or something like that, where one could find extensive details on that marvellous invention, the Maxim machine gun, and on the various types of armoured ships, which were called *Monitors*. A special issue had been devoted to Queen Victoria's jubilee: 1837–1897. The links of kinship between the reigning houses of Russia and Britain were retraced in detail, and an impressive picture was given of the progress of British industry and especially of the British navy during these sixty years.

There were also satirical drawings whose captions I did not always understand or rather understood in my own way, since I could not bear not to understand. I remember in particular one drawing where I met for the first time with a problem which was to preoccupy me a lot later in life: time reversal. The drawing, or rather the sequence of drawings, represented an entirely mechanized meat-packing Chicago plant. The customer was bringing in a pig, introduced at one end of the machine, only to come out at the other end as a lot of hams, sausages, and other salamis. What if the customer dislikes the merchandise? No matter! One stuffs all the baked meats into the exit opening, and lo and behold, out comes the porker through the entrance wagging its tail. After giving the matter some thought I deemed the drawings mendacious, the industrialist unscrupulous who made such promises, and the customer downright foolish who let himself be taken in by such tomfooleries.

One thing only disoriented me: the ladies' fashions. The numerous illustrations, including advertisements, showed the ladies wearing gigantic hats, dressed up in skirts and cloaks trailing to the ground, and, most surprising, exhibiting an unnatural hourglass narrowing at the waist. It goes without saying that I was not seeing anything like it around me. It was one of the rare mysteries for which my fertile mind had no explanation to offer.

So much for general culture; what about science? One set of books played a capital role in my awakening to science: the *Children's Encyclopaedia* that I was presented with for my seventh birthday. Translated or rather adapted from English, it must have appeared before the Revolution if I judge by the excellent quality of the paper and also (although my memories on this point are a little shaky), by the old spelling (reformed after the Revolution). There were ten volumes of it, of one hundred and fifty to two hundred pages each, lavishly illustrated and dealing with the whole of natural phenomena, from astronomy to life sciences, and passing through explanations of storms, hail, rainbows, boiling and freezing, the hot air which makes balloons go up, etc. I learned that light takes eight and a half minutes to come to us from the sun and that diseases are propagated by minute beings diversely called microbes or bacilli or bacteria. I tried unsuccessfully to establish in my mind distinctions between these various types of tiny evil creatures. I learned that the healthiest food was cream (understand sweet cream, something I had never seen and whose Russian name, *slivki*, differs from that of the sour cream or *smetana* that I knew very well), followed by butter and then by eggs. It is clear that the authors of my Encyclopaedia had never heard of cholesterol. Although butter and eggs were both rare and dear I hated both cordially, perhaps precisely because, when some were available, they were forced on me. It took me a long time to get used to them. I ended up liking them when, during the German Occupation, they disappeared completely and when, after the end of the war and the return of plenty, they were cursed by the Medical Establishment.

Thanks to my Encyclopaedia I learned why lightning is seen before thunder is heard, how one knows that the Earth is round, and why the Australians, whose heads point downward, do not fall off it. I think that it was there that I received for the first time and digested with some effort the idea that concepts as firmly rooted as 'up' and 'down' could be relative. But the roundness of the Earth only transferred into space the problem of 'world's end' which bothered me sometimes (and which still bothers cosmologists today). I did not always agree with my beloved Encyclopaedia. She was offering an explanation for the sound 'paf' produced by a shot. I found the explanation futile: everybody knows that the sound produced by a shot is 'boom' or possibly 'poom'.

There was a chapter on optical illusions that I found enchanting, and some very simple experiments of 'amusing' physics, which, although I understood their principle perfectly, never seemed to work in my hands. Of one of them I keep bitter memories: the Encyclopaedia had explained that a glass of water, filled to the brim and covered with a piece of paper, could be safely turned over, the atmospheric pressure being more than adequate to overcome the effects of gravity. The simplicity of the experiment and the clarity of the explanation easily convinced me to attempt it, unfortunately over a table of polished mahogany. My father's wrath in the face of the inexplicable failure of the atmospheric pressure in keeping the part assigned to it by the Encyclopaedia, could have put me off physics for the rest of my life. Perhaps from that day dates my distrust of theoretical predictions, which I expressed much later in my maiden lecture at the Collège de France when I spoke of 'the divine surprise of seeing a phenomenon predicted by theory taking place precisely where expected and as expected'.

Another field of science where I felt at ease was mathematics, or rather its humble sister arithmetic. I was very good at doing sums in my head and I adored arithmetic problems. The metric system had not penetrated our little schoolbooks and the multiplicity of units of length (*versta, sagen, arshin, vershok*), of area (*desyatina*), of weight (*poud, fount, zolotnik, dolya*) offered to their authors cues for innumerable exercises on units conversion.

Problems of faucets running into a bath were rare (shortage of bathrooms?), as well as those of train crossings, no doubt inappropriate in a country where most railway lines were single track. The most frequent type of problem was when a 'quidam' (I never saw the corresponding Russian word anywhere except in these arithmetical problems), having bought teas of two different grades, amused himself by mixing them in given proportions, before selling them at a given price. The question asked was in general: what will be his profit? (The ideologically unacceptable character of these problems did not seem to bother the school authorities.)

Far more difficult were the problems where one was given the weight of the mixture and the profit of the merchant, and the unknowns were the weights of the two components. I learned to master them by means of 'reasonings', subtle and verbose, which run invariably along the following lines: 'if the "quidam" had done this . . . he would have earned that . . . but he wants . . . therefore . . . etc.' When much later I gained access to algebra, the purely mechanical way of solving this kind of problem with two equations and two unknowns, shocked me, as a traditional craftsman might be shocked by mass production.

If I add that I had no aptitude, only ineptitude playing the piano, drawing, singing, and dancing, activities to which a child belonging to the intelligentsia was invariably exposed, I shall have rounded off the field of my abilities and interests. I may add yet that I had an excellent memory: it was enough for me to read a poem two or three times and to reread it once in the evening before going to bed, in order to be able to recite it without a hitch the following morning (only to forget it a day or two later). One sees that in spite of my few weaknesses I was well equipped for succeeding in school.

I did not go to school before eight for reasons I do not remember . . . It may be that, coming from a bourgeois family, there had been obstacles to my admission at a time when schools were desperately short of teachers, and the children of workers, and others ranking as such, had to be served first—but I cannot swear to it. Before going to school I had a lady teacher who came to our house for two hours every day to make me study. She was named Vera Semyonovna; that is what I called her and I do not think I ever knew her last name. I liked her very much, her and her teaching, and I spent with her two happy, uneventful years. She taught me to write legibly, for my handwriting had been abominable, she taught me grammar and syntax, made me learn a lot of poetry by heart and write little essays. She also made me solve a lot of arithmetic problems of the type I described earlier. In history we stopped at the abolition of serfdom (around 1860), and geography was limited by the confines of Russia.

It is in the autumn of 1923 that I entered the Soviet school which I attended until our departure from Russia in the summer of 1925. In 1966, there was in the Soviet Union a second printing of a book published first in 1927, called *The Journal of Kostia Riabtzov*. The hero, Kostia Riabtzov, is a boy aged fifteen at the beginning of the book, and his journal described the period from September 1923 to March 1925, which coincides almost exactly with my own schooldays in Russia. There are enormous differences between Kostia, an adolescent of fifteen and a fictional character, and myself, a boy of eight and real (although at times I am inclined to doubt it, so far away from me it all is, and not only in time). The problems of puberty and of his relations with the adolescent girls in his class, which take a large place in Kostia's journal, are perforce non-existent in my memories of the Soviet school. The problems of puberty were yet to come for me as for all boys, but, as I made it clear from the start, there is no room for them in this narrative, while relations with adolescent girls in my class simply did not exist for the very good reason that, like all the boys of my time in France, I went to a *lycée de garçons*.

It seems to me that in certain aspects, Kostia, my elder by seven years, is more naïve and more impulsive than I; born in the working class and not immersed in books like myself, he is also more ignorant. But what I have rediscovered in that book, is the rather extraordinary atmosphere which prevailed in the Soviet school during these two years.

It was a period of intense pedagogical experimentation. Discipline was to be maintained by an elected Committee of pupils and the programme of studies for the term to be discussed with it. I remember very well that this also took place in my own class of brats, where it is true that I was the youngest by far and the oldest was some five years older than I. Social and political activities took up a considerable part of the curriculum. Among these, in the foreground, there was the so-called 'Wall newspapers', in which everyone was expected to participate, and on which those who could draw were employed almost full time. There was the making of political posters, and the drawings of portraits of Lenin, from which I was unanimously excused after the Committees had unanimously decided that *my* Lenin looked like a nanny-goat. There were circles of all kinds and many guided visits to museums and factories.

Thus at the beginning of 1925 we visited Lenin's Mausoleum, a wooden structure at the time. I do not think there are many people in France now who, like me, have seen Lenin lying by himself (1925), then with Stalin (1956), then alone again (1961).

I do not think that I had heard Stalin's name at school, and Trotsky alone, the heroic Father of the Red Army, the Victor of the White Armies, the Bard of the Permanent Revolution, found room in our folklore next to Lenin. I remember the death of Lenin in January 1924, the very real grief that I felt, and the Siberian cold spell ($-35°$C, exceptional even for Moscow) which prevailed during his funeral.

There were in our school numerous meetings in which we discussed with the teachers our impressions of the guided visits, and ways to improve the workings of the school, be it discipline or studies. The pupils were invited to present their complaints, usually concerned with the heating, the state of the lavatories, and above all, the shortage of pens, ink, and paper, and of books. I do not know whether anything useful ever came out of these palavers but they were fun and I enjoyed them a lot.

The shortage of books was indirectly the cause of an incident which affected me painfully. Shortly after school started, the teacher opened a book and started to read from it very slowly, after having invited us to write down what he was reading. As incredible as it may seem, I explained to myself this strange proceeding by the fact that he was the only one to own the book. I never did dictations with Vera Semyonovna and I had never heard of that exercise, which, I must add, was quite unnecessary to me. Saturated with reading as I was, the spelling problem simply did not exist for me! (It took a cruel revenge on me two years later when I collided with the French language.)

My neighbour got out of his desk another copy of the master's book and suggested that I copy from it with him the text that was being dictated. I thought it an excellent idea: so much more convenient than writing down what the teacher was droning! Great was my indignant surprise when the teacher fell on us, called us cheats, and refused to believe my denials, which were indeed hard to believe.

I now want to jump five years ahead for a moment, from eight to thirteen, to France from Russia, to German from Russian, and to artful cheating from wounded innocence. Our German teacher was very proud of an exercise he had invented and which proceeded as follows: he dictated very, very slowly a German text which we were supposed to write down directly in French. When the dictation was over, we were left some time to put it back into the original German from whatever French we had written during the dictation-translation. It did not take me long to realize how much more efficient it would be to take down the dictation directly in German and *then* to translate it unhurriedly into French. (Time reversal again.) The only precaution was to take the dictation on the second page and then write the translation on the first. It is amazing that I was the only one to have thought of it, that I got away with it through four or five dictations, and when finally caught by the teacher, surprised at last by the remarkable quality of my translation, that I brazened it out, asserting that I had thought this was not cheating but mere efficiency. The German teacher, a strange fellow, to tell the truth, did believe me and simply enjoined me to stop being efficient. Back to Russia.

As far as studies were concerned, those of my comrades who wanted to study, could do so; our teachers were competent and conscientious, always ready with explanations, during class or afterwards. Those who did not want to study just didn't: with the meetings of the Pupils' Committee, the editing of the Wall newspaper, and the manifold social activities, they had enough excuses to miss class instead of disturbing the teachers and those of their comrades who wanted to study. There were no exams either during term or at the end of the year; those who could prove their proletarian origin were automatically promoted into the next form, the rest did work because the threat of exclusion was always hanging over their heads. More than once we had been told that the Revolution could do better than educate ungrateful 'boorjuys'.

Whatever the virtues and the weaknesses of the system, it hardly survived at all after our departure from Russia. (I am speaking now of what I have read rather than what I know at first hand.) As early as 1927, examinations, compulsory attendance, and authoritarian discipline were introduced. The number of school hours was practically doubled (we only went to school in the afternoon), the Pupils' Committees remained, but became a tool of the authorities to keep an eye on the masters.

The number of Pioneers, who were a sort of Red Boy Scouts, wearers of a red necktie, and paragons of orthodoxy, increased considerably. In my time, there had been only one of them in my form the first year, and five or six, mainly girls, during the second. We looked on them as eager beavers who tried to make up for their academic mediocrity with their little red ties; an unfair accusation since one of the first girls to wear a red tie was regarded as ranking second in the form. I say 'regarded as', because there was no official ranking of the pupils. One can guess *who* was 'regarded as' first. I did not deserve much credit; the dice of the family environment were loaded in my favour from the start.

The most serious threat in this evolution of the school was that of a reform, planned for the autumn of 1925, denying the bourgeois elements access to the so-called secondary cycle of studies—the very one I was due to enter if we had not left Russia. Even if my mother, in view of her Service in the Red Army, could hope to escape this ignominious classification, my father was the 'fabrikant', the 'boorjuy' par excellence. I think that the threat of this reform, though, in truth, I do not know whether it was ever carried out, was the decisive reason for our departure. That their children could not pursue their studies beyond elementary school was unacceptable to my parents.

It is hardly possible today to speak of life in the USSR without mentioning the problem of anti-Semitism. All I can say is that I never personally suffered from it. It did happen that in an argument with children in our yard (never in school) someone would invoke my personal responsibility in the death of Our Saviour on the Cross, but the complete absence of State anti-Semitism made these remarks quite harmless; more serious might have been an occasional reference to bourgeois origins, but the son of a heroic (what else) doctor in the Red Army knew the answer to that one.

If, before leaving my life in Russia, I try to pass an overall judgement over these first ten years of my life, I am tempted to use a somewhat unfortunate expression, coined by the head of the French Communist Party, shortly after the invasion of Afghanistan: 'The global balance-sheet (of the Soviet regime) is positive'. So was my own.

I was happy in the midst of my family, I adored my mother and I admired my father, I was happy in my school, happy above all, in the midst of my books and my reveries. As they say rather horribly nowadays, in France I mean, I was comfortable 'inside my skin'. I shall not say the same of my first twenty years in the West, but this is another (and long) story.

II

FRANCE, CHILDHOOD, ADOLESCENCE, YOUTH

Mademoiselle Bertin

The shock of the West—'Tis my fault, my very great fault'—Clovis embraced the cult of his wife

When we alighted, my mother, my sister, and I, on the platform of the Gare du Nord in Paris on 25 June 1925, we were met by uncle David, my father's elder brother, who had been residing in France for more than twenty years. He looked amazed, or pretended to be, at the sight of the kettle that my mother was holding in her hand, an indispensable accessory on any long journey in Russia. I have remembered this trivial incident because from the start it gave the tone of our relationship with my father's family—this uncle, and one of his sisters, also settled in Paris many years ago. They were French, better, Parisians, whereas we were people come from the East, worse, from Sovietia, whose ignorance of civilized customs was a source of indulgent merriment.

They were right, to be sure; from the beginning the child that I was discovered surprising usages. At the restaurant where my uncle took us that night, they served artichokes, a vegetable I had never seen before, with a thick white sauce. An observant child, I immediately noticed that the leaves of the artichoke were used to gather the sauce from the plate and to carry it to one's mouth. However, two things intrigued me: why of the two extremities of the leaf did one use the one least suitable to its office of a spoon, and even stranger, why did one use every leaf just once? Vexed by the burst of laughter which greeted my question, I decided to make no more remarks. A large bowl of lettuce, another dish unknown to me, was brought in and immediately seized upon by my uncle. Apparently he did not like what was on top, because instead of helping himself or, still better, his neighbour, my mother, he turned over the salad to fetch something better at the bottom. What he found there did not please him either, because he kept turning it over, looking for God knows what, until, utterly disgusted with his efforts, he gave up and passed the bowl to my mother. I had never seen such deplorable manners.

A last surprise awaited me that night. I discovered that the blanket of my bed was sewn to the mattress, and that I had to squeeze myself into the narrow space between the sheets, which was most inconvenient. The idea that I was in a country of thieves where one had to sew the blankets to the mattress lest they be stolen crossed my mind. I must remind my reader that in Russia, as in Central Europe, one did not tuck in the blankets, but covered oneself with a quilt enclosed in a linen cover.

In spite of these few comical incidents I easily adjusted myself to surroundings very different from those I had known in Russia; the short stopovers in Riga and Berlin had already eased the transition.

But there was still the great shock of school to come.

I did not know a word of French upon my arrival in Paris. I am telling a lie: I knew: *bonjour, au revoir, merci,* and a collection that was less immediately useful in an urban context: *la poule, le coq, le canard, la vache, le chat, le chien.* This little domestic zoo was the heritage of an afternoon spent, around my sixth year, in a private kindergarten run by two old maiden ladies who tried to survive as best they could. Their method was to show the children pictures and make them repeat the names in French. Speaking Russian was not allowed. It may have been a good method, but I landed there among children who had been frequenting this place for some time already and were used to it. This attempt, drowned in my tears, was short-lived for I categorically refused to return to a place where I was addressed in an unknown language. The least one can say is that more of the same was in store for me.

Our flat in Paris was in the XVth arrondissement near the Avenue Emile Zola. The nearest *lycée* was Buffon. Considering my ignorance of French, it had seemed wiser to send me for the first year to a private school, pompously called Ecole Secondaire de Breteuil, located on the Boulevard Garibaldi in the shadow of the Lycée Buffon. I never had any curiosity to return there and I do not know what happened to it.

This was my first encounter with a French school, in October 1925. I was ten and I was put in the sixth form†, which corresponded to my age and to the general level of my education. Alas, the scene in the kindergarten was replayed with few changes. Most unfortunately, the first lesson turned out to be Latin. The teacher wrote on the blackboard a column of words in French with the Latin opposite, or vice versa, I did not know, for I could not tell the one from the other.

It was too much for me, I burst into tears and cried all day long. At intervals a master would come to me, speaking some kind of gibberish in which the word 'kamarad' kept recurring. I understood that he was encouraging me to play with the other children but I obstinately refused. The following day, after consulting with the Head of the school it was decided to move me into a lower form. It was not done by halves, for I was put into the ninth form. I believe, but I would not swear to it, that the Head took me for a mild case of mental deficiency.

† In French secondary schools the forms are numbered backwards: the last but one, called the first, is followed by a last year with two options: *Philosophie* and *Mathématiques Elémentaires.*

It was then that I encountered Mademoiselle Bertin, my first love, if not my first mistress. Mademoiselle Bertin was young and beautiful. She ruled with a firm hand over the ninth, the eighth, and the seventh forms, all housed in the same room. There must have been about twenty of us, more than half of whom were in the seventh. If by any chance Mademoiselle Bertin is still among us (she was born with the century), I would like to express to her my gratitude and what I never dared to tell her, my love.

From the beginning my mother asked her to tutor me in French. For arithmetic, whose French name, *calcul* (which means more generally calculation), I found ridiculous. I did not need anyone, and sometimes I even slightly irritated my beloved Mademoiselle Bertin by doing sums in my head ahead of her.

(A parenthesis about *calcul*: years later, after Latin, which had been my bogey on the first day, had become my best friend in school, I was greatly puzzled by a quotation I had found in my big Latin dictionary: 'He produced a "calcul" while passing water', for I did not know that 'calcul' also meant 'stone'. Quite recently, while standing in a lavatory at Saclay next to two young theoreticians who were arguing furiously about some calculations while performing their natural functions, I could not resist the pleasure of reminding them of that celebrated quotation.)

I remained one week in the ninth form and one month in the eighth. At Christmas I was ranked first in the seventh form, not 'regarded as first', as in Russia, but physically recognized as such, by the medal that Mademoiselle Bertin pinned herself to the lapel of my jacket. I nearly fainted from happiness and pride, but when I came home, my mother, after congratulating me, advised me to take it off. 'Intellectuals do not wear medals' was her brief comment.

It took me six months to vanquish my ferocious enemy, Spelling, of whose existence my Russian childhood was not even aware, and to pass finally from the sixty mistakes of my first dictation to none.

In my apprenticeship in French I sometimes fell victim to strange misunderstandings. In history, for instance, there had been (I have forgotten the century) a *Ligue du Bien Public* or 'League for the Public Good', which I interpreted as 'The League for the good Public', an elitist organization whose blatant class content repelled me.

A mystery it took me a long time to penetrate was that of *Tismafo, tismafo, tismaverigrayfo*'. In our school we had catholic prayers every morning, and longer on Fridays, when all the pupils uttered the strange sounds that I have just attempted to transcribe (suitably modified for the English-speaking reader). My mother did not know their meaning, and for a long time I dared not question Mademoiselle Bertin about rites in which I was not expected to participate. I did so eventually and discovered that it was: ''Tis my fault, 'tis my fault, 'tis my very great fault'.

I delighted in parsing long sentences and the complicated concords of

French participles surrendered to me before long. I was not deterred by the bisexuality of *amour*, *delice*, and *orgue* (their gender is masculine in the singular and feminine in the plural). I learned to love the Magnificent Seven: *Bijou, caillou, chou, genou, hibou, joujou, pou* (jewel, stone, cabbage, knee, owl, toy, louse), which in the plural take an 'x' rather than an 's', and the Beautiful Five: *Pondichéry, Chandernagor, Yanaon, Karikal, Mahé*, the five French trading posts, regretfully surrendered by de Gaulle to independent India—places whose natives can even today claim French citizenship if they so choose. I knew by heart the eighty-nine *Départements* into which France was divided, and the three hundred-odd subdivisions or *sous-préfectures*. I rejoiced in the sound of Clermont-Ferrand, Tonnerre and Yssingeaux, Briançon and Barcelonnette, and Mont Gerbier-de-Jonc where the Seine (unless it is the Loire) starts its course.

How much more alive and picturesque the history of France was than that taught in my Soviet school, where a few figures like Vladimir Prince of Kiev, Ivan the Terrible, Peter the Great, and Catherine the Great barely stood out, before yielding their place in history to the workers' fight for their liberation led by Lenin and Trotsky.

I quickly learned that our ancestors the Gauls were not afraid of anything except the improbable falling down of the sky, that the proud Sicambre (the Frankish Chief Clovis) broke the vase of Soissons, before bowing down to embrace the cult of his wife (a time honoured double-entendre), that Philippe-Auguste erected a wall around Paris, that Saint Louis dispensed justice under an oak, that Joan of Arc drove the English out of France and was burnt for her pains, that Charles IX took pot shots with his arquebus at the Protestants, also known as Huguenots, that Henri IV, promoter of a fowl-in-the-pot for every Frenchman on Sunday, thought that Paris was worth a Mass, and was slain by Ravaillac, that Louis XIV was *le Grand Roi* for whom there were no more Pyrenees, that Louis XV, who, as one was supposed to know, was *not* his son, was the *roi bien aimé* in spite of his deplorable conduct, that Mirabeau (the revolutionary leader, whom I somehow mixed up with a novelist named Octave Mirbeau whose books my mother was reading), told the Marquis de Dreux-Brézé to go and speak to his Master of the will of the people and of the strength of the bayonets, that the people took the Bastille, that Louis XVI was guillotined with his wife, the 'Austrian', after an escapade to Varennes, that Danton told the people: 'Boldness, boldness, and yet more boldness', and then the executioner: 'Show my head to the people', that Robespierre's jaw was broken on the ninth of Thermidor, that Bonaparte crossed the Alps and climbed the Pyramids, then was victorious at Austerlitz and Moscow (but they could not make *me* believe that, thanks to Tolstoy I knew the other side of the story too well), then through the fault of Grouchy and the perfidy of the English, ended up at the island of Saint Helena, before running off for a while from the island of Elba (thanks to Lermontov's poem, 'The Ghostly Ship', I knew all about Saint Helena), that he was avenged by Napoleon III (why III?), who took Sebastopol, that the Prussians of Bismarck entered Paris but that Thiers liberated the Territory, that Joffre performed a miracle at La Marne and Foch at Rethondes (where the Armistice was signed) and that Monsieur Gaston Doumergue, nicknamed 'Gastounet', was the Head of State in 1925. Such was the history of my new country, from its origins to its most burning contemporary issues, as taught to me by my dear Mademoiselle Bertin. As for 'General Science', I think that, with what I had learnt from my *Children's Encyclopaedia*, I knew as much about it as Mademoiselle Bertin herself, if not more.

The other subjects were drawing, handwriting, and gymnastics. No problems in drawing—hopeless I was, and hopeless I stayed. In gymnastics I held my own, a decent average for running and jumping, rather clever with ball games, on the weak side for apparatus work.

I took a liking to team games, such as prisoner's base, and cops and robbers. I took part timidly in the soccer games which went on in the schoolyard. I became the happy owner of a bicycle and practised in the quiet street where we lived. Curiously, I shone with an unexpected sparkle in the 'Science of dullards', handwriting (just like Hamlet, according to what he tells Horatio, but then he tells him so many things). Armed with a steel pen, I happily devoted myself to the joys of downstrokes and upstrokes. I came out first in the final term handwriting examination, thanks to the phrase: 'Hoche pacified the Vendée'. I kept my sheet for a long time; my capitals, H and V, were pure marvels.

I can now congratulate myself on arriving in France without a word of French; I am convinced that I owe to this that I spoke it straightaway without any foreign accent. The rapidity of my progress was nothing abnormal, I am saying this without false modesty of any kind, for it was the case with most children of Russian émigrés.

Thus, within a year I was brought back to the right level. (Almost, for I was due to enter the sixth form at eleven, with a year to catch up on. Good heavens! It was nothing compared to the delays circumstances were to force on me in the future. I later caught up easily with that one by moving directly from the fourth form to the second.)

I had become like the other children, up to date with his studies, at ease with his comrades, in a word integrated. Well, maybe I was, but I felt this integration as a regression. I felt in a vague way, or if I did not feel it then I feel it now, that I had somehow been made more infantile and more ordinary than I was before. It was the first breakup in an existence which was to know more of them.

Les Cinq Glorieuses

Dress and hairdressing—'Version Latine': a scientific subject—Giving up Greek: first rash decision—Literary dissertation: school of verbiage—The Sweet Power of Physics—Maths: good and bad—The passion to be first

The following year I went to the Lycée. Living in the district of Grenelle it would have been natural to go to Buffon. This district, where we lived for ten years, was working class. Frémicourt Street, which I took to go to school, housed an enormous taxicab garage and no less than twenty-five bistros. Garibaldi Boulevard, which I followed next, was inhabited at the time by a large number of Moroccan workmen. Once, coming home on a Saturday night with a pal, a big chap from the fifth form, we passed a low building in front of which stood a few Moroccans. 'What are they doing?' I asked. 'They are waiting for the brothel to open', he said and laughed. I laughed too and, coming home, asked my mother: 'What is a "brothel?"' She did not know. I looked it up in my little dictionary, but it was not there. During a visit to uncle David's, I looked it up in his large dictionary and found '*Maison publique*'. Do not think this answer baffled me. I knew what it was, as I was reading Tolstoy's *Resurrection* at the time and the heroine of it ends up in a '*Maison publique*'. I did not know *exactly* what it was, but I understood it to be a place of crude amusements and ill-bred merriment. It did not quite fit with the patient wait of the sad, resigned Moroccans that I had seen on the pavement.

On the advice of my uncle, who lived in the elegant XVIth arrondissement, on Avenue Henri Martin (which is now Georges Mandel), I was sent to the Lycée of Janson de Sailly which was definitely for the 'League of the Public Good', in the very personal sense I gave to that expression in the last chapter.

Two years ago they celebrated the hundredth anniversary of the Lycée Janson and I was invited. My membership of the Academy had not escaped the organizers, and I could have expected a seat at the VIP table, presided over by a former Prime Minister. I did not go, and now that I am leaning back over my past, as the French saying goes, I regret it a little. No doubt there will be a hundred and fiftieth anniversary, but for me it is all over, whatever the future advances of medicine.

The Lycée Janson, where I studied till I went to university, was indeed frequented by the 'Good Public' or, as coarse people say, '*du beau linge*' (for smart underwear). The lycée was in two parts: the Petit Lycée went up to the fourth form (inclusive) and the Grand Lycée took it from there. In the morning, on coming out of the metro in the Avenue Henri Martin, one could see a few chauffeur-driven, sumptuous cars—Hispano-Suiza, Voisin, or Delage—stopping in front of the entrance to let out my schoolmates. We (those who came by metro) never failed to ask the chauffeur if he was free, in the hope of annoying him by taking his car for a taxicab.

Besides the good French bourgeoisie, there were glamorous foreigners at Janson—South Americans, Egyptians, Persians, and Lebanese, their pockets bursting with money. Most of them were *pensionnaires*, that is boarders, and they formed among us a category apart. All pensionnaires were considered *dessalés*, that is knowing, or at least claiming to know, all there was to know about sex. They were also the Brummels of our crowd. The fashion was then for hair styles à la Rudolf Valentino. The hair was plastered on the head and maintained in that position by some kind of goo (Gomina Argentina was the most famous), so as to form a surface looking like a mirror or a skating rink. To make sure the hair stuck fast to the cranium, the pensionnaires appeared in the morning with a hairnet that they took off just before the first lesson. Some made attempts to keep it on even then, provoking the indignation of the teacher. The overcoat, atrociously padded at the shoulders, was pinched at the waist, while fitting snugly down below. The delicate transition period between childhood and adolescence, that is between short and long pants, was taken care of by plus fours which, as their name only partly indicates, were expected to be very ample and to come down very low. (Plus eights would have been more appropriate.) When I entered the fourth form, I extorted from my mother the promise of a suit with plus fours, which we ordered in the bespoke department of the *Belle Jardinière*—a large store, which we both considered, mistakenly I am afraid, to be the *ne plus ultra* of elegance. The suit was of a broken check pattern with a half belt on the jacket, and plus fours whose ample folds fell below the calves and could have housed all the treasures of Arabia. For a long time I was only permitted to wear it on Sundays, a restriction I did not mind, for I wanted to protect this treasure from the rude contacts of the school playground.

My transition from the Ecole Secondaire de Breteuil to the Lycée Janson was uneventful, for the changes were material rather than intellectual. Mlle Bertin was replaced by several men teachers (an inconstant lover, I quickly forgot her), the ring of the little bell which announced the beginning and end of classes gave place to the roll of a drum, the single sixth to half a dozen parallel sixth forms, the exercise books for homework were replaced by separate sheets, called 'copies', but all these changes were of little importance, and in my brief existence I had already seen changes far more important.

Our teachers were all *agrégés de l'Université*, that is they had all successfully passed a tough competitive examination called *Agrégation*. (Nowadays only a small proportion of teachers are *agrégés*, most of them have less prestigious degrees). All were meticulously dressed: bowler hat, grey spats, wing collar, cane or umbrella for the eldest, trilby hats for the youngest. M. Perrichet, our teacher of *calcul* in the sixth form, shocked his elder colleagues deeply one day by appearing bare-headed.

If I give so many details of the clothing habits of pupils and masters, it is because of the, possibly mistaken, impression that the changes which have occurred there during the last sixty years are far deeper than the minute changes in the content and methods of the teaching itself. Childless myself I only know what my friends used to tell me about their children, and tell me now about their grandchildren. But let us go back to my own studies.

From the beginning I felt attracted to Latin and I preferred what we called the *version* (from Latin into French) to the *thème* (which is the opposite). I found in the *version Latine* what became the foundation of my career as researcher and teacher: the need to understand and then to express clearly what I understood. I do not think I am exaggerating in saying that for me Latin was the only properly scientific apprenticeship of my secondary education, and probably the best school of intellectual self-expression.

In the fourth form, our Latin teacher, who shared these views, used to dictate a model translation to us after a test. 'You need not stick closely to the letter as long as you are faithful to the spirit', he used to tell us. 'Misunderstanding is the only danger'. I thought that he took liberties with the text which he denied to us, and he went too far at least once. It was all about the reception of Scipio Africanus by the people of Rome massed on the banks of the Tiber. 'I think we could say: "the quays were dark with people", yes, I think we shall dare to say that'. As I raised my hand in protest, he said with some annoyance: 'Don't be pedantic, Abragam, I think we may say that' 'But, Monsieur, in the preceding phrase it said that they were all wearing white dresses: "candidas togas".'

The decisive factor which kept me away from classical studies was an impulsive move, the first of a long series, which made me give up the study of Greek when it started in the fourth form. From the first lesson I felt a violent antipathy for the Greek master, whose grimaces and tics I found unbearable. I persuaded my mother, to whom I dared not tell the truth, that Greek was a waste of time which would be better employed on more important studies.

In her time she had taken Latin but no Greek, so she believed me and went to see the Head about my transfer into a form without Greek. In the face of his unwillingness to permit it, she had to tell a lie and to allege that there were reasons related to my health. Learning of my transfer, the Greek master told me, between two grimaces, how much he regretted the departure of a pupil who appeared so apt at following his teaching.

I was less attracted by the courses of French language and literature than by Latin, although I did not dislike dictations and, later, studies of literary texts, and I enjoyed writing narrative essays. A little incident showed me that I had not yet mastered all the intricacies of my new idiom. We were asked to write a piece of folklore, the celebration of a christening in the country, the very thing for me. I began to gather information among my schoolfellows who might have attended such an event. One of them told me: 'They give the brat a "lavement" of holy water'. 'Lavement', coming from the French verb 'laver', which means 'to wash', did not surprise me in the least. I was familiar with the rite of baptism through immersion in holy water, its being called 'lavement' seemed perfectly natural, and I put it in my essay. Little did I know that 'lavement' has only one meaning, which is 'enema.' I am convinced now that the idea of misleading me had not even occurred to my friend and that he was simply being witty, for he could not have imagined that I did not know the meaning of the word 'lavement'. Neither did it occur to the teacher, who bitterly reproached me with the mocking of rites which I did not have to believe in, but was under obligation to respect. I do not know whether he believed my protestations of innocence, but the important fact was that my schoolmates did not believe a word of it, and my prestige in our form as a daredevil and a wit grew considerably as a consequence.

From the fourth form on, and to an even worse degree from the second, we were exposed to that odious activity, literary dissertation. I quickly learned the little tricks which enable one, with the help of a literary textbook, to whip up enough pages of trivia to get an acceptable mark, without even bothering to read the authors to be commented on, but I found the whole exercise hateful and despicable.

We were encouraged to attend classical matinées on Thursdays at the Trocadero theatre. (In those days children did not go to school on Thursdays.) The old Trocadero, torn down in 1937, had very peculiar acoustics: if you had missed a line, you were offered a second chance and sometimes a third. I remember the famous '*Qu'il mourût*' ('Let him die') of Corneille, which went round the theatre several times.

The teaching of French Literature counts among the worst memories I have of my second and first forms. It is not enough to say that I learned nothing from it; it put me off the French Classics and even the Romantics. I can read Swift, Shakespeare, Gibbon, Johnson, and Defoe for pleasure (let alone the Russian Classics), but since the Lycée I have hardly ever opened Rabelais, Corneille, Racine, Bossuet, Fénelon, Lamartine, or Vigny, reread *Ruy-Blas* or *Hernani*. It is because I have heard and written too many platitudes about all of them, and Molière, who escaped this disgrace, must have been blessed with the cat's metaphorical nine lives.

In maths I had phases. In the sixth and fifth forms, arithmetic (sorry, *calcul*)—taught by M. Perrichet, the fashion innovator who came to the Lycée bare-headed—did not offer much more than what I had learned from Mlle Bertin or indeed what I had brought with me from Russia.

In the fourth form I started geometry on the wrong foot. My new teacher was mediocre; he took an immediate dislike to me and I to him. I do not know who started it, possibly I. My behaviour towards the Greek master, had shown how intolerant I could be. I shed bitter tears (at thirteen!), which I did my best to hide, over the poor showing I made in the first term examination, a real disaster for a pupil used to top marks. I recovered from it, in spite of the teacher, rather than thanks to him, because plane geometry turned out to be far more amusing than any maths taught to me before. I ended the year much better than I started, to such an extent that, with the assent of all my teachers, I was allowed to skip the third form and pass directly into the second form. A new shock awaited me there: my ignorance of algebra, a subject that one started in the third form. Fortunately my new maths master, a good teacher and a kindly man, whose name, Anatole Decerf, has remained a legend at Janson, pulled me up all the way to first place, in spite of a programme I found rather boring; which was the opposite of what had happened in the fourth form.

Physics, which one did not start before the second form (!), turned out to be sheer happiness. I must thank my young and brilliant physics master, Robert Massain, for revealing to me the Sweet Power of Physics. It was his first year of physics at Janson, as it was mine. With him I rediscovered everything I had learned to love in my *Children's Encyclopaedia*, but in a quantitative form. I had the joy of seeing him again, thirty years later, at my maiden lecture at the Collège de France. He died in his eighties in the spring of 1987.

Yet it was under him that I met with one of the most painful experiences of my schoolboy life.

In the first term examination, after a set of routine questions to which I knew the answers, I dried up over the problem. My anguish redoubled at the thought of disappointing M. Massain, who had already gauged me as his best pupil. The key to the solution was an algebraic formula; it was elementary, but taught in the third form and for that reason I had never seen it. My neighbour kindly whispered it to me, and I promptly solved the problem. You can guess what happened: I came first and he second. Conscience-stricken, I wanted to confess to M. Massain. My kind neighbour, as free of the competitive spirit as I was full of it, dissuaded me by assuring me that he bore no grudge against me, and by pointing out that we would both be punished if I spoke. I was easily dissuaded.

My physics teacher in the first form was an obnoxious moron. He took advantage of the obscurity of his lectures to encourage the pupils of his class to take private lessons. The 'beneficiaries' of these lessons, if not the wiser in physics, were at least guaranteed passable marks. I must have liked physics a lot since he did not put me off it.

There is not much to say about the maths taught in the first form— space geometry and endless variations on the algebra of the second order polynomial. It needed all the talent of Anatole Decerf, who had stayed with us in the first form, to make it palatable.

For foreign languages, one had the choice of German and English. I chose German, which I am not able to read and even less able to speak after five years of it. In the defence of my teachers it must be said that, from the second form up, having learned that for the Baccalaureat I could take Russian, I badly neglected my German. (The Baccalaureat, the final examination, usually abbreviated to 'Bachot' or 'Bac', is in two parts. The first Bac takes place at the end of the first form and the second at the end of *Philo* or *Math. Elem.*)

I congratulate myself on not having chosen English in school. If today I have a tolerable accent in English, a language which I use a lot, I owe it to my choice of German in school.

I will round up this too long survey of my secondary studies with history and geography.

I have always been bored to death by geography, but managed thanks to my excellent memory. I much preferred history, which we learned from the excellent series of textbooks by Albert Malet and Jules Isaac, who educated half a century of schoolchildren. In the fourth form I had a teacher who fascinated me, named Charles-André Julien. A few years later he became a university professor and a respected teacher of a generation of French historians. Far more than his sartorial daring, which put to shame that of M. Perrichet, it was his way of treating his pupils as adults (in the fourth form, and in 1928!) that surprised us and enchanted me. Alone among his history colleagues he made us understand that there was more to history than kings and battles, that there were people and their customs, their civilizations, and their economic evolution.

A bizarre consequence of my jump from the fourth form to the second is a gap, which was never filled, going from the battle of Bouvines (1214) to the murder of Henry IV by Ravaillac (1610). I know roughly what went on before and what happened after, but between the two there is a Black Hole.

The time came for the first Bac, I was confidently ready for it and I was not disappointed, for I was successful in all the subjects. I was helped a little (but not much as it did not count for much) by top marks in Russian. At the written Russian examination I sat next to a boy of Russian origin (like all those who took that language), named Hofman. I saw him again a few days later at the oral examination in the company of his father, a quiet gentleman with a beard. Hofman senior asked me if I was feeling quite ready for the oral examination. I replied modestly that I was sure at any rate to know more Russian than the examiner, and that this should suffice. Naturally Mr Hofman, a distinguished Slavist and specialist of Pushkin. turned out to be the Russian examiner. I impressed him by mentioning Batiushkov, a little known and mildly erotic poet, contemporary of Puskin. That got me top marks.

And so, with a flourish, I ended my first five years at Janson—five years of uninterrupted successes, five years of consecutive *Prix d'Excellence*, five glorious years, 'les Cinq Glorieuses'. (In French history *les Trois Glorieuses* are the three days of the Revolution of 1830 which brought Louis-Philippe d'Orléans to power. *Sic itur ad astra!*. Yet the Tarpeian Rock was not far from this Capitol!)

A false start

Second rash decision: choosing medicine—In Math. Elem. I fall apart but pull myself together—Disgust of the disciples of Asclepius—Fear of the sight of sickness—I pull out in time

I have always been lazy. I am not being falsely modest. The image of the 'bright chap', who gets ahead of the hard-working swot and succeeds without working, is a legend supported by these same 'bright chaps', who actually work hard on the sly, in order to impress their parents and their little pals. Nothing great, or even simply very good, can be achieved without hard work, in Science at least; but it may well be the same in Arts. In any case, all the great physicists I have ever known have worked like beasts of burden. It goes without saying that hard work, although necessary, is not enough: to succeed, one needs other gifts as well. But, among those who do possess these other gifts, there are those who work hard naturally without straining themselves—and one should realize that this too is a gift in itself, perhaps the most precious of all—and others who are bored by work. I was one of these, and it is in that sense that I say I am lazy. I did not work more than others, perhaps a little less, but it cost me more. To overcome my sloth I needed to be pushed by something. If I look back on my 'Cinq Glorieuses', I must admit that this 'something' was seldom interest in the subject. Latin 'Version', plane geometry (in spite of the teacher), history in the fourth form (thanks to the teacher), Physics in the second form (thanks to the subject *and* the teacher), and that's all. The rest of the time I was moved by the spirit of competition, which was actively encouraged by the system.

This competitive atmosphere had been weighing on me for a long time. Before passing from the fourth to the second form I told my mother: 'At least if I am not among the first any more, I will have an excuse, and nobody will blame me.' Alas, my Nessus tunic continued to cling to me, and I remained the first both in the second and in the first form. In *Math. Elem.* I let go.

There were several reasons for it happening just then. When I was in the first form I started thinking about my future. For the 'bright chaps' then, (and, unless I am much mistaken, it is still the same fifty years later), there were two imperial roads: *Philo* and *Khâgne* or *Math. Elem.* and *Taupe*. (This needs explaining: in France after the second Bac, prize pupils remain in the Lycée to be groomed for two hectic years in special classes, for tough competitive examinations which lead to the so-called 'Grandes Ecoles', from which emerge, among others, the high-ranking civil servants of my newly beloved country. Science classes are called *Taupe* and literary ones *Khâgne*, do not ask me why). There was no *Khâgne* at Janson, and anyway for me a *Khâgne*, that is Classics without Greek, would have been, as Anatole France puts it, a bed with no pillow or a woman with no bosom. And what does the *Khâgne* lead to: being a schoolmaster? No thank you! I was well acquainted with the *taupins* (the inhabitants of the *Taupe*). Pupils preparing entrance to the Grandes Ecoles, 'Polytechnique', 'Centrale' (another engineering school), 'Saint-Cyr' (a French Sandhurst), 'Agro' (School of Agronomy), all wearing caps of various colours, decorated with little insignia known only to the initiated, had a playground separated from the other pupils, the *bizuths* (freshmen, beginners, the lowest form of animal life). When the *taupins* played in their covered playground a game called *balle au mur*, or 'ball against wall' (a game I was very good at), it sometimes happened that their ball landed in our playground. The *taupins* then howled: '*Bowl, bizuth!*' (why was it necessary to shout 'bowl' rather than 'balle', the French for 'ball', I do not know, but such was the usage of Janson—perhaps it sounded more English and thus more chic), and the *bizuths* threw back the 'bowl'. One day, as the 'bowl' was slow in coming back, the *taupins* came to fetch it and chastise the *bizuths*. It was not a good idea. I was only in the second form then, and inclined to admire the *taupins* from afar. I saw that many were bespectacled and puny. My friend Aziz, a *pensionnaire* and a mere third-former, but making up in brawn for what he lacked in brain, seized one of the most vehement *taupins* by the collar, turned him around and promptly kicked his bottom. The *taupins* left with their 'bowl', promising to come back, but never did. This may have been for me the first blow to the prestige of our great Ecole Polytechnique. More importantly, in the first form, I heard from the elder brothers of some of my friends that our little contests were child's play compared to the cut-throat competitions that took place inside the *Taupes*, and that did not tempt me.

What else then? I admired the great barristers of my time, and I may have had some of the qualities required to become a good lawyer. But the young men of today do not know what the Faculty of Law and the Bar of Paris were like in the thirties: they were somewhat to the right of Genghis Khan. My origins and my political ideas, for I was beginning to acquire some of these, turned me away from law.

There was still medicine; this is the choice I made and not solely by process of elimination. I had just finished reading *Arrowsmith*, a novel by Sinclair Lewis, which is the story of a doctor, his research in various scientific institutions, the disappointments in his career, and his great love, ending up with the death of his young and dearly loved wife, a young nurse who perishes during a plague epidemic that they fight together. I have never reread this novel, which at sixteen had moved me deeply. I would be, nay I was, Arrowsmith, but I would be more persistent in my research and I would protect my darling wife better.

What sealed my decision was the opposition of my mother, who said that medicine was a wretched profession (after all she knew it from the inside), and that I was choosing it through sheer laziness and an inclination for easy ways out. The obscure feeling that she may have been right reinforced my determination.

When lessons started in *Math. Elem.*, the maths teacher asked each of us what Grande Ecole he wanted to try for. I proudly announced that I would be a doctor. There were very few like me in my class, for in those days the future doctors took *Philo*. The teacher, who was a good chap but who saw his class as a channel for the best to enter a *Taupe*, took little interest in me from then on, and in order to shine I needed some empathy with the teacher. I have already said what I thought of my physics teacher, who was the same one I had in the first form.

There was also something else. I was sixteen, the age of Romeo, but I was no Romeo. Need I say more? There is no need to draw a picture, for what would there be to draw?

It was in *Math. Elem.* that I met Laurent Schwartz, who was to become one of the most distinguished French mathematicians. Like me he had obtained all the prizes in previous years, and our respective teachers in the first form looked on our meeting in *Math. Elem.* as a contest of Titans. They were wrong; one of the Titans had feet of clay, and it was me.

There was no contest. I did not get a single first place in our tests, and of course not a single prize. I would be lying if I said that my pride did not suffer. Still, being a non-contender in the race, I suffered less than if I had been defeated in a close contest.

Like the fox with the sour grapes in the fable, I consoled myself with the thought that, being a future doctor and benefactor of humanity, I did not need these vain toys, of which I had had my share for so long.

After the second Bac, which through sheer habit, I imagine, I managed to pass with fairly good marks, I was ready for the jump into the unknown—the university—while my comrades remained prisoners of the Lycée.

'. . . *something about university attracted me; the words: "student, professor, lecture, lecture theatre", were filled with a mysterious charm; I had a premonition of something free, young and intellectual in a student's life; I did not thirst for amusements and wild parties, but for I know not what new sensations and aspirations which I was incapable of defining, or even of naming, but which I fully expected to find within the walls of the university . . .'*

These lines, written by the great Russian journalist Pisarev in 1862, provide a good description of my own feelings when, seventy years later, aged seventeen, I crossed the threshold of the Annexe to the Faculty of Sciences, located on rue Cuvier, next to the Jardin des Plantes, where the courses in PCN took place.

PCN, short for Physics, Chemistry, and Natural Sciences, was a one-year programme in these subjects, under the auspices of the Faculty of Sciences and sanctioned by a diploma. It opened the door to medical studies proper, which took place at the Ecole de Médecine in the heart of the Latin Quarter. In those days the examination which led to that diploma was the only serious hurdle that the would-be doctor had to clear in the course of his long studies, before putting up his plaque on the door. French doctors who are my age may be shocked if they read these lines, but this is how it was. Those who did want to pursue serious medical studies—and there were fortunately for our country, many of them—could no doubt do so, but those who did not want to work could still become doctors after eight or nine years, or even more, provided they had the patience and their parents the money.

This is why students of PCN worked, or rather crammed, zealously. The lazier students went to some of the large towns in the provinces, where the final examination was notoriously easy, before coming back to Paris to the Ecole de Médecine with the precious diploma in their pocket.

This cramming was my first disappointment—or rather my second, the first being my exile to this Annexe by the Jardin des Plantes, where the joyful sounds of the Boul. Mich. (Boulevard Saint-Michel) and of the Sorbonne filtered but faintly. Even worse than in *Math. Elem.*, there were constant control examinations or *colles*, which one had to prepare and in which one had to shine (not true, one did not have to shine, but in spite of my disappointing *Math. Elem.* I still had not shed my bad habits).

A few words about the professorial lectures. There were four subjects, four professors, and four sets of lectures: physics, chemistry, zoology, and botany. In my maiden lecture at the Collège de France in 1960, this is how I described my impressions of the physics taught on this course: 'A long and gloomy trail, lined with cathetometers, polarimeters, saccharimeters and catskins' (for the study of static electricity, you know).

I did not know the age of the Chemistry Professor, but he looked very ancient. His white hair and beard inspired more veneration than his teaching.

The Professor of Zoology was decidedly 'modern'. In connection with the contractions of the muscles and the electrical currents that one could detect on these occasions, he liked to tell us of the profound unity of the natural sciences and of the prominent role that physics and chemistry were to play in the future. Unfortunately, between these flights of oratory, he had to cram us with the frightful terminology of the classification of animal species; even now, more than half a century later, names float in my poor brain like a tale told by an idiot, signifying nothing: 'Gephyreans and Malacostracans, Flagellates and Flagellants (that's a lie, the second is a sect), Nematods and Trematods.' Some are 'Anourous' and others are 'Inerm' (what a beautiful name for the heroine of a novel!)

Strangely enough, it was the subject to which I felt least attracted, botany, which I found the most satisfying. The reason is simple: the professor who held the chair, Antoine Guillermond, was an authentic scholar, but I had never heard of him so I did not realize this. His delivery was hesitant and his voice was weak; the lack of attention of his mediocre audience, which he must have felt beneath him, got on his nerves, but I did read his mimeographed course on vegetable cytology, which was more of a course on general cytology, and I found it exciting. It was the only one out of four.

Besides the formal lectures which took place in the morning, in the afternoon we had practical work or TP (short for *travaux pratiques*): three hours for each subject, four times a week. For physics TP, there is nothing to add to the description I gave earlier. The zoology TP showed me that I might become a doctor, but a surgeon, never; I was unable to make an incision with a scalpel without trembling. Besides, some dissections, involving creatures like rats, ascarids (an intestinal worm which can reach fifteen centimetres in length), snails, and others I prefer to forget, used to provoke a physical disgust in me—a bad omen for my medical future.

Once dissected, a drawing of the innards of the animal had to be made, and I have explained that my draughtsmanship was beneath contempt. For the first time in my life I found myself at the bottom of the class, a painful experience. In botany too, I lacked the manual dexterity with a razor to cut thin transverse slices of stems, previously inserted in the pith of elder (*sambucus nigra*). Then I had to place the results of my cuttings, successful or not, under the microscope, in order to draw what I saw or did not see.

The chemistry practicals were the only ones I enjoyed: so-called 'qualitative analysis', where one had to identify in a powder or a solution four elements—two cations and two anions, was great fun.

Still, none of these frustrations would have been enough to make me drop medicine; something else was needed.

I rapidly discovered that the milieu of my fellow students was no less reactionary or xenophobic than that of the Faculty of Law. Their feelings were no doubt less explicit, less flamboyant, one might say, but ran, perhaps, even deeper than those of the future lawyers. It was among the law students that the fascistic leagues, *Camelots du Roi* and *Jeunesse Patriote*, recruited their members. My colleagues in the PCN were too taken up with their studies and too far removed from the Boulevard Saint-Michel to go there and noisily accost passers-by with the right wing *Action*

Française and other publications *ejusdem farinae*, but their conversations left little doubt about their feelings and their ideas.

More serious in my eyes was the rather sordid materialism of many of them. These young people, almost adolescents, who had not yet had a taste of medicine, who were still dissecting invertebrates, earnestly compared the costs of medical practices in Paris and the provinces. Those who did not look so far (but who had a more realistic vision) were busy finding out under which senior consultant in hospital they should try to land. What was Arrowsmith doing in the middle of people like that?

The *coup de grâce* to my medical career came from the discovery that I simply could not bear to see sick people. 'Not such a good start for a medical profession' was the verdict of our family doctor, to whom I had confessed my problems. A guided visit to a hospital, with one hundred patients lying side by side in an immense room finished me off. I took my decision that very evening: I should not become a doctor.

I made it a point of honour to pass the final examination in June 1933 with a final mark which was a compromise between 18 (the maximum mark was 20) in physics, and 6 in zoology for the dissection and drawing of the genital apparatus of the snail, a gastropod as bisexual as the nouns *amour*, *délice*, and *orgue*. The year had not been completely wasted: when I had started PCN I had also taken the precaution of enrolling on a course of *Mathématiques Générales*, and passed the examination successfully in October 1933. I could thus veer towards physics, which, deep down, I think I had never given up.

When I finished PCN I began a twelve-year period crowded with events which was to end in 1945 at the age of thirty. I am tempted to divide it into two parts of six years each: the 'lonely years' and 'the dark years'.

Masters and examinations

*Old Masters—Hunting the tapir—Distractions—A tooth for Palestine—
Return of the Father*

Having gone back to physics and mathematics, my wisest course would
have been to go back to the Lycée. There, in a *Taupe*, under close
supervision and in an atmosphere of fierce competition, I would have been
groomed for success in a battle for a place at Ecole Polytechnique or
Normale Supérieure, Sciences. (In my ignorance I had thought for a long
time that Ecole Normale was for Arts only.) I would have been put back
on the rails of the System from which I had strayed for a year, and, under
firm guidance, would have reached the normal goals of those known as
'first class material': *Agrégation de physique,* or *Corps des Mines* (a
prestigious scientific branch of the Civil Service). I have little doubt today
that I would have succeeded, for, in spite of my relatively poor showing in
Math. Elem., I still remained 'first class material'—an animal, which, in a
suitable environment, could absorb and memorize just about everything. I
am certain that even if I had persevered in medicine I would have been
'first class material', though probably not a good doctor which is something different.

If I had had someone whom I trusted and respected to advise me, I
might have gone to Canossa, that is back to a *Taupe* in Janson. I do not
think that I would have learned more than what I have learned in books
by myself, but I would not have been so lonely.

Left to my own devices, I indignantly rejected the idea of such a return.
What, me, a *student*, go back to being a *pupil*! Start playing 'ball against
wall' again in the playgrounds of Janson, and shout in my turn: '*Bowl,
bizuth!*' Never!

I enrolled at the Sorbonne for two courses: *Physique Générale* and
Mécanique Rationnelle, which together with the *Mathématiques Générales*
that I had passed, and the SPCN, would give me the four credits, which
were the minimum for a *Licence*, the first University degree. I forgot to say
that, conscious that my medicine was foundering, I had enrolled for the
SPCN, a souped-up version of the PCN. Compared to the standard model,
it involved some miserable combinations of physics, chemistry and mathematics as well as a course in geology, and in contrast with the ordinary
PCN, which was strictly for future doctors, it counted as a credit for the

Licence of Sciences. The geology enriched my vocabulary with some high-sounding names of fossils. I loved (onomastically speaking) *Nummulites* and *Trilobites* (especially *Trilobites Conocoryphes*). I did pass the SPCN examination.

But let me go back to the new academic year (1933–4) and begin with mechanics. We had two professors, Chazy for dynamics and Garnier, whom I was to meet again, forty years later at the Académie des Sciences for kinematics. Chazy had written up his course in a book, and read passages of it at each lecture, something everyone could do at home for himself. The lectures of René Garnier were a visual treat. I thought him a handsome old man (ye gods, he was forty-seven then and died at ninety-two!). He had beautiful handwriting, and always filled three blackboards, from the top left corner of the first to the bottom right of the last. In spite of the magnificence of the show I gave it up after a few lectures. After the examination for *Mécanique Rationelle*, I learned, to my joyful surprise, that I had passed it with top marks (*mention très bien*). No course had given me less to do, nor vanished faster from my memory.

Physique Générale was more serious, and I worked at it for a whole year. My teachers were Eugène Darmois for electricity, Charles Fabry for thermodynamics, Croze for waves and optics and Aimé Cotton for a course called 'Radiations' which strongly impinged on optics. It was the most important certificate at the Faculty of Sciences, with an enrolment of over three hundred and fifty for the year 1933–4.

I soon gave up Darmois' course after he had demonstrated to us that the electric field was normal to the surface of a conductor, *without making the assumption that the surface of the conductor was equipotential*, tantamount to proving that *any* vector was normal to *any* surface. He waved aside my timid objections and I gave up the attempt to follow such a revolutionary course. He too, later on, made the Academy.

Croze's course was less flamboyant and much more boring, and I bade it adieu before he even got to optics.

Charles Fabry was in a different class. His lectures were admirably clear, and he himself was full of wit and charm. I still remember his comment on the Second Principle of thermodynamics: 'In spite of the conservation of energy, one has a faint feeling that winding a watch and putting it into boiling water is not quite the same thing'. At the oral examination he told a young polytechnician, who was in front of me: 'You are like all your colleagues, full of yourselves but empty of everything else'. His course is the only one I followed from beginning to end. His one weakness was to skip lightly over difficult points. He was a member of the Academy, of course.

I do not think I fully appreciated Eugène Cotton's course, though there is no doubt that he was a remarkable scientist. He spoke softly and could not be heard at the back of the lecture room. Besides, most of his lecture-room experiments required darkness, which did not help in taking down what he said, and since there were no mimeographed lectures, I did not retain very much from his teaching. He too was a member of the Academy.

Of the six professors of physics and mathematics I have named, five were members of our Academy, and two at least, Fabry and Cotton, were scientists known the world over for their discoveries or inventions. Why is it that, with the half-hearted exception of Fabry, I found so little satisfaction in their lectures, and even less cause for enthusiasm? Is it my fault or theirs? I do not want to draw conclusions. The practicals in *Physique Générale* showed a slight improvement over those in PCN, by their ideological content (if I may say so), if not by the quality of the equipment. After the inevitable cathetometer, there was a perceptible progress from totally out-dated electrostatics using catskins and electrom-eters, to slightly dated electromagnetism using galvanometers. In optics, only two out of every ten Fresnel mirrors which were for the use of the students worked well enough for the lucky ones to observe beautiful interference fringes. On the others the adjusting screws were worn out, and one could only see the thick diffraction fringes, unless, before the arrival of the teaching assistant, one slipped a coin to the lab mechanic who had a trick for producing them at will.

I had no problem with that experiment at the examination, and passed with a *mention bien*. After my depressing interlude at the PCN I had, in one single year, landed one *mention bien* and one *mention très bien* for two of the main courses of the Faculty of Sciences.

Zorro was in the saddle, Zorro was riding again! Zorro was going to come a cropper before long.

But, before I describe this second year of *Licence*, a few personal notes. When at the end of the last chapter I spoke of six lonely years, I was referring to my studies, where, like all my fellow students, I was completely isolated. At the end of lectures or practical work, everybody cleared off home, only meeting his fellow students at the next lecture; and since, with a few exceptions, I was skipping all the lectures, I was seldom seeing anyone, students or professors. Outside my studies I naturally had friends like anybody else. We met either at their places or mine—but more often at theirs after my family had moved to the suburbs, to Croissy-sur-Seine, which is twenty minutes by train from Saint-Lazare station.

I said at the beginning of these memoirs that my father was supposed to join us after a few weeks, in 1925.

Ten years later he was still not there. At the beginning, judging from his letters, his little factory must have been prospering, and I think that by some oblique means he must have managed several times to slip some money to my mother. (I never had the curiosity to question my mother about our means and she never spoke to me about it.) Little by little we found out that he was having a difficult time, that he was being pushed out of his factory (the fact that he had managed to stay there for so long was a bit of a miracle), and that his application for an exit visa had been turned down *sine die*. Then one day we learned that Uncle Boris was seriously ill and that he was going to join him, which was the code for telling us that he had been expelled from Moscow and exiled to a region in the north of Russia. After some time we learned his address and were able to write to him. Do not misunderstand, he was not in a camp; he could correspond with us and he had not given up the hope of obtaining an exit visa. I have already spoken of the moral and physical qualities of my father—courage and physical resistance, manual skill and incurable optimism. He adapted himself quickly to his exile, which lasted several years, till 1936 when he was at last able to join us. During the ten odd years that he lived separated from us, he subscribed to innumerable editions of complete works that he was sending to us by mail. Thus he sent us the *Great Soviet Encyclopaedia*, in sixty-five volumes (!), the *Shorter Encyclopaedia* in ten volumes, a *Medical Encyclopaedia* in ten volumes, for the benefit of my mother, and a *Technical Encyclopaedia*, of comparable size, presumably for me. There was also a superbly unreadable *Literary Encyclopaedia*, the complete works of Lenin in thirty volumes, a magnificent edition of Tolstoy in sixty-five volumes with all the literary variations and his diaries and correspondence, and all the classics from Pushkin to Maxim Gorky. Books were and still are very cheap in Russia (whenever you can find them) and my father wanted to rebuild a library like the one we had in Moscow. All this disappeared during the German occupation, for the benefit of God knows who. Most of it must have found its way into stoves. I did not miss Lenin much, but I did miss our edition of Tolstoy, which is a bibliographic rarity nowadays. I will describe Soviet publishing methods later.

At the start of the school year 1933–4 I began to look for *tapirs*, (a strange slang expression for private pupils) an activity which I pursued with some interruptions for over ten years, till 1944.

Dunces from the XVIth arrondissement (a district where live well-to-do people), be blessed! Blessed be too, O ye second-order trinomials, O Ohm's law, O divergent lenses and virtual images! How many books, dinners with pals, theatre or cinema performances, how many holidays do I owe you. I discovered, why be falsely modest, that I was an excellent teacher, that I liked to teach, and that (to repeat a phrase of E. M. Purcell, the discoverer of NMR, which I shall make mine): 'Anything I understand I can explain.' My renown among the mothers of the XVIth arrondissement spread rapidly and the *tapirs* grew in quantity if not in quality, especially since I charged 20 francs at home (but who was going to come to my home at Croissy?), 25 at the *tapir's*, thus offering serious competition to the *professeurs agrégés* who charged 75 or even 80 francs an hour.

Here is an example of the kind of pearls of wisdom produced by my *tapirs*. During a study of a trinomial, depending on a parameter m, a numerical value, say (3/2), had cropped up, and it appeared to me that the *tapir* did not see clearly whether it was a value taken by the parameter m or the variable x. 'Who takes this value?', I asked the *tapir*. 'You, Monsieur', was his respectful answer.

It was all very well, but at some three *tapirs* a day, at various hours and in various places, one may make some money, but one loses a lot of time and nervous energy, and one's own studies suffer. The *tapirs* were not the only distractions. (In the French version of this book, where the word *distractions* meant 'amusements', I had to put them in inverted commas.) The political situation of the country was becoming a matter of concern, and the episode on 6 February 1934, when the House of Parliament was nearly invaded during a fascist manifestation, was a sombre omen for me and my friends. More dark clouds were gathering: the advent of Hitler and his treatment of the Jews, the Spanish war, the Italian invasion of Ethiopia and its repercussions in the Latin Quarter, where right-wing law students were disturbing the lectures of Gaston Jèze, the law professor who had presented the case of Ethiopia at the League of Nations.

I said at the beginning of these memoirs that, like Panurge, 'I had a natural aversion for blows'. Not always! One day as a column of the JP (*Jeunesse Patriote*) was marching down in the middle of the Boulevard Saint-Michel, shouting: 'France for the French, send the Jews to Palestine', I lost patience and, from the pavement where I was standing, addressed them in a few well-chosen words. Half a dozen courageously detached themselves from the column and started beating me up. I was rescued by a squad of policemen, who extricated me from my aggressors and took me to a police station, where I refused to lodge a complaint (after all I had provoked them). After dressing my injuries (of no consequence, apart from a front tooth which must have remained on the pavement), they let me go home by myself.

Thinking about this incident today it occurs to me that the charming young men who howled: 'Send the Jews to Palestine' must have been Zionists in the proper sense of the word. It is their worthy descendants who howl today: 'Palestine for the Palestinians!' and 'Death to the Israeli assassins!' You can't win!

To add to all these distractions, I may add, without departing from the reticence which guides me in these memoirs, that I had fallen in love with an Israeli girl (or should I say Palestinian, as the State of Israel did not exist then). She was the sister of a friend of mine, and had come to Paris to study history. She was determined to go back to Palestine, but I was far from being indifferent to her, and she would have willingly agreed to my accompanying her, for better or for worse—following, in short, the advice of the young men who had given my dentist so much work. I hesitated for a very long time, I was very unhappy, she was too, '*Invitus, invitam dimisit*', she left, I stayed and forgot her as was natural at my age. She must have forgotten me too, for during a trip to Israel in 1968 with my wife, I saw her again, now a happy mother of two. But she was cruelly fated to die of cancer a few years later, after losing her son in the Yom Kippur war.

Such were the distractions that were preying on me during my second year of *Licence* (1934–5), during which I tackled courses in 'Differential and Integral Calculus' (abbreviated to CDI) and 'Mathematical Physics'. Let me give the score straight away: I failed in both. My distractions explain and excuse it in part, but not completely.

CDI was a tough nut, without doubt the most difficult course of the *Licence*, which accounted for 75 per cent of failures at the exams. It was taught by two mathematicians of great prestige: Gaston Julia and Arnaud Denjoy, both, it goes without saying members of the Academy. For reasons I now forget (assuming I ever knew them), it was René Garnier who was giving the part of the course allotted to Julia. This was a frequent practice at the Faculty of Sciences. You could often read in the official notice announcing the lectures:

Course X, Monsieur Y Professor, Monsieur Z in charge of the Course.

I have already spoken of René Garnier; his lectures had the great quality of being comprehensible. If only M. Denjoy had followed the example of M. Julia! But alas! The conscientious M. Denjoy wished to teach the Course which was his responsibility himself. His teaching could be summed up as follows: his lectures were incomprehensible (and, as a minor compensation, inaudible), and his examination questions were impossible. It was understood that in order to pass the exam, one had to solve all of Garnier's problems and try to scratch the surface of Denjoy's. Naturally, after my first taste of Denjoy, I stopped going to his lectures. As for Garnier, the first part of his course, which was called 'Complementary Geometry and Algebra' and was destined to fill some gaps for those who had not passed through a *Taupe*, had just been published by Gauthier-Villars (a publisher still thriving today), at an exorbitant price—like all their books—and so there was no point in going to Garnier's lectures either. As a friend told me: 'You could enlist in the Foreign Legion; all you need is a day's leave for the exam.' For this purpose (not so I could join the Foreign Legion, but so I could stay away from the lectures), I treated myself to the *Goursat*, a monumental work from Gauthier-Villars in three volumes, by the former holder of the Chair of CDI, a mathematician of global repute in France—if I may be permitted this ambiguous expression.

When, later, I learned the meaning of Dirac's delta function, I thought that it was an adequate description of the commercial policy of Gauthier-Villars: selling an infinitely small number of volumes at a price that was infinitely high. All their books were paperbacks, and since they were meant for everyday use, they started falling to pieces after a few weeks and had to be sent to the binder. Moreover, following a prejudice, like that governing the virginity of brides (I take back the word 'prejudice,' not wishing to offend beliefs that I respect), their books were uncut, and, when leafing through them at the stands of booksellers, one had to be content with incomplete gratification—as described by the novelist M. Marcel Prévôt of the Académie Française (alas almost forgotten today) in his novel *Les demi-vierges*. The *Goursat* was formidable. After carefully cutting its pages and thus reducing its resale value by 30%, I tried to read it, if 'read' is the right word. I am not a mathematician and my judgement—that of an unsuccessful candidate—is questionable, but I am convinced that this is not the right way to teach mathematics. Be that as it may, whether the responsibility lies with Messieurs Denjoy and Garnier or myself, I flunked the exam. I had never fallen so low, and never did it again. I expected it, yet the shock was so severe that I did not even turn up to the October session. What I was lacking was the intellectual gymnastics (if again 'intellectual' is the right word) to which the *taupins* are subjected for two years and thanks to which, every examination problem (I do not mean every *new* problem, for it is not a matter of novelty—quite the opposite in fact) has a familiar taste. It may well be that it is the humiliation of my failure which, after more than fifty years, inspires these virulent lines.

Mathematical physics was another matter. The course was based on the Calculus of Probabilities and three options: 'Complements of Probabilities', 'Theoretical Complements' (?) and 'Mathematical Physics'. I got into it by mistake. I had seen the lecturer's name on the notice board, but for *Francis Perrin* I had read *Jean Perrin*. Jean Perrin was an illustrious French physicist who had received the Nobel Prize in 1926 for his work on 'the discontinuous structure of matter'. Francis Perrin was his son, a theoretical physicist in his thirties, of whom I will have a lot to say later on. I understood my mistake when, instead of the noble visage crowned with the white hair and adorned with the white beard of Jean Perrin, as popularized by the Press, I saw a shortish young man with a little moustache (he was going to grow a beard later, after breaking his jaw in a diving accident). I thought of leaving, but the lecture room was small and it would have been embarrassing. I stayed and did not regret it. The first part of his course was devoted to classical statistical mechanics, and I found it delightful. For the first time since I had started mooching around the university, I had the impression that I was learning something new. The second part, quantum statistical mechanics, I had to drop, as I was ignorant of quantum mechanics. I did not even try the examination, but I promised myself that I would come back next year.

Such was the end of the disappointing second year of my *Licence*. There is nothing much to say about the third year (1935–36) except that I finished off CDI and also passed mathematical physics. For this second examination I had bought an excellent book from the publisher Hermann, who was not giving away his books either, but who at least had the intelligence to cut them and put a slightly stronger cover round them (fifty years later he was to publish my *Reflexions d'un Physicien*). This book was Eugène Bloch's *The Old and the New Theory of Quanta*. It finally taught me what these quanta were and enabled me to follow Francis Perrin's course. At the final examination I came second (only two had been admitted).

In the summer of 1936 we had had the great joy of my father's belated arrival. His first words on seeing me on the platform of the Gare du Nord where we had alighted eleven years before him, were an astonished 'But you are not short!' I had indeed grown to a normal height, the same as his, whereas I had been very small for my age when I left Moscow at ten.

Our relationship was difficult at times, which is probably inevitable when one leaves a child of ten and finds a man of twenty-one, who, indeed, now belongs to a different culture. He found it difficult to accept that sometimes I came home very late, and even more difficult on a few occasions when I came home very early; I in turn found his reactions hard to take. But the most serious problem was that I was entering a difficult period of my life—the second part of my six 'lonely years', in which, as I had occasion to say in a publication celebrating the fortieth anniversary of the Commissariat à l'Energie Atomique: 'I was desperately searching for a direction, for a guide, for companions in my research'.

For my poor father, who was greatly attached to external marks of success (which was only natural in a man who had worked very hard all his life for himself and his family) this search looked very much like idleness. Poor Father! He had arrived at a bad time; if only he could have been here during my 'Cinq Glorieuses' at Janson, or through some miracle have lived long enough to see me wearing the *Costume de l'Académie*!

In search of research

... and of time lost.

A painting by Watteau—The trajectory of the self-taught man: beating about the bush—Discovery of the good authors—The Great Seminar(y)—The discovery of fire—A 'de luxe' tapir—Death of a killer— Marine zoology

I have in front of me a yellowed piece of paper, dated 1945, and signed by the Assistant Secretary of the Faculty of Sciences in Paris, certifying that Anatole Abragam had enrolled at the Faculty for the years 1936–7, 1937–8, and 1938–9, to prepare a thesis with a view to a Doctorate of Science, under the supervision of Professor Perrin. Where is that thesis? There is no thesis, there is no subject for a thesis, there is not even a single calculation and *a fortiori* not a single experiment, *there is nothing*. Whose fault is it? Mine, no doubt, to a large extent. If I had been more talented, if I had been fired by that passion for research, so exalted in the books written for the enlightment of studious youth; if I had also been less exacting in what I aspired to accomplish, I might at the end of those three years have produced some tangible evidence that the modest enrolment fees had not been completely wasted. But I was far from being the only one to blame: there was one great impersonal culprit—the System. But behind the impersonal system there were people, and of these people I must speak. The first, the most responsible for that state of affairs, the one under whose 'supervision' I was 'preparing' my thesis, was M. Francis Perrin; I cannot avoid speaking about him. I have hesitated for a long time before writing what follows, and perhaps I will tear it up if I cannot manage to say what I want, the way I want.

Francis Perrin is eighty-seven at the time of writing (1988). I described in the last chapter under what circumstances we first ran into each other. After an interruption which lasted from 1939 till 1946, we kept seeing each other more and more often as I rose in the hierarchy of the CEA (Commissariat à l'Energie Atomique) where he was *Haut Commissaire* (High Commissioner), that is the head of science, from 1951 till 1970. In 1960 I was elected to a Chair in the Collège de France where he had been a Professor since 1946, a further opportunity for seeing each other. Finally, in 1973 I was elected to the Académie des Sciences, where I can see him every Monday.

Today, my uppermost feeling toward Francis Perrin, a man I have known and associated with for over half a century, is one of deep-seated affection based on his kindness and his sense of humour. Next comes my admiration for his amazingly quick intelligence, which 'twigs' on the spot, for the scope and expanse of his knowledge, for his vast culture, for his capacity to take an interest in every thing and to understand everything.

Then comes my gratitude for all the things he did for me at the various stages of my career. He was responsible for my entering the CNRS (Centre National de la Recherche Scientifique) in September 1946, and then the CEA at the end of the same year. He supported my candidacy for a Fellowship in England. He nominated me for several of the scientific prizes that I obtained during my career. He was in charge of the reports and one of the sponsors of my candidacies for the Collège de France and for the Academy. If this feeling of gratitude lags behind my feelings of affection and admiration it is (false modesty be damned) because, whenever he had backed me, I had always been the best candidate by far.

Last comes the bitterness for the manner in which he failed me during the three years when he was 'supervising' my work, a bitterness which after all these years still lurks in a little corner of my mind.

What had he done? Every year, for three years, he signed a paper asserting that I was working on a thesis under his supervision, he signed an attestation making it possible for me to work in the library of the Institut Henri Poincaré, at my request he introduced me to Louis de Broglie whose seminar I wished to attend, he brought me to the 'Tea', where scientists gathered around Jean Perrin and I was introduced to Pierre Auger (of whom I will say a word later on).

In 1938 he lent me his personal copy of *Reviews of Modern Physics*, with the seminal article by Hans Bethe on nuclear physics (the library copy had been stolen), a copy that the war had prevented me from returning to him. What else? His advice on finding a subject of research had been to read the *Physical Review*, to see if something there would interest me. True, in the autumn of 1936 *Physical Review* was not yet the big monster it has now become, but even so, as I said earlier, I needed far more talent than I actually possessed to make use of his advice.

He was elusive and unreachable. I never knew where he was nor what he was doing, and since I dared not telephone him at home, our contacts were rare and brief. Clemenceau is reported to have compared Raymond Poincaré to Aristide Briand in the following terms: 'Poincaré knows everything but understands nothing; Briand knows nothing but he understands everything'. I was tempted to say of Francis Perrin: 'Francis knows everything and understands everything, but what does he do?' (When he saw these lines in the French version of this book, last year, he told me that I was being both too kind and too harsh to him, that he neither knew nor understood everything but that he did do a few things in his lifetime. This indeed is quite true: for example he was the first to calculate the critical mass of natural uranium, and I believe he suggested before anyone else that the atomic nucleus was made of neutrons and protons. But he had misunderstood me. When I said: 'What does he do?' I meant: 'Where the hell is he when I need him!')

I think I would have been less resentful if he had not been so intelligent and so charming. I remember a famous painting by Watteau (the Press had talked about it a lot when it was stolen and then recovered sometime later). The painting represents a youth, charming and agile, who gambols while playing with a *diabolo*. The painting is called *l'Indifferent*. This is the character that my friend Francis reminds me of, Francis, whom after more than fifty years, from strength of habit, I still call *Monsieur*. I will return to him more than once in these pages.

I do not know what to call my three years of 'research' (1936–9)—part two of the six 'lonely years' (1933–9) Since my first disastrous geometry test at thirteen, I have not wept over my intellectual failures, and so 'the weeping years' won't do. Perhaps 'the foggy years', for the memories I keep of these three years are far more blurred than those of the previous three years. Is it because during the years of my *Licence* the examinations served as milestones and marked the passage of time; is it because, in obedience to good Doctor Freud, my memory tries to obliterate what it dislikes? I don't know and I don't care. I feel lost in their chronology and will be content to recall, with a few comments, the books I studied and the characters I met during this period. I fear that it will be frightfully boring to anyone who is not a physicist. Too bad—I have to exorcise this past!

Relativity and quanta were the enchanted universe which I longed to penetrate. I shied from tackling, head on, the books of Louis de Broglie, and even more so the various works in English and in German which stood on the shelves of the library in the Institut Henri Poincaré. De Broglie scared me, I could barely read English, and even less German, even though it had been my choice of foreign language at the Lycée. (I discovered long ago that the two main stumbling blocks in German are: first to find out whether in the end the sentence means yes or no—a problem of parity of the number of negatives—and, second, to find the verb.) For relativity I at first chose a ridiculous book, called *General Relativity and Absolute Differential Calculus*, by a M. Galbrun, 'Mathematician and Actuary' as he called himself. I cite this first attempt just to show what kind of absurdities one can be led to when entirely on one's own.

Overwhelmed by the abundance of indices, I soon gave it up. I think that this capacity for being rapidly discouraged by indigestible books saved me more than once, then and in later life also.

I passed on to a treatise on relativity in two volumes by von Laue. Von Laue is a great physicist, but, perhaps through the fault of the translator, I found his book difficult to understand.

Studying von Laue helped me discover the gaps in my knowledge of electromagnetism, and I turned to a book by Léon Bloch (brother of Eugène Bloch, whose book was my first initiation in quantum mechanics): *Précis d'Electricité Théorique*, a book swarming with equations and therefore necessarily 'advanced'. (I was a bit of a snob, I am afraid. It was much, much later, that I was to discover how much physics one can explain with very few equations.) Léon was not as good a teacher as brother Eugène, and after fifty pages he remained on a shelf in my room, a constant reproach to my fickleness. (The two brothers perished during the Nazi occupation.)

I also turned to the books of Bouasse. I want to say a few words about this evil spirit of French physics. Bouasse held the chair of Physics at the Faculty of Toulouse. It is a good thing that his impossible character had kept him away from Paris: he would have done even more harm there. He had produced a large number of very thick books, principally on acoustics, electricity and magnetism, of which he said with apparent logic: 'My books must be good since they sell well'. I never used the acoustics ones but I did use some of the other books. They were not bad for engineers and for physics teachers, and for students of the *Agrégation de Physique* they may have been ideal. These qualities were spoiled by colossal ignorance and a rabid hatred of modern physics. Not only quanta, but even electrons could not find favour with him. As for relativity, he foamed at the mouth at the mere name of Einstein, whom he called Newton II (he was being ironical). The narrowest conservatism, an unbridled chauvinism, and a hatred of his colleagues in the capital, were expressed in the incendiary prefaces which preceded his books. Bouasse had a deleterious influence on generations of engineers, teachers in secondary schools, and even a few university professors. He bears a large responsibility for the backwardness of large parts of French physics.

For a long time I had been eyeing a book on the library shelves. It was a work in two volumes, sumptuously produced by Springer, in German alas—*Elektrodynamik* by Ya. Frenkel, a Soviet physicist. 'It must exist in Russian' I thought to myself, and decided to acquire it. My father was not in Russia any more, but one of his brothers-in-law was the head of a small translation bureau in Paris. He obtained a catalogue of Soviet scientific books for me and ordered a good many of those I wanted. As I have said before, they were very cheap (Frenkel's *Electrodynamik* cost 15 per cent of the Springer price). It was a great boon and I obtained many Russian books at a low price—or rather books in Russian, for they translated a lot from foreign languages.

Frenkel's book was a bit of an unweeded garden and sometimes downright obscure, but brilliant and imaginative, far more modern and alive than that of Léon Bloch, and I studied a sizeable part of it.

In relativity I procured two books by Arthur Eddington: *Space, Time,*

Gravitation, a delightful popularization, such as only the English (well, the Anglo-Saxons) know how to write, and *The Mathematical Theory of Relativity*, which I studied seriously. At the same time I was following Léon Brillouin's course on tensors at the Collège de France.

This left quanta, and I circled around the subject without daring to embark, such was its reputation for difficulty and abstraction. Besides, I argued to myself: 'Since quanta have called into question all the physics that preceded them, the least I can do is to find out what exactly has been overturned, before studying what was put in its place.' Such scruples were meritorious but did not take me very far. I have said earlier that the study of the *Old and New Theory of Quanta* by Eugène Bloch had brought me to the right level for the course of *Mathematical Physics* by Francis Perrin, which was true; but only the Old Quantum Theory was needed for it, and a holy terror still paralysed me at the gates of the New Theory. The same scruples drove me to delve further into the details of the Old Theory before starting on the New. My scruples were absurd, for if the Old Quantum Theory is very simple in the form given to it by Bohr and Sommerfeld, it becomes very complicated and very shaky if one tries to generalize it further. This is where some intelligent counsel could have helped me, but there was no one to give me that kind of advice, and I pursued my convoluted and solitary quest. Still on the Old Theory, I studied a book by Léon Brillouin, *l'Atome de Bohr*, and I acquired the Russian translation of a book by Max Born from 1923, called *Theoretical Atomic Physics*, in which, using complicated calculations, Born tried to get out of the Old Theory all it could yield and even more.

At last I understood that the time had come to launch myself into the New Theory. Even then, I did not immediately tackle the second part of Eugène Bloch's book and the books by de Broglie, but lingered once more, starting on two bizarre works, which both claimed to be a painless initiation: *Microénergétique* by someone called Bricout, auxiliary master of the Ecole Polytechnique, with a preface by Charles Fabry, and a book by a Mr Birtwhistle (I am not sure of the spelling), translated from the English by 'two young and brilliant French scientists' (said the preface by someone senior, whose name I forget), Maurice Ponte and Yves Rocard. Maurice Ponte died in his eighties some time ago, a member of the Academy, and Yves Rocard is the father of the French politician Michel Rocard.

Bricout was rejected almost immediately. Coming out of the library, I ran into Francis Perrin, who was in a hurry as usual. I seized on this rare opportunity and told him that I was going to study the *Microénergétique* by Bricout. 'Who?' he said. 'Bricout', I said. 'Why?', he said, and disappeared. It was the end of Bricout, and I should in fairness have cited this exchange as another piece of advice from my supervisor.

Birtwhistle, whom I had bought for a song at the large bookshop Gibert (there was a high pile of them on the stalls), remained incomprehensible, (perhaps only uncomprehended by his translators) and went the way of Bricout.

I finally dared to start on the first de Broglie: *Mécanique Ondulatoire*. I was pleasantly surprised to find it quite accessible, albeit a little complicated. The second: *La Quantification dans la Nouvelle Mécanique*, the best of de Broglie's books, seemed very clear to me. On the other hand the third, *l'Electron Magnétique*, which deals with the relativistic theory of Dirac, is mediocre to say the least.

For those who know what it's about, I'll say that he demonstrates the tensor character of the various operators one can form from Dirac's matrices in an incredible clumsy manner, using an explicit representation of Dirac's matrices.

After that I had no difficulty in finishing off the second part of the book by Eugène Bloch.

Three more books complemented my education in quanta. The first was a big two-volume treatise on wave mechanics (in Russian) by Ya. Frenkel. One should know that Frenkel had been a brilliant Soviet physicist, who in his time launched a quantity of new ideas, many of which turned out to be valid—for instance his theory of a certain type of defect in solids which bears his name. He published an enormous amount, and some of his Soviet colleagues said that he did not always reread what he wrote carefully enough (it goes without saying that I discovered all of this much later). It was in his book that I saw for the first time the expression 'phonon gas' which, being used to the numerous misprints in Soviet books, I took, for a while, to stand for 'photon gas'.

The second book, written for Soviet students working for a doctorate, was by the Soviet physicist V. Fock. I open here a parenthesis about Fock. He had been one of the founders of Russian theoretical physics after the Revolution (and also a great teacher, as I could see for myself from that book).

*We owe him a considerable improvement brought to an approximation used to calculate electronic wave functions, invented by the British physicist Hartree. In that method each electron moves in the average field produced by the other electrons. The calculation must be 'self-consistent', meaning that, by recalculating the average field from the wave functions thus obtained, one should recover the values of the field, injected at the start. Hartree's method was imperfect insofar as it did not take into account the indiscernibility of the electrons. Fock introduced this indiscernibility and showed that *his* wave functions were the 'best' in a variational sense, that is they yielded the lowest, and therefore the best value, for the energy of the atom.*

I am afraid I have let myself go a little here, because I wish to come back to Hartree–Fock functions later, in connection with a little incident which occurred during my thesis examination in Oxford in 1950.

Let us go back to Fock's book. Unlike my other Russian books it was lent to me by a man named Jean-Louis Destouches, who had got it from de Broglie, to whom it had been sent as a homage by Fock. This book was a marvel of clarity and brevity. In two hundred odd pages it put in the hands of the student all he needed to *use* quantum mechanics as a tool, rather than as something to worship. I cannot better describe the impression it made on me than by saying that I formed then and there the project of returning to Soviet Russia to study under Fock.

I do not remember exactly when this insane project took shape, perhaps at the end of 1938. My comrades, to whom I told my plans, congratulated me warmly on my knowledge of Russian, which was going to make it possible. My father, who had kept his Soviet passport and who seldom spoke of Soviet Russia in a derogatory manner, told me that he could imagine less unpleasant ways of taking one's own life, and revealed to me for the first time a few things about the Soviet Union that he knew at first hand. Although I was often in revolt against my father, I listened to him for once and gave up my plans. It is always difficult to estimate retrospectively one's chances of survival, considering what happened in France in 1940 and later, but I believe that by following his advice I did not choose the worst option.

The third book is *The Principles of Quantum Mechanics* by Dirac. I can sum up what I think of it (and I weigh my words), as follows: 'It is the greatest book on physics ever written'. It is a very mathematical book, but with very little *visible* mathematics. Dirac gives the impression of knowing a very small amount of mathematics and of inventing what he needs as he goes along. One can cite his delta function, which Laurent Schwartz 'made an honest woman out of' fifteen years later, by giving it a mathematical legitimacy with his distribution theory. I remember a conference with Dirac after the war at the Institut Henri Poincaré, at which he worried about the convergence of a certain series. 'He is getting old,' I told my neighbour.

One knows since Weyl and Wigner that group theory had been the keystone of quantum mechanics; Dirac uses the permutation group with a tranquil shamelessness while giving the impression that he has never heard of it. He brings to an end, and with such majesty, the debate between 'Quantum Mechanics' and 'Wave Mechanics' by introducing from the start an abstract formulation which makes the whole debate irrelevant. In thirty pages he gives a formulation of the relativistic theory of the electron, beside which the painstaking attempt of de Broglie fades away.

I think I had a nerve to choose the following title for my first book, published in 1961 by Oxford University Press: *The Principles of Nuclear Magnetism*. In 1981 The Oxford University Press had the imprudence (impudence?) to announce 'two great classics from Oxford University Press in paperback for the first time'. I proudly showed the announcement to my friend and colleague Charlie Slichter from the University of Illinois. 'Dirac must be tickled to death' was his comment.

I also studied some mathematics in my little corner. I had ordered from the USSR the Russian translation of *Modern Analysis* by Whittaker and Watson (at a fifth of the price) and had formed the project of studying it thoroughly, and of solving all the exercises. I had been encouraged in this demented undertaking by a Zionist friend who had just come from Palestine, where he had been jailed for three years by the British for activities of which they disapproved. It was during his imprisonment that he had accomplished this task which he recommended to me. I realized rapidly that he had benefited from a particularly favourable environment and gave up my own attempt. Those familiar with the work in question will, I am sure, understand me. But I acquired the Russian translation of *Mathematical Methods of Physics* by Courant and Hilbert, which allied depth and rigour with simplicity. One was a long way from the cutting in four of epsilons by M. Goursat.

During my 'Three Foggy Years' I must have had more 'good reads' than those I have recalled in these few pages, but I think I have let most of them float to the surface of my memory.

I did not mention the philosophico-scientific popularizations by Henri Poincaré, Émile Borel, Jean Perrin, Louis de Broglie, Arthur Eddington, James Jeans etc., which provided some relief from more austere pursuits. Naturally this 'reading' of mine was practised with pen and paper, checking the calculations as I went along and covering a prodigious amount of paper with writing. It goes without saying, at least for me, that one cannot do that kind of thing, with no palpable satisfaction apart from filling one's noodle with knowledge, eight hours a day and six days a week. I had periods of fatigue and even of complete discouragement where, apart from my *tapirs*, I did not do anything. I went to the cinema or to the swimming pool, or just lay down on my bed and read mystery stories.

No wonder poor Father had decided I was a lazy bones and a ne'er-do-well, and there were moments when I was not far from thinking so myself.

Naturally before I had locked myself in 'Splendid Isolation' I had made attempts to get integrated into the scientific life of my country. I had been, as I said at the beginning of this chapter, introduced by Francis Perrin to Louis de Broglie.

At this point I want to digress for a while from my own destiny to say something about this great figure of French physics, too little known outside France.

Louis, Duc de Broglie (1892–1987), made one of the greatest discoveries of the twentieth century, the wavelike nature of all matter. His formula: $\lambda=(h/p)$ stands on a par with Planck's $E=h\nu$ and Einstein's $E=mc^2$. He came from an illustrious family of soldiers and statesmen. His ancestors, of Italian origin, the Broglia, a younger branch of the Gribaldi family of

Piedmont who hark back to the XIIth century, came to serve the King of France in the XVIIth century. Louis de Broglie is directly descended from François-Marie Broglia, (1611–1656), the first to serve in France, a brilliant and valiant soldier, posthumously made a *Maréchal de France*. The next three direct descendants, Victor-Maurice, François-Marie, and Victor-François were also *Maréchaux de France*. François-Marie was made the first Duc de Broglie by the King of France, and his son Victor-François was rewarded for his services by the Emperor Francis I with rank of *Prince du Saint Empire Romain Germanique*, a rank extended to all his direct descendants of either sex. (When, after his Nobel Prize in 1929, the name of Louis de Broglie became widely known to many not conversant with the finer points of nobility rules, some were surprised to see him referred to as the *Prince* Louis de Broglie, whilst his elder brother Maurice, no mean scientist himself, only had the title of *Duc*. The explanation is of course that here *Prince* is not a French title, unlike *Duc*, which takes precedence over it. Louis de Broglie became Duc after his brother Maurice died without male descendants.)

After Victor-François the family switches to politics. His son, the liberal Louis-Victor, refused to emigrate and died on the guillotine, but the next two gave France two Prime Ministers, the second of them being the grandfather of Louis de Broglie, Charles-Victor-*Albert*. Then at last came the scientists: the elder brother Maurice (1875–1960), and Louis himself.

Maurice de Broglie was a distinguished scientist. After the death of his father, the Duc Maurice, who was a naval officer, installed a private laboratory in his town house in Paris, obtained a long leave of absence and finally resigned from the navy in order to devote himself entirely to physical science—much to the disappointment of his family. It did not seem right for a Duc de Broglie to tinker with strange pieces of apparatus— even if at the beginning it was practised only as a hobby in his own house with his own mechanic—instead of becoming a general, a statesman, or at least an admiral.

It is experimental science that he practised—X-ray Physics, photo-electric effect, and later electron diffraction—with great distinction. In 1911 Maurice de Broglie attended the first Solvay Conference, of which he was one of the secretaries. He took with him his younger brother Louis, aged nineteen, who saw there for the first time the greatest theorists of his time, H. A. Lorentz, Henri Poincaré, and Albert Einstein, who impressed him deeply.

As befits a scion of an illustrious family, Louis de Broglie was first educated at home by a private tutor, Father Chanet. At the age of fourteen he entered (twenty years before me) the Lycée Janson, but, unlike me, went there accompanied by his faithful Father Chanet. At eighteen he started historical studies at university, but switched to Science after the intellectual shock of the Solvay Conference, and passed his Licence of

Science. This brings us to the year 1913, but then a gap of six years opened up in the scientific career of Louis de Broglie. He was called up for military service and was naturally kept there when the First World War started. He spent it under the Eiffel tower in a military wireless station, and it was only in 1919 that he was demobilized at last and took up science again. One cannot say that his beginnings were so much more auspicious than my own.

He spent a lot of time in his brother's laboratory and started working on the theory of X-ray spectra and the photoelectric effect. It was in 1923 that he made his immortal discovery, which was published in three short notes in 1923 and in his doctor's thesis in 1924. Few people realized at the time the deep significance and the extraordinary daring of de Broglie's ideas. It is a fair guess that his thesis examiners would not have given him his degree if one of them, Paul Langevin, had not had the good idea of showing the thesis to Einstein. Einstein understood immediately the significance of the work and wrote to Langevin: 'He has lifted a corner of the great veil.' (A personal recollection at this point. In the sixties I met Van de Graaff, the inventor of the electrostatic accelerator. He told me that as a young student in Paris he had attended the public thesis examination of Louis de Broglie. 'Never had so much gone over the heads of so many', was how he put his impressions.)

The discovery can be summed up in a few words. It is known that the photon which is a wave is also a particle. Why should not the electron, which is a particle, and for that matter any particle, also be a wave? That sums it up, all that is left is a few equations, and it is worth a full Nobel Prize in 1929 at the age of thirty seven.

Then followed all the honours that France could bestow on its illustrious son: a Chair of Physical Theories was created for him in 1933, the same year that he was elected to the Académie des Sciences; he became its Life Secretary in 1942, and was elected to the Académie Française in 1944.

He was also elected Foreign Associate of the US National Academy in 1948, and Foreign Member of the Royal Society in 1953. He became Duc de Broglie on the death of his brother Maurice in 1960, as mentioned above.

De Broglie ran a well-attended weekly seminar where young and not so young theorists expounded their views. It was not customary to interrupt and ask questions before the end of the seminar, and the discussions at the end were brief and devoid of passion, which gave a somewhat stilted course to the whole proceedings. It must be regretfully admitted that the disciples who congregated around de Broglie were not of the highest intellectual calibre, and perhaps not always of the highest intellectual honesty. One of the manifestations of this was the atmosphere of admiration, not to say of adulation, with which they surrounded him. Thus, for instance, it was bad form to speak of 'quantum mechanics' rather than 'wave mechanics', since the latter form was the one based on de Broglie's waves. It was also understood that wave mechanics was a highly abstract and difficult field for the chosen, rather than, an everyday tool for the rank and file physicist as it was at the time in other countries. Although de Broglie may not have encouraged such behaviour, perhaps out of kindness he never reacted against it sufficiently strongly to put it down once and for all. Also, with advancing years, as the direction of his research separated him more and more from the mainstream of research pursued abroad (where he never went), he must have felt some comfort in being surrounded by young (and not so young) disciples, who agreed with his conceptions and devoutly developed them in seminars and articles. The situation was reminiscent of the image of Gulliver tied down by Lilliputian midgets.

Needless to say I knew very little of all that when Perrin introduced me to him for the first time. He greeted me with great courtesy and invited me to take part in the proceedings. I was terribly impressed. At the thought of shaking hands with a man who was a prince of physics and a prince by birth I was seized with an almost religious emotion. He was wearing a dark-blue suit which even then seemed slightly old fashioned, with a wing collar and a pearl in his tie. He had a curiously high-pitched voice and he seldom spoke. Strange as it may seem, I thought that this man, covered as he was with honours and glory, was shy.

At the thought of finding myself in the mainstream of theoretical physics of our time I was overcome with joy. My disappointment was all the more cruel.

I shall mercifully omit here the portraits of some of the participants in the de Broglie seminar which I drew in the French version of this book, in particular that of Jean-Louis Destouches, de Broglie's prize disciple, sometimes known as the Incitatus of wave mechanics. Some are dead, others forgotten, all totally unknown outside France.

The case of Louis de Broglie raises the painful problem of the genius who makes one great, very great discovery, but one only, and then has to live with it for the rest of his life—over sixty years for de Broglie. This problem is marvellously illustrated by a cartoon I saw many years ago. It shows a cave man immersed in deep thought in the pose of the *Penseur* by Rodin. Next to him are two more cave men, and one of them is saying to the other: 'All right, so he discovered fire, but what has he done since?' Louis de Broglie *did* discover fire and he was the first. Others might have discovered it if he hadn't but he *did*, before anyone else.

And what then? One must go on living, confronted by other geniuses, Schrödinger, Heisenberg, Dirac, Pauli, and then the *poetae minores*, Born, Jordan, Kramers and all the others. But the second great idea does not come, will never come, and the physicist who has one idea of genius and who cannot bear to stop at that, locks himself in an impossible quest, is little by little circumvented and confined by flatterers, by incompetents, by cranks if not by crooks, and lo and behold, French theoretical physics goes right down the drain.

I did not realize all of this immediately. It took me six months to see that I was wasting my time at this seminar, and so I left, unsure what do next. Besides Louis de Broglie and Francis Perrin there was in my time a third theoretical physicist of international repute, Léon Brillouin. (If I do not count Paul Langevin it is because during my 'three foggy years' he was only concerned with politics—generous and courageous politics, but politics all the same. The reason why I do not count Edmond Bauer, an outstanding theorist of physical chemistry, who had published in the late thirties, with Fritz London, a penetrating essay on 'Measurement in Quantum Mechanics', a man as learned as he was modest, is precisely that because of his great modesty I had not heard of him.)

Brillouin did not make any discoveries of the Nobel Prize calibre (though that was not what he thought, and he made the mistake of putting his opinion in writing, which did not do him any good) but he had to his credit several important results. He gave his name to a number of phenomena and concepts (Brillouin zones, Brillouin functions, Brillouin scattering, Kramers–Brillouin–Wentzel approximation method). Recently a laboratory of neutron physics at Saclay was named after him. He made contributions to solid state physics, statistical mechanics, wave propagation, information theory and its relation to the entropy concept. He was the most international of French physicists; well known in foreign parts and well informed on what was going on there.

Physically he was very handsome, with an unlined youthful face under snow-white hair. At the Collège de France, where he held a Chair, he had given two courses on tensors and their applications. I had liked his lectures, and timidly offered him my services. He got rid of me with a laconic: 'See my assistant'. His assistant, named Mariani, had the reputation of being a very good tennis player, but I had heard him speak at the de Broglie seminar and it had been enough to discourage me from speaking to him about research. *Exit* Brillouin.

Having investigated what theoretical physics could offer me, I turned to experimental physics. This was even briefer. I went to see my former master, Charles Fabry. He agreed to take me in his lab, called 'The Teaching Laboratory of the Sorbonne', but just as the course of CDI, nominally under the responsibility of Julia, was given by Garnier, the man in charge of Fabry's laboratory was Eugène Darmois. I found myself in familiar waters and I was not optimistic. Darmois told me that he would put me on a study of the Raman effect and explained to me what it was. I left him somewhat bewildered, having ceased to understand what little I thought I understood about it before. The man responsible for me 'in the field', that is, in the laboratory which seemed to me an image of utter devastation, was Ivan Peychès who later made a brilliant career as an industrial chemist, but who, for the time being, was far too busy finishing up his own thesis to devote any time to me. He put me in the hands of a young man who had been working under him for some time and who did not seem to have a care in the world, least of all that of guiding my research on the Raman effect. One may well say that I was not made of the right stuff and that I should have stuck at it. I did not stick at it and left after three days.

My second attempt took place with Pierre Auger, whom I had contacted at Jean Perrin's 'Tea' on the advice of Francis Perrin. Pierre Auger is now ninety and his mind is as sharp as ever. He is known for two important discoveries made before the war: the so-called 'Auger effect' (where the energy of excitation of an electron is used to expel another electron rather than to emit an X-ray), and the large showers of cosmic rays. After the war he pursued an international career as Scientific Director of Unesco.

On our way out of the 'Tea' Auger gave me a brief description of the research he was pursuing on cosmic rays, and delivered me into the hands of one of his collaborators, a M. Fréon, who was a man of few words. I came back to see M. Fréon the following morning. He took me to a bench covered with counters and suggested that I write down, every ten minutes, the numbers appearing on the counters. 'What do we do next?', I asked. 'When we have enough data we'll see about their treatment.' I took data all morning and did not come back in the afternoon. Once more I did not stick at it.

Before I take leave of my studies during the 'six lonely years' (the war was going to tear me from them before long) I want to make two remarks which go beyond my own personal experience.

The first thing that strikes me on rereading what I have just written is that none of my masters seem to have found favour with me. In part this may be due to the fact that, with the exception of Louis de Broglie, whose case is very special, there was no one whose work and stature had earned my admiration, rightly or wrongly. But the main culprit, as I said before, was the system which prevailed in the French university of my time.

Who among my teachers had sought to find out how his teaching was received? Who, like all the American professors that I was to meet later, had set hours to see the students and listen to their problems? What professor advised those who wanted to do research about the books and articles they should read, or the courses they should follow? In my own experience the research candidate was a football: Francis passes to Auger who passes to Fréon, Fabry passes to Darmois, who passes to Peychès who passes to Anon.; Brillouin passes to Mariani. No doubt I have my own little bit of responsibility in this disaster; I have said it before and I say it again, I could have tried to stick at it. I am only half sorry that I didn't; those who did fared no better than I (scientifically speaking, of course). I had been told that Frédéric Joliot, the Joliot of the thirties, was a different matter, and I am quite willing to believe it. I dream sometimes that if I had met him at the right time, at his side and with his inspiration I might have done something. Maybe. But one cannot remodel the past.

My second remark is of a more general, dare I say epistemological nature. In the list of the books that I studied to initiate myself in relativity and quanta, there had not been a single original article by any of the great men, Lorentz, Einstein, Planck, Niels Bohr, de Broglie, Schrödinger, Heisenberg, Pauli, who created these sciences, but only textbooks and monographs, written by others, who had applied themselves to digesting the original papers for the benefit of the students. Dirac's monograph and to some extent the first book of Louis de Broglie—at least for me— represent two unusual examples of creators who took the trouble themselves to explain the results of their discoveries in manuals and monographs.

This is a fairly general point. From the moment the results are sufficiently well established and sufficiently well understood to be undisputed within the scientific community, books are written to describe and explain these results, and no one, except historians and philosophers (assuming they are able to do it), reads the original articles. Some may regret it but that's the way it is.

The contrast with philosophy is striking: can one imagine a philosopher with an interest in the ideas of Marx, Freud, or Hegel, who could content himself with manuals or commentaries without studying the originals? In the discussions between these gentlemen one reads (or hears): 'You missed completely Hegel's meaning' or 'read your Marx again' or 'Freud never said that.'

Working physicists do not worry these days about what Bohr or Heisenberg or Einstein might have meant in their writings, or said in their meetings, and even less Huygens or Lagrange. What they did say or write has fallen into the public domain; their names, their results, and their ideas are more alive today than their writings. I am not familiar with the writings of Pascal on vacuum, of Descartes on refraction, or Newton on equilibrium profiles of free surfaces of rotating fluids; and I do not feel the need to be.

If I were not frightened of blasphemy I would say that their flesh and their blood have penetrated into us to quench our hunger and our thirst, and that we don't need their personal contact any more. Is that not their greatest claim to fame?

Two summers of this period remain in my memory: '37 and '39. In the summer of '37 the Office of the Association of Science students, where seekers of *tapirs* used to leave their names, informed me that a M. Marcel Schlumberger wished to see me at his office. It is generally known that Marcel Schlumberger, an enterprising genius, and his brother Conrad, an inventive genius had, after the First World War founded a firm which is today one of the largest multinational concerns of our time. Well, I did not know about it. M. Marcel Schlumberger explained to me, briefly but clearly, the principle of the electrical oil survey methods which are still today the backbone of the Schlumberger empire, before telling me what was expected of me. His son Pierre (at least I think it was Pierre), aged twenty-three (a year older than me), had just got married and proposed (I now think that it was father Marcel who had proposed it to him) to spend his honeymoon on their estate called Val-Richer, in Normandy. Nothing there that concerned me so far. But Pierre had just flunked his examination in *Physique Générale* at the summer session, and his father asked me to spend two months at Val Richer to *tapirize* his son, at the rate of two to three hours every morning, for a salary of 1500 francs a month, food and board thrown in. I had to see to it that, at the end of that period, the heir to the Schlumberger empire would land the diploma which would make him look good among the staff of the paternal business. Young and innocent as I was, I understood immediately how risky this enterprise was. It was clear that this young man, very wealthy and newly wed, would feel very awkward facing a tutor, who was his junior by a year. But the financial side was too attractive, and I accepted. It was not a success.

As has been evident from the book so far, I did not hesitate to put the blame for my failures on others whenever I felt it justified, and I see no reason not to continue. I took my task very seriously. Every night immediately after dinner, I retired to my room to prepare the lesson for the next morning, surrounded by my best textbooks and a vast collection of problems, and I worked very hard. I have little doubt that if I had had to pass the examination in the autumn I would have been among the first, if not *the* first. But unfortunately the candidate was somebody else. My *tapir* was not stupid, perhaps a bit on the lazy side, but I must recognize the fact that his father had put both of us in an impossible situation. The newly-wed arrived late for the morning tutorial, his eyes still swollen with sleep, and his mind obviously on something else. In spite of my efforts, and possibly his, our relations remained strained. In the afternoons I never saw him in that vast mansion. As for the other numerous members of the household, I might as well have been transparent: nobody seemed to notice my existence. I spent the afternoons walking by myself in the grounds of Val Richer, when the weather, which was very wet that summer (as it possibly was every summer, for this was Normandy) permitted; or I stayed in my room, to work on my own research programme, or to read old 'plays of the boulevard', of which there was a large pile lying in a corner. I was not very happy.

I had one single moment of brief but intense satisfaction. Every year they organized at Val Richer a *battue* for wild rabbits. For that purpose a guard pushed specially trained ferrets into their burrows and the con-veniently placed hunters let fly at the unfortunate coneys, who bolted toward them when the ferrets drove them out.

Time reversal

I think everybody knows what a ferret is like. It is the most bloodthirsty animal there is, which kills for the pleasure of killing. The whole problem of training a ferret is to moderate its murderous instincts enough so that it will drive as many rabbits out of the burrow as possible, instead of butchering as many as possible and then, gorged with blood, falling asleep in the burrow. The training is long and unpleasant, for the wicked beasts are always trying to bite the hand of the trainer.

They told me that a fully trained ferret was worth 800 francs, more than half of my monthly salary. In a burst of kindness they gave me a shotgun. They loaded it for me and told me where to aim when the rabbits came out.

I had done some shooting in fairs and I was not, I think, a bad shot; but I had never shot at a fast moving target like a bolting rabbit. I raised my gun, took aim, fired and with my first shot bagged a . . . ferret. I wish I could say that I did it on purpose, but that would be telling a lie. It seemed to me that by slaying that evil beast I had exorcised in a single shot all the frustrations accumulated during my stay at Val Richer. I offered my humblest apologies and surrendered my gun.

As could be expected, my *tapir* flunked. When we parted he himself signed the cheque for my second month's salary. That too was a new experience for me, a *tapir* signing a cheque. I have often wondered what would have happened if the *tapir* had succeeded. Would Marcel Schlumberger have been sufficiently impressed to offer me a job in his business?

The summer of '39, also devoted to work in principle, was far more pleasant. I retain sweet memories of it and, God knows, I was going to need sweet memories to keep me warm during the six years that were to follow. It was also the first and last time in my life that my SPCN (remember the SPCN and the trilobites?) had been of any use to me. At Roscoff in Brittany, there was, and I expect still is, a zoological station where, every summer students from all parts of the world congregated to work in a marine environment on various aquatic creatures—hard or soft, sea urchins, jellyfishes, octopuses, lamellibranchia and *tutti quanti*. A pal of mine, who was working on a zoology thesis, told me that summer sojourns in that station were an opportunity for wonderful holidays in an atmosphere of gaiety and camaraderie. The participants in the sessions were housed and very well fed at special rockbottom rates in a Roscoff Hôtel (Ecu de France, Hôtel de France?) thanks to an arrangement with the zoological station. My friend was confident that, with my SPCN and a word to his supervisor, he could pass me off as a zoology student. He succeeded, and I was made part of the joyful crowd of zoologists, whom my physico-mathematical skills (whether they were alleged or real), impressed deeply. Their work involved boat excursions (officially called 'expeditions'), in the course of which my comrades were expected to fish out all the beasties which were the goal of their studies, and in which I participated with pleasure. There were many foreign students and the proportion of girls, more than half, was far more than I saw at my own lectures and seminars. In the evenings there was dancing, for those who could dance. I had always been a wretched dancer, but it was great fun all the same.

What struck me most was that the names of the zoology bosses—Prenant, Teissier, Drach, Pérez—were pronounced in a context which suggested that regular and useful contact existed between them and their students. Even the tensions and competition that I was able to detect between some of the members of the group seemed to me a symptom of being alive, preferable to the isolation and emptiness of my own studies. It may have been a case of 'the grass being greener on the other side', but I do not think so.

There it was, the kind of student life dreamed of by me and by those before me who had fired my imagination, Pisarev and Arrowsmith.

I remember three girls who had the same name, so to speak: an English girl named Little, a Swedish girl, Eva Klein, and a French girl, Claudine Petit. Little was the best looking of the three, always surrounded by boys. She could get by in French but sometimes used strange expressions. Her favourite was: '*Les Français sont ventre à terre.*' I never found out whether she meant that the French were always in a hurry or that they were potbellied. Klein, in contrast to the usual image of the Swedish girl, was slightly on the plump side and sweet-tempered. Claudine Petit, the youngest, was seventeen and a slip of a girl. Later, in the Resistance, of which she was a heroic member, this morphology saved her more than once: in the metro she could give her pursuers the slip by squeezing through the crack left by the automatic gate when it was shut. I met her after the war (reasonably 'well-covered') and at the time of writing these lines, nearing retirement.

Little was far too popular, but I made friends with the slender Claudine and in a less avuncular manner with the sweet Eva Klein. It was with sorrow (shared, I think) that I saw her leave for her native Sweden, which in this troubled year seemed a haven of peace.

After the Roscoff station, three of us—Claudine, another very energetic girl, Simone Galetti, and I—spent a fortnight exploring the youth hostels of Brittany. Sometimes we asked for hospitality in a farm and were treated to a lard omelette and buckwheat crêpes dripping with salted butter, washed down with Breton cider. I remember that once when we arrived in a farmyard bending under the weight of our rucksacks, a kind old soul asked me: 'And how much do they pay you, my boy, for tramping around like that?' Claudine was Communist (at the time), Galetti was a Trotskyist, and both deplored the woolliness of my political beliefs; but we were agreed on the need to fight the Brownshirt Plague. Then we returned to Paris. A new phase, tragic, or rather tragicomic, was beginning.

III

MAN'S ESTATE

Armageddon
or the gaieties of the squadron

Ridicule does not kill

Lost illusions—Grass-roots France—Artillery: the scholars' arm—
A cycling jaunt—The shipwreck

Shortly after the declaration of war I was called up to Châteauroux, to the Depot of the 372nd regiment of 'Heavy Artillery on Rail Tracks', which I shall henceforth abbreviate to HART. (The French version of that acronym gave rise to an untranslatable play on words which I do not regret omitting, for it did not amuse.)

The French army turned out to be a terrible disappointment to me. I had long ago gauged the value of our university; our politics, ignoble like those of Charles Maurras and Pierre Laval, or hare-brained like those of Edouard Daladier and Leon Blum, filled me with disgust or pity; and our Press, especially after Munich, seemed to me to match our politics. But I believed, laugh if you wish—this shows what systematic brainwashing can do even to people who are not completely devoid of critical sense—as I say, I did believe that we had the best army in the world. Our generals had learned the lesson of the massacres of the last war; our planes, our tanks, and our anti-tank guns were the most modern; and behind an impassable Maginot line, the Nation in Arms—led by officers, regular or reserve, who were the best in the world—stood ready to crush the worst tyranny that the world had known. I too felt ready to play my modest part in this tragedy.

I had hoped that our government, which would have compiled timely lists of all the scientific skills of our country, would call me up for scholarly defence activities, such as acoustic location, anti-aircraft artillery, mine detection or possibly even more sophisticated scientific pursuits, such as deciphering enemy codes or perfecting communication devices. But I was ready to serve and to fight Hitler anywhere. I did not dislike the idea of finding myself in HART. I was full of curiosity at the idea of seeing these gigantic guns, which, aimed with scientific accuracy, would launch huge projectiles at the rear of the enemy, devastating his factories and head-quarters. The idea that, by its very nature, this kind of artillery would be located at a distance from the line of fire, did cross my mind, but I resolutely chased away such cowardly thoughts.

An NCO who was waiting for us at the Châteauroux station, marched our civilian herd to the barracks, in imperfect step. The barracks, yards and rooms, were exactly like those I had seen in *Les Gaietés de l'Escadron*, a popular military vaudeville written by Georges Courteline, around 1900, and made into a film in the thirties. It did not take me a week to realize that *everything* was as in *Les Gaietés de l'Escadron*. Need I say that there was no trace of an artillery gun? In fact there was *nothing*. I exaggerate; there were boots, socks, long underpants, puttees, breeches, shirts, woollens, and greatcoats, everything khaki (except the underpants), but no jackets and no forage caps. Since there can be no army without a military salute, and in the French army no military salute without headgear, we were issued with black berets. Mine was very small and could barely be seen over my hair, which was dark and thick (in 1939!). The first officer I saluted, howled: 'Never salute with an uncovered head!' 'It is covered, *mon Lieutenant*', I replied meekly. I forgot to say that there were *Gras* rifles, that is of a model from before the First World War, when it was replaced by the *Lebel* rifle.

After the medicals, we started on the '*classes*', or '*école du soldat*', which was intended in principle to transform a herd of civilians into a troop of soldiers—that is an ensemble capable, not of fighting certainly, but of moving in a group with a minimum of order under the command of an NCO. Two other techniques which were crucial for defence had to be mastered: '*Le lit au carré*' or '*square bed*', and the puttees. The formative role of puttees has been forgotten today. Any fool can wear trousers, leggings or jackboots, but puttees, that's another matter! To wind them hard to a close fit around the calves and not to 'go limp' like a greenhorn while marching, is not learned in a day. The officers cheated, they wore elastic bandages which clung to the calf and did not 'go limp', but these were strictly forbidden to the enlisted man (or to give him his proper name in the artillery, the 'second gunner'). I had had some military instruction in my last student year, but square beds and puttees were new to me, and mastering them took some time.

Then came the training with rifles: *Présentez armes, reposez armes, arme sur l'épaule, bayonnette au canon* etc. Then came 'theory', that is the military ranks, the rights and duties of the 'second gunner', the gamut of punishments, the duties of sentries etc. It lasted three months, during which not a single shot was fired. Our military instructor at the university had told us that, once recruited, we would be promptly sent to the Artillery School at Fontainebleau, and, after specialized training there, into the fighting units with the rank of officer cadet. It was not quite going that way. I saw that they had mobilized far too many men and that they did not know what to do with them. Instead of killing the enemy we were killing time.

Looking back, I do not regret this absurd period for two reasons. If I had been sent to a 'fighting' unit earlier, even as an officer cadet (and entitled as such to elastic puttees), I would have wasted my time much the same during the phony war, that is up till mid-May; and after that I would have been taken prisoner if I did not run fast enough, or 'at best', killed. But, more importantly, for three months I had lived in my barrack-room side by side with a kind of people whom otherwise I would never have encountered, and who interested me. If ever there was a grass-roots France, or *France profonde*, this was it. There was a majority of farmers' sons, a few farmhands, several sons of cattle merchants, two butchers' sons, a plumber, and a character who I think was a pimp. There were, not counting me, three 'intellectuals': a seminarist, a travelling salesman, and a trainee accountant. What was a *Docteur ès Sciences* doing there? (Oh yes, I had lied; I was not going to explain at great length, the way I have done in the previous pages, *why*, I was not yet a *Docteur ès Sciences* after three years, and I had found it simpler to appropriate that degree which I never obtained.)

The butchers and the cattle merchants had the florid complexions and the assured bearing of men raised on abundant and varied flesh. At all times, even to the showers, they all wore a small pouch on a leather string around their necks, which held their money. When, after the various vaccinations, we got permission to go out in the evenings, they scorned the regimental fare in favour of Châteauroux restaurants, or of private feasts, organized in the barrack room with sumptuous hampers received from home. The presumed pimp stuck closely to them, and I imagine that in exchange for some of their viands he gave them advice drawn from his professional competence. They were the aristocrats of the barrack room. They did not know yet what radiant future was in store for them, with the defeat and all the years of the black market to follow.

The farmhands were the pariahs. I was struck to see how puny and sickly they looked. They were the butt of raggings and practical jokes from the rest of the barrack room. One of them who had the beautiful name Chantre (which means 'Cantor' in English), once confided to me that what he liked about the army was eating well and getting up late. (Reveille was at six-thirty and the food—beans, lentils, badly cooked rice, cabbage, potatoes, beef or mutton stew with more suet than meat—was definitely not for delicate palates. All the same, a year later, with the food shortage that accompanied the German occupation, I might have sided with good old Chantre.)

Every time that poor Chantre was *homme de jour*, the same witty practical joke was played on him. It was part of the duties of the *homme de jour* to get up before the others, sweep the barrack-room, and run to the kitchens to fetch the bread and the dishwater called coffee which were our breakfast. The joke was to wake him up around 11 p.m., one hour after lights out, and to persuade him that reveille had sounded and that he had better hurry. The poor fellow, half-awake, swept the room in a daze, then rushed across the dark and empty yard toward the kitchens, which were of course locked. What fun!

No one was completely illiterate but some were not too far from it. A farmhand who presented himself as Arsac (or Arzac; the reason why I don't know which will appear presently), was asked by the sergeant: 'How is it written?' 'It ain't written' was the reply.

'Theory' also raised some problems. To the perfidious question: 'How many stripes does a two-stripes lieutenant have?' my friend Jacquemin replied: 'Got one, that's for sure'.

Another, whose powers of induction deserved better than the mocking reception which he got, began his recitation of military ranks correctly: lance-corporal, corporal, lance-sergeant, sergeant, but then extrapolated boldly to 'lance-lieutenant', 'lance-captain', all the way up to 'lance-general.'

A last story sticks in my memory. Standing in the yard for a potato-peeling fatigue duty, some of my little pals started on a well-known song, whose refrain goes approximately like this:

> And my grandmother
> Is full of bother
> To see them dry out so fast . . .

An NCO who was passing by thought he heard them singing the 'Internationale', which, shortly after the Sovieto-German pact, was an offence of the utmost gravity. The affair went rapidly all the way up to the captain who, in the light of our protestations of innocence, called the seminarist—professionally trustworthy, so to speak—and asked him to say in front of his comrades what they had been singing. The seminarist, flustered and blushing, replied: 'I cannot say it.' The affair was finally cleared up and did not go higher than the captain.

Christmas came and with it the Christmas furlough, and we still had no jackets. The supply people hurriedly unearthed some unfamiliar dark-blue jackets with a red border. Some told their families that it was a commando outfit.

After the Christmas furlough I was sent to an SG (Special Grouping) at Nemours, some fifty miles from Paris, as a candidate SRO (Student Reserve Officer). Three months' training in the SG was to be followed by an examination for admission as SRO to the artillery school at Fontaine-bleau. After three months' training at Fontainebleau there was a second examination. Those who passed would then be sent into fighting units with the rank of cadet officers, those who failed with the rank of sergeant. (Incidentally in the artillery and the cavalry a sergeant is not called sergeant but *maréchal des logis*. Similarly, lance-corporal and corporal are called *brigadier* and *brigadier-chef*, nothing to do with the British brigadier who is a general. Finally a cadet officer is an *aspirant*, and an *adjudant* is a warrant officer.)

All of this was going to take us to the end of June 1940. Time was on our side; 'With your scrap iron we shall forge victorious steel,' and 'Nous vaincrons parce que nous sommes les plus forts', proclaimed the posters covering the walls; nobody was in a hurry, except the Germans, but that we did not know.

The departure for the SG at Nemours presented a moral dilemma for those likely to be selected. It was understood that on no account would they return to HART, but would go instead into field artillery, which was supposedly more dangerous. Among the 'intellectuals' from my own room, the only ones to be considered as 'officer material', the travelling salesman and the would-be accountant preferred the relative safety of HART to the glamour of officer stripes, while the seminarist and I bravely opted for field artillery.

The population of the Nemours SG was very different from that of the Châteauroux depot, as much by their education (everyone at least had the Bac) as by their state of mind. I think that the majority, and I among them, earnestly wished to learn as much of the fighting trade as could be taught to us. We learned how to take a Lebel rifle apart and put it back together again, and each of us fired two dozen shots in target practice. We were *shown* machine-guns and *told* how to use them.

We finally saw the '75', the famous 75mm French field gun, and studied it in considerable detail. The 75 had been the best field gun in the world in 1914, but this was 1940. We learned everything about it, or nearly everything: its 32 lubricating outlets, the weight of its breech (26 kilos), and the number of its grooves (I forget). We learned the answer to the tricky question: 'Where does the shell go after leaving the muzzle?', which is: 'It enters the domain of Exterior Ballistics'.

I said that we knew *nearly* everything about the 75. Indeed. To the question: 'What is the composition of the liquid in the hydraulic brake of the 75 field gun?', the answer was, and still is, for all I know: 'The composition of the liquid in the hydraulic brake of the 75 field gun is a secret.' Even if it is a secret, one knows that it freezes between $-15°C$ and $-20°C$, which makes the 75 unusable in a very cold climate. This problem arose in connection with the war that was raging then between the USSR and Finland, in which our High Command was anxious to help. They decided to send the Finns not the useless 75, but its predecessor, the de Bange field gun. It was a beautiful medieval weapon, and it elegantly solved the problem of the liquid freezing in the hydraulic brake by having no brake at all, that is by *recoiling without coming back to its initial position*. Thus the rate of firing fell from four per minute for the 75, to one every three minutes. I had fired the de Bange at Fontainebleau, and I know what I am talking about. Lucky old Finns!

We also had courses of GIAF (General Instruction on Artillery Fire), in which we learned how to calculate the various parameters of an artillery shot taking into account the coordinates of the target, wind velocity, type of ammunition, shells and fuses, etc. We also learned to take topographical bearings, etc. On the whole it was far from ridiculous.

On the other hand, what *were* ridiculous or at least inept, were the living conditions. We were housed (I am speaking now of my own outfit of thirty people, but conditions for others were identical) in the damp, cold basement of a disused brewery, which bore the proud name of *Lutèce*. The beginning of 1940 had been very cold, nearly every one had influenza or tonsilitis or both, and no one was admitted to the sick bay with a temperature of below 39°C. We slept on straw mattresses lying directly on the ground, the washing facilities were rustic to say the least, and it was a brave man who washed below the neck. The only advantage of the intense cold was that people did not even smell. It was there that I had a set-to with our instructor, a career *maréchal des logis*. Having found my boots badly polished, he called me a dirty fellow. I immediately challenged him to a contest of cleanliness by proposing that we both take off our boots and socks and compare our feet. (In a heroic move I had washed mine that very morning). He did not take up the challenge and from then on left me alone. It could be said: 'Why were you complaining? This was war and you should have considered yourself lucky to be in the rear'. First of all, by and large, we *did not* consider ourselves particularly lucky to be in the rear, we were willing to fight; and secondly, that was no reason to treat people like pigs, through lack of competence and foresight.

One day when the urge to malinger was irresistible, I went to the sick parade and complained of pains in the chest. Our medic took it very seriously, diagnosed a mitral stricture and prescribed for the following week an examination at the Nemours hospital, after which, according to him, I would undoubtedly be recognized as unfit for military service. 'Don't rejoice too much' he added, 'you are not going to live long'. Like all malingerers, I had hoped to be let off from work, but as we say in French: 'The bride was too beautiful'. I went back to the barracks with my tail between my legs. It so happened that the next day a case of scarlet fever was detected in our barracks, and we were all quarantined. The military training went on, but there was no question of going out, to the hospital or elsewhere, and so I walked miserably around with my mitral stricture for the three weeks of the quarantine—which is an oxymoron (a posh word, like onomastics), since 'quarantine', or *quarantaine*, means 'forty days'. When at last I was able to present myself to the resident at the hospital and tell him my problem, instead of examining me he asked for the name of my medic and then burst out laughing. 'It's his pet craze,' he said, 'he sends us two or three mitral strictures every week.' God had punished me for my attempted malingering, but lightly.

We got on well in our SG, and in spite of my interest in 'grass-roots France', communication was easier with these boys, most of whom were students like myself, deferred conscripts, and of the same age as I. I particularly remember one of them, a taciturn character, who owed his nickname, Groucho, to his big moustache and his sly wit. He was always the last to wake up, but the first for roll call. His secret was that he slept fully dressed (puttees included), and in the morning he put on his forage cap, lit a cigarette and was ready to face a new day. As I said before, the cold was our saviour.

At the end of the SG there was a competitive examination. I came out first out of two hundred and fifty candidates, demonstrating that besides my civilian talent, which had received no tangible reward for nearly four years, I also possessed military virtues.

So far everything in my budding military career was going as expected. All that remained was the last stage before the fighting—Fontainebleau— where the unexpected happened.

After Nemours, my first impression of Fontainebleau was a contrasting one of extraordinary comfort, almost of luxury. We had beds with sheets, showers, a hairdresser, and decent food. To counterbalance this, the military discipline was much more finicky. No negligence in dress or general appearance was tolerated. I could not have challenged an instructor at Fontainebleau to a contest in feet cleanliness. As far as I remember, all our instructors were regular officers. Spurning puttees, even the elastic ones that I coveted at Châteauroux, most of them wore riding boots and spurs and carried riding crops under their arms. A horsy fragrance floated over this artillery school.

The SRO could choose between automobile and *hippomobile* (that is, horse drawn) artillery. It goes without saying that the military virtues were all on the side of the so-called *hippo*. Like puttees, the horse was 'formative' and therefore priceless. Incidentally, a major is called 'squadrons leader' in the cavalry and 'squadron leader' in the artillery. A single *s* lies between them.

I chose the *auto* artillery, for I have always liked to keep a distance between horses and myself. I remember, while writing this, that in the autumn of 1934, having obtained my first four credits for the *Licence*, I was offered a job through a friend, as a private tutor in Chile. The employer, a Frenchman, owned a vast isolated hacienda, and was seeking a student to look after the education of his two children—a boy and a girl, aged twelve and fourteen. I might have been tempted if he had not added: 'You will love it: one practically lives on horseback.'

At Fontainebleau I discovered two new exercises: the miniature firing range, called Rémy, after its inventor, and the *ecole à feu* or 'firing school'. The Rémy was a wonderful toy. Imagine a miniature three-dimensional landscape, with roads, villages, church steeples, and rivers, on a scale of one to a thousand, which you observe from a distance of a few metres with field glasses. The instructor points a target out to you and gives you its coordinates on the map. You calculate it in your head, as quickly as possible announcing the parameters for the aiming of an imaginary gun, and you give the command to 'Fire'. A little cotton tip, simulating the impact of the shell, appears on the miniature landscape in the vicinity of the target. As fast as possible, you change the parameters in order to get nearer to the target and you 'fire' again. You are judged on the number and duration of the shots it takes to hit a target. Nowadays, when everybody is trained for everything by computer simulation, it looks rather quaint, but I think that in 1940 it was good practice. Anyway, I liked it and was rather good at it.

A little incident that occurred at the Rémy showed me that our colonel was not stupid. One day when he had come to watch our practice, the instructor naturally put on his prize pupil. It took him half a dozen shots that day, instead of the usual two or three, to get his target. A mark of 12 (out of 20) was his reward for this mediocre performance, causing our champion's average marks to plummet. Somewhat vexed, he made the mistake of mentioning that he was normally a far better 'marksman' and that it was only the presence of the colonel which had flustered him. 'I congratulate you on your frankness and I change your mark to zero', said the colonel. 'If an officer permits himself to get flustered in what after all is just a game, what will he do when he is firing and being fired at for real?' The colonel had just shown the difference between military skills and fighting virtues. In the firing schools one fired the 75 for real in an artillery polygon. Each of the SRO had had the opportunity to command at least a dozen firings. I was not bad at that either.

Yet, in order to be a good artillery officer I lacked one military skill and one fighting virtue.

My main military weakness was my appearance. In spite of my efforts, I never managed to have my boots properly polished, my jacket completely buttoned, my cap at the right angle, or my salute snappy enough. At the SG, where most of the instructors had come from the Reserve, and where it was materially impossible to look smart, one did not pay much attention to such things.

None of this mattered to me, I did not care a hoot about being one of the first (I *had* changed); all I aspired to was to be firing at Germans. But I did have a weakness, of which I had always been conscious, but which was particularly serious in an artillery officer, as I was to discover at Fontainebleau. I was completely devoid of a sense of direction. In field practice, for which we were given a theme, we had to be able to answer at any moment: 'Where is the enemy?' 'Which way is north?' It did not take me long to lose the north and with it the enemy. I was first in my group when I arrived at Fontainebleau, but I was rapidly losing some of my feathers.

In spite of my weaknesses, my relations with the instructors were not bad. They would have been better if I had had the impression that they were taking some interest in the war that was on. But the way it was developing, and it was certainly beginning to develop in the most disturbing way, seemed to be the least of their cares.

One day, one beautiful day—it must have been the end of May or the beginning of June, (the Germans had entered Paris on 10 June and it was some ten days earlier)—a day when instruction in 'Presenting the Sabre' was planned for the morning and a topography examination for the afternoon, we were abruptly informed of our transfer to the artillery school at Poitiers (the second French artillery school), where the two aforementioned exercises would take place with some little delay. The means of transport would be bicycles, and we were marched then and there to get them and the rations for our cycling jaunt.

We left for Poitiers, pedalling two abreast, in impeccable order, along the roads of France. The weather was splendid, and if I had not been worried sick about the outcome of this war I would have wonderful memories of this three-day cycling promenade. We did see a few German planes in the sky but they must have had better things to do than to bother the flower of the French artillery. We stayed for one day at Poitiers with an aborted attempt at 'Presenting the Sabre' and a topography examination. We then moved, still on our bikes, towards the *province* of Limousin, ending up in a village called Saint-Cyr (ironically the same name as the French Sandhurst).

We stayed there for three months awaiting the orders and the decisions of the authorities. The officers were far more preoccupied by their future assignment than they had been by the outcome of the campaign. The attitude of some of them had turned decidedly unpleasant. A captain explained to us that we had been beaten because we had given all our anti-tank guns to the Spanish Republicans. I nearly protested, but thought better of it and shut my mouth. It was not the last time that I would be shutting it. An SRO said that he had heard of a General de Gaulle, who had made an appeal to join the British and go on fighting. He was put under close arrest. After the armistice most of the SRO continued to follow some kind of phantom instruction, for they were still thinking of their Cadet Officer stripes, incredible as it may seem. I could not bear the sight of these damn fools and of their instructors. I had fortunately saved my faithful *Courant and Hilbert* from disaster, which gave me some solace. One of the classrooms in the village school of Saint-Cyr had been converted into the guardroom, and I managed more than once to get punished with confinement there, so as to be able to read quietly by electric light in the evenings. That kind of behaviour is not without consequences, and at the end of the session I left the prestigious school of Fontainebleau, which I had entered among the first, with the rank of *brigadier-chef* which, as I explained, is equivalent to Corporal—a rank which in France does not even count as an NCO but as an enlisted man. *Sic transit.* It was not the worst of my worries. When I went to the Demobilization Office at the end of August I was told that I could not return to my Parisian domicile. I protested for form's sake, for naturally I did not intend to throw myself into the lion's jaws. I gave my demobilization address as that of an hotel in Cannes on the Côte d'Azur, where I knew that I would find (for a few days at least) my sister and her husband, who had also recently been demobilized. My parents had remained in their house in Croissy.

I reached Cannes in easy stages; as a demobilized *brigadier-chef* I was not entitled to use all the trains. I have wonderful memories of the journey between Sète and Marseilles. I travelled with two other soldiers in a magnificent convertible placed on a platform railway car.

I arrived in Cannes. Another phase had begun.

The verdigris years

Primum vivere.
J'ai vécu (Sieyès)

Llanabba School—Into the lion's jaws—The encounter—Hardships and perils—From the sea to the mountains—The hut of Providence—A perilous examination

In September 1940—a disastrous month and year for the country, if not for the few (many?) clever ones—where did I stand? I was twenty-five years old. After ten years of a Russian childhood, which had left its mark on me forever and which had been in a way the happiest period of my life, I had been living in France for fifteen years. Behind me I had a year of primary school and six years of secondary schooling, which had on the whole been excellent (barring a little disappointment in its last year), an aborted attempt to become a physician, three years of successful, albeit rather slow study for a *Licence*, then three solitary years spent in search of research. Three years full of frustrations and disappointments, but not completely barren, as a yet distant future was to show. Lastly, a year of 'soldiering', in which I learned a lot of quite useless things but in which I acquired an experience of my fellow men that I had previously lacked, by rubbing shoulders with human beings very different from myself, such as farmhands and career soldiers; a year in which, as a member of the 'nation who had stood up in arms', I had not seen a single German (but some were in store for me), had not heard the whistle of a single bullet, nor the explosion of a single shell, but in which my artillery school and I had pedalled from Fontainebleau to Saint-Cyr en Limousin fast enough not to be made prisoners—and that was not to be sneezed at.

I did not think any of these things at the time. *Primum vivere*. The so-called 'status of the Jews', on the verge of being proclaimed, was going to make a second-rate citizen out of me, before making me a prey to the carriers of the brown plague and their tricoloured allies. In a sense I was privileged in comparison with the likes of me who held a teaching or a research position. Not being blessed with one, I was not threatened by the traumatic experience of losing it. Lacking a position, I had to look for a job and in that respect there were favourable circumstances. With the installation of a 'demarcation line', which had cut France in two, a goodly crowd of well-to-do citizens, not only Jews had thought it wise to 'wait and see' for a while; so they stayed with their families in the south of

France, rather than returning to their homes in the north, which they had abandoned in their exodus. And what better place to wait and see than the Côte d'Azur, if one has the wherewithal! Their children, who included an above-average proportion of asses, were in need of tutors, individual or collective. For years, asses had formed the bulk of my *tapirs*, if I may hazard this expression, and I counted on them to feed me some more. To respond to the demand of the newcomers, private institutions had sprouted here and there on the Côte d'Azur, run by characters who were more or less competent and more or less scrupulous. For these new headmasters the 'Status of the Jews' was a blessing. Where could you find a workforce that was cheaper, more docile and, as a bonus, better qualified than all these Jews looking for a job?

On my arrival in Cannes I was contacted by Nora. Nora was the daughter of that family doctor whose advice I had sought before giving up my medical studies. She was a pretty fair-haired girl (a fairness which owed some of its glamour to art), elegant, lively and active. She did not pass unnoticed. (In 1943 she was arrested by the Gestapo under circumstances I do not know. Her unfortunate father had the mad idea of going to the Gestapo headquarters to ask for her release. She was sent to Ravensbrück, but came back at the end of the war. He did not return). She was teaching in Saint-Raphaël, a sea-resort about thirty miles from Cannes, in a private school run by a gentleman whom I shall call M. Hood. M. Hood was in need of a Latin teacher and Nora suggested me for the job. I accepted immediately and left for Saint-Raphaël. Ten years later I was to discover an English novelist named Evelyn Waugh, a hateful man but a humorist of genius. His first book, *Decline and Fall*, describes with surrealistic drollery a private school, Llanabba School, where an Oxford student, unfairly sent down for 'indecent behaviour', finds a job as a junior master. I too was guilty, if not of 'indecent behaviour', of indecent 'essence'. If I had a quarter of half Evelyn Waugh's talent, I too could have done something very funny with the Collège de Saint-Raphaël, run by M. Hood. I shall make no attempt at being funny, it would spoil everything. I shall be content with a faithful description and invent nothing.

I arrived at Saint-Raphaël around 6 p.m. and went straight to the 'collège', a large villa, where the principal, as he wished to be called, greeted me amiably in his office. M. Hood was tall man, in his thirties, with longish hair, combed back and curling on the neck, an aquiline nose, and a prominent Adam's apple. He looked like the writer Roger Vailland, judging by photographs of him that I was to see in later years. He was wearing beige slacks and a blue shirt, wide open on the chest and with sleeves rolled above the elbows. He did not correspond exactly to my own image of the principal of a college, even a private one, even on the Côte d'Azur. In fact I had never met anyone like him, certainly not in the barrack-rooms of my military life. I asked what his field was, which he said was geography, but to my surprise he did not ask about my diplomas. 'Nora must have told him' I thought. We spoke briefly of the employment conditions: a monthly salary of 800 francs, lunch and dinner at the college and a room at the Pension des Myrtes, a family hotel nearby. I would be teaching Latin in all the forms and share the supervision of the study periods with the other masters.

I was still a little dazed by my return to civilian life and all the uncertainties I had to face, and I did not even think of discussing the conditions of my employment nor of asking for further information about my teaching duties—information which the principal, for his part, seemed unable or unwilling to provide.

After this brisk rounding off of our discussion, M. Hood put on the wireless, a handsome set, from which wafted a waltz air, and asked me if I was fond of music and had a sense of rhythm. Before I had time to reply, a man entered the office, a stocky chap, wearing a navy blue sweater and sailor's trousers of the same colour, and with the thickest eyebrows I had ever seen, for they made one continuous line from one temple to the other. 'My bursar, M. Maurice' said M. Hood, without considering it necessary to complete the introductions. I certainly did not expect what happened next. The bursar took the principal by the waist and they started whirling round to the reckless rhythm of the waltz music coming out of the wireless. 'Not bad for a start' I thought. After they had waltzed for a while, and I had politely declined to waltz with either of them, in came an old lady whom the Principal introduced as his aunt, the Marquise de . . . (I have forgotten the name). The Marquise de . . . , who turned out to be the actual bursar of the establishment, for M. Maurice was in fact the cook, said that it was time to have dinner.

We went to the dining-room where, apart from the four of us, there was only a little boy, the grandson of the Marquise de . . . ; M. Hood tried unsuccessfully to entice him to sit on his knee. The dinner too was unforgettable. I was prepared for the restrictions required by the situation of our country, but this first dinner—pumpkin soup, pumpkin gratin, and pumpkin marmalade—was even less palatable to me, because I had always hated pumpkin in any guise. Years later, seeing Americans feasting on pumpkin pie made me doubt that they were a civilized nation. M. Hood seemed to share my tastes, for he spurned the pumpkin in all its forms and was served dishes in earthenware pots, which were anonymous, and no doubt different.

After dinner I took my leave and went looking for my new lodgings. The Pension des Myrtes turned out to be a largish pleasant building facing the sea, some two hundred metres away. I was met by the owners, who showed me to my small but quite decent room.

The following morning I made my way to the college where I met the members of the teaching staff. The oldest by far was M. Bettelin,

('Bettelheim' to close friends, among whom he did me the honour of counting me after a few days). He taught history, a job he did not really need for his living, but he preferred to have an official income, however small. We got on very well, for he considered, not without reason, as it turned out, that he and I were the only more or less professional teachers in the Hood institution. He confided to me: 'Is it not strange, these masters who are one lesson ahead of their pupils?'

As far as I remember Nora taught French, but she did travel a lot and was often away. The main teacher, or at least self-appointed as such, was a maiden lady of uncertain age, whom I shall call Mlle Rubinstein (she bore the name of another pianist of similar origin). She taught physics and mathematics with great zeal and little competence, and stood in for Nora during her frequent absences.

Mademoiselle Rubinstein was extraordinarily ugly. Her hair was red, her complexion pale and freckled, and her eyes, of a dull bluish tint, bulged slightly. As to her build, it could best be described by the little incident she reported to us herself: a civil gentleman had offered her his seat with the comment: 'In your condition you should not be standing up' 'What condition, may I ask?' she replied indignantly. To crown it all Mlle Rubinstein was hopelessly in love with M. Hood. Hopelessly indeed! Even if the lovelorn girl had been the pretty Nora, there was no chance of her love being returned. Apart from all that, she was an excellent person, always ready to be of service, as long as one did not say anything against M. Hood, to whom she reported everything.

A young Swiss girl, a Miss Vögeli, was in charge of the younger children. She could draw very amusing caricatures of M. Hood and M. Maurice dancing together, but unfortunately returned to her native country before long.

There was the gym master, a wretch who kept complaining of being hungry and also disappeared rapidly. M. Hood asked me to replace him in his duties, and I accepted in exchange for an extra slice of meat at lunch, whenever there was some, and a plateful of pasta. I liked potatoes better but there were none.

There was a 'butler', as M. Hood called him, who helped M. Maurice in the kitchen and did the cleaning. They called him Clément, but I discovered that he was Russian and that his first name was Klim. He had emigrated after the Revolution and forgotten most of his Russian; still, on some subjects he knew more Russian than I: I had never heard the incredibly dirty word he used to describe the little habits of the principal and the bursar. He was a slightly mysterious and menacing figure (not unlike Philbrick, the butler in Llanabba school) and he too disappeared one day, God knows where.

I made the acquaintance of my pupils, with whom I got on famously. My knowledge was more than adequate for their modest needs; the experience gained with *tapirs* over several years of practice and the authority acquired during my year in the army insured their obedience and their devotion to me. They never dared to misbehave in my class the way they did with M. Bettelin and Mlle Rubinstein.

The inevitable occurred after a fortnight. Mlle Rubinstein fell ill and I replaced her for maths and physics. When she came back, the pupils refused categorically to start again with her and insisted on continuing with me. M Hood, who was getting fed up with Mlle Rubinstein's devotion, tried to take advantage of it to get rid of her, but Nora, Bettelin, and I made him keep her.

After a month, new pupils appeared who were older and wished to take Greek. M. Hood attempted to talk me into teaching Greek. 'You know so many things, surely you could teach Greek.' I did not give in to these despicable flatteries: I had my reasons for not wanting to teach Greek, but I suggested someone else to him, a friend of Nora's, who had stayed in Paris and who had studied Greek in his Lycée years. Nora wrote to this chap, Richard, and he came a week later. Having heard that he had passed his *Bac de Philosophie*, M. Hood wished him to teach philosophy as well to the oldest pupils. Richard yielded to his entreaties, in exchange for the same bonus as I got for my gym: an extra slice of meat and a plateful of pasta.

I taught at Hood's for three months, from the start of the term till Christmas. The hardest part was to make him pay your salary. The trick was to burst into his office while a pupil's mother was paying the school fees. To avoid a scandal, and being unable to allege lack of money, he usually complied unwillingly.

At Christmas I decided to cross the demarcation line and to visit my parents at Croissy. Before relating the circumstances of that visit, I want to describe briefly how I left Hood after my return from it.

There had been a terrible snowstorm in the Côte d'Azur, something which happens once every ten years, and the trains were running with considerable delays. I nearly froze on my way back and returned three days after the beginning of term. Hood was furious and threatened to deduct two weeks from my January salary because of the alleged problems this delay had caused the school. By taking such a step he was giving me good cause to leave him for his competitor in Saint-Raphaël, a man I shall call Grosjean, who had been trying for some time to get me to work with him.

Richard had given me the itinerary he had used to come from the north zone, occupied by the Germans, to the south zone, the so-called 'free zone', ruled by the Vichy government. I went the same way, by train to Loches, a dozen miles south of the demarcation line, and by train again from Tours (about the same distance to the line on the north side) to Paris. The tricky part was crossing the line between Loches and Tours. By loitering in a café by the Loches station, I discovered that a carrier, for a few francs, would take candidates to the crossing within a mile of the line, which had to be crossed on foot across the fields. North of the line a pal of his would pick you up and take you to Tours.

Even more than crossing the line on foot, I dreaded the two trips in a van; I had acquired enough experience of mankind to believe that each of the carriers would willingly betray his charges if he saw some advantage in it. However, everything went well, and I had no trouble in reaching Paris.

It was dark when I arrived there and I spent the night at the house of my aunt Raissa, a sister of my father (her husband and two of her three children perished later in Nazi camps, as well as the wife and one of the two daughters of my uncle David). I went to Croissy via Saint-Lazare station the following morning. Paris was full of German soldiers and vehicles, which I found less unexpected than the darkness at ten a.m. Paris was on Berlin time.

My parents were of course happily surprised to see me, but my mother was so worried for my safety in the lion's jaws that, after feeding me, she was all for sending me back immediately. My father, an incurable optimist, made fun of her and she let herself be persuaded enough to permit me to stay three more days at Croissy. I must say that my father, an old hand at survival in Soviet Russia, was not in the least surprised by the hardships and shortages which from the autumn of 1940 had fallen on the Parisians. When he came to Paris we used to laugh indulgently at his habit of never throwing out any odds and ends, such as pieces of string, bottles, empty tins, nails, wrappings and God knows what else. When everything became in short supply, these absurd reserves became life savers.

At the beginning of the war he had stocked up on firewood and now, whenever he went for a walk in the country, he picked up some dead wood which he stored in our garage (we never had a car). Needless to say, on his initiative my parents had made timely and abundant reserves of flour, pasta, cooking oil, corn flakes, sardines, tinned milk, etc., and lived now in a state of almost complete autarchy. In the living room, where they slept now, he had installed a wood-burning stove with tins hanging from all the joints of the flue to prevent their dripping on the floor. In short, he had recreated the atmosphere in which he had lived and survived for several years in the Soviet Union. I suggested that they move to the less dangerous 'free' zone. My father would not hear of it and I saw his point. He had kept his Soviet passport, and as long as Hitler and Stalin were bosom friends, it was his best protection. He was in greater safety than his brother and sister, in spite of their French citizenship of long standing. He should be forgiven for not having foreseen that Hitler would attack the Soviet Union six months after my visit, on 22 June 1941; after all, Joseph Stalin, who had access to a wider range of sources of information, had not foreseen it either. The following day men from the Gestapo came to take him to a camp in Compiègne, where my mother was able to visit him twice, and from there to Germany, after which we had no more news. In 1944 a postcard from the German authorities informed us of his death in a camp, the name of which I have forgotten. All I know is that it was not an extermination camp like Auschwitz, but a camp for enemy residents, as I was to learn later from someone who had been staying there with my father and who had returned. Poor Father, unlike so many members of his family, had died a 'natural death', that is of cold and starvation, as if in an 'honest' Soviet camp and not in a gas chamber. He was seventy years old.

After this digression I come back to January 1941. To return to the south zone I put my bicycle on the train, and cycled from Tours to Loches with no perilous mercenary assistance.

Then a marvellous event took place in my life. I met Suzanne Lequesme whom I at once liked infinitely. Her eyes were green, her friendly smile was constantly ready to break into a laugh which revealed her dazzling teeth, her complexion was roses and cream. Actually, she was far from being as healthy as she looked, for she was just recovering from an attack of rheumatism which had kept her in bed for several weeks, and was to leave her with some repercussions for life. I had caught sight of her in the living room of the Hôtel des Myrtes a few days before my departure for Croissy, and had made up my mind to get better acquainted with her upon my return. The people with whom she had come from Paris went back, leaving her in the care of the owners of the hotel. They took good care of her, except for their persistent, although vain, efforts to convert her to Pentecostalism, the religion which they practised and preached with a zeal I found somewhat excessive. She told me that she was waiting to be able to walk again before leaving for Paris. She had a country accent from the Sarthe and she rolled her R's as strongly as a Russian. That too enchanted me. I believe it took me longer to get her to like me, but I may be permitted to think that I succeeded in the end, since in order to stay with me, a poor private tutor and Jewish to boot—decidedly not a very attractive match on the material side—she gave up her plans to return to Paris.

It turned out that she was an outstanding cook, and once up and about, she agreed to take over the kitchen of the Hôtel des Myrtes while waiting for better times to come.

It was not a time for attracting the attention of the authorities and we were married only in October 1944, during a furlough, for, ever the incorrigible militarist, I was a soldier again. As they don't quite say in fairy tales, they lived happily ever after and had no children. I close here this chapter of my life, which still lasts today.

The Collège Grosjean where I was now exercising my talents, was not as picturesque as M. Hood's college. All my former colleagues, Nora, Richard, Bettelin, and Mlle Rubinstein had disappeared, one after another,

God knows where; as did M. Hood himself, who cleaned out after gettiing most of the parents to pay a term in advance. It was an unstable time, and people disappeared without anyone being surprised.

After my father's arrest at the end of June 1941, my sister went to fetch my mother from Croissy and brought her to Saint-Raphaël, to live with Suzanne and me. We stayed for a while at the Myrtes and then moved into a small apartment towards the end of 1941. I did some accounting, and discovered that I would make more money while working less if I left Grosjean and was prepared to give private lessons, which I did from the beginning of the last term of 1941. I do not regret the year spent between Hood and Grosjean; it gave me some experience of class teaching which turned out to be precious many years later.

Among my pupils (the word *tapir* is insulting for such an intelligent a boy) I had Alfred Grosser, who was to become the well-known Germanist and political expert. He was a charming youth, lively and cheerful, and completely devoid of pedantry, which contrasted with a maturity far beyond his years. I taught him Latin, which he knew almost as well (or as badly) as I, and mathematics. In spite of a difference of ten years in age, he was more of a friend to me than a pupil. Not all my *tapirs* were like my friend Alfred. One day, when one of them, whom I was grooming for his Second Bac, had demonstrated even greater stupidity than usual, I asked him: 'But how did you manage to pass your First Bac?' He replied with angelic candour: 'Well it was like this. During my First Bac the Germans were approaching, and we had been moved rapidly from Rennes to Toulouse. On our arrival in Toulouse, I was exempted from the oral exam there, on the strength of a statement under oath that I had passed the written exam in Rennes.'

During the years we spent in Saint-Raphaël, our little trio—Mother, Suzanne and I—had three worries: the defeat of the Germans, our daily bread and, for two of us at least, the danger of losing our freedom. (We did not see beyond the loss of freedom, for, like most people, we did not suspect the real nature of the Nazi camps.) Like many people also, we listened assiduously to the BBC, with its *cortège* of little joys and great disappointments, or, as a BBC comedian was to call it many years later, 'fresh disasters'. The Battle of Britain, won by the heroes of the RAF, gave us our first reasons to hope. We managed to pick up Soviet radio and listened to their communiqués, which, being in Russian, were not jammed in France. Those today who marvel at the blindness or the indulgence of so many towards the Soviet regime, have not known or have forgotten the dark years when hope lay in the east.

I only understood much later that the Soviet disasters at the start of the war were just as bad as ours, and that, without the immensity of its territory, the rigour of its climate and Hitler's folly, the Soviet Union could have known the same fate as France.

Unlike a large majority of the French (or so some would have us believe today), I did not take an active part in the Resistance. My only effort in that direction had been an unsuccessful attempt to embark on one of the French warships, which, I thought, could not fail to make for North Africa after the Allied landing there, and the invasion of the southern zone by the Germans which followed. After bidding farewell to my mother and Suzanne, I left for Toulon where the French fleet was stationed. I loitered in the port for two days and one night at the risk of being picked up by the police ten times over. I finally convinced myself that the fleet would not sail and went home full of a terrible disappointment, mixed with cowardly relief. Two days later the French fleet scuttled its ships.

In Saint-Raphaël the problem of daily bread was a constant worry to all except a small minority. In spite of its tourist attractions, the countryside surrounding Saint-Raphaël is a desert. The peasants, who in other parts of France sold or bartered their produce on the black market, simply did not exist there and the only sources of food were the distributing agents—that is, the small shopkeepers who sold rationed goods, or sometimes dishonest municipal employees who peddled food coupons. It was not enough to be prepared to pay black market prices, one had to be known and accepted by those who dispensed the blessed food, which called for patience and humility. Those dispensers were the equivalent of what today is known elsewhere as the *Nomenklatura*.

On the fringes of this aristocracy of food dispensers one could find all those possessors of other material goods in great demand, the haberdasher with his thread and needles, his cotton and sometimes even his wool, the wood merchant who had the wood for the gas-producing engines which were mounted on lorries to get round the lack of petrol, the electrician who had batteries, bulbs, and electric wire, the ironmonger with his pots and pans etc. All the consumer goods had found a refuge under the counter and came out only for 'friends'; that is, for those who had something to offer in exchange or were prepared to pay triple. Nowadays with good reason no doubt, one pities the small shopkeepers driven to bankruptcy by the supermarkets, but one must recognize and I still find it hard to forget, that for their predecessors the 'Verdigris Years' had been not only the golden age of prosperity, but even more so, that of power and respectability. The *Nomenklatura*, what else!

I discovered one day to my astonishment and delight that I was entitled to fifty grammes of bread per day, over and above the ration of ordinary mortals. The clerk who had issued my ration card had somehow interpreted my profession of 'physics teacher' as 'physical education teacher', and presented me with the extra fifty grammes of bread alloted to teachers of gymnastics to make up for their physical exertions. If I had described my profession in my demobilization papers as 'teacher of physics and mathematics', as I had intended, I would have lost the blessed fifty grammes. I had omitted 'mathematics' only because there was no room for it on the form I had to complete.

I had been forced to give up swimming in the sea, which I was very fond of, because it increased my appetite even more. I shall never forget a day in the spring of 1941, when hunger had made me particularly morose; Suzanne disappeared, to reappear a few minutes later with an earthenware pot filled to the brim with chickpeas swimming in olive oil: she had not hesitated to steal it for me from the pantry. It brought tears to my eyes for I knew what such an action had cost her.

Until September 1943 Saint-Raphaël had been in the zone occupied by the Italian army, an occupation which was relatively light to bear, and which sometimes even tempered the zeal of the Vichy government. But in the summer of 1942, Vichy had invited all the Jews who were French citizens to get registered at their local police station 'in their own interest'. Some Jewish friends of mine, French by birth, had been telling me that by not going to register I was taking the risk of breaking the law. But I could not see how the risk taken by not registering could exceed that of being filed as a Jew by the police, and so abstained. The future was to show that I had made the right choice. Needless to say, my mother, who on top of everything had the papers of a Russian refugee, did the same as I. A few days after my father's arrest in the north zone, she had been summoned to the *Kommandantur* of Saint-Germain-en-Laye and a German major asked her why she had not registered as Jewish. She replied that she was Russian by birth, of orthodox religion, and that she had no reason to register. 'But you are married to a Jew' said the Major. '*Es kommt in besten Familien vor*' ('It happens in the best families'). Wisely, she did not wait for the major to ruminate at length on her answer, and left for the south zone, as I have already described.

With the departure of the Italians and the arrival of the Germans, the situation became much worse. As well as the Germans, the troops of the Vichy *Milice* (Militia) made their appearance. They were even more dangerous than the German soldiers, if not the SS, whose officers could be seen lolling on the terraces of Saint-Raphaël hotels. A few Jews disappeared, leaving no trace behind. Raids were organized at cinema exits, and young people who could not prove that they were lawfully employed were assigned to the STO or *Service du Travail Obligatoire*, and sent to Germany to work in factories there.

In the autumn of 1943 I decided that I was becoming too well known in Saint-Raphaël and that the time had come for a change of air. I left one September day for Grenoble where I knew a friendly couple, the Glikmans, he an engineer and she a doctor, with two big boys aged fifteen and seventeen.

I had dinner on the train. The man who was facing me in the dining car and whom I must have impressed favourably, confided to me some information which he claimed to have obtained from a highly placed friend in the Préfecture du Var. 'All these Jews' (he used a different word), 'who are lolling on the beaches, believing they are safe, will be collared during a large raid and sent to a camp. You know, I believe the raid could well be scheduled for tonight'. 'One at least will get through', I thought to myself on leaving my charming neighbour. His information turned out to be correct, and a few gullible people, who had registered in Saint-Raphaël, disappeared that night.

Arriving in Grenoble at 5 p.m., I learned at the station that a curfew had started at 4 p.m. I spent a night in Grenoble station which I do not count among the most joyful and comfortable of my life; the more so because, being accustomed to the mildness of the Saint-Raphaël climate, I found the night rather chilly. The following morning, dirty and exhausted, I made my appearance unannounced at my friends' house and was greeted without apparent surprise. It was a sanctuary of hospitality, with people constantly arriving for a change of air, lodgings, and sometimes papers. They found a room for me at a grocer's whom they knew. It was a long and narrow room, isolated in a back yard, with a stove for which thanks to his relations the good Glikman managed to obtain a few bags of metallurgical coke on which I was able to survive till the end of January 1944.

I gave shelter there for one night to Laurent Schwartz whom I had encountered in the street; for reasons of his own, into which I did not inquire, he did not wish to sleep in a hotel. As a good Samaritan I offered him half of my bed, for which I made him pay by asking him to explain a point of the theory of functions of real variables, which I was studying at the time. My feelings for Laurent Schwartz are a mixture of admiration and annoyance. Admiration, first of all, for his mathematical gifts which, strangely enough, did not reveal themselves before *Math. Elem.*, which for great mathematicians (as for great musicians) is rather late. (It is true that I am not well placed to speak of late revelations). Admiration for the courage, both physical and moral, which he exhibited over the years, by taking stands which were physically dangerous (during the Algerian war), or morally uncomfortable (when opposing some teachers' unions, in spite of their common political affinities). My annoyance stems from his fixed ideas, which change from time to time, but are unshakeable until he himself has decided to change them. (This may not be quite true anymore. Age does erode fixed ideas.) Particularly annoying was his attitude during the student unrest of 1968, which I am bound to admit that he shared with Alfred Kastler, Jacques Monod, Jean-Paul-Sartre, and *tutti quanti* (but not with me).

But let us go back to Grenoble in the autumn of 1943. I soon discovered that the distance from Grenoble to Saint-Raphaël was far greater than what appears on the map. In Saint-Raphaël the Germans were the Germans and 'behaved correctly'. In Grenoble the Germans were the 'Chleuhs' and they were the enemy (I am quite unable to tell why the Germans were given that nickname of 'chleuhs', which I understand to be that of a certain tribe of Morocco, but that is what everyone called them). In Saint-Raphaël there had not been a single attempt at sabotage, although ten miles from there a viaduct was bombarded unsuccessfully several times by the Allies in an attempt to stop all railway traffic to Italy. In Grenoble there were saboteurs' explosions every day. In Saint-Raphaël the Germans walked unarmed; in Grenoble they never showed up unless they were in a group and armed. It was a different country, almost another planet. If I add that, as a bonus, so to speak, one was far less famished in Grenoble than in Saint-Raphaël, it will become clear why I was feeling more at ease in Grenoble in spite of a more perceptible atmosphere of danger. I visited the Faculty of Sciences, (it was the first time in four years that I was setting foot inside a university) and decided to enrol for the course of advanced analysis. The programme consisted of a course by Brelot on Bourbaki's general topology and another by Lelong on integral equations. Of the two, Lelong was the better teacher, but his lectures, although very clear, did not tell me much that I did not know already. Bourbaki, on the other hand, was a revelation. I had never seen mathematics like that, and I liked them.

I met a young mathematician named Samuel who, although extremely young, was acting as Brelot's assistant, and he literally dazzled me with the clarity and the brilliance of his explanations. 'If this boy manages to pull through, he will go far', I thought. This restriction, 'if he pulls through' did apply to quite a few of those I was associating with in that winter of 1943 in Grenoble. Samuel did pull through: he is a university professor in Paris. Did he go as far as I had predicted forty-five years ago? It is for the mathematicians, not for me to say. All I know is that on atomic energy he has recently taken stands which I find unreasonable to say the least. One must say, in his defence, that he is far from being the only mathematician to behave unreasonably. And, since I am on this subject, I would like to remind the mathematicians, who are fond of charging the physicists with all the deadly sins in the matter of weapons of mass destruction, that the two greatest 'assassins', to use their vocabulary, were two mathematicians, John von Neumann and Stanislaw Ulam, and that even today it is the mathematicians who are top dogs in the mass destruction Establishment.

In his autobiography, Ulam explains that most of the mathematicians who commit themselves in this manner only do so in order to find sponsors for their research in pure mathematics. He illustrates his thesis by a little Jewish story. A Jew, who is behind with his dues to the synagogue, is stopped at its door by the verger (if that is what they call them in synagogues), who asks him to pay his dues. 'I am only entering for a minute, there is so-and-so who owes me some money'. 'You liar' replies the verger: 'as if I did not know that you only want to get in there to pray'.

At the university I made the acquaintance of two of my future fellow academicians, the astrophysicist Pecker and the crystallographer Bertaut. Pecker was short, garrulous, hare-brained, and charming. He is still all these things after forty-five years. Bertaut too was already the Bertaut we know at the Academy today. I also met the Dean of the Faculty of Sciences, René Gosse, a marvellous man, who was both wise and kindly. A few days later I was horrified to learn that he had been murdered by the *Milice*.

The situation in Grenoble was getting more and more dangerous, and early in 1944 my friends the Glikmans and I reached the conclusion that the time had come to take a higher view, so to speak—in an Alpine village where one would not see the Germans so much. We chose a little village at the foot of the massif of Sept-Laux (the Seven-Lakes), called Fond-de-France, where they had never been seen so far. There was an inn where the Glikmans and I stayed for a while, before finding a more permanent refuge. A few young people, boys and girls, were staying in this auberge, most of them members of the Resistance or at least claiming to be. They did not look very serious to me, apart from two, who were peddling meat on the black market.

I was beginning to wonder whether it would not be nobler and also cheaper to join one of the *maquis* in the vicinity, when I received a letter from Suzanne saying that the Germans were emptying Saint-Raphaël and that Mother and she would be sent to a God-forsaken place in the neighbouring hills. I immediately wrote back telling them to come and join me. They arrived a few days later, exhausted by their journey but happy to be with me. There was no question of staying on at the inn, and I found a house a little lower down the valley, in a village called La Ferrière d'Allevard. The house was too big for the three of us and we shared it with the family of a colleague of Glikman named Polonski, whom everyone called Polo. They had two little girls, Irène and Nicole, aged three and one, who were both very cute and intelligent.

Living with the Polos did not raise too many problems, if one does not count Mrs Polo's habit of regularly forgetting that her children's milk was on the fire, and of stating when she contemplated the disaster: 'I am not going to commit suicide over a thing like that'. In spite of this little shortcoming she was an intelligent and upright person, and we felt much closer to her than to her husband who worked in Grenoble and only came home for week-ends.

We lived peacefully at La Ferrière for three months, though in a state of constant anxiety. The Germans had already showed up in the valley, though never higher than Allevard, a small town a dozen kilometres from La Ferrière. Polo and I were the only Jews in the village, and although he took good care to show up at church every Sunday with his elder daughter (his wife had refused to take part in that farce), I very much doubt that he ever fooled anyone.

I discovered the joys of Alpine agriculture with the owners of our house. They raised potatoes on the hillside and every year the vegetable soil which had slipped down from the lowest furrow towards the valley had to be carried up to the top of the field on one's back. It was too steep for the mule. Suzanne, who had been raised on a farm and knew quite a bit about hard work in the fields, had never seen anything like it. My other occupations were *Courant and Hilbert* and *Bourbaki*. The beauty of *Bourbaki* is that, in contrast to conventional mathematics, you can do all the exercises in your head without paper and pencil. I took long walks in the mountains while I did them. But at the beginning of June 1944 something happened.

One morning, when I was still in bed (I think it was Sunday) I heard my mother cry in Russian: 'Tolya' (this is the diminutive of 'Anatole' in Russian), '—the Germans!' I bounded to the window and saw that the street outside our window was full of them. I started to pull on my clothes in great haste, to the amazement of Suzanne; she did not understand what my mother had cried out and I did not immediately think to translate it for her. I got out through the back door which opened onto a path leading to the mountains; I had picked it out long ago for just such an occasion. Polo was following me. At that moment I saw, between the mountain and me, more Germans who had fanned out with bayonets on their rifles. I remember very distinctly thinking: 'I am cornered like a rat', in those very words. Then I saw a tool shed about thirty metres from there, and slipped into it like a rabbit into his burrow, with Polo behind me. I put out my hand to grab the key which was over the door, and locked it from the inside. I do not have pleasant memories of the day I spent in there with Polo. I remember that after a while he started to hiccup in a particularly noisy manner. They say that the best way to stop someone's hiccups is to give him a fright, but I did not see how I could have frightened him any further. Strangely enough, seeing his fright gave me the calm that I badly needed. Still, when an invisible hand started to turn the handle in an attempt to open the door—unsuccessfully since I had locked it—my heart was in my mouth. Our visitor went and did not return. Later there arose the problem of emptying our bladders. There was no question of peeing on the floor; it sloped towards the edges and a trickle would have revealed our presence. I saw empty bottles in a corner and suggested using them as receptacles. I would like to inform some of my gentlemen readers who have never peed in a bottle: it is not terribly convenient, but it can be done. At last, when dusk fell, I heard Suzanne calling out some Russian names of little animals, which I had taught her when we had first met and I was very anxious to amuse her—such as: little rabbit, little donkey, etc. It was her way of letting me know that the Germans had gone and that the coast was clear, without saying my name.

It became obvious that it was unsafe for the men, Polo and myself to remain in the house, for it was likely that the Germans would come again. I do not know where Polo went. I never saw him again, but I know that he made it safely to the Liberation. I am sure that the memories he had of our forced companionship were as unpleasant as mine. Suzanne and I left the following day to set up in an old isolated house in a small hamlet called Le Burdin, which was perched in the mountain, some five hundred metres higher up than La Ferrière. My mother stayed at La Ferrière with Mrs Polo and her children.

The day after we moved we saw her coming up. There were tears in her eyes, but they were tears of joy. She had come to tell us that the Allies had landed in Normandy. (We had no radio at Le Burdin.) We decided against making any moves, for new forays into the valley could be expected from the Germans and their hateful allies the *Milice*. Until August 15, for more than two months, Suzanne and I led an idyllic life, which was interrupted only once, for three days, by any intellectual activity—about which more later.

In our retreat we naturally had no water in the house, and we went to fetch it at a nearby spring. The cooking was done in the hearth with twigs we gathered around the house. For light we had a candle, which we did not use much, for the days were long at that season and we went to bed early. We slept on a straw mattress, which had to be shaken vigorously every day.

We had a hen which we baptized *Gudule* (the name of a vicar's servant, borrowed from Anatole France). When fed with crusts of cheese, spoilt rice (of which we had two packages), and various leftovers, all cooked for her by Suzanne, the hen turned out to be an outstanding layer, and we did not lack eggs almost all the times we were there. She used to come as far as the threshold, and seemed to listen to what we were saying. My mother used to warn us that she was a Gestapo spy. Alas, one day we decided to eat her to celebrate the advance of the Allied troops, and Gudule was sacrificed on the altar of victory. It was a great disappointment; all Gudule's physical being was devoted to the laying of eggs, and under her abundant plumage she was mere skin and bone.

In the woods further up the mountain, one could find plenty of chanterelles and wild strawberries, but mostly blueberries, which the local people gather with a 'comb', that is a rectangular box, without a top and with one of the sides missing. On this missing side the bottom of the box is edged with teeth in the shape of a comb, which pick up the blueberries. In good spots one could gather a kilogramme of blueberries in a few minutes. The gathering of chanterelles demands greater care and persistence. I remember the day when we were going to give up on a spot where we could only find two or three chanterelles; a peasant woman came along and in a few minutes she had picked more than a kilo of them in that very spot.

In the course of this idyllic existence I again asked myself now and then whether I should not be joining the nearby *maquis*, representatives of which could be seen more and more often, walking the paths and even the roads, carrying Sten guns. However, as far as I could see, their main, and perhaps their only occupation seemed to be *staying* in the *maquis*, instead of working in Germany with the STO, which in itself deserved praise. (I certainly do not wish to generalize: I am speaking only of those I saw around me.) But since I was not with the STO either while I was at Le Burdin (and, anyway, the STO would not have been the lot reserved for *me* by our German friends) I saw no special reason for sleeping in a *maquis* rather than in my bed.

Let me describe that intellectual pursuit I mentioned earlier. I have already said that I had enrolled at the Faculty of Grenoble for the course of advanced analysis, and the time had come for the examinations. After doing all these Bourbaki exercises I was feeling prepared, and I had made up my mind to go to Grenoble to pass the examinations. They were to take three days in all, with the written paper separated from the oral by a day. I fully realized that it was dangerous. The buses which went down to Grenoble were frequently inspected by the gendarmes or the *Milice*, and in Grenoble itself there were raids by Germans all the time. The university district was particularly dangerous. I am in general an easy-going person and inclined to give in, but this time nothing that my mother and Suzanne said to me could change my mind. A psychoanalyst might suggest that by this reckless behaviour I was trying to compensate for my frustration at not having gone to a *maquis*, but I don't believe it. In November 1942 all I wanted to do was to get aboard a French warship bound for North Africa, and now all I wanted to do was to pass an examination for which I was feeling well prepared. 'Very well' said Suzanne, 'I will go to Grenoble with you; I don't want to stay here and wait for you to return'. A friend of the Glikmans, a Mrs Ross, had a small room in Grenoble and let us have the key. Going down to Grenoble turned out to be uneventful, and we got without a hitch to our room, which was even smaller than we had expected. The bed was so narrow, even for one person, that we had to push it to the wall in order not to fall out. On the way to the University, everything went well. The topology examination took place in the morning, and the integral equations in the afternoon, and I solved both problems. Coming back, I was nearly caught by a German patrol which I saw advancing toward me. I escaped thanks to one of those lateral alleys, of which there are many in Grenoble, and into which I plunged to emerge in a different street. The oral took place two days later, and I came out first with the highest marks, which soothed my bruised ego. On 15 August 1944 we heard that the Allies had landed in the south of France. The same day or the day after I saw a French officer in uniform in the main street of La Ferrière. His presence there so soon after the landing looked like a miracle. Actually there had been no miracle: he belonged to the forces of the interior, more precisely to the FTP (*Francs-Tireurs et Partisans*), a communist branch (as I learned later), of the FFI (French Forces of the Interior). I happened to be wearing a beret, so I saluted him and expressed my wish to join the troops of which he was a member. He told me to come back in the afternoon with my kit. I went to announce my decision to my mother and Suzanne, who received it without enthusiasm but did not protest. The Verdigris Years had ended. A second military year was beginning, and, apart from the happy ending, it was to be as disappointing as that of five years before.

Second service

Whatever did he climb on that galley for?
Molière

I enlist—History stutters—Stripes blossom up—Warriors are resting

This absurd year gets on my nerves in retrospect, and this irritation tends to shroud my memories in a fog which I shall do my best to clear up, in order to exorcise what is hidden underneath—nothing tragic or dishonourable, I hasten to add, but, as I have said, absurd.

On the afternoon of this day in August 1944, I found myself, equipped with the essentials of life (which included Bourbaki's book of algebra) standing with several young people in front of La Ferrière's Town Hall. Lieutenant Rossi, for such was his *nom de guerre*, invited us to climb aboard an open lorry, and we left for Fond-de-France, a journey I knew well. There a skip took us up to the summit of the Sept-Laux, where I saw some buildings belonging to the Electricity Board of the Alps, which were being used as barracks by some hundred FTP. They asked for my name (I could have chosen a *nom de guerre*, but didn't), the address of my next of kin, and my military experience. I said I had served in the artillery, and was told that I would be shifted there later. I signed an enlistment for six months, which was to be validated by the army later. We were then lavishly equipped with green ski pants of excellent quality, and leather zip jackets which had come from Vichy Youth camps. I had not suspected that the *maquis* were so well organized. I was also given a Sten gun with one magazine, and two hand grenades. There was no demonstration of how to use them and I assumed that everybody knew. I asked a big chap who had fought in the Spanish International Brigades to instruct me in the use of the Sten gun (I knew about the grenades).

A guard was put around the camp and I did guard duty a few times, Sten gun in hand and hand grenades hanging from my belt. I was ready to empty my magazine or to hurl my hand grenades at any assailants, but the occasion did not arise. Apart from that we were doing absolutely nothing, and, always prone to discouragement, I began to ask myself: 'What the hell am I doing here?'

After ten days we were sent on leave for forty-eight hours. Back at home, Mother and Suzanne admired my ski pants and my jacket. Mother wished to know if there was a chance of my arsenal going off by accident. I assured her that as long as the magazine was not on the Sten and the safety pin was on the grenade, both objects were perfectly safe. Back at camp we had some shooting practice with the Sten, during which each of us emptied one magazine. Apparently oblivious of the safety rules I had described to my mother, one of us managed to shoot himself in the foot.

We were then put on open lorries, and we made for the Massif de l'Oisans. I remember that we were cheered by crowds massed on the roadside. We were annoyed to discover that these gatherings were for the benefit of the American soldiers, who generously threw chewing gum and cigarettes as they passed. By way of revenge we fooled the crowds by throwing them the little wooden cubes which were the fuel for our lorries' gas engines. Their disappointment was a source of merriment to us.

After a time they shifted me to the FTP artillery, the bulk of which was one German anti-tank gun; we used the four shells that had come with it for firing practice.

During a three-day leave in October 1944, Suzanne and I got married.

I remember staying for one month (before or after my marriage?) in a fort above Briançon, into which a mortar shell landed without hurting anyone. Above all I remember being bored, bored absolutely to death! None of it was serious. Somewhere there must have been people fighting the Germans, but where were they?

All around me I saw a proliferation of FFI officers with lots of stripes, all anxious to know whether these stripes would be validated by the regular army. I was willing to believe that some of these stripes had been earned in combat, but hardly all of them; and anyway, as a *brigadier-chef* from 1940, what did I care? There is a well-known anecdote about General de Gaulle inspecting a troup of FFI officers, all with lots of stripes, except for one, who only had a single stripe. 'What's the matter?' asks the General, 'can't you sew?' Later most of the FFI ranks were declared *'fictifs'* (fictitious) by the army, with no one knowing exactly what it meant.

Finally, it must have been in December 1944, I was summoned by a very nice Artillery Commander, named Bérenger. He explained to me that the country was in need of a new army, of which the FFI would form the backbone, and to that end the FFI fighters (I had become an FFI fighter) had to go back to school before becoming the new officers of the new army. The school would be based in Lyons, in a barracks called Lyon-la-Doua. The nominal head of the school would be a colonel but he, Bérenger, would be in charge. I pointed out to him that I had enlisted to fight the Germans. 'Don't worry' he said, 'the war will last a long time and your turn will come.' At the thought of starting all the things I had done in 1940 again, my heart sank and I decided to wait for my six months enlistment to end, and then go home. I made one last attempt, which was quite irregular, to get into the 'real' army, the one that fought the Germans. Seeing a battery of 105 bore field guns (they had replaced the beloved 75s) which had stopped by the roadside before heading north, I went to its captain. 'Captain, I was trained at Fontainebleau in 1940; may I come with you?' He answered: 'I have all the men I need, though I could use one "purveyor" perhaps.' I must explain that in the crew of six gunners who manned a field gun, there was first of all an aristocracy of two, the *pointeur* or 'gun layer', who aimed the gun, and the *artificier* or 'primer', who primed the shell with the appropriate fuse. Then came the middle class, with the *chargeur* or 'loader', who loaded the gun, and the *tireur* who fired it. Last came the plebs, made up of the two *pourvoyeurs* or 'purveyors,' who were chosen for brawn rather than brains, and whose only task was to wheel the gun round under the command of the *pointeur* and to lug the shells under the command of the *artificier*. My urge to fight could not have been irresistible, for I spurned the humble, although essential, task of the 'purveyor'.

With a heavy heart I left for Lyon-la-Doua, where they again taught me all I that I had learned in 1940 at Nemours and Fontainebleau. The only difference was that now we did not even have French 75 field guns at our disposal, but Italian 75 field guns, which had been captured from the Italian army. Many of my fellow students were NCOs from the regular army, which the Vichy government had been allowed to keep after the armistice of 1940, and for them this school represented an unhoped for opportunity to get a commission. There was also an *adjudant* (warrant-officer) of a very special kind, a very nice chap with whom I made friends immediately, who held a degree in philosophy and was tipsy most of the time (FFI needless to say). One day when a captain was giving him a rocket for not being at his post, he replied: 'As a "fictitious" *adjudant*, I am there "fictitiously".'

At the end of my six months I went to see Commander Bérenger and told him that I was thirty, that I had my career to think of, and that I did not wish to renew my enlistment which had expired. He let me go and I went back to La Ferrière with the firm intention of preparing myself for civilian life.

Two days later I was called up as a reservist by the military authorities in Grenoble who, since my unfortunate enlistment, had my name in their files. Reservists were being called up to serve as guards in a prison camp, which was to be installed in a place called Pont-de-Claix near Grenoble. Nobody knew whether this camp would be used as a temporary reception centre for French prisoners repatriated from Germany, or as a prison camp for German soldiers. Meanwhile it was quite empty apart from me and another nine unfortunate reservists, all in their early thirties. 'Better Lyon-la-Doua than this place!', I thought and wrote an eloquent letter to Commander Bérenger asking him to free me from the degrading tasks of a gaoler by taking me back to Lyon-la-Doua. He got me out remarkably quickly, I went back to school, and graduated with one of the top marks, having at last secured the rank of *aspirant* (officer cadet).

There was a big celebration at the end of the course and for the occasion I composed a poem which could be sung to the tune (well known to the medical students of my youth) of '*Caroline la putain*' ('Caroline the harlot'). Alas I remember only one verse, which in English would read something like this:

> They gave to us the gun that wins.
> That was the great Italian gun.
> It had done marvels at Bouvines
> And firing it is still great fun.

It was indeed, and I got top marks with it. After finishing at the school (I may be confusing the dates—this might have been a training period before the final examination), we were sent to Alsace with the 4th DMM (*Division Marocaine de Montagne*). It was my first meeting with men from the French army who had actually seen some fighting during this war. I stayed for two days in an observation post where nobody fired at me, and I finally had the pleasure of directing gun fire at a target which the captain pointed out to me; he claimed it was an enemy observation post. He said that I had got it. I took his word for it, because I could not see how he could have known—and I had jolly good eyesight in those days. The following day the 4th DMM was sent to Mulhouse for a rest, and we went along. I don't know what Mulhouse is like in peacetime, but it was absolutely sinister then. Among the tasks entrusted to me, the most unpleasant was to lead the town patrol, pacing the streets at the head of four men with helmets and rifles, on the lookout for undisciplined soldiers who had to be taken to the barracks. I had never been so pleased that Islam forbids the use of alcohol. Among these Moroccans, formidable men who had fought fiercely in Italy, I did not see a single drunk. One also had to watch out for something else, which Islam apparently does not forbid; and this is how I found myself with my patrol standing at the entrance to an establishment, which was reserved for Moroccan soldiers, in charge of keeping the peace if necessary. At no time did I have to intervene. The men were standing in line, strangely calm and silent, and I could not help going back in my mind to a similar wait I had watched twenty years before. I found the sight and the memories equally distressing.

After Mulhouse I was garrisoned in Belley, a quiet provincial town some eighty kilometres from Lyons, where I took it easy until my demobilization. My military duties were slight, everybody was waiting for the war to end, and my superiors left me alone. The Belley region is famous for its gastronomic delights, and with some of my former pals from Lyon-la-Doua we had a few memorable feasts. I discovered with them the practice of drinking *fillettes* by the metre, that is setting up a row of the small bottles, called *fillettes*—having drunk the excellent local white wine contained therein—until the total length of the row reaches (or exceeds) one metre.

I had just one little set-to with an artillery commander, but to explain what it was about, I have to give a short artillery lecture first.

In artillery, one distinguished (I am using the past tense because I don't know what they do nowadays) gunfire into two types: 'percussion fire', where the fuse mounted on the shell makes it explode when it strikes the target, and 'fuse controlled fire', where the fuse starts the explosion at a given height above the target. In my time it was regulated by the combustion time of the powder contained in the fuse, and this regulation was the duty of the second aristocrat of the gun crew, the *artificier*. At the officers' mess the conversation had turned to the new so-called 'proximity fuses', which automatically measure the distance between shell and target, and make the shell explode when this distance has reached the required value. Perhaps I knew, but more likely I had guessed, that it was done by the duration of the round trip of an electromagnetic wave emitted by the fuse and reflected by the target. (Naturally I did not know that it was called 'radar'.) The commander saw fit to explain that it was done by means of a mercury altimeter inside the fuse, and I was foolish enough, me, an officer cadet, to contradict a commander. What was the good of having had two years of military training! Needless to say, when, a few days later, we heard about the explosion of an atomic bomb over Hiroshima, I kept my mouth shut and let my superiors say what they pleased.

I started to think seriously of what I would be doing after my demobilization. I shall speak of it at greater length later, but I want to relate here an amusing incident. As an officer cadet, I was now entitled to private lodgings in town and had found a room in the old house of Brillat-Savarin, the famous gourmet, a native of Belley. Browsing through his books I found the recipe for a melon marmalade that I thought would interest Suzanne. In her reply she did not mention the marmalade but asked me what was to be done with an application of mine for a scholarship, addressed to Monsieur de Valbreuze, Director of the Ecole Supérieure d'Electricité. I wrote back to explain to Suzanne where she should forward the application, and gave up on the melon marmalade recipe, which must still be lying unused in Belley. (Unless Madame de Valbreuze had the curiosity to try it out. During the two years I spent in that school I never had the opportunity of taking the matter up with the director.)

A few days later I was demobilized and returned to Paris.

The Three Musketeers

Catching up

*Supelec—The budding CEA—A mature d'Artagnan—The Big Atomist—
The School for Secrets—Atoms and red tape*

In 1985 the Commissariat á l'Energie Atomique (Atomic Energy Commission, abridged to CEA henceforth), celebrated its fortieth anniversary. The journal *Energie Nucléaire* had asked some of its great (?) veterans to reminisce briefly about their early years with CEA. My recollections begin with a rhetorical question: 'In the autumn of 1945 I was thirty, I had successfully passed seven examinations in seven university courses, I had nothing published and no job; how did it happen?'

One could hardly accuse me of not having answered this question, and in great detail, in the preceding pages. But once the past had been exorcised (a word which keeps showing up in these recollections with an alarming frequency), and I had returned to a life, which, now the 'verdigris years' were over, was not only civilian but also civilized, the present was taking me by the throat. I have described in the last chapter how I had applied, via Suzanne, for admission and a scholarship to the Ecole Supérieure d'Electricité (*Supelec* henceforth). My seven university credits exempted me from the entrance examination and my status of valiant soldier got me the scholarship. What were my reasons for knocking at the door of *Supelec*? I have just given my first reason in the last sentence: a good chance of a scholarship and of admission without examination, and that by itself was something. Besides, the thought of a return to the Sorbonne filled me with repulsion, and what's more, a return to do what?

But there were more positive reasons. My friend Glikman, a radioelectric engineer himself, held that school in great esteem. In the radioelectricity section, the one I had chosen, the duration of the course had just been lengthened from one year to two, which was not exactly good news for someone like me who had already wasted so much time: but it must be recognized that it was a sound decision. It had been made necessary by the advances which had built up in the field of radioelectricity during the last ten years—not only abroad as a fallout from military research, but even in France where, with the General Ferrié, Camille Gutton and others (even Louis de Broglie), there existed a great tradition, and where the radioelectric engineers had been less idle than the physicists.

And this is why at the beginning of October 1945 I was for the first time entering the premises of *Supelec*—located then in Malakof, a Parisian suburb—with the intent, successful, I hasten to state, of getting out two years later with a degree as a radioelectric engineer. Had the bell tolled for my hopes to become a physicist? But who knows for whom the bell tolls?

Supelec was not then, and as far as I can tell, is not now, what is known as a *Grande Ecole*, comparable by its prestige and the quality of its recruits to *Polytechnique* or *Normale*. I think I can positively state that it was far superior to them then (I do not know about now) by the quality of the tuition it offered.

First of all, and this was the newest part for me, it was superior by the quality of the practical work, which was varied and abundant, well supervised by competent junior and senior staff, and above all provided with modern equipment in excellent condition. It was this practical work which, for the first time since my childhood (at thirty !!!), restored my faith in the predictions of physics. The hysteresis cycle of a transformer core, the response of two coupled circuits, the characteristics of a pentode, the radiation diagramme of a horn, all the things I was measuring in the lab: they qualitatively and quantitatively really resembled the curves drawn in the lectures, and this was *without cheating* as I had done during experiments performed at the PCN or in the course of General Physics. It was a revelation to me. For the first time in my life I was taking pleasure in experimental work. I was a butter-fingers, I scalded myself with the soldering iron, occasionally I received an electric shock because I had forgotten to earth my apparatus properly, I burned out a measuring bridge once, but I knew that all of it was *my* fault and that reality was indeed in agreement with the equations.

Everybody had heard about the great physicist Fermi, whom theoreticians and experimentalists both took for one of their own kind. I am a little like that myself, but not quite. Experimentalists take me for a theoretician and theoreticians for an experimentalist. It is not as bad as it sounds; and if I have been able to talk to both kinds, to understand and sometimes to inspire both, and if I have been able to create a laboratory and to direct it for thirty years, I owe it at least in part to *Supelec*. 'But yet I run before my horse to market.'

Most of the formal lectures were good too, far superior on the whole to those on general physics at the Sorbonne. There was one course, however, on radioelectric equipment, of which I do not have good memories. During the first lecture, our professor, wanting to give the future engineers the latest news on the atomic structure of matter, mentioned the presence of electrons inside atomic nuclei. I could not refrain from pointing out to him that in 1945, and after the Hiroshima bomb, it was a somewhat obsolete idea. He did not take my innocent remark in good part, and it cost me several places in the final examination. May I add that this professor was a colonel, a fact which did not inspire any indulgence in me, now that I was a civilian again. A good third of the students were regular officers, and all of them captains ... Several of them made their career in the CEA.

Let's talk about the CEA. Newspapers did nothing else: not so much about the CEA, which so far existed only on paper, but about the Atom, the tool of death—but also possibly, through its peaceful applications, a benefactor of mankind. And what country was better placed to succeed in the atomic race than France, mother country of Becquerel, Pierre and Marie Curie (well, up to a point, for she was born a Pole), Frédéric and Irène Joliot, Jean Perrin and Paul Langevin, and their worthy successors Francis Perrin and Pierre Auger!!

There was a lot of truth in this journalistic clamour. The work done in 1939 by Joliot and his coworkers Halban and Kowarski, on uranium fission and the number and characteristics of the neutrons emitted in a single fission, the first calculation by Francis Perrin of the critical mass for a chain reaction, were at the forefront of what was being done everywhere. But it is also true, however, that Joliot—who had refused to leave France during the war years, and was confined in his laboratory of the Collège de France under the eye of the Germans, the rather benevolent eye of Gentner, the German physicist in charge of the supervision of this laboratory—did nothing for science, at least nothing worthy of his genius. He had been a courageous member of the Resistance but there had been plenty of those— if not millions as some try to persuade us, at least tens of thousands—and not one a Joliot. What a waste!

In the autumn of 1945 (at least I think it was then) Joliot gave, in the great theatre of the Sorbonne, a lecture on the Atom, its menaces and its promises. My most vivid memory of it is that I was nearly smothered to death in the incredible stampede of all those who tried to get in. Many women fainted.

I learned from the newspapers of the creation of the CEA and of the leading parts to be played there by Professors Frédéric and Irène Joliot, Auger and Perrin. I decided to seek out Francis Perrin. I found him in the Luxembourg Palace, seat of the Senate, for he had been appointed Senator (I believe it was called something else at the time) by de Gaulle, whom he had joined in Algiers in 1943. We spoke in the midst of the racket made by pneumatic drills; the Germans had strongly fortified the Luxembourg Palace and it was being brought back to normal. Francis told me that this new organization, the CEA, of which Joliot would be the High Commissioner, and he himself one of the Commissioners, would be needing scientists and that there would be room for me. Meanwhile, until things became more definite, he could get me a position at the CNRS (Centre National de la Recherche Scientifique).

Francis Perrin also spoke to me of three young polytechnicians, Claude Bloch, Jules Horowitz and Michel Trocheris, who wished to do scientific research in the CEA. He said that I could team up with them. I will have more to say about these three people a little later.

After this interview with Francis, the first in seven years I returned, somewhat reassured on my future, to my *Supelec*—or rather to the compulsory summer practice session, which took place between the two school years, for this was summer 1946. On the advice of Francis I chose to spend a month at Bellevue in the laboratory of Szolem Rosenblum, a well known nuclear physicist who had discovered the fine structure of the alpha spectra. The reason for the location of his laboratory in Bellevue rather than at the Radium Institute, founded by Marie Curie, was the need for strong magnetic fields, which were available at Bellevue from the large magnet that had been installed there by my former professor, Aimé Cotton. The strong magnetic field produced in the large gap of the magnet imparts different curvatures to the trajectories of alpha particles of different energies, and, by separating them, allows an analysis of the fine structure of their energy spectrum.

Rosenblum received me with great kindness and put me in the hands of Eugène Cotton, the son of Aimé Cotton, who was finishing up his thesis on the subject. Eugène Cotton, who was only a few months older than I, put me in the picture about the experimental setup. The alpha source and the detector were placed inside a glass container, where a good vacuum was maintained, and the container itself was placed inside the gap of the magnet. Data were to be taken shortly, as soon as the vacuum of the container had proved satisfactory. There was no leak detector, and the quality of the vacuum could be judged from the colour of an electrical discharge in the residual gas. The vacuum was established by means of a vacuum pump, the famous Holweck pump—a mechanical jewel, according to Cotton. I was delighted to take part, for the first time in my life, in new experimental work, the meaning and importance of which I fully realized. But oh woe! On this particular day the container shone with a beautiful purple hue, denoting a very poor vacuum, due to a leak. The purple obstinately refused to turn pale despite an increase in the speed of pumping. 'Must take it apart,' said the mechanic who assisted Cotton. I shall abridge this sad tale. After a month, the container was still as purple as the humble rosette of the *Palmes Académiques*, which in our country adorns the lapels of worthy schoolteachers after long years of loyal service to education.

I began by going to Bellevue every day, then every other day, then twice a week, then not at all. I was present at the dismantling of the 'mechanical jewel' and admired its innards, but there was not enough material in that for the report on the practice session that we had to submit before the autumn. I left Cotton, who was naturally even more worried that I, in search of another practice session elsewhere. The most interesting ones were all taken by then, and I ended up *in extremis* in the Thomson laboratory, where they gave me the task of wiring the frame of a radioelectric circuit. (This was naturally ages before modern solid state electronics.) The work particularly involved piercing large circular holes in the bottom of the steel box which was to house my electronic *chef d'oeuvre*. I discovered a tool known as trephine or trepan, and got an idea of how neurosurgeons get to the brains of their patients. This was 'formative' work, as 'formative' as the puttees and the horse in our army. Just my bad luck. During the last two days I managed to make a few measurements, and wrote up a report which was more or less acceptable by stretching it out as much as possible.

During my second year I worked hard, harder, I think, than during any other period of my life. The reason was simple. From the autumn of 1946 I had been working at the CEA full time, while studying at *Supelec* full time. The high point had been the design of a fifty kilowatt radio transmitter, for the final examination.

To finish it in time, I did something that I have never done again: I remained seated at my desk for twenty-four hours, without interruption. My efforts were rewarded with the best mark in my class. I remember that immediately after completing my assignment I returned to the CEA, where Professor Jacques Yvon, who was to become my new boss, was expounding his cogitations on the slowing down of neutrons. I was literally falling asleep every two minutes and Horowitz, seated next to me, squeezed my arm each time to prevent me from snoring or even collapsing, which would have been an insult to Jacques Yvon.

I came out of *Supelec* seventh out of forty. I would have probably come out second or third but for a work practice grade that was barely average, and a very poor one from my friend the colonel, who favoured electrons in nuclei. This was my last examination, (the last but one if one counts the viva of my thesis in Oxford), in a life which counted more than its fair share of them.

It was at the beginning of October 1946 that I met three young men who were to become my regular working companions for a year and, after that, colleagues and faithful friends: Claude Bloch, whom a terribly premature death took from us at the end of 1971, Jules Horowitz, and Michel Trocheris.

When Claude Bloch left us, he had been Director of Physics at the CEA for a year. Michel Trocheris retired in July 1986 after being the head of the Controlled Fusion Department for many years. Horowitz retired in December of the same year. He was Director of Fundamental Research, after having been in charge of the atomic reactors division till the end of 1971. But we are not there yet.

Our first meeting took place at Châtillon near Paris, in a disused fort which the CEA had appropriated and was converting into a series of laboratories set up in the blockhouses of the fort. A small building, which, although new, was already exhibiting signs of decay after a few months, contained some offices.

Shall I confess that my first impression of my future companions was a mixed one? I have recounted earlier what my master Fabry used to say of Polytechnicians: 'full of themselves and empty of everything else.' My future friends could not be summed up totally by this description, for if indeed their opinion of themselves was not without fullness, the knowledge they had absorbed, and more importantly that which they proved capable of absorbing in record time, were far removed from the concept of emptiness. They were no ordinary Polytechnicians. The war and the German occupation had lost them a few years (nothing like me though), since Trocheris and Horowitz had graduated at twenty-five and Bloch at twenty-three, instead of the usual twenty-one for lads as bright as these. Those lost years had not been completely wasted for them; all three had acquired a knowledge and a maturity far exceeding those of a young Polytechnician at graduation. Their graduation ranks had been: first for Bloch, third for Horowitz, and a very honourable rank that I have forgotten for Trocheris.

What is more, all three had the firm intention to do research, and in that too they were no ordinary Polytechnicians.

One might have feared, and I had certainly feared at the beginning, that these three lads, who had a similar uprbringing and had known each other for a long time, would distance themselves from a man who was their elder by six to eight years, whose chequered background I have described, and who, most ridiculous of all, was still going to school for another year. Nothing like that did happen.

They soon realized that I knew what they knew, and even a few things they did not know; that what they could understand, I understood also; that what they were capable of doing, I could do; that, like them, I wished to learn and work; and this is how, quite naturally, they immediately adopted me as one of them. We became something like the Three Musketeers, in which the eldest by far and the only non-Polytechnician, I became some kind of d'Artagnan in reverse. This esteem that each of us extended to the other three was accompanied by misgivings towards our superiors which they did not always give us cause to abandon.

Our first meeting at Châtillon took place under the auspices of Commander Ertaud, a naval officer in his early forties, who has assembled a considerable body of literature on the behaviour of neutrons inside matter. Our first task was to go through it and absorb the essentials. A few days later we were summoned to the Collège de France by the greatest (I would say the biggest, considering his bulk) French specialist in atomic energy, Lew Kowarski.

The role of Kowarski in the development of atomic energy, in France (with Joliot and Halban) before the war, in Great Britain, and later in

Canada during the war, and in the CEA after the war, is part of the history of atomic energy and is not an object of dispute. It has been described in many publications. But the story I am recounting is mine, not his. What I shall relate about Kowarski is only the story of some personal contacts which—why hide it—appear more comical than unpleasant after all these years. With respect to fundamental research in the CEA, which is the only aspect of that establishment I have ever been concerned with, his great merit—his only merit but a significant one—lay in bringing the CEA to accept the need for sending young recruits abroad, to be trained there.

As far as I am concerned personally, his only service to me was to have written a letter of recommendation on my behalf to a British colleague. But he had an evil genius, which forever pushed him into spoiling whatever good turns he did for one, and nipped in the bud any feelings of gratitude that one might have harboured.

That day he was waiting for us on the steps of the hideous modern building of the Collège de France: the one behind Chalgrin's graceful edifice which housed Joliot's laboratories. He kept his hands behind his back, as if to discourage any attempt at hand-shaking. At a later time he told me that he felt more Anglo-Saxon than French, and that in Anglo-Saxon countries one did not shake hands. True, but we were in France and we do shake hands when we meet or part, even if the British are sometimes taken aback by it. Horowitz was a few minutes late and innocently stretched his hand out to Kowarski who could not but take it. Then he led us to an empty chemistry lab with a blackboard, and gave us his celebrated lecture on secrecy which he was to repeat many times to new recruits. I still remember his instructions about always keeping a piece of cloth or a sponge in one's left hand (assuming one is right-handed), and systematically erasing with this hand all that one was writing with the right hand. Such was the procedure we were supposed to follow when going through the secret notes that he had brought with him from Canada on the behaviour of neutrons in matter, be it a fissile medium or a moderator.

My three companions had been charmed by their first contact with Francis Perrin, as I myself had been ten years earlier; for this little man *was* a charmer. They considered him to be the natural mentor of the CEA theoreticians, and expected guidance and directives from him. It was a domain where, taught by long and bitter experience, I had few illusions and indeed we saw little of Francis Perrin.

He came to Châtillon one day and my friends insisted that he give us a problem to work on. He suggested that we try to improve Bohr and Wheeler's theory of nuclear fission, for he said that he had never 'liked that theory'. This advice offered to beginners was a similar example of his old advice to me: to look for a problem by reading the *Physical Review*.

Our only encounter with Joliot took place in the lift of the Collège de France. He smiled at us on entering the lift and said: 'You must be the young students from the 'School of Physics and Chemistry' (a school from which he had graduated himself) 'who have come to visit the lab.' We did not have time to disabuse him of this notion.

That winter we often met in the large flat where Trocheris lived. He had kept a childhood magic lantern, which, with a sheet pinned to the wall, made a passable microfilm reader. Many of the prewar publications which we studied were in German, and Horowitz's knowledge of that language proved precious to us. We could all read English but each of us pronounced it differently. Unable to agree on how to pronounce 'hitherto', we decided to pronounce it 'Hiro-Hito', linking the Emperor of Japan to our atomic adventure. I think we could have been quite happy working in this flat if only it had not been so beastly cold. (It was the winter of 1946 and the repercussions of war were still with us.) One of Trocheris' sisters, for he had several, and I was under the impression that they took turns, used to bring us strange herb teas which we swallowed boiling hot, in an attempt to keep warm. What a good time we were having!

As a basis for our work we were using the Smyth report, which the Americans had declassified and which could be found in bookshops. It had stripped the secrecy from many ideas and results, including some of the notes brought back by Kowarski on the theory of nuclear reactors.

In fact, once one *did* know that a reactor moderated with heavy water, with a geometry of cylindrical bars of natural uranium immersed in the moderator, *could* diverge—something that Kowarski had demonstrated in Canada by building the *Zeep* reactor—it was enough to know the values of a few cross sections to be able to design a reactor of zero power. This is a general feature of all great new scientific and technological enterprises. To *know* that something has been done, and therefore is feasible, is half the secret.

Kowarski's notes had mysterious names which resembled codes: *Pryce–Guggenheim* notes or *Volkov* notes. I did meet their authors later. Pryce, of whom I will have much to say, had become Professor of Theoretical Physics at Oxford, Guggenheim Professor of Physical Chemistry at Reading, and Volkov Professor at the University of British Columbia in Vancouver.

In one batch of these notes we found the numerical (relative) values of the radial distribution of neutrons in a cylindrical cell as a function of the distance 'measured in reduced units' to the axis of the cylinder. These numerical values were an atomic secret. Claude Bloch showed easily that these values were those of a Bessel function, steady state solution in cylindrical geometry of the diffusion equation, and reduced the atomic secret to a smoke screen.

I remember another formula in Kowarski's notes called the *Wigner–Kowarski* formula. When we asked Kowarski for some explanations of points in this formula which seemed unclear to us he said: 'I can explain the Kowarski part to you, but I cannot answer for the Wigner part.' I was under the impression that the Kowarski part was the replacement of densities and cross-sections in the Wigner formula by their numerical values, but I would not swear to it.

Before long we decided that dissecting documents relating to atomic energy and the corresponding calculations was not enough to keep us happy, and we decided to do some pure physics as well. I must admit that I was surprised to see my comrades eager to tackle straightaway unsolved problems of quantum mechanics and electrodynamics—such as the theory of the S matrix, which was then much talked about—before getting a little more familiar with the solutions of problems which had been solved already. I think the truth lay half-way between my timidity and their temerity. We started with von Neuman's book on 'Mathematical Foundations of Quantum Mechanics'. The book was in German and we were absorbing it slowly through Horowitz, but before long a translation into French by Al Proca had appeared. The impression I retained from our collective reading of that remarkable book was that it was a very fundamental work, that it was a very good thing that someone had completed it to insure the solidity of the foundations of quantum mechanics, but that perhaps it was enough to know that such a work did exist and authorized the use of quantum mechanics in complete safety. We studied a few more items of pure physics, which were of lesser scope.

Apart from Kowarski, two other scientists, both chemists, Bertrand Goldschmidt and Jules Guéron, had come back from Canada with the aura of atomic prestige, but we did not have much to do with them. I remember that our little group had been asked to translate a set of mimeographed lectures which had been given by Victor Weisskopf at Los Alamos. These lectures which were very elementary and remarkably clear, like everything that comes from Weisskopf, naturally contained no secrets of any kind. Our French version was revised by a maiden lady, the daughter of a very great mathematician, who pronounced our translation unfaithful.

In the face of our indignant protests, such as: 'Why doesn't she mind her own business!', Jules Guéron was called up as an expert to arbitrate in the conflict. He explained to us that we should have adhered more closely to the original text, for atomists accustomed to dealing with confidential documents know full well that it is sometimes necessary to read between the lines, and that in a free translation there is always a danger of letting confidential information slip through. This nonsense finished him off for good, in our eyes.

I may add that he had a sententious and sybylline way of speaking, which reminds me of Jules Renard's remark: 'A sentence which should be read twice, not because it is profound but because it is obscure.' (I cannot resist the pleasure of throwing in that other remark of his, which was made about a young writer, but fit some of our young physicists as well: 'Remember that name well, for it will not be heard again.') Guéron's son, who did his thesis in my lab many years later, had inherited his way of speaking, which made me say to him once: 'The advantage you have over your father is that I can make *you* repeat what you say.' I would like to add that all through his career Jules Guéron has been an honourable man and dedicated to his job.

Bertrand Goldschmidt was far more subtle but very lazy ('bone idle' says my dictionary. In French we say: *paresseux comme une couleuvre*, 'as lazy as a grass snake', presumably because this harmless reptile likes to lie in the sun doing nothing). He says now that he is not lazy. Maybe he isn't, and belongs to that lucky crowd of people who manage to do a lot of work without seeming to. If so, he is very good at it. He gave up scientific work at the CEA fairly early to devote himself to para-diplomatic activities, both internal and external, which became properly diplomatic when he was appointed Director of International Relations at the CEA. He has written several books on the history of atomic energy.

From the summer of 1947 the members of our Gang of Four started to move in different directions. Claude Bloch had chosen to enter the prestigious Corps des Mines. His obligations to it were purely nominal and they left him plenty of time to do physics, but he had to stay in Paris till 1948. On an initiative of Kowarski, Horowitz was sent to the Niels Bohr Institute in Copenhagen. Trocheris left for Manchester where Professor Léon Rosenfeld, a French speaking (actually polyglot) disciple of Niels Bohr, had established a school of theoretical physics which attracted many young French physicists.

'*Et moi? Et moi?*' (title of a popular French song). Kowarski, to whom I had addressed that question, possibly phrased differently, said that someone had to stay at home to mind the shop, and when I asked him why me, he explained to me for the first time that, not being a Polytechnician, I should be modest. If my polytechnician comrades treated me as one of them, Kowarski, *plus royaliste que le roi* (out-heroding Herod, says my dictionary), clearly thought otherwise. He encouraged me to look outside the CEA for the funding of a future trip abroad, which might take place in 1948 when the other two would be back. I did so, but more of that later. Feeling a little lonely and wondering what he meant by 'minding the shop' I rang up Kowarski to ask for instructions. 'You and Ertaud have a look at the problem of oxide' (of uranium) was his brief reply. I had not seen Ertaud for quite some time and, what's more, Kowarski had deliberately put him on the sidelines. I decided to act as if I had not called him. I had no more dealings with atomic energy except for a brief period after 1950.

I was hired formally as a CEA employee as from 1 January 1947. Because of that my card bears the number 284. If I had been hired as soon as I started working there, that is in October 1946, I would have belonged to the aristocracy of the two-digit cards. (The nine one-digit cards had been allotted in 1945.) Even so, 284 is not so bad for an agency which at one time had thirty thousand employees.

My farewell to the CNRS did not go smoothly in spite of the fact that my allegiance to it (from October till December 1946, while I was working at the CEA) was purely formal, as a means to pay me some money until I could be hired by the CEA. Early in January 1947 I wrote to inform them that I was no longer a member of their organization, having been hired by the CEA as of 1 January, and asked them to stop paying my salary from that date on. At the end of January I received my salary. I wrote back asking them how I could pay it back to them. No answer, but a second payment at the end of February. I wrote again. Still no answer, but a third payment at the end of March. I don't remember if I wrote once more. However, in April I received from the CNRS a very nasty letter accusing me of having done them out of three months' salary, demanding the immediate return of these sums, and threatening me with administrative and possibly legal proceedings. Cloaked in my virtue, so abominably hurt by these insensitive and clumsy bureaucrats, I went to their office to protest. The bureaucrat who received me opened the drawer of his desk, got out my three letters and magnanimously admitted that I was 'in order'.

The CEA administration also made a few mistakes at the beginning. At the end of January a list was posted at the Fort de Châtillon inviting the people whose names were on it to go to the cashier to get paid. If, as expected, my name was the first on the list, I did not see those of Horowitz and Trocheris. (Bloch was getting his salary from the Corps des Mines.) 'We have already been paid by standing order,' they told me. Slightly surprised by this difference in treatment between me and my Polytechnician friends, a difference to which I may have become oversensitive, I went to see the cashier to get paid and to obtain an explanation. 'It's all right,' said the cashier, counting my notes, 'you are not staff, that's why.' 'I am not staff! What am I then?' He consulted his list. 'You are a top grade glass blower: there are only two of you in the whole CEA. And don't you worry, you get as much as your friends on the staff.' But I firmly intended to worry: the possibilities of advancement for a glass blower on the top scale were limited, and in spite of my age of thirty-two I still aspired to promotion. I managed with some difficulty to have my professional status redefined.

The rapid expansion of the CEA had led at an early date (I have forgotten that date) to the signing of a collective agreement between the Administration and the personnel. This agreement contained two clauses, one for staff, and one for 'other ranks', so to speak. This gave rise to the terminology: 'a clause one' or 'a clause two', to refer to *people* of either category. There was a third category for 'higher staff' (*cadre supérieur*).

These happy few had an individual contract not covered by the collective agreement.

The collective agreement was a bulky brochure which carefully listed the professional qualifications of all those employed or employable by the CEA. There was a big distance between a mere typist and a bilingual executive secretary. It contained a few pearls of which I will transcribe some here:

Second class usher: receives visitors and keeps them waiting according to instructions.

First class usher: receives visitors tactfully and keeps them waiting if necessary.

Minister's usher: Nothing was said in the agreement about *his* duties.

An even more picturesque example was that of the archivist.

Second class archivist: One capable of filing a document.

First class archivist: One capable of filing a document and retrieving it. (I am not making this up).

When I became head of a section, they gave me a secretary. As soon as she had learned to decipher my English handwriting (in French she had no problems, as my handwriting is reasonably legible), she went on maternity leave. The administration 'lent' me an experienced executive secretary for the duration, who had a nominal qualification far above what I was entitled to. It was a poisonous gift. This person of respectable age, who typed slowly and could barely decipher English, owed her exalted classification to her extraordinary 'security rating'. She had been cleared to handle papers marked 'Confidential, Defence' and even, it was rumoured, those marked 'Secret'. On the other hand she was quite incapable of ordering a piece of equipment, a task far below her rank and far above her competence. After she had replaced some things in my scientific writings— 'white Gaussian noise' by 'white Russian noise' and 'adiabatic transition' by 'diabetic transition'—I despaired and asked the central administration to get me a temporary secretary. Strangely enough, such a demand had to be made on a 'purchasing form', which to me smacked of slavery. After waiting in vain for a month, I asked a new and dynamic member of the central administration about my 'purchase'. He told me that he had changed the rules, and requests for a temporary secretary should now be made on a 'manufacturing form'. I asked him whether the use of such a form would not lead to exceedingly long delays.

He replied, deadpan, that it would be faster than with a 'purchasing form'. I never found out whether he was right, because my own secretary came back from leave.

From the start the CEA had been bicephalous (two-headed, if you prefer), with a General Administrator, representing the government, and facing him, a High Commissioner (*Haut-Commissaire*). So far there have been eight General Administrators: Raoul Dautry, Pierre Guillaumat,

Pierre Couture, Robert Hirsch, André Giraud, Michel Pecqueur, Gérard Renon and the present incumbent, Jean-Pierre Capron, and four High Commissioners: Frédéric Joliot, Francis Perrin, Jacques Yvon and the present incumbent, Jean Teillac.

Traditionally, the High Commissioner is a scientist, an advocate of fundamental research, and politically slightly left of centre (Joliot excepted).

The General Administrator is a Polytechnician, belonging to the prestigious Corps des Mines (Robert Hirsch excepted), with varying interest in fundamental research, and his political colouring is that of the government.

Over the last forty plus years, the balance of power, which was even between Joliot and Dautry, has been leaning more and more towards the General Administrator, following in that the will of successive governments, up to the present state of affairs, in which the position of High Commissioner—apart from one or two specific responsibilities, the most important being safety—is purely representative.

Speaking of High Commissioners, I have already described my sole encounter with Joliot in a lift, some time after having nearly been smothered to death at his celebrated public lecture on atomic energy. I have also attended two or three of his scientific lectures at the Collège de France and I will say a word about them later. I have already spoken of my relations with Francis Perrin and I will come back to him. I will speak in some detail of Jacques Yvon, who was an honourable man (not in Mark Antony's meaning) and whose memory I respect greatly. The advent of Teillac came after I took official leave of the CEA: he is a good friend.

Speaking now of the General Administrators, I have nothing personal to say about Dautry and Guillaumat, whom I only saw in public. I will come back to Hirsch and Giraud. I had few dealings with Pecqueur, and none with Renon and Capron, but the memory of my only contact with Pierre Couture still amuses me.

In 1959 I was promoted Head of a scientific department bearing the acronym DPNPS (Département de Physique Nucléaire et Physique du Solide) and a few days after this important (for me, that is) promotion I was due to leave for a conference in the US. Two days before my departure I was informed that the General Administrator wanted to see me about a confidential mission in the US. At the prescribed time I was ceremoniously introduced into his spacious office, where I had never set foot before, by his usher (whether 'first class' or 'minister's', I cannot tell). The General Administrator bade me sit down, and after some hesitation said: 'This is what it's all about and I wish it to remain confidential.' Then he opened a safe and got out a submachine gun (oh no, you did not misread me) which he handed to me. 'It's for my son', he said blushingly. 'I would like you to buy another one like it, if you can find the time while you're in New York—he has managed to break this one.' I then saw that it was a toy, although it looked very much like the real thing, and promised to do his errand. I hardly could have done it today with the new regulations in airports.

During my first year with the CEA my military past nearly caught up with me. In the autumn there had been some very tough, communist-led miners' strikes in the north of France. To maintain law and order, the Minister of the Interior, the socialist Jules Moch decided to call up all the cadet officers, who had recently graduated from a certain number of military schools, including my own beloved Lyon-la-Doua (whose merits I had so eloquently celebrated in a poem). The official list of those schools had been made known on the radio and in the newspapers. I need hardly list here all the reasons which made me reluctant to get back in uniform for the sake of keeping law and order in the north of France, however noble and patriotic this task appeared to the Minister of the Interior.

I thought of asking for a meeting with my scientific patron Frédric Joliot; for even if, as I had reason to believe, he was not fully aware of the importance of my work in the CEA, he might have intervened on my behalf with the authorities, because of his sympathies for the communist party which was behind these strikes. Thinking some more, I decided that there was no law obliging a citizen to listen to the radio or read the newspapers, and I decided to wait and see. It was a wise decision, no gendarme came to fetch me at home; and by this time the statute of limitations must have come into play.

Physicists' stories

As they see themselves

Alexandre Proca, who had translated von Neuman's *Mathematical Foun-dations of Quantum Mechanics* into French, had started a seminar after the war where young French physicists could meet every week. At his suggestion, in the summer of 1947, the CEA had sent Horowitz and myself to an International Conference on Theoretical Physics organized by Professor Rudolf Peierls, who held the chair of Theoretical Physics at the University of Birmingham. It was not a very large conference—a larger one, to be attended by all the primadonnas of theoretical physics was scheduled for the following year—but for us greenhorns, this first contact with international science was thrilling.

At the opening of the conference, Peierls made a short speech, which must have been permeated with British humour, for the audience laughed heartily more than once. I am touching here on the first barrier which separated us from international science, the language barrier. I had been training myself strenuously for this experience by listening to English records based on the *Assimil* method, and by reading English and American mystery stories during the interminable journeys between Croissy and Châtillon, (I had to go on foot, then by train, then metro, then bus, then on foot again, which took more than three hours of my time per round trip). It had not been good enough. I realized that I understood the English of foreigners better than that used by the natives.

In fact, I have noticed with respect to English—but it must be true for other languages as well—that in the learning of a foreign language there is a decisive stage when you begin to understand the speech of natives better than that of foreigners. One knows then that the goal is not far away.

We were certainly far from it that year in Birmingham. Among the speakers there was a short dark man, whom no one in the French delegation could understand, nor place his accent. Some said he was Irish, other said Scottish. 'Nonsense,' I said, 'he's short and dark, he must be Welsh.' We looked up his name in the programme. It was Ferretti, a distinguished Italian theorist.

A few words about Peierls. Born in Berlin in 1907, he settled in Britain in the mid thirties, where, liked and appreciated by all, he soon made himself at home. He must have had a gift for languages, for he speaks French and Russian, the latter learned from his Russian wife, tolerably well. With respect to his English, our difficulty in understanding his introductory speech, and its sprinkling of humorous remarks, was proof enough of his successful assimilation by his second homeland.

He has brought important contributions to nuclear and solid state physics. Nuclear physics is indebted to him for an original quantitative model of Bohr's hypothesis of the formation of the compound nucleus, but his best known contribution to nuclear physics is related to the atomic bomb.

He had tried to improve an earlier calculation of the critical mass of natural uranium by Francis Perrin. Otto Frisch, who had worked on uranium fission, asked him to try the same calculation for pure uranium 235, of which there is less than 1 per cent in natural uranium. Peierls did the calculation on the back of an envelope, as physicists like to say. (There should be a future in manufacturing envelopes with large backs for theoretical physicists.)

The result of the calculation was staggering: one pound!! It turned out later that this estimate was somewhat optimistic (or pessimistic, in view of what happened later), by a factor of five to ten. Peierls realized immediately that an atomic bomb was feasible if one knew how to separate isotopically that much pure uranium 235. He also understood immediately that what he had done, German scientists in the service of the Nazis could also do. Straight away, in order to convince the British authorities, he took certain steps, which became the detonator, if I may use that expression, of the British military programme. Taking part in the Allied war effort, he spent most of the war years in Los Alamos. A ludicrous detail: after the war, in the McCarthy era, when the US authorities had adopted a paranoid approach towards their own and foreign scientists, Peierls was refused a tourist visa to attend a conference which was open to a broad scientific audience. Yet he was able to attend it, because at the same time a very secret conference, concerned with the declassification of some secret documents from the last war, was taking place, and Peierls had been sent to it by the British government as its official representative.

It often happens that high level scientists are best known for work which they themselves consider minor at the time of doing it. Peierls is best known today by young solid state physicists because of a remark he made at a summer school at Les Houches on the fundamental instability of a linear chain of atoms; he later incorporated this remark into a short book on solid state physics. Materials have been discovered in which such linear chains of atoms exist, interacting weakly with each other, and in which the 'Peierls instability' had been observed.

Peierls is basically what Freeman Dyson has called (applying it to himself) 'a problem solver'. He is also a marvellous teacher who has educated several generations of theorists. It is true that in his youth he himself was in contact with some very extraordinary people. At twenty-five he had worked or at least communicated with scientists like Bohr,

Sommerfeld, Heisenberg, Pauli, Bethe, Landau, Gamow, Felix Bloch, and many more of their ilk. He is also a kind and generous man, whose keen sense of humour keeps away from him fools and crooks.

A word about Otto Frisch, whom I met in Cambridge. Having met in Cambridge (Mass) an American physicist by the name of David Frisch, I am ashamed to admit that I asked him if there was 'a Frisch in every Cambridge'.

It was in Birmingham that I met the formidable and delightful Genia Peierls, who left us in October 1986—Lady Peierls after her husband had become Sir Rudolf. Rudolf had met Genia, a Russian girl, during a trip to Russia and they got married in Leningrad a few months later, with less than forty-five years of age between the two of them. Genia was an adorable woman, adored by all, who had been a second mother and then grandmother to her husband's innumerable students: intelligent, courageous, cultured, and generous, she did not pass unnoticed, or unheard, (nor did she want to)—partly because of her voice, which had the volume, if not exactly the tonality, of a foghorn.

In Oxford they like to tell how, once, when she was speaking to her husband on the phone, someone in the next room asked: 'What's that noise?' 'Lady Peierls is calling her husband at the lab.' 'Why doesn't she use the phone?'

I ran into her once in the Latin Quarter in a bookshop run by Russian emigrés. She started to tell me what exactly she disliked about Solzhenitsyn, at the risk of us both being lynched by the customers present in the bookshop, or for that matter in all the Russian bookshops in the Latin Quarter.

I met her for the first time in Birmingham, one afternoon when the 'conferees' (horrible but convenient word) were free to roam about. She was walking in the sun, a sun which had made up its mind to shine after a cloudy morning. Beside her, and carrying some of Mrs Peierls' clothes which the sun had caused her to discard one after the other—'my seven veils' she said—the great Dirac himself was walking sagely. Seeing a man whom I had admired so much, walking so near me that I could have touched him, I was filled with emotion. I had already been to a conference he gave in Paris at the Institut Henri Poincaré, of which I had understood everything during the first ten minutes, and next to nothing during the fifty that followed. He had spoken excellent French except for one amusing mistake: of a hypothetical, *hypothetique* in French, he kept saying *hypothéqué*, which means 'mortgaged'—an expression which remained part of the slang which Horowitz and I used.

There are countless stories about Dirac. If one added all those, authentic or apocryphal, about Pauli, Bohr, Einstein, Wigner and the others, it would fill a book twice the size of this one.

One of the best, and the best known, of Dirac's stories is the one where, after one of his conferences, a listener raises his hand and says 'I did not understand your conclusion.' Dirac remains silent and the chairman asks: 'Would you care to answer this listener's question?' 'It is not a question, it is a statement.'

Two other stories are interesting, insofar as they show a side of his attitude to students which is somewhat different from the usual behaviour of Anglo-Saxon professors.

In the first story a young research worker (M. H. L. Pryce), tells Dirac of his wish to work with him. 'Thank you very much, but I do not think I need help' replies Dirac.

The second, told by Peierls himself, is about his daughter Gaby who had been staying with the Diracs. Planning a small party for her, Mrs Dirac asked her husband whether he had any students that could be invited to it. After thinking for a while, Dirac said: 'I had a student, but he died.'

Naturally all these stories sound much better if the storyteller can claim to have been a participant himself, or at least a witness, which may tempt some people into tampering with the facts. This is a temptation which should be resisted.

A French colleague told me once of having been to Dirac's house. According to him, Dirac who had just married Wigner's sister, introduced her to him as Wigner's sister rather than as his wife. I had heard that story before; it had been told many times and I knew for certain that it had not happened to that colleague. When he told me the story, I felt myself blushing and I think he guessed why. In France little children are told that when they tell a lie their nose twitches; but Jules Renard says 'My nose twitches when so-and-so tells me a lie.'

To me the most beautiful of all Dirac stories is this one told by Peierls: to the question: 'What's your hobby?' Dirac replies 'Thinking'.

Now to conclude, two Dirac stories, their only merit being that they genuinely are *my* stories.

Shortly after I had come to Oxford to work with Pryce, Dirac gave a lecture to a small audience, which was a repetition of the one he had given earlier at the Institut Henri Poincaré. He then handed round a few reprints of the lecture.

He asked me in English: 'Can you read French?' 'Yes,' I said in English. Had I out-Diracked Dirac? In '49 Suzanne and I went to Cambridge for a couple of days. Coming out of the railway station, Suzanne said: 'Look at this funny tall man striding along with his head in the clouds'. 'Aren't you lucky, the first man you see in Cambridge is Dirac.'

I have no recollections of Dirac saying anything during the conference. Among those who took part, besides Peierls, I remember Pryce, Casimir and Wentzel. It may not be too late to say that the main theme of the conference was to do with the divergencies of the quantum field theory, which had worried the theoreticians ever since Heisenberg, Pauli and Dirac had laid down the principles of quantum electrodynamics around 1928. All the speakers wished to introduce the concept of a minimal length, below which the laws of electrodynamics should be modified, but no one saw clearly how to it.

In 1947 Gregor Wentzel was one of the best specialists on these problems. In 1943 he had written an excellent book on the subject which I would be digesting, all through the forthcoming year, but I understood very little of what he had been saying at the conference. What struck me most was the incredible quality of cigars he smoked during the sessions.

Casimir has been the great man of Dutch science for the last forty years. His career has a strikingly wide range, extending from important experimental work on the electronic properties of metals and on magnetism at very low temperatures (or rather at what were called very low temperatures when Casimir did his experiments), to very abstract theoretical results of group theory (the Casimir operators). In the years to come, what interested me most in his work was his theory of the interaction between the nuclear quadrupole moment and the electronic shells of the atom.

As precocious as Peierls, and belonging to the same generation of physicists, he too had already known and worked with most of the great physicists I mentioned earlier, before he was twenty-five. Around the age of forty-five he made a decisive change in his career by going into industry, where for many years he was Director General of the Philips laboratories. He is a man of vast experience, considerable culture and charm, much sought after as a speaker, and a great storyteller.

Here are two of his stories in which I played his straight man, but came out of it rather well, I think.

While I was Director of Physics at the CEA he came to visit us at Saclay. During lunch he told the story of two firms which had been in ruthless competition while, unbeknownst to their leaders, both were owned by Philips. 'You did not fool us,' I said, 'we do know that the CEA is a subsidiary of Philips.'

More recently, at a dinner of veterans in magnetism, organized by the German physicist Mössbauer, of whom I shall have much to say later on, Casimir reminisced about our great ancients, Bohr and Pauli. According to Bohr, he said, there is an important difference between a trivial truth and a profound truth. 'A trivial truth is a statement the opposite of which is a falsehood; a profound truth is a statement the opposite of which is also a profound truth.' Then he spoke of Pauli, to conclude by saying, 'You know, deep down Pauli was a modest man.' 'A profound truth,' I said.

I had promised myself not to tell any stories about Pauli, but so that those of my readers who have not heard of this very great physicist, might be able to see the point of the previous story, here are two Pauli stories.

The first one is undoubtedly true because it had many witnesses. In

1919, Einstein, then at the zenith of his fame, gave a conference, attended by the young, in fact, the very young (nineteen years old) Pauli, who had already written the best account of theory of relativity. At the end of the conference Pauli got up and said: 'You know, what Dr Einstein says is far from stupid.'

The second story had no witnesses, at least no witnesses that one could interrogate and so I cannot vouch for its veracity. After his death Pauli is greeted in Paradise by God himself who tells him: 'Pauli, you have been a good man and a good physicist; what can I do for you that would give you real pleasure?' 'Well, God, I would like to know the secret of the Universe; I have been looking for it all my life.' 'That's easy,' says God. He takes Pauli to a blackboard, whips a piece of chalk out of his robes, and writes down three equations. 'Here you are, Pauli.' Pauli looks at the equations, frowns, shakes his head and says one word: 'Dummkopf.'

I will speak at length of Maurice Pryce, who had been my thesis supervisor, in another chapter. All I shall say here is that I was struck by the contrast between his youthful fresh face and his prematurely grey hair.

I do not wish to leave Birmingham, where I have been now playing hookey for a few pages, without speaking of a confidential mission entrusted by Kowarski to Horowitz and myself. He had asked us to talk to Klaus Fuchs—a British theoretician of German origin and a former coworker of Peierls', who worked at Harwell—and to try to extract from him some information relevant to the building of our reactor, taking advantage of the postprandial general goodwill that would prevail at the closing banquet. Kowarski thought that Fuchs, a seasoned nuclear specialist, might be willing to lend a hand to young and inexperienced theorists taking their first steps in the great field of atomic energy.

We decided that since Horowitz could speak German fluently it would be wiser to tackle Fuchs in that language rather than in our halting English. After dinner I saw Fuchs and Horowitz seated together in a secluded corner. From where I sat it seemed to me that Horowitz was doing most of the talking. When their conversation ended Horowitz came back to me. 'He would not say much; his advice was to take an empirical approach, not to put our trust into extensive calculations, and to try to measure as many parameters as possible.' 'There was no need of Fuchs for that. I could have told you that much in French.' Obviously Horowitz had not been able to gain the confidence of our 'informant'.

Three years later we learned that Fuchs had been arrested, and that when Horowitz had talked to him he had already been a Soviet spy for many years. 'We did it all wrong,' I told Horowitz. 'I should have been the one to approach him, and in Russian.'

On my return to Paris I had made up my mind to spend a year with Peierls as soon as possible.

A year of transition

... allowed

First contact with accelerators—From Birmingham to Oxford: the third rash decision

In the autumn of 1947 I began preparations for spending the next year in Birmingham. Following Kowarksi's advice I got in touch with the British Council. I presented them with my various credentials and was granted a Fellowship for one year or rather ten months, at a monthly rate of thirty-five pounds, renewable for one year at most. It was not much, but it was better than nothing.

I then went to the Headquarters of the CEA, which was temporarily housed in an immense flat in the Avenue Foch, the most elegant district of Paris, to inquire about the possibility of an additional grant from the CEA. I was received by M. Pernot, a very pleasant gentleman, who, after hearing me, suggested a different scheme. I would be sent to Britain by the CEA on an official mission, with a salary higher than the one offered by the British Council, say fifty to sixty pounds, and I would pay back to the CEA whatever monies I would be getting from the British Council. That way I would not lose my superannuation benefits for the years I would be spending abroad. Naturally, in practice, to avoid unnecessary book-keeping, the CEA would simply pay me the difference between my salary and the British Council grant. The whole scheme would still have to be approved by the scientific authorities.

On leaving M. Pernot, elated by his offer, I commented with some surprise on the number of sanitary appliances present in most of the rooms of the flat. M. Pernot explained that the flat had been equipped by the Gestapo as some kind of Valhalla for its warriors, and that these utensils were the remnants thereof.

'Upon my leave wrung by laboursome petition', Francis Perrin 'sealed his hard consent', and my mind thus set at rest, I was able to devote it to science. Horowitz had gone to Copenhagen, Trocheris to Manchester; and so it was with Claude Bloch, whom the liberal Corps de Mines left free to do very much what he pleased, and with Philippe Meyer, a young man who had returned from the US, where he had been studying at Harvard, that I undertook to digest Wentzel's book on *Quantum Field Theory*, which I mentioned in the previous chapter.

Another brilliant polytechnician, Albert Messiah, who also wanted to do physics, made a brief appearance among us. I don't think that he belonged to our little group, and anyway he soon disappeared for a stay of several years in America.

To tell the truth, I was getting fed up with studying books; I had been doing little else for the last ten years.

This is why I was pleased to hear that the CEA was taking an interest in the construction of particle accelerators. These machines had superseded the radioactive sources of alpha particles which had also been the sources of some of Joliot's striking successes. In 1947 he had at his disposal a cyclotron of a few MeV (millions of electron-volts) at the Collège de France, and an electrostatic generator of an energy between 1 and 2 MeV in his other laboratory in Ivry.

But following discoveries made in the US, and to a lesser extent in the USSR, new types of accelerators were making their appearance.

*First contact with accelerators

The first of the new machines had been the frequency-modulated (FM) cyclotron. To remind the reader—in an ordinary cyclotron a charged particle rotates inside the gap of an electromagnet with an angular velocity Ω, proportional to the magnitude of the magnetic field and inversely proportional to its mass. At each turn the particle receives an accelerating kick from an electric field oscillating at the same frequency Ω as its angular velocity, acting not unlike the ringmaster in a circus, cracking his whip in time with the revolutions of a horse in the circus ring. This is the so-called 'resonance condition'. With the increase of the particle energy, its mass also increases according to Einstein's relation between mass and energy, and its angular velocity, inversely proportional to mass, goes down, and breaks the resonance condition. To maintain that condition the frequency of the kicks produced by the electric field must be modified (modulated) accordingly in the course of the acceleration cycle. This idea, so simple in theory, if not in practice, has been responsible for an increase in energy from a few MeV for the old cyclotrons to a few hundred MeV for FM cyclotrons. This is how the CERN synchrocyclotron still works after more than thirty years.

But why no more energy than this?

The difficulty resides in the fact that the greater the energy of the particle, the greater the radius of its trajectory which spirals outward from the centre of the gap and unrolls itself with an instantaneous radius which is proportional to the particle's impulse and inversely proportional to the magnetic field. With increasing energy, and therefore also impulse, this radius grows and the surface of the gap which houses the spiralling trajectory becomes very large, leading to a prohibitive size and weight for the magnet.

This is why another type of machine had to be invented, the 'proton synchroton', where the frequency of the accelerating electric field and the magnitude of the magnetic field are modulated simultaneously in a manner which maintains at all times the resonance condition *and* keeps constant the radius of the orbit. It is then sufficient to produce the magnetic field in the narrow annular space surrounding the fixed orbit. This is the principle on which the CERN supersynchroton or SPS works, producing protons of an energy of 450 GeV (One GeV is a billion electron-volts). Thanks to a very clever device (which it would take too long to describe here), invented at CERN by Simon Van der Meer, two large groups of physicists, led by Carlo Rubbia and Pierre Darriulat, were able to discover the so-called intermediate bosons W and Z, predicted by the so-called electroweak theory due to Glashow, Salam and Weinberg. The large Fermilab Tevatron in the US, which produces protons of 1000 GeV (that is one Teravolt or TeV), works on the same principle.

The LEP (Large Electron–Positron collider) which is being built at CERN will also function on the same principle. It will accelerate electrons (and positrons) to an energy of 50 GeV in the first stage and to 100 GeV later.

It is essential to understand that the acceleration of electrons is considerably more difficult than that of protons. This is connected with the fact that their rest mass is nearly 2000 times smaller than that of protons. It so happens that the electromagnetic energy radiated by a charged particle in circular motion is, all other things being equal, inversely proportional to the fourth (!) power of its rest mass. For electron energies like those of LEP, the radiated energy can only be maintained within manageable limits by vastly increasing the radius of the particle's orbit, in order to reduce its centripetal acceleration, which is responsible for the radiation of electromagnetic energy.

A very peculiar feature of radiated electromagnetic energy is the width of its spectral density. For an ultrarelativistic charged particle (one with a kinetic energy many times that of its rest mass) the frequencies contained in its radiation spectrum are not only the radiation frequency itself, but also its harmonics up to an extraordinary high order, extending into the visible and the ultraviolet and even into the X-ray range.

This characteristic of synchroton radiation, considered at the start to be a curiosity, if not a nuisance, has recently acquired a considerable importance: for it is a powerful continuous source of ultraviolet radiation, and, even more importantly, of X-rays, with applications to solid state physics, chemistry, and biology, sufficient to justify the building of electron synchrotons specially designed for that usage.

The theory of synchroton radiation was well known in 1947. In that theory, the accelerated electron and the radiation field had both been treated classically. It occurred to me that the number of the 'hardest' photons emitted by the electron in one turn was not large and might exhibit important fluctuations, a fact which the classical theory was unable to take into account. I undertook a semi-classical calculation, in which, contrary to the usual procedure, I treated the orbit of the electron *classically*, but I quantized the electromagnetic field the way I had seen it done in Heitler's book on quantum theory of radiation. It was the kind of first calculation that a thesis supervisor might have suggested to his student. I had no supervisor, and so suggested it to myself. I saw it through, and was more pleased than disappointed at seeing that I had obtained the same results as those of the classical calculation. It showed that I had correctly done a calculation of little interest. I published it in the *Journal de Physique*: it was my first publication.

The head of the accelerators department at the CEA was so impressed by this calculation that he wanted to present it at a conference. With some difficulty I talked him out of it.

I also took an interest in high energy linear electron accelerators. Their principle can be understood in simple terms by placing oneself in a frame moving with the velocity of an electromagnetic wave, created by electronic power tubes in the waveguide where it propagates. An electron which is moving with the same velocity as the wave will *imagine* that it is motionless and that it *sees* a static electric field. The effect of that field is to accelerate the electron, but if it is ultrarelativistic and therefore moving with very nearly the velocity of light, even though its energy increases, its velocity remains practically unchanged and it does not fall out of step with the wave. This led me to inquire into the structure of an electromagnetic wave propagating inside a waveguide, with *exactly* the velocity of light c. I showed that, with the exception of a structure of circular symmetry— unfortunately the only one to occur in practice—a wave of velocity c cannot be derived from a wave of lower velocity by a continuous change of parameters. I published this result as a short note in the *Comptes Rendus de l'Académie des Sciences*. To use Pauli's oft-quoted saying, 'It was not even wrong'. I doubt that it had any readers beside myself.*

Meanwhile, Horowitz in Copenhagen was in the middle of some real advances in physics. In his letters he told us of a discovery made by the American physicist Willis Lamb, which, according to Niels Bohr, was of paramount importance and would lead to a complete renewal of the quantum theory of radiation. Undoubtedly quantum field theory was the raft aboard which I had to climb.

Two things worried me though. Firstly this raft was terribly over-crowded. Practically all those who belonged to the Proca seminar were doing nothing else. The same was true of the great majority of the French physicists who were working with Rosenfeld in Manchester and with Peierls in Birmingham—my next destination.

But there was something else. In 1947, during my stay here, I had taken a good look at the good city of Birmingham. The provocative ugliness of its architecture, the tasteless dreariness of its streets, the guttural idiom spoken by its inhabitants—which to my ear, accustomed to the stereotyped accents of the *Assimil* records, sounded like anything but English—the unspeakable food, (at least for a Frenchman, even one whom four years of German occupation had not cosseted much) all this led me to wonder whether the game was worth the candle. Had I lived through two years in the army, four years of German occupation, and all the postwar hardships, just to shut myself off, at thirty-three years of age, for one year and most likely two, in this sinister exile?

I realized long ago that I was largely overreacting; Birmingham was not that much uglier than other large English cities, and could even offer some pleasant districts; the food was much the same everywhere; and the university people, with whom I would be dealing, would not be speaking in the horrible local accent, but rather that of the BBC, or with accents hailing from Germany or from other parts of Central Europe.

Be it as it may, on an impulse I went to see the British Council people to tell them that, after thinking it over, I was not very keen any more on going to Birmingham, and to inquire whether I could not go somewhere else. They were very understanding. 'Where would you like to go?' 'I haven't quite decided yet. Where could I go?'

They opened their files. 'There is not much left. Oh yes, there's a new Professor of Theoretical Physics in Oxford, Maurice Pryce, who might have room for another student. We don't quite know yet what he is doing, but it is probably far removed from your interests in quantum field theory. He is collaborating with the experimentalists at the Clarendon Laboratory, who are working in the field of magnetic resonance, if you know what that is.' I did not know what it was and I didn't care. I had heard 'Oxford'. On my way back from Birmingham, I had made a detour through Oxford and spent three days there. Oxford is like Venice or Florence. Too many people whose job it is have written too many beautiful things on these almost too beautiful cities, for me to add my own awkward ramblings to them. Suffice it to say that I came back from Oxford fascinated by so much beauty. The idea that one might not only breathe that beauty, but also be doing physics there had not occurred to me.

'Oh yes, I have been interested in magnetic resonance for some time; could you put my name down for Oxford?' 'We shall put you down as a candidate, but you must get Professor Pryce's agreement as soon as possible. Besides, you will lose your place in Birmingham, as they have several other candidates.'

Pryce! For a long time Kowarski had been telling me about his friend Pryce, whom he had known in Cambridge during the war, and who was the author of the famous 'Pryce–Guggenheim' notes. He was delighted to recommend me to Pryce, who accepted me into his flock. He said that I could come as I was, with my hands in my pockets, with no other rewards for my pains than the fame that my discoveries would bring me (I am afraid there had been a grain of irony there from my future spiritual guide); or I could work for a Doctor's thesis, but then I would have to be accepted by a College. Caution made me choose the latter and I took the required steps. The Registrar of the University (or whoever it was who looked after these things) informed me that my diplomas would have to be translated into English by a sworn translator, unless they were in Latin, in which case a translation was not necessary.

Oxford

Ay, marry why was he sent into England?
... there the men are as mad as he.

*Everyday life: the Colleges—Academic bathing—Lady Godiva in
reverse—An interlude: Edinburgh and Paris: meeting my betters—
The Clarendon and Cherwell—Pryce, Bleaney, and others—*ESR,
Hyperfine Structure, the thesis.

The details of Oxford mores which follow were included in the French
version of this book, for the enlightenment of my compatriots. Their
usefulness in a book published by the Oxford University Press may appear
questionable. I decided to let them stand, because with any luck, a copy of
the English version might find its way into North Dakota, South Carolina,
West Virginia or even, who knows, Eastern Europe, where such details are
not as widely known as they are on the banks of the Isis.

In 1948 Oxford University could be compared to a feudal monarchy:
the colleges were the feudal lords, rich and powerful, and the university
proper was their suzerain, feeble and impecunious. Degrees were granted
by the university, but only to those that the colleges had been willing to
accept. The resources of the colleges came in large part from the income
of their considerable real estate. The colleges favoured very long leases,
which lawyers like to call 'emphyteutic' (what a word!), and which last
ninety-nine years. For a private person such leases are tantamount to sales,
but not for a college, which counts in centuries.

Gifts and legacies from former members who have done well in life are
another source of income. I have heard one story of such a gift.

A rich businessman passing through Turl Street dropped into the lodge
of the college where he had been an undergraduate. The old Head Porter
who had retired years ago but happened to be standing in the lodge,
greeted him with a: 'How are you Mr Sanderson, Sir?' (I have changed the
name).

Mr Sanderson was so gratified at being remembered and recognized that
he gave one million pounds to the college.

If the colleges are all equal within the university, some are more equal
than others—more prestigious and richer. What the prestige rests on is not
always obvious; it may be the antiquity or the proportion of famous
former members, but wealth is never far behind.

The college where I ended up was Jesus (another example of my Judeo-
Christian tradition). While not one of the most prestigious, it is far from

being one of the lowest. On Fortune's cap it is not the very button, nor the soles of her shoe. It was founded by Queen Elizabeth (the one who beheaded Essex, not the one who opens horse shows), and counts among its Honorary Fellows: Lawrence (of Arabia, not of Lady Chatterley), the former Prime Minister Harold Wilson and, since 1975, myself. Jesus has close links with Wales. A large proportion of its undergraduates are Welsh, and it is claimed that if you stand in the middle of the quad and shout for Jones or Evans, a hundred heads will pop out of the windows. Their favourite song is: 'Lloyd George knew my father, Father knew Lloyd George', which can go on for ever.

Pryce had first tried to get me accepted into his own New College, but was told that I 'would not be happy there'. Jesus, his second choice, greeted me warmly. Did they think Abragam was a Welsh name?

Each college is governed by the body of its Senior Members, or Fellows, familiarly known as dons, who co-opt themselves. The head of the college, elected by the Fellows, is diversely called: Principal, President, Warden, Master, Provost, Rector, Dean (I may be forgetting some).

Among the undergraduates, the scholars are those most successful in a tough competitive examination, which entitles them to a grant; those who have passed well but not quite so well as the scholars, are called exhibitioners (*Honi soit qui mal y pense*). The simple mortals are the commoners. There are also those who work for a higher degree such as a thesis, and of whom some but not all, God knows why, are the 'advanced students'. I was an advanced student between 1948 and 1950. All these people wear black gowns of various shapes and lengths, depending on who they are. Commoners wear a ridiculous little *pet-en-l'air* (a bum-freezer, says my dictionary), an advanced student's gown goes down to the knee, thank God, while dons' gowns are long and ample and flutter behind them as they stride. In my time undergraduates had to wear their gowns after dark, and were forbidden access to pubs. Two Fellows appointed by the university saw to the observation of all the rules by those *in statu pupillari*. They patrolled the streets after dark, escorted by underlings called *bulldogs*. Most of this has become folklore, but was still strictly enforced in 1948. College meals were taken in Hall, the Fellows being seated apart at a High Table. Their food was quite decent and had little in common with that consumed by the undergraduates, with whom I sat on long narrow benches. If the food is mediocre, table manners are excellent: the space available on the bench for each eater is so narrow that elbows have to be kept close to the body, as befits well-bred gentlemen.

Another tradition connected with meals taken in Hall was the *sconce*. The sconce is a penalty that a senior can inflict on a junior colleague for a breach of the rules. The exact nature of the rules belongs to an oral tradition and can only be learned through experience. The offender has to order a large tankard of ale from the buttery, which then goes around the table, everyone taking a sip or a gulp in passing.

Let me give two examples of breach of the rules that I remember: pronouncing the name of Queen Elizabeth was one (again meaning the First—the other was still a Princess); wearing a scarf at meals was another. I had to plead guilty to that one, once. Neither the temperature in Hall, nor my foreigner's ignorance of the rules were accepted as extenuating circumstances. I paid my fine with good grace, but there was always a recourse for the *sconced*. One possibility open to him was to drain the tankard himself, at one go, in which case the *sconcer* who had pronounced the sentence was himself *sconced*. The second was to appeal to the High Table if one found the sentence unfair. There was a catch, though: the submission had to be made in Latin, and if the dons found the Latin wanting the sentence was doubled. During my two years at Jesus I saw a few examples of the first procedure, none of the second.

I had very little in common with the undergraduates, whose modest repasts in Hall and decorous debates in the Junior Common Room I sometimes shared. They were, on the average, ten to twelve years younger than I and sometimes seemed to me like beings from another planet. If I made a point of eating in Hall at least twice a week, it was because the college charged me for a minimum of two meals a week, whether I ate there or not—something I could not afford to disregard—and also because I wanted to practise my English.

Our landlady, Mrs Burns, was a young widow with two charming little children: a boy, Ronnie, aged four, and a girl, Susan, not quite two. Suzanne got along very well with our landlady, who was only too pleased to have her advice and sometimes her assistance in cooking the meals, which benefited a lot from it. I remember that in exchange for a small reduction in the rent and board Suzanne took the children out for two hours a day. She had always adored children, and Ronnie and Susan grew very fond of her.

At four Ronnie spoke in a little voice which was remarkably clear and slightly pedantic, and he sometimes unwittingly said very funny things. Asked once whether he was ticklish, he replied indignantly: 'Of course not, I am English!' Another time, one of the lodgers had been trying for a long time to induce him to say 'thank you' when given a sweet. Having finally dragged a half-hearted 'thank you' from Ronnie, he said absent-mindedly 'Don't mention it'. 'Make up your mind!' said Ronnie angrily. He was supposed to pick up some French from Suzanne during their walks, but unfortunately it worked the other way round: a couple of weeks after our arrival Mrs Burns was amazed to hear Ronnie cry out to her: 'Mummy, me go upstairs?'

Susan did not speak yet, but I had never seen a small child with such a precocious gift for music. She could pick up and hum any tune, whether heard on the radio or sung by Suzanne, who used to sing all day long. Susan took a special liking to me and gave me a very moving proof of her love. This child adored butter, a rather scarce commodity which had to be used sparingly. She slipped a whole quarter of a pound of it into my pocket, without my noticing, and was deeply wounded by my outburst of temper when I withdrew a hand covered in butter from my pocket.

The other lodgers were a Chinese, an Indonesian, and a Pakistani. Mr Pahlia, the Pakistani, was slender, taciturn, and melancholy. He honoured me with his trust and once confided to me that he had left a fiancée behind, who was rich and beautiful; when I asked him why he had to forsake her, he said: 'She was very, very pregnant.' He also described the Oxford climate as: 'very vet vetter.' All this goes to show that the language spoken in our boarding-house was, in the words of George Mikes: 'the purest accent without the slightest English'. I had brought along my *Assimil* records and pestered Suzanne to listen to them during the day.

There was one lesson devoted to a description of the human body, which began with the phrase: 'The top of the head is covered with hair', which for some reason filled Mrs Burns with mirth, and had become a kind of private joke between her and Suzanne. This phrase will reappear in my story.

Next to the Clarendon Laboratory where I worked, the spacious University Parks spread out; this is where Suzanne used to take Ronnie and Susan, and where I liked to walk, thinking about a problem, before returning to the lab.

In the spring the Parks became a Mecca for cricket. In 1948 the Oxford eleven was said to be one of the best in the United Kingdom, and the show was free. For foreigners cricket is undoubtedly an acquired taste, something you learn to love; and I must admit that for me this love had never been *l'amour fou*. I am not going to explain the rules of the game, assuming that a foreigner *can* understand them. All I can say is that I took a greater interest in the proceedings after I realized that the batsman and the bowler were playing *against* each other. A match lasted for three days, with an entr'acte at tea-time each day. What struck me most was the impression of leisurely relaxation given by the players, reminding one of a slow motion film. Anyway it was a beautiful sight, all these players in immaculate flannels against the emerald green of the grass. No hairy calves, no shorts or sweatshirts, but long sleeves carefully rolled up before throwing the ball or hitting it with the bat.

There was, until very recently, another form of entertainment in these Parks, which attracted me more (for I am very fond of swimming)—a bathing place with the charming name of 'Parson's Pleasure'.

The Parks are crossed over a major part of their length, by a branch of the Thames, and a stretch of more than a hundred metres on both banks is reserved for the members of the university who wish to romp in the water or to get a tan by lying in the grass. High fences protect them from prying eyes; these fences are all the more necessary because bathing trunks are not worn. Ignorant of this custom, I came in wearing trunks, which I hastened to remove under the baleful gaze of those present. I must add that the place mostly attracts dons of respectable years who are more interested in peripatetic conversation than in competitive swimming. I still remember a degree ceremony in the Sheldonian Theatre towards the end of my second year in Oxford—Sir Maurice Bowra wearing the splendid robes of the Vice-Chancellor, giving out the diplomas to the happy doctorands with a light slap of the Bible on each head. I could not help envisaging his majestic paunch which I had seen at Parson's Pleasure that very morning.

Did I say that ladies are not expected? It is not written anywhere, but it goes without saying. The ladies have at their disposal another bathing place called, I am told, 'Dames' Delight', where the rules are no doubt different, but into which I never attempted to penetrate. There is one problem at Parson's Pleasure: its location on the two banks of a river, along which glide flat-bottomed boats called 'punts'. Male undergraduates propel them with long poles, trying to dazzle their female conquests by posing as gondoliers. There, between 1948 and 1981, I have been able to observe the evolution of morals and manners. The female passengers of a boat which is going to pass through Parson's Pleasure were expected to leave the boat beforehand, and to walk ashore, before rejoining the boat after the dangerous stretch. During my first stay at Oxford one could see a few boats containing some wenches, who were forgetful or just plain lazy, gliding between the two banks covered with venerable masculine nudes.

Rigid, they looked neither right nor left but straight ahead, for all the world like so many Lady Godivas in reverse. More numerous in the sixties, they permitted themselves a peek, followed by snickers of even derogatory comments. In 1981 there were as many girls as boys in the boats, and no one paid any attention to anything.

At the risk of appearing obsessed with this question of elderly academic nudes, I want to recount a last episode which seems to me typical of a certain kind of Englishness. During the particularly harsh winter of 1962–3, I again spent a few months in England. The Thames was frozen solid and one could walk safely on the ice. As Suzanne and I were taking such a walk, I told her: 'At last I will be able to show you the inside of this forbidden place, Parson's Pleasure.' We crossed this part of the Thames on foot. An elderly gentleman in tweeds was busy breaking the ice with a pick. 'Must be an angler,' said Suzanne. We walked for another quarter of an hour, then retraced our steps. 'Look,' cried Suzanne. 'Do you see what I see?' A bluish shape, wrapped in what from a distance looked like smoke, stood up in front of us, before disappearing into one of the cabins. There will always be an England!

An interlude

*In 1949 I attended a conference on nuclear physics in Edinburgh, organized by Max Born. Among the Founding Fathers of modern quantum mechanics, Max Born comes immediately after the greatest—Bohr, de Broglie, Heisenberg, Pauli, Schrödinger, and Dirac. Some may object to this presentation and wish to replace 'comes immediately after' by 'is one of'. His contributions to the field are numerous and important, the most profound being the probabilistic interpretation of wave mechanics, in which the modulus squared of the wave function of a particle represents its probability to be found in a given point of space. This *'immaterial'* interpretation of wave mechanics, which Schrödinger and de Broglie had been reluctant to accept, was firmly laid down by Bohr and finally accepted by all (except de Broglie who recanted); it bears the name of 'the Copenhagen interpretation' which is unfair to Born, I think. He was awarded the Nobel Prize, but only in 1954, long after his glorious juniors, Heisenberg, Dirac, and Pauli. When Born, much more of a mathematician than the young Heisenberg, had pointed out to him that the algebra of his non-commuting symbols was nothing more than matrix algebra (taught today in the first year at university), Heisenberg exclaimed: 'Oh dear, will I have to learn that too?' Before the war Born had tried unsuccessfully to build a non-linear electrodynamics which would remove the divergencies from quantum electrodynamics. In 1949, the wave of modern physical theories had rolled over him, but he was still leading an active group of theorists and was trying to promote a 'reciprocity principle', which unfortunately did not come off.*

When I met him in Edinburgh he had a noble visage crowned with white hair, and a pleasant and kindly manner. Our encounter was unfortunately marred by a ridiculous incident for which I was not responsible, but which prevented me from approaching Born—whom I revered—as much as I would have wished during the conference.

I happen to hold the dubious record for the greatest number of introductions to Max Born. I was one of the first to arrive at the opening party of the conference and Born, who was standing near the entrance, greeted me warmly. A little later Proca, who considered himself to be the mentor of the young French delegation which counted besides me, Louis Michel, Claude Bloch, and no doubt others, took me by the arm and dragged me over to be introduced to Born, who smiled at me but less than the first time. That was it until the arrival of Maurice Pryce, who had married Born's daughter. What could be more natural for him than to introduce his father-in-law to someone who was in the process of becoming his favourite disciple. Born's smile of welcome looked more like a grimace than a smile. But the agony, Born's and mine, was not over. Towards the end of the reception I was sitting by myself in the corner of a settee, when

Mrs Born, a beautiful and sweet old lady, sat down next to me and put me at my ease by asking me kind and tactful questions about life during the German occupation. Fate would have it that Born, tired out after this long party, should be passing by. 'Max,' called out Mrs Born, 'come here: I want you to meet this young Frenchman.' Born covered his face with his hands and disappeared. 'He is very tired,' said the sweet Mrs Born, to explain the strange behaviour of her husband.

It was in Edinburgh that I first heard the greatest, Niels Bohr. At the end of the session devoted to the foundations of quantum mechanics he made a brief but striking contribution.

I had shamelessly propelled myself into the front row because I did not want to miss a single word of what the great man was going to say; I had been warned that he was not easy to understand. (I learned later that at large international conferences with simultaneous translation, when Bohr spoke in 'English' there was another channel with simultaneous translation of his speech into ... English.) He spoke for a few minutes in a low guttural voice, which was more like a deep whisper, hammering out each word with tremendous emphasis, and punctuating his speech from time to time with a gesture of the hand. Even a layman could not have missed the importance of the far-reaching conclusions which he was drawing from the day's session. I did not miss the importance but I missed the meaning; in fact, I did not understand one single sentence. When the applause subsided, I asked my neighbour, Leon Rosenfeld, a physicist of Belgian origin who spoke French, English, German, Dutch, Danish and 'Bohr': 'What did he say in his conclusion?' 'He said that we have had a long and interesting session, that everyone must be very tired, and that it is time for refreshment.'

The high point of the conference was a talk by Cecil Powell on his work, which put an end to a long controversy and got him the Nobel Prize the following year.

*I will briefly touch on the theme of the controversy. The Japanese physicist Hideki Yukawa had, before the last war, proposed a theory of nuclear forces based on an exchange of massive quanta between nucleons, patterned on the theory of electromagnetic forces, which are mediated by the exchange of light quanta or photons between electric charges. The infinite range of the electromagnetic forces implies a mass equal to zero for the photons, whereas the finite (and short) range of nuclear forces corresponds to the massive character of the Yukawa quanta.

Shortly after Yukawa had published his theory, charged particles with approximately two hundred times the mass of the electron were discovered in cosmic rays and thought for a while to be the Yukawa heavy quanta. However, the ease with which these particles went through matter precluded any strong interaction with nuclei and the possibility of their identification with Yukawa particles.

In a study of remarkable ingenuity and thoroughness, which used photographic emulsions to observe cosmic rays, Powell had been able to identify the true Yukawa particles now known as pions. He showed that a pion would decay into a muon and a neutral particle of zero mass, called a neutrino. The neutrino had been a gleam in Pauli's mind, almost as an ad hoc postulate to save the conservation of energy which the continuous electron spectra in ß-decay seemed to contradict, long before proof positive of the neutrino's existence had become available.

These problems were far removed from my own concerns of the time, but I could not help but be captivated by the clarity of the thinking and the elegance and simplicity of the experimental means in Powell's discovery.*

It was also in Edinburgh that I first met Leprince-Ringuet, a representative of a new generation of rulers of French physics, who had entered the Académie des Sciences before he was fifty, and had scoured the world high and low in search of cosmic rays. He was a great traveller and a physical fitness fiend. More of him later.

I have a photograph of this conference where three characters can be seen, linked by a single word: East. The first is Janossy, known for his theories of cosmic rays, who gave up his British position and returned to his native Hungary shortly after leaving Edinburgh. The second is our old friend Klaus Fuchs, still waiting to be unmasked in 1949.

The third, the most gifted, and certainly the most attractive of the three is Bruno Pontecorvo, a brilliant nuclear physicist, who had worked in British and American nuclear laboratories and who suddenly disappeared, to reappear a few days later in the Soviet Union—where I had the pleasure of seeing him again in 1965. Why this talented and exuberant Latin— who, unlike Fuchs, had probably never been associated with any really important atomic secrets—should have chosen to lock himself in a country where, despite the honours lavished on him, he is not and cannot be happy, is a mystery to me.

A great conference on theoretical physics took place in Paris in the spring of 1950. I have kept a photograph of this conference too, which fills me with melancholy. All these young representatives of French theoretical physics, whom I knew when they were full of the hopes and the ambitions which so few fulfilled, are retired now, or gone before their time. Gone too, is that extravagant genius, Richard Feynman, who did everything his own way—a way which became a freeway for his innumerable followers once he had shown . . . the way—and who was the life and soul of the conference. Let me remind the reader that one of his great discoveries (by no means the only one) for which he shared the Nobel Prize with Julian Schwinger and Sin-itiro Tomonaga in 1965, was the renormalization of quantum electrodynamics: a subject I will return to at the end of this book.

Ever since I embarked on the hazardous task of helping my past emerge from the depths in all its boring grandeur, I have become a great reader of autobiographies. This is how I came to read the one Richard Feynman wrote, or rather dictated into a tape-recorder, with the alluring title: 'Surely you must be joking, Mr Feynman.' Shall I avow my cruel disappointment?

I found it vulgar and unfunny. I felt like crying out to him: 'Not you, Mr Feynman!' I felt like Salieri, in Pushkin's poem 'Mozart and Salieri' (those who have read Pushkin less than I have, can replace him by the film *Amadeus*)—Salieri, the hard-working second-rater, confronted with the exuberant genius of the young Mozart, but also his shocking bad taste and terrible practical jokes. What I remembered of his humour in 1950 was made of finer stuff. One of the asses from the sorry crowd of those who busily sheltered de Broglie from the outside world gave a presentation, aimed at Feynman, of his own version of quantum electrodynamics. At the end neither Feynman, nor anyone else, said anything; so he asked for Feynman's opinion. 'No comment,' said Feynman. Our speaker asked for and obtained the Chairman's permission to repeat his talk in English. '*Pas de commentaires*,' said Feynman.

The Clarendon and Cherwell

Oxford and Cambridge—Rome and Carthage, Athens and Sparta? No! If these two proud metropolises of knowledge have been content for so long to confront each other only on the waters of the Thames or the lawns of the playing-fields, it has been as a consequence of what today's geopolitics call a sharing out of spheres of influence—arts for the one and sciences for the other, or, to put it differently: 'Oxford for manners and marmalade, Cambridge for sausages and sums.'

For more than half a century, one man had played a vital part in this sharing out—R. B. Clifton, the incumbent of a Chair which even today is still the main Chair of Physics in Oxford: 'Dr Lee's Chair of Experimental Philosophy', which carries with it the Directorship of the Clarendon Laboratory.

(In the sixties, one of his successors, my great friend, Professor Brebis Bleaney, about whom I will have much to say later on, was visiting me at Saclay, where foreigners must show their credentials at the gate. On the slip he had been asked to fill in he wrote: 'Professor B. Bleaney, Dr Lee's Professor.' 'Where is the other one?' asked the security officer. 'If this is Professor Bleaney, then where is Dr Lee, and if this is Dr Lee, where's Professor Bleaney?')

During the fifty years from 1870 to 1920, three professors filled the prestigious Cavendish Chair in Cambridge: James Clerk Maxwell, Lord Rayleigh and J. J. Thomson! During the same period Oxford had R. B. Clifton, whose name nobody knows any more, even in Oxford.

Accompanying R. B. Clifton's application for the Professorship, there were only *two* publications, but twenty references from personalities such as Bunsen, Kirchhoff, Stokes, and W. Thomson, later Lord Kelvin, all praising his abilities as a teacher, but keeping remarkably silent on his capacity to direct scientific research.

It seems that during his long and peaceful career Clifton had one great passion—his collection of scientific instruments, lovingly polished and carefully kept under lock and key—and one great fear—that a fire would start in his laboratory, which was locked for that reason every day from 4 p.m.

I owe this information to the kindness of my excellent friend Professor Nicholas Kurti. More details on what guided the destiny of Oxford Science for over half a century, can be found in his fascinating article (*Nature*, 22 March 1984).

However, when, in October 1948, I crossed the threshold of the Clarendon, it had long since ceased to be the Castle of the Sleeping Beauty into which Clifton had turned it. The first man responsible for this awakening was F. A. Lindemann, Lord Cherwell, who remained Dr Lee's Professor till 1956. He was a strong character who could arouse implacable hatred or blind devotion in those who had to deal with him. Since I had some few contact with him, and since (besides his important role in the rebirth of the Clarendon where I spent some of my best years) he played a far more direct and by no means negligible part in my own career, I wish to say a few words about him.

Before the First World War, and between the two wars, he had had a career that was honourable but no more, in a field that was not yet called solid state physics. His tall figure, with a face that was whiskered at the time, appears on old photographs of early Solvay conferences. He was a great friend of Maurice de Broglie and a frequent guest at *Broglie*, the family seat in Normandy.

Two episodes of his life, which will weigh on opposite scales in the judgement of history, might throw some light on this complex character.

His father, of Alsatian origin, had made his abode in Britain long before Frederick's birth. While travelling abroad, his mother gave birth to him in Baden-Baden. *Who's Who*, which devotes a long entry to his prestigious career, mentions the date of his birth but not the place. Cherwell, who all his life had willed himself to be the most British of the British, never forgave his mother for the humiliation of being born in Baden-Baden.

During the First World War he was detailed as a scientist to the Farnborough Air Force Establishment, where the young men who risked their lives every day on their marvellous flying machines looked down, in more ways than one, on those who crawled on the ground. An aeroplane accident which was frequent and often fatal for the pilot in those days was when his plane went into a spin. Lindemann made calculations, from which he drew the surprising conclusion that to get out of a spin the pilot should attempt to get even further into it.

One can imagine the contemptuous remarks which greeted this suggestion, when he submitted it to the pilots and to his superiors.

Cut to the quick, Lindemann learned to fly, then deliberately put his plane into a spin and got out of it using his own method. This story, almost too good to be true, is confirmed by biographers, who were far from being all on his side.

Another feature of his career is the manner in which he used his influence and his considerable personal fortune to help the rebirth of Oxford science. From the early days of Hitler's rise to power he realized what a boon Jewish scientists of stature could become for Britain. In his luxurious limousine, a Mercedes-Benz or a Rolls-Royce, he made several 'survey' expeditions into Germany and 'imported', like some precious merchandise, a certain number of physicists, who were the backbone of the Clarendon for thirty years and who worked on defence during the war.

The leading figure among them was Franz Simon, later Sir Francis—probably the only individual to have been awarded the Iron Cross for having fought in the German Army during the First World War, and a CBE for his contribution to the defence of Britain during the Second. Simon was a great specialist in thermodynamics, and played an important part in the studies of isotopic separation of uranium 235 through gaseous diffusion. He died prematurely in 1956, shortly after succeeding Cherwell in Dr Lee's Chair.

His disciple, Professor Nicholas Kurti, who was one of the pioneers of cooling to ultra-low temperatures by nuclear demagnetization, is one of my best friends. His *violon d'Ingres*, or hobby, is *cuisine* and he appears on British television, more often since he became emeritus, to explain the part played by physics in the making of the most delicate dishes. Needless to say he is a skilful and dedicated cook himself.

He is also an inexhaustible source of amusing but instructive stories and a vigilant guardian of Oxford lore, with which, although he was born in Hungary, he is more familiar than most natives. He did his *Licence de Physique* in Paris and speak excellent French.

Among other physicists of the same origins as Simon I have known Kurt Mendelssohn, another great cryogenist, and Heinrich Kuhn, a remarkable spectroscopist; but there were others.

I am not through with Cherwell; far from it. During the war he was highly valued by Churchill as his chief adviser, but many think that his advice was not always the best possible. A relentless supporter of strategic bombing, he pleaded for preferential bombing of working districts. The benefits, he claimed, were twofold: the density of population was higher and you killed far more people that way, and also working people were far more important to the German war effort than the rich bourgeois of the residential districts. (Marxist thinking!)

I owe a friendly Jesus don, called John Griffith, a little known story about Cherwell which he told me in 1981. I am reporting it from memory (like all my stories) and if these lines fall under his eyes, I hope he will pardon the inevitable inaccuracies. I had a double link with Griffith: in 1948, as Tutor for Admissions, he had to appreciate whether I was enough of a Welshman to be admitted *in statu pupillari* to Jesus; in 1976 he was the public orator whose task it was to celebrate my merits, but more of that later.

In the thirties John Griffith was a schoolboy at Winchester College, the prestigious public school. His father, a Fellow of Brasenose, was a close friend of Cherwell. Here is his story about Cherwell, who was still Lindemann at the time.

In 1931 Lindemann had been engaged in bringing Einstein to Oxford. Having landed in Britain, Einstein, while driving with Lindemann in his Rolls-Royce, began to feel queasy, possibly under the combined effects of a stormy crossing and the softness of the Rolls-Royce suspension. They were passing Winchester, and Lindemann suggested that they should stop and visit the famous school. They were met in the lodge by the Head Porter. Lindemann told him that he wished to show the school to Professor Einstein, who had expressed an interest in Winchester's educational methods. The Head Porter was respectful but firm: 'I am sorry, sir, but it can't be done. This is Monday and the young gentlemen are working.' Somewhat taken aback, Lindemann asked the man whether he knew that Professor Einstein was the greatest scientist alive. 'This may well be, sir, but this being Monday and the young gentlemen being at work, it can't be done.' Neither was the Head Porter impressed upon learning that Lindemann was a friend of the Prime Minister.

Beginning to feel that he was losing face in front of Einstein, he threatened to report the Head Porter to the Board of Governors of the School. 'I have my orders, sir,' replied the Head Porter staunchly. Suddenly, on an impulse, Lindemann said: 'I would like to give a message to young John Griffith, from his father who is a friend of mine.' 'Oh, you know John Griffith, sir? I'll send for him and he'll show you round.'

Two more Cherwell stories in which I have been personally involved.

A few days after my arrival at Clarendon, I found myself in the hall, face to face with the great man. I had come in as he was going out, dressed as usual in bowler hat and black suit, with a watch chain across his stomach, grey spats, and a tightly rolled umbrella. He stopped and addressed me, which for him was an unusual thing to do. I seem to remember that he spoke for quite a while. I must say here that he always spoke in a soft, barely intelligible voice. His rare lectures never carried beyond the second row. To put it plainly, he mumbled. If I add that my mastery of spoken English was in its infancy and that I was terribly intimidated, I may be believed when I say that I did not understand a word, not a single word, of what he was saying to me.

He seemed to expect an answer, but all I could do was to look at him. He too was looking at me. I do not know how long it lasted, but it seemed an eternity. Then he left without another word. This first meeting had not been a success. The comedy of the situation made its recollection bearable after a while.

A few years later, in 1954 or 1955, Bleaney wrote to me asking whether I would accept the Oxford Chair of Theoretical Physics (the Wykeham Chair), if it were offered to me. According to Bleaney, a majority of the Clarendon physicists would like me to come, but the final decision did not rest with them. I wrote back to say that I would be very pleased to accept the offer, which indeed was more than I could have hoped for at the time. I heard nothing more for two months, and then learned that my name had not met with approval. It was twenty years later that I heard from a reliable source that Cherwell had vetoed my candidacy. 'With origins like his, he would poison our relations with Harwell.' But for the caprice of a potentate, I might have ended in the shoes of a Professor Emeritus at Oxford instead of a *Professeur Honoraire au Collège de France*. Although not made by me, this may be considered to be the fourth rash decision of my career. Had fate chosen so badly for me after all? '*Je ne regrette rien*'

Maurice Pryce, who had been my mentor for two years, was bilingual in English and French, but in a peculiar manner. His English was that of an Oxbridge Professor who had first gone through a public or grammar school and Cambridge University. Nothing unusual in that; a large majority of those I associated with at Oxford spoke, or tried to speak, like him.

But his French, although perfectly fluent, was that of a Norman peasant, and reminded me of some of my army comrades of 1939. His mother was French, and in his childhood he had spent many holidays in Normandy, playing with peasant boys and then taking their accent back to England— the way some people keep childhood photographs from a foreign country. It has often been said that England is a country of two nations, speaking two different languages (albeit with an infinity of ramifications in each); and it is true that a single sentence *read* by an Englishman will betray his 'national' origin. The example of *Pygmalion*, a play which is untranslatable into French, is well known: but it seems to me that *Dr Jekyll and Mr Hyde* offers a better picture of this partly subconscious English duality.

*ESR (paramagnetic electron spin resonance)

I was thinking of this English dichotomy while Pryce, jumping from one tongue to the other, sometimes the professor and sometimes the rustic, was trying to initiate me into the mysteries of ESR. This was not without a few hitches, for he was not accustomed to talk about physics in French. ESR was then, and was to remain for many years, the most dynamic of the Clarendon activities.

In a few words, and very crudely, this is what it's about.

An atom behaves like a little magnet; it has a total magnetic moment, associated with the orbital angular momenta of the atomic electrons and with their intrinsic angular momenta, or spins. The spins couple with each other, the orbital angular momenta also, and finally the total angular orbital momentum is coupled to the total spin, according to the rules of atomic physics derived from quantum mechanics, to yield a total atomic angular momentum to which is associated a total magnetic moment. In a strong magnetic field, the number of orientations of the atomic magnetic moment, with respect to the field, allowed by quantum mechanics is finite. To each orientation corresponds a different energy and a frequency, related to it by the famous Planck's constant h. This phenomenon is called the Zeeman effect after the Dutch physicist who discovered it at the end of the last century in optical spectra. To promote the atom from an energy E_1 to an adjacent higher energy E_2, it must be supplied with an energy equal to the difference (E_2-E_1), associated with the Planck frequency $(E_2-E_1)/h$. It so happens that for magnetic fields of the order of a few kilogauss, easily produced with electromagnets, such frequencies fall into the microwave range, which the development of radar during the last war had put after the war into the hands of British physicists, as military surplus materials. When I arrived at the Clarendon, Brebis Bleaney, the most brilliant of the lot, was busy creating the Oxford school of paramagnetic electron spin resonance, which under his leadership would dominate the field for over thirty years.

One should also speak of the atomic nucleus, which for most nuclear species is itself endowed with a magnetic moment, but a very tiny one, thousands of times smaller than an atomic moment. This small nuclear moment can take in turn a finite number of orientations with respect to each orientation allowed for the atomic moment, giving thus to each of the Zeeman atomic levels a finer structure which is usually called *Hyperfine Structure*. This hyperfine structure reflects the strength of the magnetic interaction between the atomic and nuclear magnetic moments, or, if one prefers, the strength of the magnetic field produced by the atomic electrons at the site of the nucleus. The nucleus can thus be used as a microscopic probe for the study of atomic wave functions near the nucleus, a fact which gives a great importance to this tiny phenomenon. All of this, which is very simple in the case of free atoms, such as those of an atomic vapour, and was known long before the war, becomes far more involved, but also far more interesting, when the atom is embedded in a piece of bulk matter such as a crystal. There, the interatomic interactions induce profound changes in the electronic wave functions, especially in those of external electrons. In particular the magnetism of the atoms (or atomic ions) becomes anisotropic, that is dependent on the orientation of an applied magnetic field with respect to the crystalline axes.

John Van Vleck had shown in the thirties that the interatomic interactions could be described with reasonable accuracy in a model where each atom *sees* a fictitious crystalline electric field simulating the effects of interatomic couplings. Van Vleck and his school have been able to explain within this model most of the magnetic properties of salts of the iron group and the rare earths group.

The phenomenon of paramagnetic ESR discovered in 1944 by the Russian Zavoysky who had however not extracted anything important from it, had been yielding far more detailed information in the hands of Bleaney and his colleagues than that derived before from static measurements of magnetic susceptibilities.

There are cases when two magnetic atoms or ions in bulk matter are so close to each other that their wave functions overlap. Because of the quantum-mechanical indiscernibility of the electrons, the question whether an electron belongs to one or the other atom becomes meaningless. Dirac had shown that the possibility for two electrons, belonging to two such atoms, to interchange their positions was mathematically equivalent to their exchanging the orientations of their spins; which in turn can be shown to result from a scalar coupling between the spins, called *exchange* coupling. Heisenberg was the first to show that in this exchange coupling lay the origin of the enormous phenomenological molecular field, which the French physicist Pierre Weiss had proposed at the beginning of this century, as an explanation of ferromagnetism.

Pryce had proposed to me that I make a *theoretical* estimate of the strength J of the exchange between two neighbouring copper ions in a crystal of copper sulphate. The existence of this exchange modified the shape of the ESR spectra of these ions (first observed by James Griffith and Desmond Bagguley) in a way which allowed an *experimental* estimate of J. A comparison of the two values could be interesting.

This was the first time in my life, at thirty-three years of age (and if I keep harping on about my age, it is because it had become an obsession for me) that a competent and conscientious supervisor offered me a problem which, although not very fascinating, was quite meaningful.

And yet, perennial malcontent, I was not happy. I had immediately realized that this was a type of work which would take me a few months of tedious calculations, during which, as Pryce very tactfully had led me to understand, he would be able to devote more of his time to his other doctorands who were more advanced in their research, or even to his own work.*

Pryce's brilliant career did nothing to alleviate my frustrations. My elder by barely two years, he was in charge of one of the most prestigious professorships in the United Kingdom, (the very chair that Cherwell would pronounce off-limits to me, seven years later); he was also well known for the highly theoretical work on field theory and general relativity which he had accomplished in the late thirties, and for his more or less secret work on the atom during the war years.

*Hyperfine structure

I was saved from despair by the discovery of the hyperfine structure in a copper salt, the so-called Tutton salt. This discovery was made in October 1948 by a friend and colleague of Bleaney, R. P. Penrose, during a stay of a few months in the Leyden laboratory of the Dutch professor, Cornelis Gorter. It was made possible by the use of a crystal in which the copper magnetic ions had been considerably diluted inside an isomorphous crystal of diamagnetic zinc. Contrary to normal copper crystal, in which the tiny hyperfine structure is masked by the magnetic interactions between the magnetic copper ions, it could be seen plainly in the dilute crystal, in the form of four resonance lines, corresponding to the $(2I+1)=4$, orientations of the spin $I=(3/2)$ of the copper nucleus. It was the first observation of hyperfine structure in condensed matter. The electronic structure of the copper ion had been known for a long time from former magnetic susceptibility measurements, supplemented by resonance measurements carried out on concentrated salt, and it appeared possible to predict from these data the hyperfine structure anistropy in the dilute salt. Pryce made an approximate calculation 'on the back of an envelope' and found an anistropy of 'two to one', which was heading in the right direction, but smaller in absolute value than the one observed by Penrose. Pryce suggested that I try to improve on his calculation by taking some other effects into account, which were expected at first sight to be small—such as spin–orbit coupling (I will not elaborate for fear of becoming even more incomprehensible). I went to work with enthusiasm and a few days later brought him the results of a far more complete theory. Pryce liked the elegance of my presentation.

He liked its result less. I had found an anistropy of '*one to two*', that is *opposite* to the one which had actually been observed. The elegance of the presentation made the calculation easy to check. Bleaney, Pryce and the others—I at the Clarendon, Penrose and Gorter and his coworkers at Leyden—had a problem of the first magnitude on their hands. The mystery was clouded further by the sudden illness of Penrose, which was to carry him off a few weeks later. The discovery of the hyperfine structure belonged to Penrose; what we knew of his experimental results had come from a private communication from him to Bleaney, and during the long weeks when Penrose was at death's door there was no question of doing further experiments nor of publishing the strange theoretical results. It was after his death that a note appeared in *Nature*, bearing his name and giving his experimental results; then another note signed by Pryce and myself relating the glaring contradiction between theory and experiment. The calculation of the exchange constant J, first suggested by Pryce, had fallen into oblivion, and a satisfactory theory of hyperfine structure, which remained to be discovered, had become *my* problem which no one knew how to solve. After Penrose's death his experiments were resumed, improved, extended to different copper salts as well as to cobalt salts. Everywhere, the same mysterious anistropy!

In all these salts, all the magnetic properties *other* than hyperfine structure were explained perfectly by the Van Vleck's crystalline field model, and there was no question of touching its parameters for fear of destroying the explanation of these other properties. This contradiction became a real obsession for me: I was thinking about it in my office, while eating, and during the hours I spent lying in the sun at Parson's Pleasure.

It was precisely from this contradiction that the answer came. I asked myself, 'What property of the electronic shells could upset the hyperfine structure while leaving all the other magnetic properties of the ion unchanged?', and came to the answer: the electrons found nearest to the nucleus, or *s*-electrons in spectroscopic jargon, must be responsible for the effect. It was then enough to superimpose on the generally accepted electronic configuration a tiny pinch of a different configuration called an *s*-configuration in which an *s* electron extracted from a deep-lying shell was promoted to the outside of the ion. This yielded the desired anisotropy without upsetting any other magnetic property of the ion. In practice it was enough to add a single *isotropic* term to all the calculated hyperfine structures, which was adjustable but the *same* for *all* the copper salts, to bring together theory and experiment. With the means at my disposal I could not calculate the value of this correction from first principles, but I was able to show that its order of magnitude was reasonable.

The experimental result which proved the correctness of my assumption beyond doubt, was Bleaney's discovery of a *large* and *isotropic* hyperfine structure in divalent manganese, where, in the absence of my *s*-electrons, its value should have been *zero*. I published my hypothesis as a brief letter to the editor of the *Physical Review* (there was no separate journal for letters then) which established my reputation overnight among 'paramagnetic resonators' the world over.*

I did my thesis on the theory of paramagnetic resonance in the iron group. Pryce and I extracted the subject matter for three long articles out of it, which were published in the *Proceedings of the Royal Society*, and are still cited today, nearly forty years later.

The old chrysalis had at last become a butterfly, and none too soon. I had become Mr Hyperfine Structure, the one who had penetrated its mysteries. They were modest mysteries, but in the words of the Russian saying: 'My glass is small but I drink from *my* glass.' And I had had nothing to drink for thirty-five years.

In 1950 an important conference on radiofrequency spectroscopy took place in Amsterdam, attended by all the stars of the field: Van Vleck, Purcell, one of the discoverers of NMR (nuclear magnetic resonance), Ramsey the specialist in molecular beams, Gorter, Bleaney, and many more. But how different I found that conference from the one in Birmingham three years before! My talk was of interest to the audience, and was followed by numerous questions.

After I left the Clarendon in the summer of 1950, my work was extended to rare earth ions by Ken Stevens and by Roger Elliott (Sir Roger later), now Wykeham Professor of Physics.

Back at Saclay, Horowitz, (a better mathematician than I) and I showed how my s-configurations could be derived from a variational principle.

In Oxford the thesis examination takes place in front of two examiners: the internal examiner, who belongs to the university, and who is *not* the supervisor of the thesis—a very reasonable rule—and an external examiner who comes from another university, often Cambridge. Some supervisors, (Pryce was one) will not even read the thesis, which leaves the jury more freedom to decide if the thesis, according to the accepted terminology, 'is not fit for publication', and to send the candidate back to the drawing board. In that way the thesis examination is not, as it is in France, a simple formality, where the examiners will pass the candidate for fear of offending his supervisor who sits next to them on the jury.

Another rule which was in force in my time, was the obligation (unwritten, like all important things in England) for the candidate to give a one- or two-page outline of his *own* contribution to the work described in the thesis. The only *written* obligations were to have kept one's name on the college books for the prescribed number of terms, by paying the dues pertaining to it; to provide the authorities with three copies of the thesis; and to have satisfied the jury that the thesis was fit for publication. This gave the candidate 'leave to supplicate' for the degree of Doctor of Philosophy, or D.Phil., granted after the payment of some more money. (These details may have been all right for the French, but Oxonians will most likely find fault with them. I apologize in advance.)

Another piece of folklore was the 'Proctor's walk'. During the degree ceremony the proctors walk in the aisles, and if someone wishes to prevent the granting of a degree to a candidate, he may 'pluck the proctor's sleeve' and explain his reasons to him. This custom was meant to protect Oxford tradesmen against bad debtors, who might try to leave with their degree in their pocket before settling their debts.

My internal examiner was Bleaney, who asked me a murderous question: what were the colours of the various Tutton salts? I knew their energy levels and their wave functions very well, but got confused about the colours. The problem posed by the external examiner was more serious. I had written in my thesis that the Hartree–Fock functions were notoriously inadequate for the calculation of hyperfine structures. How was I to know that my external examiner would be Professor Hartree from Cambridge?

He wished to know what was wrong with *his* functions. I tried to explain that, having been conceived as the best functions for the calculation of energies, they were ill-suited to the calculation of hyperfine structures. 'Which ones are better suited to it?' he asked. 'There aren't any.' This answer satisfied him and I got my D.Phil.

Among the people who were working under Pryce more or less at the same time as I, I remember John Ziman, Ken Stevens, Roger Elliott, and above all John Ward, who became a great theoretician. I was far from understanding everything that John Ward—who was a terrible lecturer—sometimes tried to explain to me, but I understood something that Pryce may have missed: namely that Ward was a bit of a genius. There had been some talk of his being asked to rewrite his thesis, which proved to be untrue.

A few words about Pryce. He is an excellent theoretician, with an extraordinarily vast culture in scientific fields as varied as: atomic energy, nuclear physics, solid state physics, astrophysics, quantum field theory, and general relativity. (I am probably forgetting a few). For me he was the ideal guide, who took just as much interest in me as I needed, neither too little nor too much; and I feel deeply grateful to him. I owe it to him that I finally pulled away from my baseline. Strangely enough, this brilliant man has perhaps received less recognition during his career than he deserved, and than might have been expected from his striking gifts and his dazzling debut. The fact that he did not suffer fools gladly, and was sometimes a little hasty in deciding *who* was a fool, may have been part of the reason. He left Oxford, which was certainly a great loss for Oxford, and possibly also for him, and went successively to Bristol, to the University of Southern California, which he did not like much, and finally to the University of British Columbia in Vancouver, which he liked and where he settled for good. I took great pleasure in seeing him there for a few days in 1975, and again in 1987. Both times he seemed quite happy with his scientific work and his life.

A few words about Bleaney. He is known in the trade as 'the man who is never wrong', so careful and scrupulous is he in the interpretation of his experiments. But he is also an imaginative and inventive pioneer. At the age of thirty-five, an age when I was passing my belated thesis, and he had been widely known for more than ten years (he had played a vital role in the development of radar during the war), he took a sabbatical half-year to join Van Vleck and learn the theory he wanted to master, in order to interpret the results of his experiments himself. (Actually, it turned out that Van Vleck was away at the time, and so he had to learn it all by himself.)

In 1957, after Simon's early demise, he accepted the heavy load of the Dr Lee's Professorship with all it implied; but managed to keep his own research going as before. A few years ago he took early retirement from his directorship to devote himself entirely to research. At seventy-two he is still doing very nice work. His humour is sometimes merciless. He is a very dear friend.

Between Oxford and Cambridge

The ocean

The CEA—Joliot—Yvon—Weisskopf—Travel plans and visas to the 'forfended place'—How to vote

The title of this chapter is a bad play on words. The Cambridge here is not the English university which competes with Oxford on the Thames every year, but the American city in Massachusetts, seat of the oldest American university, Harvard. 'Between Oxford and Harvard' would have been a more accurate description of the two year period between my stays in these two universities; but it would have lacked the symmetry dear to a physicist's heart.

On my return to the CEA in 1950 I went to see my patron saint, Kowarski, who expressed satisfaction with my scientific achievements at Oxford; they were, he implied, more his than mine, since it was he who had recommended me to Pryce in the first place. Then he exhorted me once more to bear in mind my double handicap of having been born abroad and of not being a graduate of the Ecole Polytechnique when I made my plans for my future career in the CEA. By alienating all those who might have had some feelings of friendship or gratitude towards him, or some esteem for his intellectual gifts, which were by no means negligible, he had started on the road to self-destruction which was to take him in a few years from a key position in the CEA to a complete loss of influence; and in the end to being shelved at CERN.

Among those who had to deal with him I was far from getting the worst treatment. Fortunately contact between us dwindled more and more, apart from a ridiculous incident I shall relate a little later.

In 1950 one single event was going to shake up the whole CEA: the government's dismissal of its High Commissioner, Frédéric Joliot. I have already said that I did not know him well, and I am not the best person to speak of this man, who was outstanding in so many ways, and who became famous so young. Everything has already been said about his 'diabolical' skill as an experimentalist, but also his dynamism, his personal magnetism, and the attraction he exercised on all those who approached him. These were the qualities which are associated with his well-deserved prestige as a great discoverer, and which enabled him to launch what had been one of the great scientific and technological ventures of our country, the CEA. But if one moves away from the well-trodden path of hagiography and attempts a more close analysis of Joliot's achievements and their impact on the scientific life of our country, there are questions to be asked and conclusions to be drawn.

*Though the main work of Frédéric and Irene Joliot—the great discovery of artificial radioactivity, which got them the Nobel prize—and to a lesser extent the work of the trio: Joliot, Halban, and Kowarski, are part of the scientific history of our country, it is less well known that they narrowly missed three other great discoveries which were crowned by three other Nobel prizes.

First of all there is the discovery of the neutron, which the Joliots literally dropped in Chadwick's basket, through their failure to analyse their own experimental results properly.

Then there is the discovery of the positron, whose *traces* Joliot does *observe* in his cloud chamber, but which he interprets as electrons *moving towards the source.*

It is fascinating to observe that this is the very description in Feynman's quantum electrodynamics of the positron: 'an electron moving backwards in time.'

Lastly it is Irène Joliot who observes that the chemical properties of some alleged 'transuranians', obtained from the neutron irradiation of uranium, are similar to those of lanthanum; but, like other great radiochemists, cannot make the decisive step and admit to herself that what looked like lanthanum *was* lanthanum, and so misses the phenomenon which has marked the twentieth century with an indelible mark, nuclear fission.*

The common trait of these three near misses is a weakness in the theoretical interpretation of results obtained by outstanding experimentalists, and the responsibility for these failures does not fall so much on the Joliots, who could hardly have done better in what one cannot avoid calling the 'French desert' of theoretical physics—which I have described in the chapter 'In Search of Research', but which the example of the Joliots illustrates far better. Theoreticians who were regulars in the laboratories, 'house theoreticians', as one says today, simply did not exist in France.

Certain features of Joliot's character can be explained by structures of higher education in our country then (and now!). Joliot was an upstart, a *parvenu*. Unlike his contemporaries, Pierre Auger and Francis Perrin, who were prestigious *Normaliens*, (graduates from the Ecole Normale Supérieure), Joliot had come from the 'obscure' Ecole de Physique et Chimie de la Ville de Paris and was often reminded that he was not one of the old boys. He had never felt quite at ease in the French scientific Establishment, and even less so in the foreign Establishment.

Should one look there for an explanation of his refusal to leave France during the 'verdigris years', which personally I find hard to take? I don't want to commit myself.

One cannot get round the fact that between his last and remarkable studies on fission in 1940 and his too early death in 1958, Joliot's scientific activity had stopped. His few lectures at the Collège de France, which I attended after the war, were unworthy of him. There is no dearth of explanations: the fight against the enemy until the Liberation in 1944, the putting into orbit of the CEA 'a gigantic task' until his dismissal in 1950, but what then? After that and up to his death, the explanation lies with his commitment to a political cause and a political party which used him for their own goals. He could have been the *scientific* architect of the reconstruction of French nuclear physics after the war, but instead he deliberately distanced himself from all relations with the Anglo-Saxon world—which could have been a source of enlightenment after the disasters of the war—and helped perpetuate the deplorable scientific isolation of our country. In that sense his influence had been negative, and Kowarski's positive.

It is difficult to use the word 'victim' about someone as strikingly successful as Joliot had been; and yet I cannot help feeling that this great scientist was indeed a victim—of the environment that his country was then offering to its scientists, and also of a political party.

It is known that his dismissal from the position of High Commissioner was caused by his outspoken refusal to let the CEA participate in the study and the construction of atomic weapons. One cannot but respect this highly moral position; but one is bound to observe that the unnecessarily provocative character of his refusal was less useful to the cause of peace and the interests of the CEA and its research workers, than to those of a political party—a party whose behaviour he had still been able to denounce in 1939, after the despicable Sovieto-German agreement.

What happened in the CEA after Joliot's dismissal was not very pretty: a frantic rush by the members of the hierarchy (including Mr K) to flee the ranks of the CGT (Confédération Générale du Travail), a communist-dominated trade union. Their trade-unionist beliefs, based on a very natural desire to please the boss, did not outlive his downfall. I found the spectacle so nauseating that, although I was never much of a trade unionist, I then joined the CGT and remained a member for ten years, until my election to the Collège de France.

It took a year for the government to select Joliot's successor. Eventually, and after much weighing up, Francis Perrin was appointed. He kept his position for nearly twenty years, till the end of 1970. His prerogatives were defined in the decree with which General de Gaulle had created the CEA in 1945; they gave him considerable power, which he used for the staunch defence of fundamental research within the CEA.

When I returned from Oxford to the CEA I found a new organization. A 'Service of Mathematical Physics' had been created, headed by Professor Jacques Yvon. A former *Normalien*, some twelve years older than I, Jacques Yvon had had the classical career of a French professor, with, however, the less classical interlude of eighteen months spent in a German concentration camp. By his origins, his family background, his character, and the turn of his mind, he was as different from me as could be; and yet we had one thing in common: as scientists we had both suffered from this curse of the French system—isolation. His scientific field was statistical mechanics into which he had, before the war, introduced some new ideas and proven some important results.

He had worked completely alone, and after the war his work was gradually discovered by a few foreign scientists. In the field of quantum mechanics he was, like myself, entirely self-taught; he had also made a considerable effort in his late forties to educate himself in the fields of neutron physics and, more generally, of nuclear physics.

At bottom he was a just and kindly man, but somewhat shy and touchy, and he reacted sometimes in an unpredictable manner. I had the misfortune of having started with him on the wrong foot. He had formed the laudable project of writing a treatise on quantum mechanics, something which was sorely needed, for de Broglie's books had aged considerably. The 'Three Musketeers' were expected to serve in this project, both as helpers and as guinea-pigs. He distributed handwritten notes to us and requested our comments. I had the bad luck of spotting a statement on page two of a purely mathematical nature that was not quite correct. I gave him a counter example illustrating its falsehood. To my pained surprise, he was far more affected by it than I would have expected. 'One does not improve with age,' he said bitterly. The project was abandoned (I cannot help thinking that under pressure from more urgent activities it would have been abandoned anyway, though perhaps much later), and henceforth my relations with Yvon took on a strained character—which did not prevent him, as my boss, from always being scrupulously fair to me.

Under his direction Horowitz and I did a few calculations on the slowing down of neutrons in heavy water and in graphite, with a view to building the first French atomic reactors; but I had not become a fan of atomic energy, and Yvon kindly let me do two or three other things.

In the autumn of 1950 Victor Weisskopf, Professor of Physics at MIT, came to Paris for a sabbatical year.

It was an event of great importance for the young French theoreticians. Within the framework of the Proca Seminar Weisskopf organized working sessions in the field of theoretical nuclear physics. He and his colleague John Blatt had just completed a comprehensive treatise on this subject. The book was in print but he had brought a typescript with him, which we used in our discussions.

Since the memorable article on nuclear physics by Hans Bethe, which I had borrowed from Francis Perrin, a single book had been published on the subject, with the title *Nuclear Forces*. Its author was Leon Rosenfeld, the disciple of Bohr, who, besides his other accomplishments, could understand Bohr's English. In spite of the encyclopaedic culture of its author, and partly because of it, Rosenfeld's book suffered from two severe defects: it was almost unreadable and it soon became obsolete. The author had tried to pack it with everything that was known, or believed to be known, on nuclear forces. Having later become the author of voluminous monographs myself, what I learned from Rosenfeld's book was how not to write scientific books. There are two guiding principles.

The first had been formulated, in slightly excessive terms, by Freeman Dyson (I quote from memory). Any book published at time 't' and containing *all* the information available up to time $(t-T)$ will become obsolete at time $(t+T)$.

I have formulated a second principle myself: 'Never put anything in a book (a *book*, not an article) apart from what you understand well, or at least think you understand well.'

In comparison with Rosenfeld's, the book by Blatt and Weisskopf was a pedagogical marvel. During the academic year 1950–1, every week one of the participants in Proca's seminar gave a talk on one of the chapters of the book, followed by a discussion.

This is how I learned the little nuclear physics I still know today. My sinister years of solitude were gone for good.

Weisskopf's enchanting personality played an important part in these working sessions. Born in Vienna in 1908, and expatriated to the US after the advent of Hitler, he combined the open and unpretentious manner of the American scientist—so far removed from the French *Monsieur le Professeur*, the German *Herr Professor*, or even the donnish braying of some of my Oxford colleagues—with the famous Viennese charm which he radiated. He liked to be liked and succeeded marvellously. He is a theoretician of great stature. It is to him, in collaboration with Wigner, that we owe a theory of the width of spectral lines, and a study of divergencies in quantum electrodynamics. He proved that the creation of electron–positron pairs reduced these divergencies to a logarithmic, and therefore slow, growth. I would not swear that he never dreamed of this important result bringing him, in one of the lean years, a piece of the Nobel pie. In any case the Wolff prize, which he obtained a few years ago, provided recognition for his great merits. He worked on atomic weapons at Los Alamos during the war years, then devoted himself to nuclear physics, to which he brought many theoretical contributions. He took a great interest in the physics of elementary particles, and served for several years as Director General of CERN. I like him very much and I think he likes me.

He told us how he had been greeted by Pauli, whose assistant he was for a while in Zürich. 'I tried to get Bethe, but he was unable to come, and so it will have to be you. Find yourself some place to sit and come back in a month to show me what you have done.' A month later, looking through

Weisskopf's notes of what he had accomplished, Pauli's only comment was: 'I should have tried harder to get Bethe.'

*Horowitz and I went to ask him to suggest a problem for us to work on. 'Do you think that if I had an interesting problem I would not be working on it myself?' he asked. Yet he took pity on us and suggested that we study the electromagnetic radiation that might possibly accompany the well-known decay of the muon into an electron and two neutrinos. It was a higher order process, with a photon added to the products of the decay of the muon. Horowitz, who, during his stay of one year at the Niels Bohr institute in Copenhagen, had become an expert in dealing with traces of operators constructed from Dirac matrices, shared his skills with me; and together we easily established the shape of the electromagnetic spectrum. We came a cropper on the *total* probability of the emission of a photon in this process, for we were up against a classical divergence of quantum field theory. We published our imperfect production in the *Journal de Physique* in 1951. Although we had not attached much importance to this calculation, which was more academic than scientific in our view, we were somewhat disappointed to see citations of a *later* English publication on the same subject, and none of ours. This was my first contact with the problem of publishing in French, which later caused much ink to flow, including my own (*Reflections of a Physicist*, Oxford University Press).*

Before returning to the US in the middle of 1951, Weisskopf invited Horowitz, via Yvon, to spend a year at MIT with him. A grant of 5500 dollars, which was quite decent in those days, went with it. (It was years later that I learned from Weisskopf himself that the invitation had originally been for me. Yvon and Kowarski persuaded him to take Horowitz instead because I had just returned from two years in England, 1948–50, whereas Horowitz had been to Denmark for one year only, 1947–8).

I was pleased for Horowitz (I knew nothing of the substitution at the time); but also sad to see him leave after we had made such a good start together on the variational approach to my theory of hyperfine structure, and then on the radiative corrections to the decay of the muon.

I had a brainwave. Why not try to get a fellowship in the US for myself as well, not at MIT but at Harvard, which is so near MIT? This is how I planned it. My former mentor Maurice Pryce was spending a sabbatical at Princeton in 1951–2. I wrote to him and asked him to contact Van Vleck, one of the most famous physics professors at Harvard. I knew that I had made a good impression on him at the Amsterdam conference in 1950. Van Vleck might be in a position to get me a Harvard fellowship for 1952–3.

Everything went like clockwork, well, up to a point; the fellowship that Van Vleck obtained for me was miserly: 2500 dollars. I was told that barely decent lodgings for two in Cambridge could not be had for less than 1300 dollars. Like many wealthy people, Van Vleck, who was the soul of generosity, had no idea of how much one needed to survive.

Anyway, this was not the toughest part, either for Horowitz or for me. We still had to obtain American visas. America, terrorized by the notorious Senator McCarthy, was a prey to anti-communist hysteria, and saw Kremlin agents everywhere. I have already told the story of Professor Peierls, who was prevented from attending a conference that was open to all, but admitted to a top secret one on the declassification of atomic data. I went to the American Consulate to obtain the interminable applications forms for a visitor visa (God knows what the ones for immigration visas were like), and started filling them in. It was not simple. As far as I remember, besides the names, first names, places and dates of birth, and whenever applicable, dates of death, of all parents and grand-parents, one had to list all the candidate's addresses during the thirty years preceding the application.

Only then came the real problems: kindly list *all* the organizations, associations, political parties, trade-unions, clubs, etc., to which you had belonged at any time in your life, for however short a period. Special emphasis was naturally placed on anything that might be considered, by any stretch of the imagination, to be associated with the communist doctrine. For me, my membership of the CGT was clearly the main problem. I decided to follow the same course of action as during the German Occupation: what they don't know won't hurt them: I'll see how much they do know. I filled in my forms, took them to the Consulate with a large number of photographs and settled to wait without undue impatience, for I did not expect success.

Refusals, or to be more accurate, failures to get any answer, were plentiful. Plain refusals were rare; after a while, the purpose for the visit simply elapsed and the application became useless. My two great bosses, Perrin and Kowarski, were pawing the ground at the gate to the 'forfended place'; Alfred Kastler was perhaps luckier, in that he received a prompt refusal. Even the impeccable Leprince-Ringuet was not admitted, for having signed the Stockholm Appeal for Peace. (Some gossips said that Leprince-Ringuet had heard the Appeal from Stockholm but Stockholm had not heard the Appeal from Leprince-Ringuet, alluding to his vain hopes of a Nobel Prize.) Horowitz was also waiting for an answer.

It was then that the ridiculous incident which opposed me to Kowarski took place. The problem of his visa had become for him a real obsession. Seeing that his influence in the CEA was dwindling with the massive influx of those Polytechnicians whom he both feared and admired, he felt the need to renew contact with America. He knew, or at least thought, that he was known, understood and admired there, and hoped to recover some of his prestige there, like the giant Antaeus, who recovered his strength by touching the ground.

He liked to repeat that he felt more Anglo-Saxon than French. He also told me once, and I am quoting verbatim, that 'the people in charge of the CEA and in particular Debiesse, Perrin's principal secretary, did not have the mental equipment that was required for dealing with the problems of American visas.' Such was his state of mind when it suddenly dawned on him that my visa application might be prejudicing his own chances, that perhaps two Judeo-Russians applying for a visa to the US at the same time and from the same place was too much. This was very much like the story of the two Russian Jews, one poor and one rich, praying together in the synagogue; the first begs Providence for ten roubles, and the second for ten thousand. 'Get out,' says the rich one, 'you are undercutting my prices.'

He got Debiesse to send me an official note, informing me that in the present circumstances my application for a visa was ill-timed and should be withdrawn. I went to the Consulate to tell them so and, seeing their astonishment, showed them my note. Kowarski, who apparently had informers in the place, set Francis against me, for he too was waiting for his visa. Francis summoned me, with my immediate supervisor, Yvon, and bitterly reproached me for having shown the Americans a document which was internal to the CEA—as though I had transmitted our atomic secrets to them. It was difficult to imagine anything more ludicrous. Feeling confident of my rights, and having never been afraid of Francis, I stood my ground: 'You ask me, in writing and without an explanation, to withdraw my visa application. I had to show the Americans that it was not a whim of my own, and nobody ever told me that this note was confidential.' Yvon backed me up vigorously, and Francis, who was anything but a fool, realized that Kowarski had dragged him into a ridiculous business, and the incident was allowed to lapse.

The funniest thing of all is that a few days later I was invited for an interview with the American Vice-Consul. The Vice-Consul turned out to be a lady, whom my imitation Oxford accent impressed favourably at first, but then things went badly. She expressed the wish to see my military papers. I answered that our military legislation forbade me to show them to representatives of a foreign power. 'Surely this does not apply to the Americans!' 'I do not recall any exceptions for any particular foreign country.' She then wished to know how I had voted at the last election. 'Why, look you now how unworthy a thing you make of me! You would play upon me, you would seem to know my stops, you would sound me from my lowest note to the top of my compass.' This is what I should have answered. Instead I replied meekly: 'In a secret ballot.'

This put an end to the interview and I went home, my mind at rest, very pleased with myself and the way I had put a full stop to this business, which had dragged on far too long. Great was my surprise when a few days later I was invited to fetch my visa at the Consulate. This is how Suzanne and I left for the 'forfended place' in the autumn of 1952. I will recount our stay there in the next chapter. Horowitz did not get his visa. Why I got mine while he did not get his is a mystery to this day. Senator McCarthy is no longer with us and I do not know who else to ask. This difference in the treatment of our applications had an important impact on both our careers, as will appear later.

Besides my studies of nuclear physics I pursued two other activities during the years 1950–2. Having become a specialist on ESR in Oxford, I wanted to familiarize myself with NMR (nuclear magnetic resonance), to which the Harvard physics department was a shrine, and the beauty of which I had discovered in a few conversations with Ed Purcell at the Amsterdam Conference of 1950.

(In my dotage, as an after-dinner speaker, I always get some laughs out of the following beginning: 'I discovered NMR in 1950. To those of you who think that it was Bloch and Purcell four years earlier, I must explain that I say this the way people might say "I discovered sex at thirty-five". This is actually how old I was when I discovered it—I mean NMR.')

The other subject of my studies was the theory of particle accelerators. I knew that the CEA was considering building one with an energy higher than 1 GeV (a billion electron-volts), and if such a decision were taken I wanted a ringside seat. This is why I got acquainted with the theory of these machines, and this too came in handy in the US.

America, America

Mene, Mene, Tekel, Upharsin—The ambiguous physician—Discovering America—NMR, its Mecca and its prophets—Making friends with R. V. Pound—*Perturbed angular correlations—*The Overhauser mystery—*Strong focusing—Trains of yesteryear

In the autumn of 1952 we embarked on the *Liberté* (which had been the Bremen before the war). The hectic packing before the departure, the feverish boarding of the boat train, the customs inspection on the train, the porters running to and fro in the immense harbour station of Le Havre, everything conspired to give us a feeling of unreality as if we had been suddenly propelled into a film. As soon as the train had left the Saint-Lazare station in Paris, I felt in my pocket the keys of our Croissy house which I was supposed to leave with my sister on the platform, and this was another source of worry. Worse was to come.

After boarding the ship one could see *everywhere*—in the corridors and inside the cabins, on the lifeboats and in the ashtrays, in large characters or in small letters—the three fateful signs that I had omitted from my visa application, **CGT**. I did know of course that they were only the initials of the Compagnie Générale Transatlantique which owned the ship, but I still read them in the same way that King Belshazzar must have read the writing on the wall—Mene, Mene, Tekel, Upharsin—as a memento mori reminding me that I was expected at the other end by the Immigration Officers who, according to rumour, went through travellers' statements with a fine-tooth comb and turned back, or confined to the purgatory of Ellis Island, those who fell foul of the standards of sincerity and loyalty of the great American Democracy.

Naturally we travelled tourist class, but to people as unspoilt by luxury as we were, it *was* luxury. Its modest opulence, the numerous gadgets in our little cabin, (which was naturally windowless) the headwaiters in dinner jackets moving noiselessly in the low-ceilinged but spacious dining-room, the abundance if not the refinement of the food—could not fail to dazzle Suzanne and myself, who in the past years, especially the last twelve, had had few opportunities to become blasé. A kind steward let us have a peek at the dining-room of cabin class and one of the swimming pools of first. This was Hollywood! And the long walks on the decks, the sunsets seen from the bow, the broad trail left in the wake which we never tired of contemplating (alas, not once did we get up early enough to watch the sunrise), the rite of putting our watches back one hour every night, all of it was a pleasant intermission before our confrontation with the New World and the unknown future.

Our arrival in the Port of New York, with the Statue of Liberty and the foreground of Lower Manhattan, remains to this day among my best memories of travel. The seven-hour plane flight has completely overtaken the five-day boat journey, but I am not sure that we have gained by it. With the advent of the jet plane has come the hateful jet lag, which affects me more and more as I get older, while the period of complete relaxation, offered by the sea crossing, has disappeared.

After the idyllic crossing, the landing was a bit of a nightmare. Early in the morning the American customs and police officers came aboard; the tourist class passengers, who were the last to disembark, were forced to wait for hours in a lounge with their hand luggage. All the while, according to the French stewards, these gentlemen were drinking hard at the bar, as guests of the CGT.

The interrogation by the Immigration Officers, about which terrifying rumours were running amok, turned out to be relatively benign. After looking for my name—in vain, thank God—in a large black book (a procedure still used in 1985, the age of the computer!) he asked me questions on my destination and my means of support in the US, without ever touching on my political or trade-unionist activities, let alone the atomic ones. All through the interview he very courteously called me *doctor*, a title to which I was certainly entitled after Oxford, but how *he* knew that was a mystery. I found the answer a little later: on the sheet which he was holding while questioning me, I had written my profession as *physicien*, which in French means 'physicist', but which he interpreted as *physician*. Without this misunderstanding I do not think I would have pulled through so easily, for physicists were under strict surveillance. Twelve years earlier I had benefited from a similar confusion between teacher of 'physics' and of 'physical education', made by the municipal employee who was handing out the ration cards, which for years brought me an extra fifty grammes of daily bread. My conclusion is that 'physicist' is a noble trade, to be proud of in private, but not to be boasted of in public.

The last ordeal came with the porters on the pier. An enormous notice proclaimed: NO TIPS! Still, on an impulse, I offered a dollar bill to the man who was pushing my tin trunk on a two-wheeled trolley. 'Brother!' he shouted, lifting both arms to heaven, before sending my trunk flying thirty feet; but for its iron constitution it would have broken to pieces. I got the message and added five dollars, (remember that seven dollars was the daily amount of my fellowship). A grunt signified that my offering had been accepted.

After a few days in New York I was due to attend a conference on magnetism at the University of Maryland. We spent these days exploring the marvels of Manhattan and I am sure the reader will be grateful to me for sparing him a description of them. Just two little down-to-earth stories.

On leaving the ship we entered a drugstore where, in my best English, I ordered two ham sandwiches. 'What bread, Mack?' shot out the reply. Confronted with my stupefied look, he let loose another burst: 'White, rye, whole wheat, pumpernickel?' As I looked even more stupefied, somebody shouted: 'Show them the bread.' The attendant produced half a dozen loaves and I poked my finger at one of them.

We were invited to a restaurant, which was famous for its beef. The waiter brought Suzanne an enormous plate entirely covered with a slice of roast, nearly an inch thick. Being the only lady at the table, she assumed that she was expected to carve for the guests and was looking for the carving knife when the waiter brought, one after the other, three more such plates, one for each guest. Such was the transition from lands of shortage to the land of plenty.

At the Maryland conference I found Van Vleck and Bleaney, and met a few physicists, among them Slater, who is famous for his work on the quantum theory of atoms, molecules, and later solid state, and Stoner, a specialist in magnetism. Under a good-natured exterior Slater was hiding a fiery temper; he and Stoner nearly came to blows on a question of itinerant magnetism, and Van Vleck had to interpose himself between the warring parties.

I also met Clyde Hutchison, professor at the University of Chicago, and one of the pioneers of chemical applications of ESR. He is a charming little man who plays the piano 'especially ragtime' beautifully. I met him many times, particularly in Oxford, and always with pleasure.

Among his important discoveries one could mention the ESR of alkaline metals in ammonia solution, and the detection by straight ESR of the excited triplet states in molecular crystals.

I had hoped to present a short paper on my work with Horowitz on the variational approach to the theory of anomalous hyperfine structure. On the advice of Van Vleck, who thought the subject too complicated for a short paper, I gave it up and instead presented a not very interesting calculation of a molecule with three coupled spins. I later regretted listening to Van Vleck. If I hadn't, there would have been a written example of my early findings in this field. (Horowitz and I had sent a draft of a detailed article to Pryce, for him to complete and send under our three names to the Proceedings of the Royal Society; but for reasons I have never quite understood, it was in the pipeline for nearly three years, before finally appearing in 1955.) It would take me at least one more similar experience before I learned to make my own decisions about the publication of my work.

At the end of the conference there was a dinner party, with separate tables and a pleasantly relaxed atmosphere. An American lady who had enjoyed the cocktails asked me: 'Who is the little man over there who thinks he is Napoleon?' I turned back and saw our distinguished colleague,

Professor Gaston Dupouy, Director General of the CNRS. Professor Dupouy is not very tall but his bearing does not let him lose a single inch from his height. 'You are mistaken, Madam,' I said. 'That *is* Napoleon.' I suddenly heard a burst of laughter coming from the next table, where Suzanne was facing Professor Gorter, the Leyden professor I spoke of in the chapter on Oxford. The following morning I asked Suzanne about the reason for that gaiety.

'This Mr Gorter asked me how I learned English and I said from *Assimil* records. He asked what kind of sentences one learned and I recited the one that amused Mrs Burns so much in Oxford: "The top of the head is covered with hair."' 'You recited *that* to Gorter?' 'Yes, why not? Oh my God!' cried Suzanne, realizing what she had done. Professor Gorter's cranium was as smooth as a billiard ball.

In Cambridge we found a flat which ate up half of my fellowship, but we were told the rent was reasonable for Cambridge. I used to walk to the lab where I had been given an office, along a pleasant street called Brattle Street, on which I was usually the only pedestrian. As a result, drivers who did not know their way, used to stop and ask me directions. I got tired of it after a while, and whenever I saw a car slowing done I cried out to the driver 'I am a stranger here.' One day a car stopped next to me, apparently heedless of my warnings and the driver got out. As I was telling him once more that I was a stranger, he answered: 'I don't care—I live here.'

Harvard was then the Mecca of what personally I like to call nuclear magnetism, which is a scientific *field*, rather than nuclear magnetic resonance or NMR, which is a scientific *tool*—albeit the main one used in exploring the field of nuclear magnetism.

NMR had been discovered in Cambridge at the end of 1945 by Ed Purcell, R. V. Pound, and H. Torrey; and quite independently and almost simultaneously on the west coast by Felix Bloch, Packard, and Hansen. I have devoted the largest part of my scientific activity to the study and the teaching of nuclear magnetism. In the following chapters I shall attempt several times to explain those aspects of nuclear magnetism which have been of greatest interest to me. Let me also refer the reader to my little book *Reflections of a Physicist* (Oxford University Press, 1986) the first fifty pages of which give a general introduction aimed at the lay reader.

In that year, 1952–3, I learned and did more than in most other years of my life. There was an unusual collection of talents at Harvard and I feel like saying a few words about them.

In *Reflections of a Physicist* there is a portrait of John Van Vleck, which was written after his death for our Académie des Sciences, of which he was a foreign member; and I shall only add a few words here about my collaboration with him.

Like Pryce, four years earlier, he suggested a problem to me which I did not like very much. I told him so and he did not insist. He then proposed that I do an improved calculation of the gyromagnetic factor of atomic oxygen, which had been measured a few months earlier with high accuracy, by ESR in gaseous oxygen. Such a calculation, including all the corrections, had only been done before for atoms with a single electron outside closed shells. I considered all the corrections I could think of: the relativistic one, another caused by the finite mass of the nucleus, and a few smaller ones, I gave my manuscript to Van Vleck and forgot about it. I thought it perfectly proper for him to co-sign an article whose subject he had suggested and whose presentation he would perhaps improve. It was only after I returned to Paris that my ordeal began. Every week I received a long letter from Van Vleck, written in his slanting irregular handwriting and each one pointing out a new error in my calculation. To make it worse, he always used a language of his own for physics, and this dialogue by mail was not the simplest thing in the world, to say the least. By the time it was all over he had undoubtedly earned the moral right to co-sign the paper, and I the palm of martyrdom.

As a physicist and a human being Ed Purcell is perhaps the man I admire the most. I have never met anyone more profoundly authentic, more detached from the wish to appear other than he is. (Correction: since I wrote these lines a year ago, I have met another man like him, but more of this later.)

As a physicist he has his own way of approaching all problems, even the simplest ones; and although it may sometimes seem unnecessarily complicated, it always turns out to be fruitful in the end. Besides his discovery of NMR with its countless applications, for which he shared the Nobel Prize with Felix Bloch, he observed the hyperfine structure of hydrogen in outer space, a discovery of paramount importance for astrophysics, which is a field to which he brought many original contributions. Later he thought up some extremely ingenious methods for detecting magnetic monopoles, should they exist and be produced in particle accelerators, and he spent a couple of years lying in wait for them at Brookhaven. Unfortunately the monopoles did not show up: the best hunter comes home with an empty bag if the game is not there. I have not collaborated with him in the proper sense of the word, but we had long discussions about his work on the NMR of solid hydrogen and about negative temperatures, which may have been of some use to him and were certainly of great benefit to me.

Norman Ramsey, a disciple of Rabi, is a specialist in molecular beams. He invented a very important improvement on Rabi's methods, which enabled him to augment, by several orders of magnitude, the precision of the measurements of radiofrequency spectra of diatomic molecules, and above all of the hydrogen molecule. For many years he has applied this method to the pursuit of something which is perhaps as elusive as the magnetic monopole, to wit, the electric dipole moment of the neutron. He also produced with the hydrogen maser the most accurate, if not perhaps the easiest to use, of the existing frequency standards.

On a personal level it would be unfair to accuse him of being as indifferent as Purcell to the impression he makes on people. I may add that he has a voice and a laugh which do not pass unheard in a room full of people.

Nierenberg, another of Rabi's disciples, like Ramsey and another physicist from Columbia, Polycarp (yes) Kusch is, like both of them, endowed with a powerful voice. He explained to me once that the culprits were the pre-war vacuum pumps, which were so noisy that one had to shout to be heard in the lab. At present, he added, there is a new generation of noiseless pumps and a new generation of gentlemanly, soft-spoken beam physicists.

Since I have pronounced the name of Kusch let me throw out a little story here which he told me himself. It relates to the Nobel Prize he was given for measuring the anomalous *g*-factor of the electron, an award which, one must admit, had somewhat surprised the community of physicists. The day he heard the news, a graduate student burst into his office to announce the sudden failure of a vacuum pump. 'Later,' said Kusch. 'I have just learned that I got the Nobel.' 'Who, you?' exclaimed the graduate student. A few years later, while visiting the Watson laboratory in New York, I repeated this story at lunch to a few of the physicists of the lab. 'You are telling me!' said one of them. 'I was the graduate student.'

Nicholaas Bloembergen, a Dutchman by birth, did not belong to the initial team of the discoverers of NMR; but became part of it as early as 1947 and made a very important contribution to the famous article whose title was abbreviated to 'BPP' (for Bloembergen, Purcell, and Pound), and which played a vital role in the development of NMR, practically until the publication of my treatise in 1961: *The Principles of Nuclear Magnetism* which considerably enlarged and modernized 'BPP', and corrected it on a few points. (As Newton is supposed to have said, and I quote from memory: 'A dwarf standing on the shoulders of a giant can see farther than the giant.' Nowadays I like to claim to be the dwarf on whose shoulders all the young giants have climbed.)

Endowed with an ingenious and fertile mind, and an indefatigable worker, Bloembergen is moved, more than anyone else perhaps, by a spirit of competition which is apt to generate a certain amount of tension around him, and which took him all the way to the Nobel Prize—of which he got one-quarter in 1981, not for NMR but for his work on nonlinear optics.

I have left Robert Vivian Pound till last. I got closely acquainted with him on my arrival in Harvard and we have retained a faithful friendship over thirty-five years, though it is crossed now and then by thunderstorms of varying violence. Born a Canadian in 1919, but an American citizen for a long time now, Pound was what is called an 'early starter', just as I was a 'late beginner', with all the advantages and the few drawbacks of a lightning start.

An electronics wizard, he took part during the war in the development of radar at the famous radiation lab of MIT, where he made a few inventions which brought him renown at an early date. The war over, he took part with Purcell and Torrey in the discovery of NMR, where his skills in the detection of weak signals played a capital role.

He wrote 'BPP' with Purcell and Bloembergen, and was the first to guess and analyse the subtle mechanism of 'motion narrowing' (see 'Reflections'); he also invented a detection device of great simplicity, known in scientific literature as the 'Pound Box', which he used to discover the effects of the nuclear quadrupole moment on NMR spectra. It is he who with Purcell introduced and experimentally demonstrated the validity of the concept of 'negative spin temperatures', of which I shall speak later.

I may add that he is extremely good-looking, or at least he was thirty-five years ago, and elegant in a British way which is revived by occasional trips to England.

We got along very well from the beginning. He can be a little contrary and so can I, though in my case I need to be pushed beyond a certain threshold. It is then that the storms break out, though seldom for long.

He sometimes reproached me in the following way: 'You don't really listen to me: you simply wait for me to finish, before saying the same thing.' There may have been an ounce of truth in that; but the manner in which he likes to express himself, which I found somewhat convoluted and sibylline, was responsible for it. I may have been repeating what he had said just before, without being aware of it. The fact that I always let him have his say without interrupting must be put to my credit.

*Perturbed angular correlations

We studied this problem together. Let me explain what it is.

When a radioactive nucleus emits two radiations in quick succession, the direction of emission of the first radiation becomes a privileged direction for the spin of the nucleus in its intermediate state, and the angular *distribution* of the second radiation with respect to this direction is not isotropic. This is precisely what one calls an angular correlation, a relationship between the directions of emissions of two consecutive radiations, and its study yields information on the spins of the different states of the nucleus during the cascade and on the multipolarities of the emitted radiations. This study assumes that the orientation of the spin in an intermediate state is not affected by extranuclear fields 'seen' by the nucleus during its lifetime, be these fields electric or magnetic, internal or man-made, fixed in time or fluctuating.

The effects of an applied magnetic field and of an isotropic hyperfine structure had been known before.

However, no one knew better than I that the hyperfine structure in bulk matter could be very different from what it is in a free atom, and nobody knew better than Robert Pound that nuclei have quadrupole moments which are acted upon by the electric field gradients which exist inside bulk matter. Lastly, no one had studied the perturbation of angular correlations by fluctuating fields. In several short letters, and then in a comprehensive article published in the *Physical Review* in 1953, we gave a complete theory of perturbed angular correlations which after thirty-five years differs little from its present-day form. In particular, we explained why the perturbations of angular correlations were considerably weaker in liquid radioactive sources. It was very much the same phenomenon as the celebrated *motion narrowing*. In liquids, the perturbing extranuclear fields fluctuate very fast, much faster than in solids, and are very nearly averaged out, as far as their perturbing effects on the orientations of the nuclear spins are concerned.

In the course of the work I did notice a few weaknesses, lack of precision, and even inaccuracies in 'BPP', which were hardly avoidable in a pioneering work, and took advantage of the writing of our paper to cast the theory of nuclear relaxation in a more elegant and compact form, which was to find its final shape in my book: *The Principles of Nuclear Magnetism*.

At the same time I had been thinking about a more general problem in statistical quantum mechanics, namely the passage from Schrödinger's equation which deals with probability *amplitudes*, to the Boltzmann's equation (or its generalization, the so-called master equation) which operates on the probabilities themselves. I was told that physicists had been concerned with statistical quantum mechanics for a long time, that they were sure to have considered that problem long ago, and to have solved it if it could be solved.

Too lazy to do any bibliographic search, I listened to this advice and gave up my project. It was a mistake for which I have no one to blame but myself. Alfred Redfield and Felix Bloch studied the same problem independently, and came up with solutions which were very similar to each other—and, most likely, to what mine would have been if I had persevered in my project. After my aborted talk at the University of Maryland and this stillborn attempt, I did not let myself be caught by that kind of advice again.

Anyway, having returned from Oxford as 'Mr Hyperfine Structure', I went home from Harvard as 'Mr Perturbed Angular Correlations'. After assisting nuclear physicists in their studies of nuclear spins and radiation multipolarities, (by correcting the observed correlations for the perturbations due to the extra-nuclear environment) the theory became a tool in the hands of physicists of condensed matter who sought information on that environment for its own sake.

When I returned to France, two young nuclear physicists of the CEA, Pierre Lehmann and Antoine Levêque, were measuring angular correlations in liquid sources. I suggested that they put a drop of glycerine in their source and see what happened. They thought that I was out of my mind (how could a drop of glycerine affect a *nuclear* phenomenon!) but let themselves be persuaded to try, and were amazed to see the correlation disappear. The explanation was simple: the glycerin had increased the viscosity of the liquid source and thereby slowed down the fluctuations of the extranuclear fields, strengthening their perturbing effects sufficiently to destroy the correlation. (Pierre Lehmann, with whom I spoke about it recently, that is thirty-five years later, does not deny the result, but claims that they had read our article and did expect an effect. Needless to say, I prefer my version of the facts.)*

The Overhauser mystery

To finish up with NMR at Harvard, I wish to mention another event which was to play an important part in my future activities: the Overhauser effect. Albert Overhauser, a young theoretician from the University of Illinois, had made the following prediction: in a metal, where the conduction electrons are known to be responsible for the nuclear relaxation, the saturation of the ESR resonance of these electrons should lead to an enormous increase in the nuclear polarization. I am not going to explain the meaning of this sentence here, for I will come to this problem later in the book. Right now I'll say two things. First, that this work provoked a delayed reaction in me which directed my thoughts on to a topic that was to preoccupy me for many years—namely 'dynamic nuclear polarization'. Secondly, that Overhauser's audience at the meeting of the American Physical Society—where he had (in ten minutes) presented the calculations which had led to his amazing conclusion—was immediately split into two parts, which, however, overlapped: those who did not understand a single word of his demonstration, and those who did not believe a single word of his conclusions. In the first row of the sceptics who did not believe his conclusions shone all the stars of magnetic resonance: Bloch and Purcell, Rabi and Ramsey. Bloembergen was of two minds and so was I. As for the presentation itself, I will repeat what Van de Graaff had told me of de Broglie's defence of his thesis in Paris in 1924: 'Never had so much gone over the heads of so many.'

The real question was of course: 'Was Overhauser right?' He was: the proof of the pudding was given the same year by Charles Slichter, a physicist from Illinois, and his student, Carver. They saturated the resonance of conduction electrons in metallic sodium and saw the enhancement of the nuclear polarization predicted by Overhauser.*

There were other outstanding personalities at Harvard that year: Brattain, co-inventor of the transistor with Shockley and Bardeen, was one. I still remember my imbecile reaction to the awarding of the Nobel Prize of these three inventors: What, the Nobel for a gadget! There was Bridgman, the man of high pressures, who had said once that you could renew the whole field of physics by adding the phrase: 'at high pressure' to every experiment. Later, when I was working on dynamic nuclear polarization I suggested (not very seriously) replacing 'at high pressure' by: 'with polarized nuclei'. I also unwittingly borrowed the title of his book, which was written many years ago: *Reflections of a Physicist*.

And then there was Julian Schwinger, a powerhouse of theoretical physics, whose motto could have been: 'if it moves, compute it'. In 1947 he had solved the problem of divergencies in quantum electrodynamics, which enabled him to compute, with a fantastic precision, the radiative corrections whose effects had been measured by Lamb and Kusch. This brought him a Nobel shared with Feynman and Tomonaga.

Long before he became Harvard's youngest full professor at twenty nine, he had been discovered by Rabi, who was wont to say that his best discovery had been ... Schwinger. A pupil of a public school (in the American sense) in the Bronx, attended by the Jewish boys of the neighbourhood, the young Julian had been sent to Rabi by a friend, because his marks in school were not good enough for admission into college without a special recommendation. Rabi summoned the boy and asked him to wait in a corner of his office while he was at the blackboard with a colleague, discussing a problem which was baffling them both. 'Why don't you use the closure theorem?' piped out a voice behind them. Julian had seen the solution of a problem before his elders, and not for the last time.

That year he was giving a course in quantum mechanics which I attended. I was deeply impressed by the cool perfection of his lectures. For two hours he lined up equation after equation, never afraid of tackling a problem from what seemed the least accessible angle, if it brought him closer to the underlying physical reality. I have never attended one of Feynman's courses, but I have read articles written by both on the same subject. I can best sum up my impressions by saying that Schwinger reminds me of Bjorn Borg and Feynman of John McEnroe.

*Strong focusing

Another activity which took up much of my time during this well-filled year was the study of particle accelerators. I explained the principle of the proton synchrotron in the chapter 'A Year of Transition'; it is the process where a simultaneous modulation of the accelerating RF and of the guiding magnetic field maintains the resonance condition, while keeping the radius of the orbit constant. To confine the orbit within the vacuum chamber, the guiding field must have a weak radial gradient. However, this focusing gradient may not be too strong lest the particles be defocused and lost in a vertical direction. With accelerators of ever-increasing energy, the size of the chamber and therefore the size and the weight of the magnet grow very large. The Brookhaven Cosmotron of 3 GeV and the Berkeley Bevatron of 6 GeV weighed several thousand tons, while the Soviet machine, of an energy of 10 GeV, which had been under construction in Dubna since 1949, was expected to weigh 35,000 tons—the weight of a battleship.

In the summer of 1952 a very important invention, due to three American physicists, Livingstone, Courant, and Snyder, was going to change the art of building accelerators drastically.

They had discovered that replacing the weak radial gradient by a succession of strong gradients, alternating between focusing and defocusing, gave rise to an overall focusing, radial *and* vertical, which was very much stronger than with the old system; this led to a considerable reduction in the transverse dimensions of the vacuum chamber, and in the size and weight of the machine.

A special group of physicists was assembled at MIT, in liaison with Brookhaven, to study projects using machines of the new type. I was instructed by the CEA to seek admission to this group and to participate in its activities. I was received with open arms and worked there part time.

It turned out after some time that the principle of alternating gradients had been invented two years earlier by Christophilos, a Greek engineer, who specialized in the manufacturing and maintenance of lifts in Athens. (Was it the relatively small number of tall buildings in Athens that had provided Christophilos with sufficient leisure to invent strong focusing?) Christophilos had sent his results to the Berkeley laboratory, where nobody paid any attention to them. The discovery of this fact had two unpleasant consequences for the American trio. The 'competent' authority in the AEC (Atomic Energy Commission) could do no less than invite Christophilos to the US, and rule that henceforth all his suggestions be listened to religiously. Those entrusted with this task confided to me that his suggestions were a lot of hot air and he himself a pain in the neck. But there was worse in store for the trio. Do you know the answer to the riddle: what is the difference between the Nobel Prize and a game of bridge? The answer is: In the Nobel one never looks for a fourth. This is what happened: the discovery which had changed the course of the physics of elementary particles was never rewarded with a Nobel, and I cannot help thinking that the untimely appearance of the fourth horseman (in fact he was the first!) had something to do with it.*

The end of our stay was approaching. We had decided that before our departure we would travel across the American continent, by train for the major part of our voyage, from Chicago to the West Coast. Our good friend Van (that's what everybody called him, except a Chinese student who thought it was irreverent and called him Dr Van), the greatest authority on rail travel, drew out our itinerary: a most prestigious train called *El Capitan* would take us from Chicago to Los Angeles with a stopover at the Grand Canyon, another train from Los Angeles to San Francisco, and the last, the marvellous *California Zephyr* (alas, long since gone for good) from San Francisco to Chicago. We could not afford sleepers, and in spite of the comfort of the American trains, which was remarkable in those days, the two transcontinental trips of more than forty-eight hours each were very tiring. Nevertheless, including the visit to the Grand Canyon, it was a marvellous experience. We discovered the immensity and the diversity of the American continent, which air travellers miss completely.

Actually, transcontinental crossings by train have much in common with transatlantic crossings by boat. I remember an amusing little incident in the dining car of the California Zephyr. I noticed that my bill was fifty cents less than that of a customer who had shared our table and left a few minutes earlier. I mentioned it to the head waiter who explained: 'We are in Nevada now—no taxes.' We spent a few days in Pasadena, near Los Angeles, in the Faculty Club at Caltech. After dinner we went out for a walk and were immediately stopped by the police, who thought our behaviour suspicious. I explained that we came from France where walking was considered quite acceptable, and they let us go.

We found Los Angeles quite awful, with its smog, its heat, its immensity, and its total absence of public transportation. By contrast, San Francisco enchanted us with its extraordinary beauty, its streets rising to the sky with gradients of forty-five degrees, its absurd little cablecars, the coolness of its summer climate (nothing like the horrible summer heat and humidity of the East Coast), and with its general air of liberal gaiety—which had not yet turned into gay liberation.

In Berkeley we met more resonators, who later became our very good friends. Among them were two disciples of Felix Bloch, Erwin Hahn and Carson Jeffries. Erwin Hahn, whose discovery of spin echoes has completely transformed the working methods of NMR, is an extrovert genius with an extensive collection of funny stories of all kinds: some, whose gentle wit would enchant a country vicar, others, whose robust gaiety would cause a mule skinner to blush. Carson Jeffries, a quiet and charming man, had for many years been my friendly rival in the field of dynamic nuclear polarization, before moving towards other horizons.

At Stanford I only met Packard: Hansen had died and Bloch was away.

We spent three marvellous days in the National Yosemite Park. We rented bicycles to get around, but were slightly confused by an urgent warning to tourists, which was posted everywhere: 'If you encounter a bear on the road, roll up your windows and stay in your car'.

On our way back we stopped at Niagara Falls on the Canadian border. The Falls are far more spectacular from the Canadian side; alas, my visa to the US carried the reminder: 'Valid for a single entry into the US'. The immigration officer who was posted at one end of the bridge between the US and Canada took pity on us, and gave us permission to go to the other side for a couple of hours.

Coming back, we were horrified to discover that our friendly officer had been replaced by another. This one refused to let us pass, especially after he saw on my passport that I was born in Russia. 'What if Canada does not let us in either?' I thought. 'Shall we spend the rest of our lives on that bridge?' Fortunately, while I was rolling these sombre thoughts around in my mind, the first officer came back and opened the gate to the 'forfended place'.

There were still six weeks to go. Robert Pound arranged for us to spend a month at Brookhaven, a laboratory of the AEC. We were given a little one-room flat, and I spent most of my time thinking about accelerators, perturbed angular correlations, the celebrated Overhauser effect, and how I could scratch through the layer of Overhauser's complicated calculations which protected it. I also thought a lot about what I would find in Saclay on my return.

In Brookhaven I met Maurice Goldhaber, a talented nuclear physicist, who later became director of the place. Goldhaber was justifiably proud of his scientific achievements and of his youthful appearance (he is a few years older than I and looked a few years younger). He told me once that during a trip to the USSR, someone there asked him: 'Are you the son of the great Goldhaber?' Here's a phrase that packs a lot of information, I thought. I also met Sam Goudsmit, Chief Editor of the *Physical Review* and co-discoverer with Uhlenbeck of the anomalous magnetic moment of the spin—a delightful man, and one of the wittiest I have ever met.

A conflict arose in the lab between two American governmental agencies because of me. The deputy director of Brookhaven asked me to sign a paper, surrendering all rights to the lab for any discoveries I might make during my monthly stay there. 'I can't,' I said. 'I have already given them to the ONR (Office of Naval Research) which is sponsoring my stay.' 'This is very serious; the surrendering of rights by the lab's guests is a rule which must be enforced, and the ONR has no business to make you sign that other paper. I shall take it up with them at a higher level.'

Fortunately I made no discoveries while at Brookhaven, and never heard anything more about the affair; but you never can tell with bureaucrats. For all I know, the AEC and the ONR may still be fighting it out today.

While I am writing these lines, another awful thought comes to my mind. As an employee of the CEA, a French government agency, what right did I have to surrender mine to a foreign agency—what's worse, to a military one? As once before, I can only hope that the statute of limitations will have come into play.

A few days after leaving Brookhaven we sailed to France on the *Flandre*, a much smaller ship than the *Liberté*.

Accelerators and resonances

Full thirty times has Phoebus' cart gone round . . .

*A new set-up—The group of the orbit—Think big—Arnie—Felix or
Wotan—Birth of a lab*

Back home, I found quite a few changes. The new nuclear establishment
of the CEA, located on the plateau of Saclay, some fifteen miles from Paris
and much vaster than Châtillon, now housed most of the scientific
activities of the CEA and practically all of its physics.

The CEA had put at my disposal a capacious flat in a pleasant small
town, three miles from Saclay, with the charming name of Gif-sur-Yvette—
which prompted Erwin Hahn to ask me: 'Who is Gif anyway?' Many of
my colleagues lived in Gif now. We were on excellent terms with all our
neighbours and became very friendly with Michel Trocheris, one of the
'Musketeers', his charming wife Simone, and their five children—three of
whom (almost four) were born during the seven years we spent in Gif.

It was also in Gif that I saw Jacques Prentki again, with whom I had got
acquainted during the Birmingham Conference of 1947; he now lived in a
little house with green shutters, in scanty comfort, with his adorable wife
Marysia and their two little boys, Marc and Pierre. A close friendship
sprang up between us, which held fast in spite of their leaving in 1955 for
Geneva, where Jacques made a brilliant career at CERN.

Changes had now also occurred in the inner structure of the CEA. The
CEA had been reorganized into a few large separate units called *Departments*, each subdivided into smaller units called *Services*. (I'll drop the
italics from now on.) There were also so-called Autonomous Services
which were not part of a Department and whose head, like the Department
heads, reported directly to a director. A Service could be subdivided into
even smaller units, Sections, but there were also Autonomous Sections
whose head reported directly to the head of the Department to which he
belonged. On the whole it was not as complicated as it sounds.

One of the new Departments, the DEP (Département d'Etudes des Piles),
headed by Jacques Yvon, included the SPM (Service de Physique Mathematique) among its Services. Jules Horowitz who, through a whim of the
American administration, had been unable to come with me to the US for
a year, had become the head of this SPM, and I, a member of its staff. The
programme of the SPM was twofold: one part was still devoted to
theoretical physics as we had practised it informally before the new

structures had jelled; but in Jacques Yvon's eyes the primary task of the SPM was its participation in the construction of atomic reactors. I do not remember exactly when Claude Bloch and Albert Messiah joined the SPM after their long sojourns abroad—Copenhagen and Berkeley for Bloch, Princeton and Rochester for Messiah. With Michel Trocheris, who had returned from Manchester, they were the fundamental research 'wing' of the SPM. Horowitz himself, while keeping an eye on these activities, devoted most of his time to reactor studies, for which he had surrounded himself with a galaxy of young and brilliant Polytechnicians. One of them was Robert Dautray, who later led the brains trust behind the French thermonuclear weapon.

Horowitz continued his ascent in the CEA. When Yvon became a director, he was promoted Department Head of the DEP; then, when Yvon left the CEA to take the chair vacated by de Broglie at the Sorbonne, he was made Director of the Reactor Division (or Direction, as it was called in the CEA). He had become one of the key figures in French Atomic Energy.

Small causes, large effects: if the capricious American administration had chosen to open the gate to the US for Horowitz and to shut it in my face, our destinies might have been interchanged. With his gift for theoretical physics he would have easily made a name for himself in America and would probably have stayed in fundamental research. If I had been the one to remain in France, I might have been offered responsibility for the SPM, accepted it, and followed Horowitz's career.

I do not regret what happened. It must have been preordained that I should one day become a professor at the Collège de France: by opening the door to the US for me, at a time when it had stayed shut for so many in France, the American administration had made a first choice for me; three years later, by shutting me out of an Oxford professorship, Cherwell had made a second choice.

Shortly after my return, I was offered a task which was to my taste: leading the 'Orbit Group'. This is what it meant: as I have said before, the CEA was planning the construction of a large accelerator, and two decisions had to be made. The first was: electron or proton synchrotron, and the second: weak or strong focusing. The technique of weak focusing was well established, and had been bolstered recently by the successful completion of the Brookhaven cosmotron, with an energy of 3 GeV. Strong focusing, although extremely promising, was more risky: no machine of that type had yet been built anywhere in the world. For construction, the CEA had an Autonomous Accelerators Service at its disposal.

To its credit it had the construction of an electrostatic Van de Graaff accelerator of a few MeV, and to its debit, the cost and even worse, the duration, of the construction, which for several years had reduced the nuclear physicists of the CEA to bibliographic researches.

Rightly or wrongly, the government of the CEA did not wish to leave that Service with the responsibility for the above choices, and gave the task of preparing a decision to my 'Orbit Group', the orbit being that of the particles to be accelerated.

The group was made up of five persons. Besides myself, there were Ionel Solomon—a young polytechnician, who exceeded all my expectations and stayed with me for nine years after the completion of our report till 1962, when he left to start his own lab—a physicist from the Accelerators Service, and two representatives from two rival firms which hoped to get slices of the construction contract.

We worked assiduously for several months. I had dreamed of doing it in eighty days, in order to give our report the title: 'Round the orbit in eighty days' 'as in "Round the world in eighty days",' but it took twice as long. I had a few problems with the head of the Accelerators Service. He had been able to appreciate Solomon's remarkable gifts while I was in the States, and objected to letting him go to work with me. Debiesse, Perrin's principal secretary, with whom I had the dealings over my visa which I described in an earlier chapter, made a suggestion worthy of King Solomon (no pun intended): Solomon would study an electron synchrotron for two days a week in the Accelerators Service, and a proton synchrotron in my group for the three remaining days. Although this solution seemed to my advantage, I refused, like the true mother in the Bible, to see our beloved Solomon cut in two; but, unlike her, insisted on having him whole. I won.

Let me open an aside here on the colourful personality of Debiesse, who disappeared a few years ago. In his youth he had passed the *Agrégation de Physique* and had become 'General Inspector of National Education', in accordance, as some would say, with the principle: 'If you can't do, teach; if you can't teach, inspect teachers.' An astute politician, Debiesse had been Perrin's principal secretary for several years before becoming director of the Saclay establishment. He was very active and resourceful, and there was no problem for which he had no solution. Some of his solutions reminded me of a well-known gag in the Marx Brothers film *Duck Soup*: a large vase has fallen on Harpo's head, covering it all the way to the shoulders; having failed in their attempts to tear it off, his two cronies crudely draw a face on the vase, with a pair of glasses and a huge moustache, and consider the problem solved. Debiesse's solution to the problem of Solomon's employment was of that type. In the early sixties, when the Algerian war was raging, Debiesse had founded an 'Institute of Nuclear Sciences and Techniques'. I asked him if he was able to find jobs for the graduates from his institute. 'No problem,' he said. 'They are all conscripted into the army and leave for Algeria.' When General de Gaulle was visiting Saclay, shortly after the emancipation of the French colonies in Africa, Debiesse had assembled his latest class of students on the steps of his institute hoping to show them to the General. 'How do they look to you?' he asked me. 'All right; but why no black students?' 'You really think there should be?' I had meant it as a joke, but I treasure a photograph of de Gaulle's visit that day. In the front row there is a magnificent negro whom Debiesse had managed to produce out of thin air in a few minutes.

Even though Debiesse could in no way be considered a scientist, as he would have liked, he was an active and conscientious administrator, and the management of the Saclay Establishment owes him a lot. He was always ready to help, and not a malicious man.

After this aside, let me return to my 'Orbit Group'. Studies of strong focusing were being pursued everywhere in the world. CERN, which had been installed in Geneva a few months earlier, was aiming first of all at a 10 GeV machine, but, with the possibilities opened by strong focusing, raised its sights to a Proton Synchrotron (PS) of 26 GeV. I went several times to Geneva for talks with the constructors of the PS, and in particular with John Adams, who was in charge of it, and who some years later would build the Super Proton Synchrotron (SPS) with an energy of 450 GeV. Adams was a great builder of machines. He was an extremely handsome man, of great personal charm. He died prematurely of cancer.

It soon appeared that strong focusing was not as simple as it had seemed. More elaborate calculations showed that during the acceleration cycle, for certain values of the energy, resonances showed up (how often during this study did I curse the word 'resonance' so dear to my ears before!), which caused the trajectories to oscillate around the equilibrium orbit with an excessive amplitude, and led to the loss of the beam. It was necessary to identify all these resonances and to find ways either for getting rid of them, or for passing over them too fast for the beam to be lost. The mathematics of the problem got so arduous that I had to ask Claude Bloch to give us a hand with the theory.

My conclusions were beginning to shape up: it was feasible, but it would be hard for the team of our Accelerators Service, which had no other construction experience than that of the Van de Graaff I mentioned before, and of a conventional cyclotron of 20 MeV. The attitude of the head of the Accelerators Service also worried me: after expressing very serious reservations about strong focusing, he had become an enthusiast just at the time when its difficulties were coming out in the open.

I could not help thinking, perhaps unfairly, that he had misgivings about his ability to build a 3 GeV machine of either type; and that he thought it less disgraceful to fail over a notoriously difficult and untried project than over one, which, like the Cosmotron, had already been successfully completed elsewhere.

I do know of a few physicists who like to attempt all but impossible experiments, which will bring glory, should they miraculously succeed, and no disgrace if they fail. I call it the 'taxicab syndrome', from the following story.

A man comes home and announces to his wife: 'I saved two francs today; the bus left before I had time to board it; I ran after it to the next stop but was still too late, and ended up running after it all the way home.' 'You fool, why didn't you run after a taxi: you would have saved twenty francs.'

I finally plumped for the weak focusing solution, but not altogether because of the 'taxicab syndrome'. For a machine of 2 to 3 GeV, the economy in the cost of iron afforded by strong focusing is such a small fraction of the overall cost that the risk involved in strong focusing was not worth taking. Our final recommendation was thus a weak focusing proton synchrotron, and was adopted by the authorities. The machine was commissioned in 1958 and given the name 'Saturne'. It was entirely overhauled with strong focusing in the seventies, and is still working today.

It is worth pointing out that the British had been far more cautious than I. They made the decision to build their Nimrod accelerator with weak focusing, nearly three years later than we did, and this for a machine of *seven* GeV—for which the savings due to strong focusing would have been far more significant.

Between 1953 and 1956, electron and proton accelerators of increasing energy were sprouting up all over the world. I do not propose to record here the particulars of those that are in operation, in construction, in the project stage, or a gleam in the eye of their promoters. Their list can be found in several publications. I would just like to say a few words on the problems raised by the race toward ever higher energies.

*For accelerators of the synchrotron type, the energy is proportional to the product of the guiding magnetic field times the radius of the orbit, at least for so-called ultrarelativistic particles, that is those with an energy many times their rest mass energy. The latter is 1 GeV for protons, and two thousand times less, that is 0.5 MeV, for electrons.

For protons—with the high magnetic fields of several Teslas that can be obtained by means of superconducting magnets, and a radius of the order of one kilometre—energies of the order of 1 TeV (1,000 GeV) have been reached at Fermilab in the US; and a project for a 20 TeV circular machine, with a circumference of 80 kilometres (!!), the so-called SSC (Superconducting Super-Collider), is at present being hotly debated in the US.

For circular electron accelerators it is unrealistic to think of energies higher than 100 GeV, because of the energy losses due to synchrotron radiation which grow at the same rate as the fourth power of energy, expressed in units of rest-mass energy. (My first publication in 1947 dealt with that problem. For a given radius and energy, these losses are 10^{13} times larger for electrons than for protons.) Only linear electron accelerators, where these losses do not exist, will (perhaps) go much higher in energy.

Another point of paramount importance is that the only intelligent way to use ultrarelativistic accelerators is in the so-called collider mode.

Instead of the standard procedure of shooting a beam at a fixed target, collisions are produced between particles from two energetic beams coming at each other from opposite directions. There is obviously a tremendous loss of intensity, and the justification for an apparently very wasteful procedure is not always clear.

I shall give an elementary and admittedly crude explanation, which I worked out for myself long ago (I later discovered that I was not the only one). The key word is *ultrarelativistic*. A particle of ultrarelativistic energy striking a fixed particle is 'seen' in the laboratory frame as having a mass many times that of the target particle, and what happens in the collision is like the shock of a billiard ball against a pea, which is unable to break either one. In the collider mode two billiard balls collide and may break into pieces, which is the aim of the experiment. Naturally there are calculations to back up such rustic arguments.*

Before I leave the subject of big machines, where I am *Sutor ultra crepidam*, I would like to recount, as a warning to authors of huge projects, the sad saga of the Soviet Dubna machine. It started with weak focusing in 1949 and was destined to become the most powerful in the world. Alas it only became the heaviest—a battleship weighing 35,000 tons. In 1953, when the discovery of strong focusing burst onto the scene, wiser and braver men would have left the doomed dinosaur on the side of the road, and started from scratch on a new project. It did not happen: guts and wisdom did not show up at the rendezvous with history.

To make things worse, the constructors had left excessive safety margins, with a vacuum chamber which was big enough, according to a sick joke, to accelerate political prisoners, should there be a shortage of protons. To be fair, I must say that I heard a similar joke in Berkeley about the Bevatron, this time with graduate students cast as the *accelerees*.

Even worse, through a construction fault of some kind, the intensity of the beam was less than planned. The unfortunate Dubna physicists, who had to use the clumsy beast, showered it with sarcastic comments, like the following: 'In the Kremlin we have the largest cannon in the world, which never fired a shot, and the greatest bell, which never pealed. We also have the largest accelerator in the world . . .'

Are such mistakes a thing of the past? I am not so sure. And since I have the good fortune of being old enough to leave excessive caution to those whose career is still in the making, I'll treat myself to the pleasure of saying what I think of the 20 TeV SSC project I mentioned earlier. I am not enough of a megalomaniac to imagine that what I say or write could have the slightest influence on the course of things, and anyway the fate of the SSC will be sealed before this book comes out; but here goes.

I find this project inelegant, and unworthy of the creativity of the great

American nation. As far as I can see there is not a single new idea in the project. The SSC is nothing but 20 Tevatrons (each one of them big enough, God knows) laid end to end, to borrow an expression from Dorothy Parker. If I may make a comparison—just imagine if in the early fifties, before the invention of the transistor, they had decided to build a supercomputer twenty times larger than the largest one in existence, with twenty times more vacuum tubes.

Having submitted the 'Orbit Group' report, and free henceforth from the worries of Big Science, I went back to thinking about the 'lightest' of the physical sciences, that of the nuclear spins; in particular I went back to the problem which was to keep me busy for a large part of my active life: that is nuclear polarization and its applications. It is time to explain what it is.

*If NMR imaging is able today to 'probe the hearts and the loins physically rather than metaphorically', it is first of all because the patient shoved inside the huge gap of a large magnet, or, for that matter, any sample place inside the gap of any magnet, is subjected to the effect of the magnetic field produced by this magnet and acquires what is called a 'nuclear polarization': that is an excess of nuclear magnetic moments pointing along the field over those pointing in the opposite direction (a polarization equal to unity corresponds to *all* the spins pointing in the same direction).

This polarization depends on the absolute temperature of the sample: the higher it is, the more effectively does thermal agitation perturb the effects of the magnetic field, which would 'like' to align all nuclear moments parallel to itself; and the lower the resultant equilibrium polarization. With fields currently used in NMR laboratories, at room temperature, the sample—our patient for instance—will have a nuclear polarization of the order of a few parts in a million. But this is enough for the overwhelming majority of NMR's applications.

There are, however, other fields of physics where much higher nuclear polarizations are required: such as the study of radioactive nuclei. I have spoken of angular correlations, where the direction of emission of a first radiation affords a privileged direction for the spin of the residual nucleus, around which the *angular distribution* of the second radiation exhibits an anistropy which is a source of information. Nuclear physicists sometimes wish to be able to create such a radiation anistropy directly, without resorting to angular correlations, and this can be achieved by polarizing the spins of the radioactive nuclei. The problem must be approached from both ends: reduce the temperature of the sample and increase the field, and one must go very far in either direction to reach tangible results.

To progress from a polarization of a few parts in a million to, say, a few per cent, one can for instance pass from a room temperature of 300 K to a temperature of 1 K, and from a field of one Tesla to a field of 100 Teslas. While a temperature of 1 K was easily available in 1954, (which is the period I am speaking of here) with vigorously pumped helium, fields of 100 Teslas were (and still are) out of reach. This is why a different method had been proposed independently by Gorter and Rose in 1948. In that method, the very high field which is required is the hyperfine field produced by the electrons of a paramagnetic atom and 'seen' by its nucleus. An ingenious variation of this method, thought up by Bleaney in 1951, was responsible for the first observation of anistropic radiation in radioactive cobalt shortly afterwards. I was fretting at the idea of being away from Oxford, when researches so close to my own interests were being successfully pursued.

Another problem on which I was reflecting was NMR magnetometry of the Earth's magnetic field, which is of paramount importance for geophysics. The smallness of this field, less than half a gauss, leads to a nuclear polarization of less than one part in a billion—far too small for NMR.*

I studied all the publications appearing on NMR, and I was dreaming of a laboratory of my own where I could try out some of my own ideas. I communicated my enthusiasm to my best coworker in the 'Orbit Group', Ionel Solomon, and I was able to arrange with the CEA administration for Solomon to have a year at Harvard, with the help of Pound and Purcell, starting in the autumn of 1954. We had an understanding that when he came back we should have a first rough sketch of a lab together.

In the meantime, one of the problems that occupied me most was the Overhauser effect, whose author had shown, as I said earlier, that one could increase the nuclear polarization in a metal by saturating the resonance of conduction electrons. I wished to simplify Overhauser's very complicated theory and to extend it to non-metallic substances.

It was natural for me to come into close contact with Kastler and Brossel's laboratory at the Ecole Normale Supérieure. They were also doing resonance experiments and were interested in high nuclear polarizations. Many of the concepts they used were similar to those of ESR and NMR, but with two major differences: they operated on atoms that were practically isolated, within atomic vapours of densities millions of times smaller than in bulk matter—which was in my own field of interest—and they used optical light, both for producing high polarizations by a method that Kastler had called optical pumping, and for detecting the effects they had produced. It is known that these studies brought Kastler a Nobel Prize in 1966, which in my opinion, and also in Kastler's, should have been shared with Brossel.

In the autumn of 1954 two events occurred which had some influence on the orientation of my work. Here's the first.

Kastler received a visiting American physicist in his lab, whom I shall call Arnie, which is what he wished to be called. He was a former student of Professor Charles Townes—who had not yet made his great discovery, the laser. Arnie arrived with the prestige of a discovery which seemed fantastic, at least for those who, like me, had an interest in nuclear polarization, and which had just been published as a letter in the *Physical Review*. He claimed to have created a 100 per cent polarization of the nuclei of arsenic, in a crystal of silicon doped with this element. The principle of his method, a variation of the Overhauser effect, involved the successive saturation of the four lines of the hyperfine structure of the ESR resonance of arsenic. (I did not put an asterisk here, because if the reader did not understand a word of the previous sentence it does not in the least affect what follows.) It was all explained very clearly and convincingly in Arnie's letter. A more detailed theoretical calculation was given in a second letter following this one, from a theoretician colleague of Arnie's. Kastler had read the letter and was convinced; Brossel read it and was convinced; I read it and was convinced. I reread it, because there was a small point which was not quite clear, and understood it a little less. I read it again and again, and each time it seemed a little more obscure until it stopped making sense altogether. The situation was embarrassing: Kastler understood, Brossel understood, and I, 'the specialist' in resonance, understood *nothing*. A rising star of French physics, Pierre Aigrain, who understood anything that could be understood and even more, happened to be passing by. He was shown the letter, read it, of course understood it, and gave a very clear explanation by making use of an analogy with an acoustic phenomenon, the 'Kundt's tube'. I had forgotten the workings of the Kundt's tube, and left in a foul temper, which I hid as best I could. After spending one more day on the letter, I was able to pin down the sophism in the reasoning, which then collapsed. The experimental result observed by Arnie should have been interpreted as a transfer of polarization between the various hyperfine components of the arsenic ESR spectrum, a result which was of some interest but which naturally had nothing to do with a 100% nuclear polarization. It took me a whole afternoon's tête à tête with Arnie to convince him of his error. One mystery remained: the referee of *Physical Review Letters* had passed the letter without the slightest objection, and, what's more, Arnie's chief, a well known physicist who shall be nameless, had quarrelled with him because Arnie had refused to let him co-sign the letter. He should be jolly grateful to him.

The explanation for this blindness among so many competent people is, I think, the following: after disbelieving the consequences of Overhauser's work, which had looked so incredible and yet turned out to be true, people were prepared to believe anything in that field; even more so because Arnie's involuntary sophism was not easy to spot.

Arnie was a colourful character who deserves a few more words. Physically stocky, with a rolling gait, and a jet-black mop of woolly hair; as hairy as an ape, with a laugh beside which Ramsey's was the tinkling of a silver bell; and wearing his belt as low as the tropic of Capricorn—he was remarkably devoid of the inhibitions which in my youth went under the name of common courtesy. Firmly determined to become integrated into French civilization, he acquired a *béret basque* which he wore under all circumstances, and insisted from the beginning on speaking French. A few days after his arrival, while showing me a piece of equipment which did not work properly, he explained: '*Il y a quelque chose merde dans apparatus*', an expression which became a classic.

I could tell a legion of stories about him, like the one he told me in a jam-packed British Railways compartment, full of horrified Englishmen, (rather a funny one, I must admit, about a Jewish matchmaker trying to arrange a marriage between a young orthodox Jew and Princess Margaret); or that other story, a true one, in which the porter of an Oxford hotel would not allow a dishevelled Frenchman up to my room because he looked intoxicated to him—he turned out to be Arnie. But the one I like best is the one about a party which he organized in his Parisian apartment shortly after his arrival. He had invited the Kastlers, Brossel, Suzanne and me, and quite a few other people. It was winter and he asked his landlady for a few extra hangers for the overcoats. Ignorant of his purpose, she asked innocently: 'Do you want them with a transverse bar for hanging the trousers?' 'I don't know,' he said. 'This is my first party in Paris.'

I have held forth about Arnie, firstly because memories of him still amuse me, but even more because the thinking I had to do in order to refute the absurd conclusion of his work made me progress toward my goal, which was still far away: the dynamic polarization of nuclei in substances other than metals.

But there was another event in the autumn of 1954. Felix Bloch, the great Felix Bloch, who had been chosen as the first Director General of CERN, invited me to spend a few months with him in Geneva. The choice of the first Director of CERN had been delicate: was not there a danger from the beginning of exhibiting the ascendancy of one of the member states? The member states chose someone who was a European by his Swiss birth, but American by his citizenship, and his residence, and a great physicist as well.

There was one flaw in this choice: Bloch disliked 'Big Science' and hated administration. Since in the autumn of 1954 the big machines were at the project stage, or at best at the stage of excavation works, all that was left was administration, which filled him with disgust. He had accepted his position out of good will towards old Europe, to which, after twenty years of exile, he still felt very close, and towards CERN as a common European enterprise; but there is no denying that he was bored in Geneva. He wanted to have someone near him with whom he could talk about his beloved magnetic resonance, to 'hold his hand', as he put it, and I was flattered to be chosen for this task, from the whole of Europe. My modest accomplishments in the field of particle accelerators, of which I imagine Bloch had never heard, had no part in his choice; the reason was resonance.

He wanted me for six months; the CEA administration, which was paying for my stay, offered one; they compromised on two.

We got on very well from the start. He was everything that I would have loved to be, but never was—partly because of the circumstances of my youth (at an age where I was running after the elusive Francis, Bloch was working in contact with Niels Bohr, Heisenberg, Pauli, etc.), but mostly, alas, because I lacked a talent which was even distantly comparable to his.

There are a few pages in *Reflections of a Physicist* which were written after his death and which are devoted to his work; I shall simply recall here that besides the well deserved Nobel, which he shared with Purcell for the discovery of NMR, he had made two if not three discoveries, each of which deserved a Nobel Prize. Physically he was tall and strong, with the build of a heavyweight boxer. His nose looked as though it had been broken in the past, which added to the resemblance. He was a confirmed mountaineer and skier.

He enriched my collection of Pauli stories by telling me, as Weisskopf had done before him, of his reception in Zurich by the great man. In constrast to Weisskopf, whose only instructions had been: 'Do something and then come and show it to me', Bloch was entrusted with a well-defined task: 'Come up with a theory of superconductivity'. Bloch went to work and after fifteen days brought Pauli his results, which it took Pauli less than fifteen minutes to tear to pieces. A second and a third attempt met the same fate. He made about ten of these attempts altogether before the end of his stay in Zurich. 'Nowadays,' Bloch told me, 'whenever somebody brings me a theory of superconductivity' (remember this was in 1954) 'I simply say: "That is my attempt number such-and-such."'

He had stated two theorems (or should one say postulates?): a) all theories of superconductivity are wrong, b) all big machines eventually work. His confidence in the second postulate gave him an excuse to devote part of his time as Director General of CERN to attempt to prove the first postulate false; for he had not given up the hope that some day he might accomplish the task entrusted to him by Pauli. Both postulates turned out to be false: the big machine of Dubna never worked properly; and in 1957 Bardeen, Cooper, and Schrieffer proposed a theory of superconductivity known as 'BCS', which Bloch never really liked but had to accept in the end.

During my stay in Geneva he was putting the last touches to his work on the derivation of a master equation for a system of spins interacting with a heat reservoir, or 'lattice'. It was very much the type of thing I had planned to do myself and had rather foolishly abandoned some time earlier. It was an impressive piece of work, a little (even more than a little) on the heavy side—to be published in three long articles in the Physical Review. When he asked for my opinion of it, I replied in one word: 'Wagnerian'. Not having undertaken that kind of work myself, I made a presentation of his, more compactly and, I think, more elegantly, in my book *The Principles of Nuclear Magnetism*; but here we go again with the dwarf on the giant's shoulders.

I was not the only one to have been summoned to Geneva to provide cultural amusement for the Maestro; a heavier type of entertainment was on the programme. Bloch had arranged to ship a large permanent magnet from Stanford to Geneva. It weighed several tons, and was specially designed for high resolution NMR by two of his disciples, Jim Arnold and Weston Anderson, two strapping fellows whom it was natural to call Fafner and Fasolt—Bloch himself being Wotan of course. My contact with these two men, who were excellent physicists, especially Anderson, and jolly companions, especially Arnold, was both pleasant and fruitful for me. As soon as they arrived they uncrated the magnet, installed the electronics, and went to work. 'This way at least we'll get a little physics going in CERN,' commented Bloch.

Later, I saw Anderson on many occasions at NMR conferences. I remember in particular a meeting of the Faraday Society in Cambridge (England, of course). Its rules are rather strict: communications are sent in, a long time in advance, to be printed and distributed in good time to the participants, and each speaker has ten minutes to show his slides and comment on them.

Anderson asked me to act as a stooge for him. In one of the many NMR spectra he proposed to show, there was a rather subtle detail: two resonance lines, which should coincide, according to a first-order theory, were slightly separated by a higher order effect. Anderson was very proud of having been able to separate them experimentally; but would not have the time to explain that feat, unless an accomplice from the audience, that is me, naïvely asked why there were two lines instead of one. I did not listen to Anderson's talk, which I knew backwards, and at the end of it I dutifully raised my hand and asked the question agreed upon: 'In one of the slides you showed, there were two lines when only one is expected. Why?' Anderson blushed and answered: 'As a matter of fact, I didn't have time to show that slide . . .'

But the main benefit I got out of my stay in Geneva was the chance to have discussions with Bloch about Arnie's results and my own ideas on the matter. Bloch encouraged me to write them down and publish them, which I did in an article for the *Physical Review*, under the title: 'The Overhauser effect in nonmetals'. Bleaney, who is not prodigal with his compliments, described it as remarkably lucid. I do not wish to indulge in details now; I will say a few words about it in connection with experiments done in my lab, because before long I was going to have a lab of my own.

During my second stay in Geneva I had been asked to give a talk on one of my favourite warhorses, 'perturbed angular correlations', and it was agreed with Bloch that it would be in French, a language which Bloch understood perfectly. Two minutes before the talk, he entered the lecture room and told me: 'It would be better to give it in English, as Bohr and Heisenberg are here and would like to hear it.' If a Greek orator of Antiquity had suddenly been told that Zeus and Athena were going to come down from Olympus for a moment to hear his dissertation, I suppose he would have reacted as I did. But everything went well. Bohr slept, or at least appeared to sleep, through the talk, and Heisenberg asked a rather trivial question which Bloch answered himself.

The following day Bloch told me that he was fed up with CERN (not in these terms) and that he was going back to Stanford. He has asked the CERN Council (hence the presence of Bohr and Heisenberg, both members of the Council) for an administrative director, who would be fully responsible for all administrative actions; but the Council had denied his request, arguing that the Director General should also be responsible for such action. Arnold and Anderson dismantled and crated the magnet, and sailed off with it. They had had enough time to do one significant experiment.

Bloch's position raised adverse comments, but I cannot bring myself to blame him: you don't make a thoroughbred do the work of a cart-horse.

After Geneva I saw Bloch on many occasions. I particularly remember our discussions on the concept of spin temperature, of which I shall speak later. Bloch did not believe in the validity, or rather in the usefulness, of this concept, whereas I was of the opposite opinion. At the end of a particularly heated discussion, during which he kept interrupting me, I said to him: 'How can I possibly convince you if you don't listen?' To my surprise Bloch burst out laughing and said: 'Do you know, this is exactly the reproach that Einstein made to Born in their discussions on the essence of quantum mechanics. I have the greatest regard for Max Born and would be flattered to play his part in our discussions, but are you sure that Einstein's mantle is not too heavy for your shoulders?' I have to add that he was convinced in the end, and became one of the warmest partisans of spin temperature.

At the end of 1954 (or the beginning of 1955, I do not remember exactly), Bloch (Claude, not Felix), Messiah, Trocheris, and I undertook on our own initiative, to give graduate lectures at Saclay, each within his domain of competence. Messiah gave a course on quantum mechanics, which he later turned into his remarkable textbook, and Bloch lectured on nuclear physics. So did Trocheris, but on a special subject: nuclear models. I naturally chose magnetic resonance, ESR and NMR. Other colleagues from the CEA also gave lectures; the course by Herpin on classical magnetism was excellent.

We wrote up these lectures, they were typed and mimeographed by the Documentation Service, and distributed to our students. I remember strongly insisting on a charge for these copies, even if only a symbolic one.

'A course that one does not pay for, is like a handbill. One mislays it or even throws it away without reading it.' These graduate lectures were the precursors of the so-called 'third cycle' (*troisième cycle*) which at the time did not exist in any French university.

My audience included the whole of Kastler's laboratory, Kastler himself, Brossel, Cohen-Tannoudji, Jacques Winter, and others. At the end of my course they gave me a gift which I cherish: a set of my lectures bound in a magnificent full leather binding.

Debiesse had arranged for a newsreel crew (there was no TV news then) to come to Saclay to film one of our lectures, and it happened to be one of mine. I lectured to about thirty people, which, considering the nature and the level of the course, was rather a lot; but the lecture room could seat two hundred people. The newsreel man raised his arms to heaven and said: 'I cannot film that.' It took more than that to throw Debiesse. He rounded up volunteers, then assistants from all the chemistry and biology laboratories, and, since this was still not quite enough, he put cleaning women, gardeners, and a few security guards in white coats and sat them in the back rows.

But I wanted a laboratory.

My problem was to convince the CEA authorities of the great usefulness of ESR and NMR in the development of atomic energy. I gave a talk in front of Perrin, Yvon, Guéron, and others I think, probably including Debiesse. In it I listed all the benefits atomic energy could expect from my beloved speciality: NMR measurement of the impurity content of heavy water in light water and vice versa, ESR measurement of uranium 235 in natural or enriched uranium, the search for plutonium, ESR studies of defects induced in materials by neutron irradiation, not counting all the applications which would be of interest to chemists. Some of these applications were standard, others highly hypothetical; but I didn't care, as I did not plan to waste my time on any of them. What I did want was to buy a magnet, a wide-band spectrometer, and a klystron from the American firm Varian to build an ESR spectrometer (which was not commerically available yet), to hire a few technicians, and, with Solomon and Jean Combrisson—a physicist who was a few years older than Solomon and who had some little experience of ESR—to start doing some of the experiments I wanted to see done.

I got an 'agreement in principle' from the authorities, and instructions to submit precise recommendations at the earliest possible date.

It was not easy: I had no experience and was starting from scratch. All the advice and information I was able to gather around me was of little practical use. The few French teams which had gone into NMR in the late forties had obsolete equipment and, if I may say so, obsolete ideas. I listened with interest to what Jean Brossel had to tell me, but his field was too far removed from mine for his advice to be really useful. One should be looking for information on NMR in America, where it was born and developed at a rate that was unmatched elsewhere. That is what I thought and that is what I did.

I left for the US in the summer of 1955. My first stop was Harvard, where my accomplice Ionel Solomon had been a tremendous hit. I wish I could call him my pupil, but it would be misrepresenting the facts; he was nobody's pupil, even if he had picked up a few things from me. I had a vaster culture, I *knew* many more things, I had been thinking for a longer time on a few problems, and I am better at explaining and expressing things than he is (and, why deny it, than most of my colleagues are). I may have influenced him more than he influenced me, but even of that I am not quite sure. I am fourteen years older than he, but circumstances had made me a late beginner and him an early starter, which reduced the difference in age and brought us closer to each other. But Solomon was a *real* experimentalist, who performed his experiments with his own hands, while I could only imagine experiments, follow them up, and interpret their results. What we had in common, I think, apart from our taste for the same type of physics, was a certain way of not taking ourselves too seriously, which I like to think, has not left me completely with age, responsibilities, and various 'honours'—and which never left him.

The experiment he imagined, carried out, and interpreted entirely by himself at Harvard, is probably the prettiest thing, in a career which had included many such.

In the summer of 1955 Solomon and I planned and undertook a voyage of a month through the US in search of information and inspiration, round the best resonance labs in the country. I have not kept a list, but there were many. Besides Harvard and MIT, Rutgers, Bell Telephones and General Electric, Chicago and Illinois, Stanford, Palo Alto and Berkeley were the main ones. We sat up together every night, and, however tiring the day had been, we never went to bed before discussing our impressions and writing up a report of the day's activities.

In Palo Alto we visited the Varian firm's laboratory, which, led by Packard, one of Bloch's two teammates in the discovery of NMR, was engaged in the manufacture of NMR magnets and spectrometers.

Packard, the head of the Varian instruments division, relied for his turnover on the sales of a high resolution spectrometer for chemists, a marvel. He showed us on a screen, the expanded NMR spectrum of alcohol with the famous triplet of the three proton groups: methylene, methyl and oxhydrile. He then improved the resolution by turning a couple of buttons and split the initial triplet into a forest of lines, which are the result of couplings between the spins of the various protons. Their interpretation requires some knowledge of the principles of NMR. Having thus shown off the possibilities of his machine, Packard told me: 'I must not forget to go back to the poorest resolution which I showed you first. I am expecting two buyers, two Texans from a large chemical plant. The three alcohol groups, that's something they know, and the three lines is something they'll understand. If I show them all those other lines it may confuse them and prevent them from buying.'

We returned, I to Paris, Solomon to Harvard for another month; we were exhausted but pleased with ourselves. Physically Solomon was a beanpole, with endlessly long legs. His angular face could light up with a charming smile. As I said in an earlier chapter, he left me in 1962 to found his own laboratory. We parted friends, as we had never stopped being, and still are today. In 1988 I had the pleasure of witnessing his election to our Academy of Science.

Combrisson, who was a few years older than Solomon, and a graduate of the Ecole de Physique et Chimie, had a good practical knowledge of microwaves, which made him my obvious choice for the ESR part of our future lab. A handsome fellow, calm and thoughtful, he was a man on whom one could rely; and this is what I did for fifteen years, before he left me to work with Horowitz.

And so, in the autumn of 1955, our little trio was ready to start on an adventure which, for me, was to last a full thirty years. I had seen an old American film with the title: *Life Begins at Forty*. I was about to test it.

Nuclear magnetism and I
(*Les Cinq Glorieuses bis*)

Better late than never

*Theory and experiment—*Dynamic nuclear polarization in liquids—
Dr Frankenstein—*The magnetometer—*Spin temperature—*Dynamic
nuclear polarization in solids—The Bible*

This period of five years may well have been the most productive of my
life. I did not make any great discoveries, probably because it was not my
destiny, but I have good memories of some of the things I did. In the main,
there are three achievements that I would put to my credit during that
period. Starting from naught, I built up a laboratory which after five years
was known to the world over; I discovered two or three interesting
phenomena; and I wrote a treatise, *The Principles of Nuclear Magnetism*,
which was an immediate success when it was published in 1961, contributed to the moulding of a generation of researchers, and even now, more
than a quarter of a century after its publication, is still a reference work.

The three things are connected: if I did not have some prior ideas about
these two or three phenomena, I might not have sought a laboratory of
my own; if I had not had this laboratory and some talented coworkers at
my disposal these phenomena would not have been discovered, at least
not by me; without the ideas and the laboratory I would probably not
have written the book; and if I had not undertaken to write it, a few
amusing experiments, even though not all of them were important, would
not have been performed in the lab.

I forgot to mention a fourth point, which is at least as important as the
other three: I seldom had as much fun as during these five years.

The starting point for this success (assuming success there was), is to be
found in my double apprenticeship: in ESR at Oxford, and in NMR,
which was acquired at least in part at Harvard. More than once I found
that, by standing on a ridge and looking down on two valleys, one had a
better view of both than the narrow specialist who keeps his eyes to the
ground as he ploughs at the bottom of a single valley. I think that Pound's
and my successful study of perturbed angular correlations, which is on the
border between nuclear physics and nuclear magnetism, offers an example
of this.

The theorist (because that's what I am when all is said and done) who has a laboratory at his beck and call, where he can put his own ideas into practice, is rather exceptionally privileged, provided this type of laboratory deals with Little Science, or as I prefer to call it, Light Science. This was the case with us at that period (things got heavier in later years). An idea which has popped up can then quickly be tested, sometimes within a week, exceptionally on the same day.

In my maiden lecture at the Collège de France I spoke of the 'divine surprise of seeing the predicted phenomenon appear when it was expected, and such as it was expected.' While testing predictions, an unexpected phenomenon can appear suddenly; and the search for its explanation is also an exciting activity.

*I remember one of the very first experiments which I did with Combrisson on the ESR spectrum of arsenic doped silicon (the same silicon, and in fact the very same sample, which was lent to me by Arnie, and in which he thought he had made his great discovery of a 100 per cent polarization of the arsenic nuclei). The nuclear spin of this isotope of arsenic is $I=(3/2)$, and this spectrum should have exhibited $(2I+1)=4$, hyperfine lines of equal intensity, like those that Penrose had discovered in copper, eight years earlier. We did see four lines, but the two in the middle were almost twice as high as the two external ones.

I thought that the spins of the arsenic were not in thermal equilibrium, and I imagined a skew relaxation mechanism where the inner lines started by growing faster than the outer ones. If this happened after a long enough wait, the spectrum should eventually come to equilibrium and exhibit four equal lines. After waiting for four hours, we were overjoyed to see that such was the case. It had been a bold assumption, because at that time we were not accustomed to the idea of an electronic relaxation being as slow as this.*

If I have held forth at length on this phenomenon, which is amusing but of modest importance, it is because it illustrates the type of situation I was facing for the first time in my life—direct involvement in an experiment.

In the search for an explanation of a new phenomenon observed in the laboratory, there are several pitfalls. An explanation may be ingenious and may cover all the facts, but still not be the right one. I have already spoken of Joliot's observation of particle traces in a cloud chamber, which has an opposite curvature to that of electrons, and which he (instead of discovering the positron) interpreted as being traces of electrons moving *towards* the source.

Much more frequent is the situation where the new phenomenon is, to quote General de Gaulle, '*vulgaire et subalterne*', or, to quote Isidore Rabi, 'a *Schweinerie*'. In my lab I had stuck up a cartoon from the New Yorker, showing a bunch of scientists leaning anxiously over a piece of equipment while one of them is suggesting: 'Before throwing quantum mechanics out to the dogs, let's check the fuses once more'. We had run into many situations where, after mobilizing all the resources of our erudition and ingenuity in search of a rational explanation, we detected the *Schweinerei* in the end.

The opposite—mistaking an important new phenomenon for a *Schweinerei*—also happens, although far more rarely: in the thirties some Berkeley nuclear physicists got rid of some 'spurious' and most annoying crackling in their counters, only to discover a few months later, when they read the Joliots' papers, that they had shut their eyes to artificial radioactivity.

I have come to the point where I must try to give an inkling of what the two of three phenomena *are* which I spoke of earlier. The reader can find a few more details in *Reflections*. He can find a *lot* of details in the *Principles*. He can also, if he so wishes, omit the passages that follow altogether, although I have made some earnest efforts to meet him half-way.

*Dynamic nuclear polarization in liquids

When I said in the last chapter that the nuclear polarization goes up when the temperature of the sample goes down, and vice versa, I had not said that these changes in the polarization are not instantaneous. For the nuclear spins to acquire their thermal equilibrium polarization, they must be 'informed', as it were, of the temperature of the other degrees of freedom of the sample, which are generally lumped together under the name of the 'lattice'. The mechanism responsible for this 'information' is called 'spin–lattice relaxation', and the corresponding time constant is the spin–lattice relaxation time, represented by the symbol T_1. Under the effect of spin–lattice relaxation, nuclear spins turn over, or to use the common expression, *flip*. At each flip the lattice receives or yields the energy involved in the flip, which, measured in frequency units, is equal to the resonance frequency—or as it is usually called, the Larmor frequency Ω_n—of the nuclear spin, which is proportional to its magnetic moment.

The equilibrium nuclear polarization is determined by the ratio between the thermal energy unit kT and the energy exchanged with the lattice in the course of a nuclear spin flip—which normally is Ω_n, but which can be made different from it 'as will appear shortly' in the Overhauser effect.

Everything said so far applies equally to electronic spins, but since electronic magnetic moments are greater than nuclear moments by three or four orders of magnitude, the energy Ω_e of an electronic flip also exceeds that of the nuclear flip in the same ratio.

Electronic spin–lattice relaxation is in general very much faster than nuclear relaxation, and in many substances the main mechanism of nuclear relaxation resides in the fluctuating magnetic fields produced by electronic impurity spins, and 'seen' by the nuclear spins.

It is now possible to understand the mechanism of dynamic nuclear polarization in liquids. Suppose first, for simplicity's sake, that the coupling which exists between the nuclear spins of a liquid, say water protons, and the electronic spins of paramagnetic impurities dissolved in it, only allows 'flip-flops' to occur between these two spin species—'flip-flops' being the name used for flips in opposite directions (as is the case in the scalar coupling between nuclear spins and conduction electrons in metals). The relaxation of nuclear spins through a scalar coupling with electron spins is a two-stage process. Firstly, the nuclear spin flip-flops with an electronic spin, exchanging with the lattice the energy $(\Omega_e - \Omega_n)$ which is required for the flip-flop. Secondly, the electronic spin flips back, through its own relaxation, and 'refunds' the lattice with the energy Ω_e. The net balance of energy exchange with the lattice due to a single nuclear spin flip is thus Ω_n, as expected.

Let's recall now that when a resonant field saturates a spin resonance, it means that the spin flips induced by that field are very much faster than the 'thermal' spin flips induced by relaxation. This in turn means that while the electron spin resonance is being saturated, before the electronic spin involved in the flip-flop described above had time to make a 'thermal' flip back, it is made to flip back by the saturating field, and so is deprived of the possibility of 'refunding' to the lattice with the energy Ω_e. The net result is that the energy exchanged with the lattice in a single nuclear flip is not Ω_n anymore, but $(\Omega_e - \Omega_n) \approx \Omega_e \gg \Omega_n$. The nuclear polarization thus acquires the value it would have had if the absolute value of the nuclear moment were equal to that of an electron moment, which is thousands of times larger. This is what Overhauser had claimed, and if in his historical talk he had told his audience the foregoing, (ten minutes would have been more than enough for that) he might have been understood and believed. But this is another example of the dwarf (or rather dwarfs, for several people had been involved in the clarification of these ideas), standing on the giant's shoulders.

In the case of aqueous solutions of paramagnetic ions, the situation is complicated by the fact that the interaction between electron and nuclear spins is not scalar anymore, but what is called dipolar, and besides flip-flops, it allows other processes such as flip-flips, where both spins flip in the same direction, and flip-stops, where only one of the two interacting spins does flip. If one computes the net effect of all these processes it is found that the maximum enhancement of the nuclear polarization is: $-(\Omega_e/2\Omega_n)$ rather than (Ω_e/Ω_n); the maximum nuclear polarization is reduced by ½ and its sign is reversed.

To relieve the boredom in my audience, I had occasionally, in lectures given here and there, called this reversed polarization the *Underhauser effect*. A few years later, I was amazed to discover the name of Underhauser cited in the bibliography of a very serious textbook on ESR among authors of papers on dynamic nuclear polarization. My amazement knew no bounds when the mythical Underhauser was cited as co-author of my own articles. Had I, like Dr Frankenstein, created a monster? I have never attempted to clear up this mystery; from what I know of the author of the book, I would be inclined to put it down to innocence rather than to anything else.

All that remained was to confirm these predictions experimentally. Combrisson and Solomon took the trouble of doing so, with me looking over their shoulders and offering suggestions, which were sometimes followed. But first we had to find the right paramagnetic impurity. By leafing through a collection of tables of free radicals, I chose one that looked all right for our purpose. In the lab we called it the disulfonate, which is only part of the name the chemists give it. It had a narrow ESR line, or rather three lines of hyperfine structure. The magnetic electron of this radical is coupled to the magnetic moment of a nitrogen nucleus, which has a spin 1. This spin can take three quantized orientations with respect to the electron spin, hence the three lines. The presence of the hyperfine structure was a drawback: the maximum polarization enhancement: $-(\Omega_e/2\Omega_n)=-(\mu_e/2\mu_n)\approx-330$ for protons, had to be divided by 3, for only one of the three lines was saturated. The experimental difficulties related to the double resonance at electron and nuclear frequencies, a new technique at the time, were finally overcome, and we did indeed observe a reversal of the proton signal, and an enhancement of its magnitude of the order of a hundred in accordance with theoretical predictions.

All this was very nice, but, besides a purely intellectual satisfaction (which is not to be despised of course), of what use could it be? As I did say before, the weak 'natural' polarizations, of a few parts in a million, are adequate for most applications; and the price one paid in complications due to the techniques of double resonance was, even for a gain of the order of a hundred, too high a price to pay.*

The magnetometer

A very different problem was that of measuring the earth magnetic field. Its value is of the order of half a gauss, and the corresponding proton polarization is less than one part in a billion. The disulfonate offered a potential enhancement of one hundred, which was better than nothing, but still a bit on the short side. It was then that, during a walk in Gif, I became aware of something which kept me awake all night. The nuclear spin of nitrogen, which in high field was a nuisance because it reduced the enhancement by three, in a field as low as the earth field, turned out to be a blessing—and this is why. One can paraphrase the theory as follows: The ratio: (Ω_e/Ω_n) of the electron and nuclear frequencies is normally equal to the ratio: $(\mu_e/\mu_n)\approx660$ of their magnetic moments, except if the electron and the proton do not 'see' the *same* magnetic field; and this is indeed the case for the disulfonate. The proton only 'sees' the earth magnetic field of the order of half a gauss, but the electron does 'see', on top of it, the magnetic field produced by its own nitrogen, which is of the order of twenty gauss.

It follows that the 'Underhauser' enhancement of the nuclear polarization is of the order, not of a few hundred, but of a few thousands. Although I had re-done the calculations several times during the night, I waited impatiently for the moment when I could submit them to Solomon's judgement. He immediately understood and approved my idea, and launched himself with incredible enthusiasm into the realization of a device which, for many years, was going to be the best of the existing earth field magnetometers.*

Among those interested in a rapid and accurate measurement of the earth field, there are geophysicists, but also archeologists, those engaged in oil survey, and people connected with the Defence Department, who, for reasons of their own, wish to detect large metallic masses moving under sea-level. We had built the magnetometer as a laboratory device and, at the request of Louis Néel, a special outfit at Grenoble was entrusted with its development. The patents office of the CEA took up much of our time in order to defend its rights in the face of foreign claims; our main opponents were the representatives of Varian who held the patent rights for the devices (and they were many), which Felix Bloch had patented. We were able to overcome all the rival claims in the end. This affair was crowned with the *Grand Prix de la Recherche Scientifique*, given to me at the end of 1958 by no less a person than General de Gaulle himself, and half of which I shared out between Solomon and Combrisson. It was almost the last thing that the General did as Prime Minister, before becoming President of the Republic. During the party that followed, he talked for a few minutes with Suzanne and myself, leaving us with an impression of great kindness and simplicity. When he felt like it, he certainly could charm, and he did charm me, although I was far from having been charmed by the circumstances of his rise to power a few months earlier.

Before the presentation of the prize I was approached by a very pleasant gentleman (was it Pompidou, who was totally unknown then?) who introduced himself as the General's Principal Secretary, and warned me that the envelope which the General would be handing me would not, for some obscure reason, contain the cheque for the Prize, but that it would be sent to me a few days later. Were they afraid that I would make a scene in front of the General?

*Spin temperature

I am passing on to the second phenomenon which fascinated me during these years: 'spin temperature', which was going to play an important part in the way of thinking of many specialists in nuclear magnetism for decades to come. The concept of spin temperature originates from the fact that, in a solid, the nuclear spins are coupled to each other by dipole magnetic interactions, much more strongly than to the lattice. The hypothesis, for it is only a hypothesis, of spin temperature, is the assumption that the state of the spin system is one of internal equilibrium, reached in a time T_2, which is much shorter than the spin–lattice relaxation time T_1, and that this internal equilibrium state can be described by an internal temperature, called spin temperature, which may be very different from the temperature of the lattice. This hypothesis had never been proven theoretically, and during the year 1957 I devoted myself to checking its validity *experimentally*, by imagining an experiment that I performed with an American visitor, Warren Proctor, a former student of Felix Bloch. (Yes, for once, I had decided to dirty my hands: was I not a radio-engineer from *Supelec*?) Here is its principle.

Experiment A: the nuclear spins of a solid sample are brought into equilibrium with the lattice at a temperature of 300 K in a high field, where the spins acquire a nuclear magnetization measurable by NMR. The sample is then demagnetized down to zero field, in a time-span which is long compared to T_2, so that the spins remain in internal equilibrium at all times, but short compared to T_1 so that the spins can be considered as isolated from the lattice for the duration of the experiment. If the sample is then re-magnetized to the initial value of the field, it recovers its initial nuclear magnetization, (apart from some small losses). This is *compatible* with the existence of a spin temperature, but does not *prove* it. In particular, nothing definite can be said about the state of the spin system in zero field. If one *assumes* that the spin state is describable by a spin temperature at all times, the temperature in zero field can be calculated simply by writing down that the entropy is conserved during the adiabatic demagnetization. Let's assume for argument's sake that it is 2 K (this is what it was in our experiment).

Experiment B: The sample is cooled in zero field in a cryostat at 2 K, for a time which is much longer than T_1. One *knows* then that the spins are at a bona fide thermodynamic temperature of 2 K. One remagnetizes the sample to the same field as at the beginning of experiment A. If the nuclear magnetization observed is the same as in experiment A, the validity of the spin temperature assumption is proven. It was.

This experiment modified the intellectual stand of many physicists with respect to the concept of spin temperature. The idea had been introduced for electronic magnetism by two Dutch physicists, Casimir and du Pré, before the war, and for nuclear magnetism by Pound and Purcell in the late forties.

I think that it was this experiment, as well as a few others that we did with Proctor, which led Felix Bloch to abandon his hostility toward spin temperature. Purcell, who had believed in the existence of spin temperature ever since his experiments with Pound, said about my experiment with Proctor: 'The baby has been around for a long time, but you have brought the wedding certificate.'

Spin systems are peculiar in that their energy spectrum has an upper bound (in contrast to all systems with degrees of freedom of kinetic energy). This makes it possible to prepare systems at a negative temperature. The probability of finding a system at a negative temperature in a given energy state is greater, the higher the energy. It is clear that for a 'normal' system, meaning one with no upper bound to its energy spectrum, a state of negative temperature is inconceivable, for it leads to an infinite value for its energy; but for nuclear spins they are not only conceivable, but have been produced and studied in detail. It is important to realize that a system at a negative temperature is *hotter* than any system at a positive temperature, and that, put into contact with a 'normal' system without a bound to its energy spectrum and therefore necessarily at a positive temperature, it will give up energy to the 'normal' system in an irreversible manner, until all its energy states are equally populated— which corresponds to an infinite temperature. It is only after this passage through an infinite temperature that it may come into thermal equilibrium, with the normal system at a positive temperature. The passage through an infinite temperature, that is a state of complete chaos, is inevitable.

An unexpected application of the concept of negative temperatures will be presented in the chapter 'East and West'.

Dynamic nuclear polarization in solids

*I am coming now to the third phenomenon discovered during this period, namely dynamic nuclear polarization (DNP) in solids. Its various aspects and its applications have been the main field of activity in my laboratory for nearly a quarter of a century.

In his original paper Overhauser had laid great emphasis on the fact that the statistical behaviour of conduction electrons in metals, whose saturation was expected to lead to a greatly increased nuclear polarization, was governed by a law called Fermi statistics, which I need not describe here. In my Geneva paper I had shown that this assumption was by no means essential, and I had predicted the possibility of DNP in liquids, which I had experimentally demonstrated in my lab, as described in an earlier section of this chapter. It is well known that the spins of the paramagnetic impurities dissolved in liquids, which play the part of the conduction electrons, do *not* obey Fermi statistics.

I was not alone in making this remark about Fermi statistics; others, and in particular Felix Bloch, had noticed it, and they drew the conclusion from it that dynamic nuclear polarization by the Overhauser effect could be observed equally well in insulating solids. But *that* conclusion was wrong in general; and I had been the only one to have shown it in my Geneva paper, where I had carefully analysed the subtle but essential difference in the mechanisms of nuclear relaxation by electronic spins— between, on one side, metals and liquids, and on the other side, solid insulators. For the reader who is not inclined to take my word for it, I can only refer him, at his own risk, to the *Principles*. If DNP proved impossible by the Overhauser effect (or its Underhauser version), was there any other method?

What I (and not only I) was looking for, was not so much an increase of very small polarizations by large factors—passing from one part in a billion to a few parts in a million, as in the earth field magnetometer, or from a few parts in a million to a part in a thousand, as we had done for liquids in high fields—but large *absolute* values of nuclear polarization, perhaps approaching 'why not?' 100 per cent, and this for a series of applications that I shall outline in the following chapters. But with dynamic enhancements of the order of a few hundred at best (the earth field was a very special exception), this inevitably called for a start from 'natural' polarizations of a few parts in a thousand, that is temperatures in the one Kelvin range. One could think of the original Overhauser effect in metals, but for the fact that at these temperatures the saturating microwave field does not penetrate into the metal beyond an infinitesimal region called skin depth. As for the liquids . . . they do not stay liquid in that range. The only exception is the ^{3}He isotope of helium (^{4}He has no nuclear spin). Between 1955 and 1960 it was not available in my lab, but since then we have tried unsuccessfully, as have others, to polarize it by the Overhauser effect. The reasons for that failure are still not understood.

The solution appeared to me one day, out of the blue, and I shall try to explain it here in a manner which, although terribly oversimplified, is essentially correct in its principle.

Consider a solid insulator containing nuclear I spins and at a much smaller concentration, say one part in a few thousands, electronic S spins. Assume conditions of field and temperature, say 1 K and 2.5 Teslas, such that the S spins are almost completely polarized, say all pointing 'up', and the nuclear spins, with their magnetic moments thousands of times smaller, almost completely unpolarized, as many 'up' as 'down'.

Assume also that the spin–lattice relaxation time of the S spins is very short, so that if through any circumstance the S spin happens to flip to the 'down' position away from equilibrium, its relaxation mechanism will bring it very rapidly back to the 'up' position. All these assumptions are quite realistic. Our problem is to bring all the nuclear spins to the 'up' position.

Consider a nuclear I spin, which is 'down'. It could come 'up' by making a flip-flop with an electronic S spin which is 'up'. This requires an energy

$\Omega=(\Omega_s-\Omega_I)$ which in a liquid could be borrowed from the kinetic energy of the relative motion of the two spins, but which is lacking in a rigid solid. This energy can be provided to the spins by means of an external microwave source of frequency Ω, driving a flip-flop which brings the I spin 'up' and the S spin 'down'. However, the S spin which has come 'down' returns immediately to the 'up' position because of its fast relaxation time. The I spin which has come 'up', 'sees' around it only S spins 'pointing up', with which it cannot flip-flop. It might flip-flip though, if the energy for it, $(\Omega_s+\Omega_I)$, were available, but it is not, and so the I spin stays 'up'. All the I spins are thus, one by one, brought into the 'up' position.

The extreme assumption of a 100 per cent polarization of the S spins, made for simplicity, is by no means necessary; and it can be shown that, whatever the electronic polarization, this method in principle permits nuclear polarization to become equal to it.

An identical argument shows that if the sample is irradiated with the flip-flip frequency $\Omega=(\Omega_s+\Omega_I)$, this will in principle impart a polarization to the nuclear spins which is equal but opposite to the electronic polarization.

One should stress the importance of the fast relaxation of the S spins. Each of the S spins has to 'service' more than a thousand I spins. No sooner has it flip-flopped with an I spin than it has to come back into the 'up' position to 'service' another I spin. This fast relaxation calls for qualities, whose human analogue led me sometimes to call this effect, 'the King Solomon method' (again no pun intended on my colleague Ionel). (I remember agreeing, begged by Debiesse, to lecture to a group of High School teachers; while I was lecturing on this very method in those very terms, I saw three nuns in professional dress, seated in the front row, earnestly taking down my every word.)

In my published work I prefer to call this method the 'solid effect', to recall the immobility of nuclear and electron spins with respect to each other, in contrast to both liquids and metals.

It was in 1958 that I first decided to put this idea to an experimental test. To save time, and even more importantly, to make the interpretation of the experiment absolutely unambiguous, I gave the part of the nuclear S spin to another nuclear spin with a Larmor frequency much larger than that of the I spin. The substance chosen was a single crystal of lithium fluoride, the S spin was the nuclear spin of ^{19}F and the I spin that of the nucleus ^{6}Li. It took Proctor and myself twenty-four hours to do the experiment and demonstrate the principle of the 'solid effect'. Some time later, with Jean Combrisson, and then with a young coworker, Michel Borghini, we repeated the experiment, this time with a real electronic spin as spin S. The era of DNP had started in my laboratory.

A small point of history. Rereading my Geneva paper years later, which was written at the end of 1954, I discovered that the principle of the 'solid effect' was in there, for everybody to read between the lines. For three years no one, including myself, had noticed it. I was lucky to have been the first.*

And what about the applications of resonance to atomic energy? Well, nobody from the higher spheres spoke to me about it, and I did not deem it necessary to speak about it to anybody from the higher spheres. At the beginning, my coworker Goldman did one or two experiments aimed at that kind of thing, but since nobody was encouraging him very much, he went on to other endeavours. I know that later a resonance laboratory was started at Saclay for such applications. I neither begrudged them it nor tried to compete.

Among my first coworkers, apart from Combrisson and Solomon, I wish to cite 'in an order, which I am not absolutely sure to have been that of their arrival to the lab', José Ezratty, André Landesman, Maurice Goldman, Michel Borghini, Jacques Winter, and Charles Ryter. Each of them had his own character, his qualities, and his faults (like myself). With the exception of Maurice Goldman, who succeeded me when I retired, they all left the lab after periods of various durations. Others came to replace them. I keep a special place in my memory for Allais (I forget his first name), who had worked with Combrisson on the Underhauser effect. Tall, intelligent, very good looking, and very gentle, this young polytechnician seemed destined for a brilliant scientific career. One day he came to tell me that he could no longer bear the misery of the Third World (though it was not called that yet), and that he was leaving for India, to live in a village there and help introduce the villagers to a more productive type of agriculture. Nothing I could say in my attempts to dissuade him had any effect. I do remember that this took place at the time when de Gaulle had been brought to power by the Algiers uprising of May 1958, and when nobody knew what the future would hold. When he left I told him: 'Leave your address in India; who knows, I might be joining you yet'. I don't know what became of him.

I had foreign visitors for periods of varying lengths; among them was my friend Robert Pound in 1958, who colloborated with a young British visitor from Oxford, Ray Freeman—who has since then become a star in high resolution NMR, FRS, and quite recently (*horresca referens*) a professor at Cambridge University; another was Warren Proctor, who came for a most fruitful two-year collaboration.

It was also in 1958 that I was awarded the Holweck Prize. This was founded in memory of Fernand Holweck, who was murdered by the Germans during their occupation of France. It has been awarded every year since 1946, alternately to a French physicist by the British Physical Society and to a British physicist by the French Physical Society. Among my British colleagues, it gives me great pleasure to cite my two friends

Nichlas Kurti and Brebis Bleaney, and four others who went on to win the Nobel Prize: Dennis Gabor, Brian Josephson, Martin Ryle, and Antony Hewish. The fact that only two of the French laureates, Alfred Kastler and Louis Néel, got the Nobel, shows without a doubt that we are twice as good at selecting Holweck laureates as the British. The amount of the award is quite small, but it gives the laureate a very pleasant stay of three days in the other country with his wife and the officers of his own Physical Society. He sings for his supper (s) by giving the Holweck Lecture. In 1958 we went to Cambridge, where I had the honour and the pleasure of giving mine in the very room where Maxwell had lectured nearly a century earlier, and to Oxford, where I was received like the prodigal son.

All in all, 1958 had not been a bad year.

The Bible

I think it was in 1955 that Maurice Pryce told me that Oxford Univeristy Press (OUP) had asked him to write a book on magnetic resonance; but he did not have the time to do it, or did not feel like it, or both, and so he had mentioned my name to OUP and had been asked by them to sound me out for the job. 'It's just at the right moment,' he said glibly. 'You have just completed a course on NMR and another on ESR: all you have to do is to translate it all into English and the trick is done.' I had no experience of the trade of book writing, I had only read a lot of them; but I understood that it would not be quite so simple.

What attracted and frightened me at the same time was that this book, which was yet to be written, would be part of the illustrious collection of the 'OUP Monographs'. Before the war, it was with reverence that I used to contemplate their prestigious titles, written in letters of gold on the backs of their bottle-green bindings, standing on the shelves of the library of the Institut Henri Poincaré: *The Principles of Quantum Mechanics* by Dirac, the greatest physics book ever written, *The Theory of Atomic Collisions* by Mott and Massey, *The Quantum Theory of Radiation* by Heitler, *The Theory of Electric and Magnetic susceptibilities* by Van Vleck, *The Principles of Statistical Mechanics* by Tolman—prestigious books, fountains of wisdom where I had quenched my thirst for knowledge. Could it be that my imperfect opus would stand next to them on the shelves?

I accepted timorously. A few weeks later I received two copies of a contract which, from the quality of the paper and of the typography, was more like a diplomatic treaty than a vulgar commercial agreement; OUP was already displaying the quality of its productions.

The contract was leonine: OUP reserved an exorbitant part of the television rights for itself, and declined all responsibility in case of prosecution for obscenity. Still, I accepted, asked Michel Trocheris to commit himself on my side by bearing witness to my signature, counter-signed all the pages, and sent back one of the copies. *Alea jacta erat*!

Pryce had spoken lightly of some 300 pages to cover both ESR and NMR, while my lecture notes were already twice that size. I decided that I had to choose: ESR or NMR, that was the question. In 1955 I was far better known for my work on ESR than for my NMR; and I was advised by some friends to choose ESR where, I was told, I was an expert, rather than NMR where I was at best a beginner. I was not convinced: while I had hardly published anything on NMR, for five years I had read most of what was worth reading on the subject. Furthermore I foresaw possibilities for development in nuclear magnetism, many more than I saw in ESR. Finally, in my infant laboratory, there were lots of things to be done straight away in NMR, and nothing of the kind in ESR. I made my decision. The book would be on nuclear magnetism and, in the wake of Dirac, I dared to call it *The Principles of Nuclear Magnetism*.

Then followed four years of strenuous work. One may well ask how, during these four years, I managed to combine the writing of a book of 600 pages (we were a long way from the projected 300 pages for NMR plus ESR), with the setting-up and the running of a new laboratory, and with my personal research. The answer is that there was a symbiosis between these various pursuits; my ideas and those of my young cowork-ers, and the results of our experiments, were fed into the book even while they were being submitted to scientific journals. Conversely, the writing of the book was at the origin of some of our researches.

For example, dissatisfied with the current theory of spin diffusion, I 'ordered' a better formulation from Pierre-Gilles de Gennes and entered it into the manuscript of my book even before he had published it in a journal.

I also liked to imagine experiments, aimed at illustrating some points of the theory in a spectacular manner. Some far from trivial experiments, which were performed in the lab during that period, originated purely for that reason.

I seldom presented a calculation taken from published literature without attempting to make it shorter, clearer, or more rigorous. I have already spoken of my efforts to strip Bloch's theory of the master equation of its Wagnerian mantle. I performed a similar operation of cosmetic surgery (I am mixing my metaphors) on a very important work, which was pro-foundly original but almost unintelligible, by Alfred Redfield. I heard from some of my readers that they understood Redfield's ideas for the first time in my presentation of them.

I kept strictly to my rule of including no theory in my book to which I did not subscribe, no experimental fact that contradicted a theory to which I did subscribe wholeheartedly, no formula that I had not checked myself. I departed from the last rule twice, to regret it both times.

All those who write books intended for students know, or at least ought to know, that they owe them a great responsibility, which is greater the better the students. A good student who reads a scientific book, pen in hand, trusts its author, and, when he comes up against an error, will waste a lot of his time trying to understand or to rederive the incorrect result. I am not saying that it is harmless to accumulate errors in an original scientific publication, but at least there the experienced reader will recognize earlier, and perhaps not without some innocent pleasure, the errors of a colleague.

This is why I took great care to detect any errors. I remember a formula cited by Bloembergen and Anderson (neither a Nobel laureate yet), with a discrepancy by a factor of four (or perhaps eight), while I myself had found a third result. Before including my own version in the book I had consulted with Walter Kohn and de Gennes, who fortunately both agreed with me.

In spite of all these efforts, small errors did remain, which readers pointed out to me and which I have, I hope, weeded out through the many printings the book has known during its long existence.

I found some relaxation from my labours by inventing short epigraphs which were appropriate to the contents of the various chapters. It is thus that I honoured Marilyn Monroe (very much alive then) by giving the chapter on spin temperature the title of her picture: *Some Like it Hot.* OUP frowned at it; but I replied that to my knowledge it was the title of an old nursery rhyme, and what else did they have in mind?

In the preface I warned the reader (and the authors) that: '. . . in a book, in contrast to an article, no references need be given solely for credit . . .' By so doing, I considerably reduced the volume of the bibliography and made a few enemies.

The success of the book exceeded all my expectations and my hopes. It was translated into French (by André Landesman), Russian and Japanese, received a record number of citations for the last twenty-five years in the notorious *Citation Index*, and last but not least, sold very well.

If I have written at such length about the genesis of this book, it is not only because I lived cheek by jowl with it during the four years it took me to write it. It is also because it gets on my nerves, with the shadow it casts on the other things I have done.

Conan Doyle was deeply annoyed by the prejudicial effect of Sherlock Holmes' success on some other works of his, which he considered at least as important. Well, I feel a little like that too. All those who had anything to do with NMR, and that's quite a crowd, know my name because of the book. Only a minority of them know that ten years later Bleaney and I wrote a even thicker book on ESR, and still fewer know of my work after 1960 and of the book I published with Maurice Goldman in 1982, devoted to new developments in nuclear magnetism 'with most of them coming from my own laboratory'. But, to tell the truth, I also sometimes think that the recognition I got for these other achievements is quite reasonable and in keeping with their value; it is the success of the 'Principles' which may be excessive. Nobody is ever pleased with his lot.

All the physics and all the writing I have described absorbed me to a great extent, but not to the point of making me indifferent to the progress of my career in the CEA. More than the rank, the salary and the prestige, to which the quadragenarian I had become without even noticing it was not totally indifferent—what I was looking for was independence; I had found my way, and I did not want anyone higher up to give me advice, or worse, orders, on how to proceed along it. It was not simple: the CEA was (and still is) a hierarchical structure, descending from the summits where the two-headed eagle AG-HC soared, all the way down to the humble Section leader—the last authority to appear in the organization chart. All the positions which I occupied during my career in the CEA, all the way up to Director of Physics (and I could have been High Commissioner if I had wished), I accepted not out of a taste for power, but lest the one who would have taken it if I had refused, should exercise *his* taste of power at my expense. I think, however, that these responsibilities sometimes gave me new interests and broadened my outlook; but more of that later.

Plate 1. Moscow (1923) A Russian boy and his mother.
'It is only recently that I realized that my mother had been beautiful.' p. 8

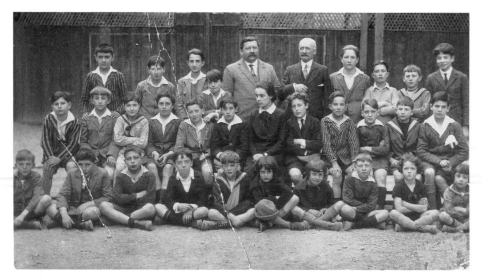

Plate 2. Paris (1926) A Russian boy and his French mistress.
Ecole Secondaire de Breteuil. The author is at the extreme left of the second row.
'I never dared to tell her my love.'   p. 25

Plate 3. (1939) A French Soldier.
'Nous vaincrons parce que nous sommes les plus forts.'   p. 73

Plate 4. Croissy (1946)   The Three Musketeers.
From left to right: Michel Trocheris, Claude Bloch, the author, Jules
Horowitz. 'They were no ordinary Polytechnicians.'   p. 106

Plate 5. Saclay (circa 1960)   Experimentalist.
'Experimentalists take me for a theoretician.'   p. 102

Plate 6. Paris (circa 1965) Theoretician.
'Theoreticians take me for an experimentalist.'   p. 102

Plate 7. (circa 1965) Felix Bloch. *Wotan*
'He was everything I would have loved to be but never was.'   p. 180

Plate 8. Saclay (1970) Suzanne and the author.
'Her friendly smile was constantly ready to break into a laugh.' p. 85

Plate 9. Paris (1958) Shaking hands: with a General.
'When he felt like it, he certainly could charm.' p. 191

Plate 10. Kent (1967) Shaking hands: with a Princess.
'I still feel in my hand this hand friendly and firm.' p. 303

Plate 11. The Vatican (1986) Shaking hands: with a priest. p. 354

Plate 12. Under the *Coupole* (1980)   Going to address a President.
'*Ave Caesar, Oraturi te salutant.*'   p. 347

Plate 13. Geneva (1987)   Chairman of the CERN Review Committee.
'Rocking the boat.'   p. 338

Plate 14. Paris (1985)   Collège de France: three Nobel winners and other worthies.
Omnia Docet

p. 226

Looking back

I had been there before
Brideshead Revisited

Mixed feelings—Portrait of a prickly genius—Portrait of an eccentric genius—The hazards of translation

An event took place in the spring of 1956, which was of great emotional importance to me: a collective trip to Russia. As far as I can remember, it had been organized on the initiative of Joliot for the benefit of some French nuclear physicists from the CNRS and the CEA. André Berthelot, the head of the CEA Nuclear Physics Service, had gone to Russia a little earlier to attend an international conference on nuclear physics, one of the first to be held there since the war, and did not wish to return so soon. It left a vacancy and I claimed it passionately.

We flew from Paris to Moscow with stopovers at Prague and Minsk, where we spent one night each. I admired what little I was able to see of the architecture of Prague, and enjoyed the Pilsen beer very much. On the Minsk–Moscow leg of the journey I was surprised to see that very few passengers buckled their seat-belts; I followed their example, for mine had been torn out of the seat.

During that flight I had a ridiculous and completely unwarranted fright. We must have been flying at low altitude, for the cabin was not pressurized. From my seat I could not see the ground and was absent-mindedly watching an altimeter that was hanging in the cabin. I suddenly noticed that we were rapidly losing height. Nobody around me seemed to be paying any attention to it. We went down to a thousand metres, then eight hundred, four hundred, two hundred. At that moment the stewardess rushed out of the cockpit and ran to the back of the plane. I thought my last hour had come. The needle of the altimeter fell to zero and stopped there. The inevitable shock did not occur and we went on flying. Apart from me, nobody had noticed anything. What a ridiculous idea, to hang altimeters in passenger cabins, especially neurotic ones!

In Moscow, at the Vnukovo airport, where we arrived in the evening, we were met by an official, who was assisted by a lady who turned out to be the head of our squad of interpreters for the whole trip. Passport control had been reduced to a minimum, and custom formalities were perfunctory; we were obviously expected and welcome guests. I shall describe in another chapter the reception I got in later years, when I went to Russia as a simple tourist; but let me now describe what can happen to someone who is not quite as welcome as we were, and who is too sure of himself—a story told me by Jacques Prentki. It happened at an international conference on high energy physics held in Kiev. One of the participants, an American, had been boasting of having worked for the Pentagon and having had instruction from specialists on how to protect his luggage against indiscretions. It involved the use of a few carefully placed hairs, a pinch of talcum powder, and other devices which he did not disclose. The cleverest secret agent could not search his luggage without his being aware of it.

When he arrived at his hotel, his suitcase was awaiting him, with both locks torn out, and tied up with a rope to keep it shut. I find this story instructive in more ways than one.

Several limousines were waiting for us at the airport, and we raced to Moscow along a road which was lit only by the headlights of our cars. Our hotel, the *Ukraine*, was a tall building in the horrible neo-classical Stalinist style, with broad corridors, vast rooms, leaking faucets, and desperately slow lifts.

This may be the right moment for analysing my feelings towards the USSR in this spring of 1956. Hardly more than a decade had elapsed since the great guns that had roared on the Eastern front had gone silent. I was filled with an immense personal gratitude to the Red Army and to the peoples of the Soviet Union. At the cost of terrible suffering, they had laid low the unspeakable horror of Nazism—a daily threat to my own life and to all those who were, if I may say so, born under the same star as I. This gratitude has not died since, even though today it does not blind me any more.

True, just before the war there had been the infamous Germano-Soviet agreement, the carving up of Poland, followed by massive deportations to Siberia. But had these same deportations not saved the lives of many by sheltering them thus from the Nazis? And when, under the German occupation of France, the newspapers had trumpeted the massacre of thousands of Polish officers at Katyn by the Soviets, who around me would have doubted for a single moment that the performers of that deed were the Nazis themselves?

The pre-war Moscow trials, the atrocious terror of 1937–1938—and no one had yet disclosed how atrocious it had been—were far away.

The trial, early in 1953, of the so-called 'white coats', the Jewish doctors accused of murderous crimes, was recent, it's true; but then, Stalin was dead, Beria shot, and Malenkov and Bulganin were greeted in Britain as representatives of a modern and moderate trend, which was only troubled by that muddler Khrushchev, who tried to take all the credit for himself. And long, long before all this was my childhood, and what I called in an earlier chapter its 'positive global balance-sheet'. Add to this the fact that, with the cold war raging, the other great power, trapped by Senator McCarthy into paranoid witch hunts, did not give the best possible image of democracy. This too earned the Soviets the indulgence of French intellectuals.

It took Khrushchev and his celebrated report for the mouths to open (in the West, mind you—in the East, Gorbachev's *glasnost* was still a very long way off); it took the genius of Solzhenitsyn to make us see and believe, to show the cruelty and, worse, the absurdity of the Stalinist regime to the eyes and the ears of all except the voluntarily blind and deaf—all things which the defector Kravchenko had said twenty-five years before him, but in vain for lack of the genuis which forces belief. But all this was yet to come, and it was with a favourable prejudice, tempered with caution, that I was preparing to rediscover my first homeland.

These mixed feelings were intermingled with an intense curiosity about Soviet science, of which we knew very little. Lysenko's fraud (a murderous fraud, as it later transpired), was still flourishing, but it was to do with biology, indeed merely with botany: was it not a simple quarrel between agronomists rather than a real scientific debate? This, I am ashamed to say, was the feeling of those of us who were not blinded and deafened by political prejudice. For the others, a goodly proportion of our group, the case was clear: Lysenko, not Darwin, was the great man of biology, and his opponents were traitors or at best poor misguided souls.

But in physics, the Russians, who had exploded an atomic bomb only four years after the Americans, and a hydrogen bomb after an even shorter delay, were obviously in the avant-garde, and there were mutual benefits to be drawn from close contacts with them. (Easier said than done, as we discovered later.) Personally, it did not take the thunderous prestige of the bombs to make me believe in the quality of Soviet physics. Had not Fock and Frenkel been among my first teachers of quantum mechanics, and hadn't I learnt the theory of relativity and the equations of mathematical physics through the Russian translations of Eddington and Courant and Hilbert? The level of physics must be high in a country where such *chefs d'oeuvre* were made available at such a low cost to so many.

But far greater than this interest in Soviet physics was the deep emotion I felt at finding myself again in the country where I was born, and had lived my first ten years.

That first night, after the sumptuous dinner—caviare, spit-roasted sturgeon, beef Stroganoff, washed down with vodka and Soviet champagne (I kept my distance from the latter)—I decided in spite of the late hour to go out for a walk. After a few hundred metres a breathless underling caught up with me and made me go back to the hotel. In spite of my fatigue I barely slept that night.

During our stay in Russia we visited laboratories, but also monuments, in Moscow, Leningrad, and Kiev. In Moscow we visited the Kremlin, the

Lenin Mausoleum, where he and Stalin were not yet sleeping apart, various museums and monasteries, and the sumptuous metro. The evenings were taken with the ballet, the circus, and puppet-shows. I was able once to go by myself to the theatre to see a play by Chekhov. I found the house where I was born, which was in a piteous state, and was photographed in front of it by Albert Messiah amidst expostulations from passers-by who reproached us for photographing a crumbling house instead of the brand new skyscrapers of the capital.

My greatest pleasure was to walk by myself in the streets of Moscow and to talk to people. I soon discovered that to them I was an unnerving problem. This chap who, judging by his accent, was obviously a Russian—how could he possibly not know the price of a metro ticket or a phone call, the spots where it was permitted to cross the wide boulevards which had mushroomed in Moscow, the workings of the soda-water dispensers at every street corner, and thousands of other details? I soon discovered in the shops that the excellence of my accent was a snag rather than an asset, and that I could get faster service and even be served ahead of my turn by faking a foreign accent.

What struck my colleagues and myself most was seeing teams of women everywhere, working like navvies with pick and spade, or lugging heavy paving stones under the nonchalant supervision of a man with his hands in his pockets. It did not fit in very well with the image of the liberated Soviet woman, being peddled by the propaganda—unless it fitted in too well. This is what Chamfort, the eighteenth-century humorist, had to say in this context:

'The Regent wanted to go to a ball without being recognized. "I know how to do it", said the Abbot Dubois, and kicked his bottom during the ball. The Regent found the kicks too hard and said: "Abbot, you disguise me too well".' Soviet women may similarly think: 'We are too well liberated'.

I was not really a nuclear physicist and took only a moderate interest in the visits to nuclear laboratories, which differed from those I had seen in the West by a more rustic type of equipment, and by the terrible quality of the buildings (they were made from what my future assistant, Jean Pellerin, once called 'precracked concrete'). What interested me more was the people, but I did not find them very open. More out of politeness toward kind hosts than out of sincerity, I expressed admiration for the realizations and the methods I saw, and the Russians must have taken me for one of the card-carriers in our 'old reliable' group, in front of whom only the right feelings should be displayed.

Our most interesting visit was to the Institute for Physical Problems, headed by Kapitza, though he himself was unfortunately away from Moscow. For the first time I saw equipment, like the large helium liquefier designed by Kapitza himself, which could bear favourable comparison with any similar equipment in the West. We met some well-known theoreticians there: Pomeranchuk, a physicist of outstanding originality, and the illustrious Landau himself, surrounded by some of his disciples. One should know that the School of Theoretical Physics led by Landau was considered by many to be the best in the world, and that, even today, the best Soviet theoreticians are pupils, or pupils of pupils, of Landau.

Lev Landau was by far the greatest of the Soviet theoreticians. He received the Nobel Prize in 1962 for his theory of liquid helium, but he discovered many other things, such as his explanation, given at a very early age, of the diamagnetism of free electrons in metals.

Landau is also the author, with Eugene Livshits, of an extraordinary series of monographs on theoretical physics, which cover practically all its aspects, and which have only now begun to age a little. Some spiteful gossip said that in this enormous series there is not one line by Landau and not one idea by Livshits. This *is* malicious gossip; without reaching the level of Landau, Eugene Livschits was an excellent theoretician. I have used most of the books in the series and learnt much from them. Their only feature which makes me uneasy is the complete absence of any numerical data, or of any reference to experimental work. I find Landau's sense of approximation all the more admirable. Exact solutions hardly ever exist in physics, and how can one discover approximate solutions in the absence of any numerical data? It is both admirable and incomprehensible!

Among the discoveries that Landau did not make, one can cite the two-lattices model of antiferromagnetism, to which Louis Néel is indebted for his Nobel Prize. Landau did think of this model, but rejected it, because he found that it disagreed with the requirements of quantum mechanics. Néel, who, to tell the truth, did not care much about the requirements of quantum mechanics—which he probably did not even know—went ahead, published his model, and extrapolated its consequences, which he brilliantly verified by experiment. Some compromises with the requirements of quantum mechanics were later found, having turned out to be a little less inflexible than was thought. It is a danger to be too learned, or *Sancta Simplicitas*—whichever you prefer. (Néel chuckled when he read that passage in the French version.)

Landau was born in 1908, seven or eight years after the greatest: Heisenberg, Pauli, and Dirac. They had skimmed, if not all the cream, at least the cream of the cream; but still had left enough of it for Landau's bread and butter. After the age of twenty, he made several trips abroad, striking all his contemporaries with his sparkling intelligence, the asperity of his character, and his full awareness of his own worth: all qualities he kept through his whole life.

This is illustrated by the story Casimir tells about Landau (or should I say about Dirac?). While spending their honeymoon in Copenhagen,

Casimir and his wife encountered the young Landau at a musical soirée in the house of Niels Bohr. Landau, who disliked music, was bored stiff and kept gesturing, making faces, and being a general nuisance.

Dirac asked him: 'Why don't you go out for a walk in the garden if you dislike music so much?' 'I did ask Mrs Casimir, who hates music as much as I, to go out with me in the garden, but she won't.' Dirac pondered this for a while: 'Ah, but perhaps she dislikes your company even more than she dislikes music.'

During our interview with Landau, a member of our group, a physical chemist, told Landau about his activities in great—perhaps too great— detail. Landau's reply was: 'I admire a good chemist the way I admire a good cook, as a craftsman of his trade. What I do dislike is a cook who dabbles in philosophy. That, to me, is a physical chemist.' I was shocked by this way of addressing a guest, albeit perhaps too full of himself; it was a remark that was not so much discourteous as unfunny. When my turn came, I was very brief about my own interests.

Pauli, whom Landau greatly admired, suffered in his later years from the same failing, often being less funny than uncouth. On the other hand, the young Pauli did not lack charm in his irreverence to his great elders, as witnessed by this little story—which this time deals with Niels Bohr rather than Einstein. Pauli had written to Bohr about some problem and Bohr, being busy at the time, had courteously replied: 'Thank you for your letter; I'll answer on Thursday'. A month later, the answer had still not come and Pauli wrote: 'Dear Professor Bohr, there is no need for you to answer me on a Thursday, any day of the week will do just as well'.

One of Landau's closest disciples, or should I say apostles, who had more Judas than Peter or John in him, once revealed to me one of Landau's favourite pastimes, near the end of a lecture. He would say: 'Let's think aloud', then start on a new subject, covering the blackboard with equations and discovering the result of his cogitations at the same time as his audience.

The apostle was greatly surprised one day to discover a jealously guarded secret in Landau's study: next day's 'improvisations' written down in advance. After hearing that story I asked myself whether, in order to gauge the validity of an approximation, Landau did not make some numerical estimates, which he never mentioned in his books. I prefer to keep my previous image of Landau, and to go on believing that he only used his marvellous physical sense.

All his pupils, and I knew several of them later on, had an ambivalent attitude towards him: they were all full of admiration and deep affection, but there were none who had not, at one time or another, had a reason to complain of his devastating criticism, and sometimes even of an arbitrary authoritarian action. It seems that Landau stopped the publication by one of his best pupils, Abrikosov, of the theory of vortices in a second type superconductor for five years, because he did not believe in it. Proof positive of the existence of the lattice of vortices was given in a neutron diffraction experiment at Saclay, suggested by de Gennes and performed by Cribier and Jacrot.

Landau's destiny had its share of tragedy. In the obituary article devoted to Landau by Piotr Kapitza, founder and director, till his death, of the Institute for Physical Problems, there is the following mention: 'Landau became a member of the Institute in 1937, and worked there, with a single interruption of one year, till his death in 1938.' What Kapitza does not say is that Landau spent that year in jail, after being arrested as a spy during the worst period of the Stalinist terror. It will be to the immortal glory of Kapitza that he threw himself into the lion's jaws by addressing himself directly to Stalin, requesting the freeing of Landau and vouching personally for his loyalty. Sakharov was not the first heroic scientist of the Soviet regime.

With the advent of Gorbachev's *glasnost*, a Soviet journal has published the letters which Kapitza wrote to Stalin, Molotov and Beria in defence of Landau. In these letters Kapitza shows himself to be not only a fearless advocate of Landau, but also a shrewd one. In his letter to Stalin he insists naturally on Landau's extraordinary value to his country as a scientist, but he also explains that Landau is far too vain, aggressive and talkative to qualify as a spy, and that his accusers must be people on whose toes he had viciously trod. In his letter to Molotov he insists on the fact that Landau's health is 'rotten' and that he might die in prison, which could prove embarrassing, in view of his reputation abroad. Kapitza's letter to Beria, who had been ordered by Stalin to release his prey, is curt: 'Kindly release Professor Landau under my personal responsibility. I shall see to it that he does not indulge in any counter-revolutionary activities inside or outside the institute.' Kapitza's refusal to take any part in the work on the atom bomb, which was put under the authority of Beria, did not improve their relations. Kapitza had said: 'How can I play the violin in an orchestra where the conductor cannot read the score?' (Oppenheimer could have objected to working under General Leslie Groves on the same grounds.)

In January of 1962, Landau was the victim of a terrible motor accident. Following a cranial traumatism, he remained in a coma for six weeks, and never recovered his intellectual powers. It was his shadow who received the Nobel Prize that year (in absentia). He survived for six years, and died in 1968.

We visited Lomonosov University in Moscow, a building very much in the same style as the Hotel Ukraine, only even bigger. Our guide was a Professor Ivanenko, an oily character, whom I disliked at first sight. I will say more about him a little later.

His name was not unknown to me: he had written the preface to the Russian translation of book by Sommerfeld on quantum mechanics. He explained the Soviet system of higher education to us, the high level of the student grants and of the teachers' salaries. Our 'old reliables' were exclaiming in admiration. I thought that our guide was juggling a little too rapidly with his figures, but did not say anything. But I could not bear the enthusiasm of the 'old reliables' when Ivanenko announced triumphantly that the students had thirty-five hours of lectures a week. 'When do they think?' I asked, which was followed by a reproving silence.

Permit me now, oh my reader, to make a jump along my world line, a few months into the future, to September 1956, and some 8000 miles to the west, to the city of Seattle on the north-west coast of the US. You will see in a moment the reason for this voyage in space and time.

A great international conference was taking place then and there. The place was alive with Nobel Prize winners, present and future: Yukawa and Felix Bloch, Wigner, Lee and Yang, Schwinger and Tomonaga, Prigogin, and many others. I met one of the most remarkable men of our time there, who deserved the Nobel Prize in physics at least as much as any of those I have just named—George Gamow.

Gamow, an eccentric genius, born in Russia at the beginning of the century, had left his native country around 1930, never to return. On the first occasion, he had tried to escape with his wife to Turkey in a rowing boat, from a beach on the Black Sea. Their boat was on the verge of sinking when they were rescued by a fishing boat. The absurdity of their attempt to escape was such that their story of tourists carried away from the beach by a current was accepted by the Soviet authorities. A second opportunity, the successful one, occurred when he received an invitation to attend a Solvay conference in Brussels.

Through great persistence and also thanks to the help of Molotov, with whom he seems to have been acquainted, he obtained permission to take his wife along. Things went wrong when, at the end of the conference, Paul Langevin told Gamow that he was behind the invitation, that he had vouched for Gamow's return, to the Soviet authorities, and that Gamow was morally bound to go back. Somebody advised the dejected Gamow to speak to Madame Curie, who was known to have great influence over Langevin. Gamow confessed his predicament to Madame Curie, she listened attentively and said: 'I shall speak to Langevin.' The following day she brought him Langevin's 'permission' to stay.

Gamow's greatest discovery is a quantitative theory of alpha-decay and, far more importantly, the discovery of its mechanism, 'tunnelling', which plays an important part in so many fields of modern physics.

He was the first to suggest that the universe started with a Big Bang, and to postulate the existence of a genetic code. He also brought important contributions to the theory of β-decay. He wrote a series of popular books on physics, the so-called 'Mister Tompkins' series, which are full of great penetration and enchanting drollery.

This is how I made his acquaintance, in the midst of the fairground atmosphere of this gigantic conference. To entertain the participants, an excursion had been organized on an enormous boat, along the Puget Sound, which passes through a magnificent landscape. From the start a thick fog descended on the Sound, enveloping both banks, and freezing the passengers assembled on the decks to the bone. The captain, who could not see further than the end of his nose, used some kind of sonar to find his way. The noise made by passengers' conversation prevented him from hearing the echoes, and he ordered us to shut up or clear the decks.

That was what I did. In a saloon in the depths of the boat, I discovered a tall blond man slumped on a couch, a tall glass of whisky in his hand, who was no other than Gamow. He was delighted to speak Russian with me, and told me the greater part of the biographical data I have just cited and which I later found in his sadly unfinished autobiography, called *My World Line*. He told me that he had just obtained the Kalinga Prize for scientific popularization, that it was to be given to him in India, that the organizers had omitted to tell him who was paying for his travelling expenses, and that he was wondering whether the amount of the Prize would at least cover that. I told him the story of the man who wins a trip to Tierra del Fuego in a television quiz game, and whom the presenter of the quiz show asks invitingly: 'And now, sir, would you like to try your luck for the trip back?' He was enchanted by this little story, which seemed to him to describe his own situation neatly. I told him a little about the people I had met in Russia a few months earlier. This made him pensive. 'Oh yes, there were three of us who were great pals in Russia: Landau, Ivanenko, and myself; we were known as the Three Musketeers. And now what? Landau is a genius, Ivanenko a police spy, and here I am;' and with his glass he pointed to himself, sprawled on the couch.

The reader will have understood by now why I could not resist the pleasure of bringing together, at least on paper, these Three Musketeers.

And while we are still in Seattle, let me describe another meeting with the incomparable Felix. The organizers of the conference had entrusted me with the task of organizing and chairing a three-hour session, where participants would present original papers on their work within the vast field of radiofrequency spectroscopy. It was my responsibility to select the papers and to retain those worthy of interest. For a while, my problem seemed to be the opposite one of finding customers to fill the three hours put at my disposal by the organizers. Felix Bloch had volunteered a talk, in the 'Götterdämmerung' style, on his theory of the master equation of a spin system I have spoken about, and I welcomed him with enthusiasm into my session. I had not counted on the numerous Japanese at the conference, who came in droves to offer me their wares. It became necessary to filter the talks tightly, and to limit each talk to twenty minutes. This is where a conflict arose with Felix, who, although he had been warned in good time of the twenty minutes limit, insisted on thirty. I would have gladly granted them to him, but I could not lose face in front of my Japanese, and stood fast. I confess that deep down inside I was more amused than anything else. When his turn came, I said in a firm voice: 'Twenty minutes, Professor Bloch.' 'But you know that this is impossible, I must have at least twenty-five!' 'Nineteen minutes, Professor Bloch.' He seemed to consider blowing his top and leaving, but thought better of it, and completed his task brilliantly in the allotted time.

End of Seattle, back to Moscow.

From Moscow we flew to Kiev, which had been rebuilt entirely after the destruction of the war. My only memories of it are a magnificent view from the steep banks of the Dnieper, a very pleasant excursion in fast motor boats on the river, and meeting the head of the Semiconductors Institute, who looked very much like Lenin—a resemblance he must have cultivated by the cut of his beard. We flew back to Moscow, and from there went by the night train to Leningrad.

Everything has been said about this marvellous city by the great Russian poets—Pushkin, Akhmatova, Blok (Alexander, not Felix or Claude), and Mandelstam—and also by the tourist guidebooks: its white nights, when you can read your newspaper in the street at midnight; its students walking all night in groups, singing their student songs and strumming their guitars along the Neva, straitlaced in her corset of granite; the Winter Palace and the Admiralty Needle; and Peter the Great on his rearing horse—Pushkin's 'Bronze Horseman'—and, and, and . . . open your favourite guidebook. We had some discussions in Leningrad with Soviet nuclear theorists. They were unable to tell us whether there were any cyclotrons or Van de Graaff accelerators in Leningrad, showing an ignorance which surprised even the 'old reliables'.

Back in Moscow, a banquet closed our visit. Rosenblum, the physicist in whose lab I had my unfortunate experience with the leaking vacuum chamber, spoke for the French delegation, which was the occasion for a piece of high comedy. He pronounced a few phrases, which the interpreter translated into Russian. Rosenblum, who was born in Russia and spoke Russian fluently, continued absent-mindedly in Russian. The interpreter, who was a resourceful girl, kept her calm, and translated what he said into French. And so they went on, chasing each other from one language to the other, amid general laughter which only poor Rosenblum did not share.

Since I am on to these interpretation problems, I'll just say that we had three interpreters, but one of them was always silent. In a burst of confidence she revealed the reason to me. She could not ride in a car for more than a few minutes without feeling sick; no sooner had she recovered from one ride than we started on another. She had a respite in Kiev: the Semiconductors Institute was so close to our hotel that we walked there. We sat down, and the Director of the Institute said a few words of welcome. 'We are here in the Institute of Semiconductors,' started our usual interpreter, when a loud voice corrected her: 'Demiconductors'. It was our mute interpreter putting in her twopenny-worth. Everybody looked at her; she went as red as a beetroot and, like Mount Kazbek in Lermontov's poem, subsided for ever.

Going up

Foreign offers—Great men and robots—Rule or be ruled—Yankee go home—Next year in Jerusalem

Although Fundamental Research has for a long time been a fully-fledged part of the CEA, as witnessed by the presence in its midst of the Institut de Recherche Fondamentale or IRF, it has not always been so. During my stay at Harvard in 1952–1953, I had been wondering about what was awaiting me at home, and the idea of a scientific career in the US had crossed my mind.

During that year I had had two offers to remain in the US. The offer of a lectureship at Harvard for the year 1953–4, for which I suspect Robert Pound was responsible, came only a few months after my arrival. The following step, which it was not unreasonable to expect, would have been an asistant professorship, a position which could be held for five years at most, according to the Harvard rule of 'up or out'. That was followed by an associate professorship for the happy few, which in those days carried tenure; or by departure—usually after a gentle hint, given well before the five years ended.

The second offer came from Westinghouse, at the end of my stay in Cambridge. This great firm wished to create, or rather to re-create, a modern research laboratory in the field of magnetism, low temperatures, and resonance; and apparently echoes of my modest successes at Oxford and Harvard had reached it. They invited me to come to Pittsburgh to talk over their offer.

I was greeted in Pittsburgh by the Director of Research, Clarence Zener, a name honourably known in the field of solid state physics, who laid emphasis on two points during our interview. The first dealt with new techniques of controlling industrial dust, which had made a clean city of Pittsburgh, whose previous record in that respect had not been blameless. The second was a blot on the firm's reputation since the pre-war depression, when Westinghouse had ruthlessly liquidated its research laboratories, considering them an expendable luxury at a time of acute crisis. 'Never again!' said Zener. My starting salary would be four or five times my present Harvard fellowship, which was a rather miserable one, it must be said.

It had never been my intent to accept the Westinghouse offer (if I had remained in the US it would have been at Harvard), and I had gone to Pittsburgh out of sheer curiosity. The smoke which had covered the city, as witnessed by pre-war photographs, had indeed disappeared—although in offices and flats one could still see electrostatic devices designed to capture the industrial dust. I was also shown an absurd monument, a kind of gothic tower, which carried the high-sounding name of 'Cathedral of Learning'. I was reminded of it three years later in Moscow, though in a different architectural style, when I discovered the absurd Lomonosov University, which I spoke of in the last chapter.

I was not through with Westinghouse. A good many years later (how many?), an emissary came to see me in Paris (he may have had other business in Paris as well), to offer me another job in Pittsburgh. This emissary was a solid state physicist, not unknown in his field, whom I had met once in Chicago. I shall call him Eves. This Eves had a rather remarkable physical idiosyncrasy. He held himself very stiffly, and all his gestures were jerky, like those of an automaton. A story goes with it: the Prince of Physics in Chicago, Enrico Fermi, one of the greatest and most admired physicists of our time, was an object of special reverence for an Italian waiter at the Faculty Club of the University of Chicago, which was patronized by both Fermi and Eves. Some practical jokers among the young scientists of the physics department had persuaded the Italian waiter, who was a simpleton, that Eves was a robot designed by Fermi. After that, every time the waiter brought Eves his order, he lingered around to see how the creature would consume its food.

The better to seduce me, perhaps, Eves had invited me to dinner in the dining room of the hotel George V, which was more famous for the elegance of its service than for the quality of its food. We were seated and surrounded by a bevy of flunkeys led by an impressive *Maître d'Hôtel*. Eves ordered trout with almonds, which he must have found flavourless, for after a while he leaned toward me and said: 'I don't care if this guy despises me, I am going to ask him for mustard.' No contempt could be read on the impassive face of the *Maître d'Hôtel* as he listened to Eves's order. He returned, majestically carrying an immense tray covered with more mustard pots of every shape and hue than I had ever seen in my life. Whether it was the way mustard is served at George V, or his own way of displaying contempt, I could not say.

Eves did not convince me and I did not go to Westinghouse.

Although I myself have never believed that Fermi built the robot Eves, I yield to no one in my admiration for him. His qualities are admirably illustrated in this little story I owe to Norman Ramsey.

A graduate student consults Robert Oppenheimer about a problem. For nearly two hours Oppenheimer gives him a dazzling lecture, of which he understands very little, but he goes away very pleased, all the same, to see that there are great minds among us, capable of mastering problems which are inaccessible to simple mortals.

He then consults Schwinger, who, in less than an hour, not only solves the problem but makes the student understand the solution. He goes away, very pleased to see that there are great minds among us who can make such difficult problems accessible to simple mortals. Lastly, he goes to Fermi with the same problem, and comes out after a few minutes, very cross with himself for not seeing that he could have solved something as simple as this problem by himself.

My admiration for Fermi will explain my behaviour in the following circumstances. At a party I attended with Suzanne, Van Vleck beckoned to us to come over and meet a short dark man with thinning hair. Seeing that Suzanne, who had been interrupted in her conversation with Mrs Van Vleck, was not paying much attention to this short dark man, I pinched her arm surreptitiously but vigorously—an action I had never committed before. Suppressing her boiling indignation, she smiled at the gentleman to whom she was being introduced but, as soon as it became possible, demanded an explanation for such unusual and outrageous behaviour. 'It is to engrave in your memory that you have shaken hands with Enrico Fermi.'

In the course of my career I received two more offers from America. The first, which came from the University of Pennsylvania in January 1958, was for a full professorship. Although Philadelphia attracted me no more than Pittsburgh, I did not turn it down straight away, for reasons to appear shortly. A second offer of a full professorship, a much more attractive one, came in 1959. The University of California was starting a new campus, devoted exclusively to research, in the enchanting site of La Jolla, near San Diego. The chairman of the future Physics Department was Walter Kohn, a physicist of great talent and an extremely nice man. This last offer was really tempting. To have been asked to become a member of the new campus was considered among US physicists as a real mark of distinction. I was at the time a candidate for a Chair at the Collège de France, and might well have gone to La Jolla if my candidacy had failed; but it didn't.

But let me go back to the CEA, and to the course of my career there. I was faced with the problem of inserting my young laboratory into the rigid structures of the CEA. Francis Perrin had thought of making it a part of the Service de Physique Nucléaire, headed by André Berthelot, a disciple of Joliot. I did not care much for it, preferring to be farther removed from my immediate superior in the line of command. There was another scheme I liked much better and was able to persuade my masters to accept: my laboratory was made a *Section Autonome* within the DEP (Département d'Etudes de Piles). This was headed by Jacques Yvon, who had far too many people under him, and far too many important problems to worry about in the field of reactors, to be breathing down the back of my neck.

Within the budget allotted to me I was my own master, free to do very much what I pleased without bothering anyone. This idyllic existence lasted for two years, but then new problems arose. The chemists at the CEA were ogling my section, considering that it would be far more logical for it to be made part of the Chemistry Department. To have a *chemist* ordering me about was unthinkable. Had Felix Bloch not said once: 'When chemists get into a field it's time to get out'? Attack is the best form of defence.

I pointed out to Yvon that in the Service de Chimie Physique, whose leader had just retired, there was far more physics than chemistry, with an X-ray group, a large colour centres group, and a few other bits and pieces. I suggested that this service should be carved up, with the chemical parts going to the Chemistry Department, and that the physical remnants, and my magnetic resonance section, could be the makings of an honest Service de Physique du Solide, which I might be persuaded to lead.

All that remained was to convince the chemists not only to stop coveting the goods of others, but to part with some of their own. One can hardly blame them for dragging their feet in the face of such proposals. I decided to play my trump card, the invitation to Philadelphia which I had not quite turned down yet. I pointed out to Francis Perrin that the situation of a *Chef de Section*, even in a *Section Autonome*, was not worthy of a man of my age with an international reputation like mine, and that there were places where my talents were better recognized. Francis yielded to my pleading, and even decided that my new Service should be called: Service de Physique du Solide et de Resonance Magnétique, or SPSRM. I managed to get André Herpin as my deputy—a solid state physicist with a good experience of crystal vibrations and classical magnetism, and a man who was easy to live with.

The reader may have drawn from the foregoing the impression that I am an ambitious schemer. I would like to assure him that I am nothing of the kind. All I had wanted all the time was to be my own master in my own laboratory. Circumstances had trapped me (and would continue to do so) into the dilemma: 'rule or be ruled'.

My new responsibilities were bringing me into contact with new problems and new physicists, and I did not dislike it. And Herpin was helping me in my new position by taking his share of the load of administrative duties. It was too good to last. It lasted a little over a year. At the beginning of 1959, Yvon was promoted from department head to director, becoming responsible for a large section of the nuclear physics service. To explain how this affected me I will, in some detail, have to describe what was at the time the flagship of the CEA's physics—its nuclear physics.

The vast Service de Physique Nucléaire, founded and headed by André Berthelot, had been split into three parts.

The first and largest, under André Berthelot himself, dealt with what today is called elementary particles physics rather than nuclear physics, and made use of the largest accelerators available at the time: Saturne and the CERN machines.

A second, called Service de Physique Nucléaire à Moyenne Energie or SPNME, was headed by Jacques Thirion, a skilful and imaginative experimentalist; its main tool was a sector cyclotron, constructed by Philips, but considerably improved by Thirion himself.

The third unit was a Service de Physique Nucléaire à Basse Energie or SPNBE, which had the use of a Van de Graaff electrostatic accelerator; its head was Eugène Cotton, whom I had met in 1946 in Rosenblum's laboratory.

All of this should have been put under the authority of Yvon. However, André Berthelot, Joliot's prize disciple and the pioneer of nuclear physics at the CEA, had managed to be put directly under the *Haut-Commissaire*, Francis Perrin, and so only Cotton and Thirion came under Yvon. As soon as Yvon's promotion to the directorship was known, Cotton and Thirion, both good friends of mine, came to see me with an unexpected request: would I be willing to serve as department head over their two services, so that they could report in the future to someone they knew and appreciated? 'What a crazy idea,' I said. 'With my lab, the book I am writing, and my own service, my hands are full—certainly not.' The following day Yvon made the same proposal to me and I declined it just as categorically, though perhaps in different words. 'Very well, I shall offer it to X . . .' said Yvon. X . . . was a nice man, but not someone I would have chosen to lead a department. The day after an awful doubt crept into my mind and I returned to see Yvon. 'What about me—my service will be autonomous, directly under you, will it not?' 'Oh no, I do not want services reporting directly to me; your service will be in the same department as Cotton's and Thirion's.' I made up my mind then and there; I asked Yvon whether I could have the job back which I had turned down the day before. Yvon granted it to me without much surprise. He may have had a better sense of humour than I had credited him with. I found myself head of a Département de Physique Nucléaire et de Physique du Solide, or DPNPS, made up of three services. The defences I had been building to protect my lab were extending farther and farther.

The increase in my work load which followed this promotion turned out to be less than I feared. My first step was to find a conscientious and trustworthy deputy. I offered the job to Combrisson, who accepted, which took a great weight off my mind. I was also lucky to have as administrative assistant a former solicitor's clerk, M. Pouillet, a man as competent and trustworthy as I could have wished. Thirion and Cotton were accustomed to running their own services and, inside the Solid State Service, Herpin relieved me of most of what was not my own lab.

Yet my new job was not a sinecure. I was the department's representative in its relations with the higher authority—which implied a good knowledge of what was going on inside the department—and I was also the representative of the same higher authority with respect to personnel in my department. No decision of consequence touching any of my three services could be made without my agreement.

Two main tasks absorbed me most at certain periods of the year: the presentation of the budget, and the annual promotions of the personnel. The annual budget began with the submission of the relevant documents, which had been prepared in the services and reviewed at departmental level; then there were discussion sessions at headquarters with the representatives of the Financial Department, where each department head, surrounded by his *Chefs de Service*, sat facing the financial director and his henchmen, for a full day of ferocious bargaining.

I considered the annual promotions of the staff as my chief responsibility. Rather than distributing the promotions, granted to the department by headquarters, on a proportional basis between my three services, I insisted on having a single promotions list for the whole department, on which were ranked all the members of staff up for promotion, after detailed discussions with the *Chefs de Service* responsible for the proposals. To get a better idea of the professional qualities of the candidates, I invited them to my office to talk about their work. From their explanations, I picked up some more knowledge of nuclear physics.

In another chapter I shall describe the collaboration between the nuclear physicists and my lab in the field of polarized targets, where my lab was a world leader.

One last remark on my administrative ascent. After the Algiers rising of 13 May 1958 which brought de Gaulle to power, a large number of the CEA staff took part in a protest demonstration. i was there . . . The CEA administration was naturally aware of it, as it was of my membership of the CGT since 1950. The fact that none of it had interfered with my hierarchic advancement deserves to be noted.

I do not know if reading about the episodes of my administrative career will be as boring as writing about them was; they represent the boundary conditions, within which my activity in the CEA developed. It had its constraints, but also accrued some possibilities for action, and I did not want to pass it over.

To round off this chapter I would like briefly to recall a few light-hearted anecdotes, connected with some travels I made during that period. Like most scientists of our time I have done some travelling and attended international conferences, most of which I have forgotten by now; but here are a few stories still floating at the surface of my memory.

Somewhere between '57 and '59, there was a conference in Bristol organized by Nevill Mott on defects in solids, including their study by

magnetic resonance—whence my presence. At that time there was a wave
of anti-American feeling among British students, and the inscriptions
saying 'Yankee go home' on the walls of the university buildings were an
embarrassment to the organizers of the conference, which was attended by
many Americans. The first American speaker was Walter Gordy, a
professor at the University of South Carolina, and he alluded immediately
to these graffiti in his Deep South accent. 'Friends,' he said, 'I am telling
you, it's no use. Back home we have been writing it for over a hundred
years, and the Yankees are still there.'

Walter Gordy provides me with a transition to a second conference I
wish to mention, which took place at Oak Ridge in Tennessee. The driver
from Oak Ridge who met me at the airport to take me to the conference
was obviously not a native, for I could understand everything he was
saying. During the drive across a hilly countryside, so different from the
flat Midwest, I saw farmers ploughing with horses, who looked very much
like French peasants. When I made this remark to my driver, he replied:
'Yeah, backward, aren't they?' The conference did not take place inside
the Oak Ridge Nuclear Laboratory, which was off-limits to foreigners, but
in a cinema in the city. There was a visit to the isotopic separation plant
on the programme, which was strictly limited to American citizens.

Jesse duMond, the great specialist in gamma-ray diffraction, who had
befriended me, told me his impressions after the visit. 'It's tremendous! Oh
dear! Perhaps I was not supposed to tell you that.'

At Varenna, on Lake Como, there is a conference centre where I gave
lectures more than once on various subjects connected with nuclear
magnetism. The site was enchanting and the food atrocious. To make up
for it, after dinner, there was great consumption of the excellent *torta
gelata*. They came in large sizes, and in principle a quorum of eight had to
be reached; but we were often content with a restricted quorum of six,
and once of four. After the meals, which were taken in the dining room of
one of the hotels in Varenna, one could get a cup of *espresso* in the next
room at a coffee machine, dispensed by a little sad-looking man. I would
have much preferred to drink mine in a café across the road, where it was
much better; but Suzanne did not want to give him offence by scorning his
coffee. This lasted until I saw the sad-looking little man drinking *his*
espresso in the café across the road.

I have kept for the end a conference on nuclear physics which took place
at Rehovot in Israel, where I gave a talk on perturbed angular correlations.
That conference was dominated, at least for the French physicists, by a
problem of air transportation. We were going to fly on the Israeli airline
El Al, whose motto, according to some jokers, is the two-millenial dream
of the Jewish people: 'Next year in Jerusalem.'

I do not wish to describe the thousand and one incidents which
punctuated this journey, in which it took us three days to succeed in

leaving Paris. The self-confidence of the airline officials was particularly infuriating: the departure of our plane, which seemed to be suffering from some mysterious complaint, could take place at a moment's notice. Those who, like myself, lived in the suburbs, were not authorized to spend the night (or rather the nights) at home, and were put up in a hotel at the airline's expense. During the day we were taken around in coaches to visit Paris. After three days, the incredible ridicule of the situation ceased to amuse me, and I was considering giving up the trip, when at last we took off. Albert Messiah sent a wire to the organizers, which read: 'Arriving Tuesday,' signed 'Messiah'. This was read out during a session, and had the reception one can imagine.

The nuclear physicist, Sam Devons, summed up the situation: 'They have an excellent public relations system and outstanding pilots, but they are slightly handicapped by a total lack of aircraft.' Perhaps I should insist on the fact that I have just described a situation which prevailed more than thirty years ago; and that today the El Al airline does not yield to any other for punctuality, and has the best record for safety against international terrorism.

Another remark by the same Sam Devons springs to mind. Visiting the holy city of Safad in Israel we saw a group of young men coming out of a *Yeshiva*, a rabbinical university, and I was struck by the intelligence and spirituality radiating from their young faces. 'What a loss for theoretical physics!' I said to Devons. 'Are you sure that they aren't looking at us and thinking: 'What a loss for the rabbinate!' he replied.

Collège de France

Omnia Docet

A place unlike any other—Candidates and elections—Modesty in the third degree—Pinning medals—Visits from above—Four physicists— Four Administrateurs—'Horizontal and vertical'—* Polarized beams and targets—* Recoilless nuclei—* Red shifts and red faces—* The magic crystal—The New Testament—The first companions.

My climb up the CEA ladder had not put an end to all my ambitions. I explained in the last chapter how my wish to be my own master in my own lab had led me to extend my authority over ever broader sectors of physics at the CEA, of which my lab was becoming, *ipso facto*, an ever smaller fraction. But I was missing something. The writing of my book *The Principles of Nuclear Magnetism* had revived a passion which had never completely left me: teaching. In an earlier chapter, I said that I could explain anything I could understand. I thought now that I could understand more and more interesting things, and I longed more and more to have a chance of explaining them. By turning down the offer from the University of Pennsylvania, which, I must admit, had served its purpose in establishing the independence of my lab, I had turned my back on teaching, and it had left me with some regrets.

The door to the French university was closed to me: I was not a Doctor of Science. (It is worth noting that I did not say the French universities but rather the French university, which is a single monolithic structure. It embraces all the French universities, regarded as equal with respect to statutes, diplomas, salaries, professors, and students. There has been talk of changing it for the last thirty years; just talk. Need I add that the French university does not recognize foreign doctorates, be they from Oxford or from Patagonia.) At forty-three, I had neither the time nor the desire to prepare a thesis. I wanted disciples, not a master: I had been looking for a master long enough.

It was Alfred Kastler who suggested that I try the Collège de France. I knew of course of its existence, the most prestigious of ... what? 'Universities' is not right, neither is 'Schools'; why not say, simply, the most prestigious college in France. I knew of three former physics professors in the Collège de France: Langevin, Brillouin, Joliot. Was I not aiming too high? However, Francis Perrin, a slightly less imposing figure, was a professor now; and I thought that, as a candidate, I could count on his support.

I wonder how many people, even in France, know what the prerequisites are to be a candidate for a chair at the Collège de France. The answer is: there are none, no degrees of any kind. In a country like ours, where you need a degree to become a postman or a railway ticket collector, let alone a university professor, this is highly singular. Of course, no degree is awarded to the students—or, to give them their proper name, the *auditeurs* that is 'listeners'.

The Collège de France was founded by King François I in 1530. The University of Paris, attached to its traditions and its privileges, had a monopoly on teaching, within its district, and was hostile to any innovation. Its four faculties: Divinity, Law, Medicine, and the Arts, claimed to embrace everything that it was useful and lawful to teach, and taught it in Latin only—even the scriptures and texts from antiquity. On the advice of the learned scholar Guillaume Budé, the King did not attempt to reform such an ossified institution; but instead elected six royal lecturers—three in Hebrew, two in Greek, and one in Mathematics. It was the beginning of the Collège de France, which numbers fifty-two chairs today.

I remember explaining the inner workings of the Collège de France to an American colleague. 'But it is modelled on our "Institute for Advanced Study!"' he exclaimed, very much the man who, after seeing a performance of Hamlet, concludes that the author has read too much Freud.

The number of professors took a long time to increase from the six royal lecturers, to the present fifty-two. If I were asked how many of the fifty-two cards are trumps, I would unhesitatingly say more than a quarter, which I think is a lot. There were forty-eight professors in 1958, thirty years ago, when I first started thinking about the Collège de France. (From now on I shall just say 'Collège', for brevity.) During the same time, the number of university professors has been multiplied by four. To those who might tax the Collège with Malthusianism, I would like to quote from Voltaire's *Candide*: 'Monsieur, how many theatrical plays have you in France?' 'Five or six thousand.' 'That's a lot,' said Candide, 'how many are good?' 'Fifteen or sixteen.' 'That's a lot' said Martin. (Out of the forty-eight who accepted me as their colleague, only one remains in the Collège today—our Mozart, the mathematician Jean-Pierre Serre, who was elected at thirty.)

King François wanted to create a *modern* institution, and one may well question the modernity of an institution which is more than four hundred and fifty years old. The guarantee of this modernity, which is still very much present today, I think, is the mobility of the chairs. What is permanent, or increasing very slowly, is the number of professorships—or in our jargon, of *chair credits*. Upon the retirement or death of a professor, it is not *his* chair which becomes vacant, but *a* chair. Keeping the same subject after a vacancy is never a matter of course; it is the same kind of decision as for changing the subject. When there is a change in the subject, the new one sometimes bears little relation to the former: thus, Frederic Joliot had followed a Professor of Sanskrit, I succeeded a Professor of Arabic Literature, and the field of my successor is Geodynamics.

In the nineteenth century, the chairs 'rotated' more slowly. From 1801 to 1862 Jean-Baptiste Biot occupied the chair of General Physics, in which he was replaced by Joseph Bertrand, until 1900. (Soviet scientists describe their elders' dislike for early retirement with the motto: 'From the chair into the grave.') In those days there was however in the Collège the wonderful custom of 'deputies'. A professor who felt the weight of age on his shoulders could delegate the task of delivering his lectures to a 'deputy', whom he paid for this office, out of his own purse, a small fraction of his own salary. Joseph Bertrand had been Biot's deputy before succeeding him.

And while I am on the subject of the professors' salaries at the Collège, there is one little-known fact about them that I find amusing.

Comparisons of costs or salaries over several decades, let alone centuries, are notoriously misleading. This is due to inflation—a French franc or a pound sterling of 1914 having little in common with their contemporary equivalents—but also to changes in technology or in the costs of raw materials, which drastically modify the relative costs of various goods and services. This being so, it is remarkable that the number of haircuts (plain, not fancy) that a professor at the Collège could buy with his salary, has not changed by more than a few per cent since Napoleon. The explanation seems to be that both trades, the cutting of male hair and teaching at the Collège, are largely independent of changes in technology and in the cost of raw materials. No doubt other examples could be found but this is the one usually quoted.

The Collège is a self-governing body, ruled by the assembly of its professors, and chaired by one of them, who is elected by his peers, with the modest title of *Administrateur*. He is in charge of the government of the Collège between assemblies, and reports to the assembly when it meets, and to the Ministry of Education whenever necessary. According to the statutes, assemblies meet at least four times a year—more often in practice—and always on a Sunday afternoon. The reason for this unusual practice is clear: to prevent the Professors from begging off, because of other professional obligations. Many of my colleagues have objected to this rule and unsuccessful attempts have been made over the years to have it changed. I rather like it myself, because I find these meetings enjoyable. To meet one's friends and colleagues, to immerse oneself in a different world from one's own professional interests, to listen to talks which are always elegant, sometimes comprehensible, and usually of moderate length, to chip in within a debate, anxiously to follow the counting of the votes for the candidate one favours—all of it is so much more appealing than standing in line to see a movie. (An Oxford colleague asked me once how often we dined together, and when I said: 'Never', he exclaimed: 'What kind of college is it?')

The chairs are divided unofficially between Arts and Sciences or, as we say, *Scientifiques* and *Littéraires*. I say 'unofficially', because officially it is understood that all chairs deal with 'Sciences', which are classified into: *Sciences Mathématiques, Physiques et Naturelles*, (which are the *Scientifiques*); and all the others are subdivided into *Sciences Philosophiques et Sociologiques* and *Sciences Historiques, Philologiques, et Archéologiques*. (both of which are the *Littéraires*). At present nearly 40 per cent of the chairs in the Collège are *Scientifiques*.

Every election to a chair involves two votes, separated by a couple of months. The first vote deals with the choice of the subject and is the important one. This is because behind every subject hides a man, and when I say 'hides', I mean just the opposite; for it is before this first vote that the candidate writes up what is called his *notice*, which is an outline of his previous career, of his published work, and of his future plans for research. After mailing this *notice* to all the professors, the candidate is expected to visit them one by one. At the assembly, the vote for the choice of a subject is naturally preceded by reports from the professors who are proposing a particular subject, and by a discussion. There are usually two contending subjects, more rarely three, sometimes only one. Although the candidate who stands behind each subject has already been interviewed by each member of the assembly for an hour or so, the rule of not pronouncing his name is still enforced, as a small concession to tradition.

After the subject has been selected, the second vote, for which the candidate wears his beaver up, is a mere formality. During my twenty-five years at the Collège, where I must have voted in more than sixty elections, no candidate, whose subject had been rejected in the first vote, ever stood again as a candidate for the subject which had won. There is nothing against it in the Statutes, and when there is little difference between the contending subjects such a step is quite conceivable. It is simply not done; or rather it is not done any more, for it did happen in an election which took place shortly before mine.

I am getting back to my own candidacy now. A vacancy had been created in the summer of 1958 by the untimely death of Frédéric Joliot, and in the autumn I asked Francis Perrin whether he would be willing to propose me to the Collège for a chair of Nuclear Magnetism. He answered that he thought it preferable to propose Hans Halban (Hans von Halban before his naturalization) for a chair of Nuclear Physics. He explained that he had hopes of obtaining the creation of a new *chair credit* from the assembly for my nuclear magnetism—which involves an increase in the total number of chairs—whereas he did not believe that he could obtain it for Halban. In this manner he would get us both into the Collège.

This was flattering, but looked improbable to me. However, there was nothing I could do about it. Meanwhile he advised me to write up my *notice* and to start on my visits.

From my first visit to the *Administrateur*, the Professor of Spanish Literature, Marcel Bataillon, I realized how ambiguous my position was: I was a candidate for a vacancy which did not exist. But my *notice* had been printed and mailed, and I decided to carry on with my visits. To the professors who wished to know which vacancy I was a candidate for, I meekly replied that I did not know, but that I counted on M. Francis Perrin to create one. This bizarre situation had at least one advantage: a normal candidate had to get through all his visits before the first vote, within a couple of months; I could pursue mine at my own pace, since I had no deadline, and that for a very good reason. These visits were a pleasurable experience. All, except one (a *scientifique*), received me with great kindness. Among the *littéraires*, great scholars like Fernand Braudel and Georges Dumézil, students of civilizations of the past, Robert Minder, the Germanist, and Louis Robert, a world authority on Greek epigraphy, were those who left the most lasting impressions on me. It was a rare privilege to have interviews with people of such quality, whom I would have had little occasion to meet under the ordinary circumstances of life. And then, as I have said, I like to explain what I understand, and it was a challenge to try and make these people share my interests—so removed from their own—at least for the time of the interview. If I was less impressed by the *scientifiques* of the Collège, it was for the simple reason that they were the kind of people I was used to mingling with.

When the time came, Francis Perrin presented his project to the assembly, but for good measure asked for the creation of three new *chair credits*, rather than one. He gave as his reason the urgent need to reduce the imbalance between the number of scientific and literary chairs, in view of the progress of the sciences. It was a rash proposal, he was of course defeated, and I with him.

Meanwhile, a formidable opponent to Hans Halban's candidacy as Joliot's successor suddenly surfaced. His name was Leprince-Ringuet, and he was an important personality in the French physics establishment. Aged fifty-seven at the time, he was Professor of Physics and head of a fairly active laboratory at the Ecole Polytechnique, and a member of the French Académie des Sciences. A former coworker of Maurice, the Duc de Broglie, he was, with the other disciples of the noble Duc, a representative of a clan which was close to the tradition of the Catholic Church and of the moderate Right, and which in the French scientific establishment opposed the progressive Left, represented by the clan of the Joliots, of Francis Perrin, and of Pierre Auger. The confrontation of Halban and Leprince-Ringuet became perforce a confrontation of these two clans. The personality of Hans Halban—a rich cosmopolitan of Germanic origin, several times divorced, a French citizen through naturalization—

facing Leprince-Ringuet, gave this contest, which I was observing without passion but not without curiosity, a character in which physics played only a minor part.

What can one say of Leprince-Ringuet as a physicist? In the chapter 'In Search of Research' I said of Francis Perrin: 'Francis knows everything and understands everything, but what does he do?' I will not risk myself by touching on what Leprince-Ringuet knows of physics, and even less so on what he understands of it; but I will state unhesitatingly that he has *done* things for physics. This is how: Leprince-Ringuet is a profoundly modest man, but he is so in an unusual way, in what I might call the 'third degree'. He is fond of saying: 'I understand nothing about theory,' and this makes him modest in the first degree. However, in saying it he is not modest in the second degree, for naturally, considering his position, he fully expects that it will not be believed. It is like the old story, in which one Russian Jew says to another: 'You are telling me that you are going to Odessa to make me believe that you are in fact going to Kharkov, while I know perfectly well that you are indeed going to Odessa, and so why do you lie to me?' But with Leprince-Ringuet there is a third degree. He does not lie to himself, he *knows* that he understands nothing about theory and very little about physics in general, and he draws the right conclusions from it. He surrounds himself with young physicists, who are gifted and highly motivated, and he gives them the means to work and develop in peace. It never occurs to him to be jealous of them, because there is no conceivable competition between him and them. If by so doing he wins the reputation for himself of being a great scientist, does it really matter? For my part, I consider that by giving his coworkers—to cite but the most brilliant, Charles Peyrou, an inventive physicist who for many years was in charge of the bubble chambers at CERN, André Lagarrigue, a modest and brilliant man whose untimely death prevented him from reaping the award for his great discovery of neutral currents, Bernard Grégory who had been an outstanding Director General of CERN, Astier, a gifted and dedicated teacher—by giving them, I say, the means of their trade and a free hand, he earned himself a positive 'global balance-sheet' in French physics.

I shall now rapidly round off the story of this election. In the first contest for the selection of the subject, Halban stood behind 'nuclear physics' and Leprince-Ringuet behind 'high energy nuclear physics'. 'Nuclear physics' won by a narrow margin of one or two votes. Leprince-Ringuet decided to remain a candidate for the chair of 'Nuclear Physics', established by the first vote. One of the professors (the same one who had given me a more than chilly reception when I had visited him), who was away in the US at the time of the first vote, returned to lead an impassioned campaign on behalf of Leprince-Ringuet, and managed to reverse the slender majority of the first vote by the same margin. It was thus, by breaking an unwritten tradition, that Leprince-Ringuet became a professor at the Collège de France. Grégory, Lagarrigue, and, most of all, Astier carefully prepared his lectures and explained them to him.

And what about me? Everything went very smoothly. In 1959 the Chair of Arabic languages and Literature became vacant, Perrin proposed 'Nuclear Magnetism', no other subject was offered, and it was voted in, with a few abstentions from those who are against a single candidacy as a matter of principle. Whether is was my reputation, or the desire of Perrin's colleagues to make up to him for the two snubs inflicted during his former presentations, I cannot say; but I am inclined to think that there was a little of each. Unlike poor Halban, I met with no competition for the second vote.

Having described how one becomes a professor at the Collège, and before speaking about what I did while I was one, a few lines about the standing of this institution in France and abroad. Rightly or wrongly, it is regarded by the French intellectual establishment as the *ne plus ultra*, and it is the dream of every university professor to become part of it.

For the *scientifiques*, its reputation can be backed by some statistical data.

At the time of writing these lines, the Collège has thirty scientists, of which seven are Emeritus, or as we say, *Honoraire*. All but six of them are members of our Académie des Sciences, which, in contrast to the Royal Society, has only one hundred and twenty members. Thus 20 per cent of its members come from the Collège. It could be argued that these figures are less impressive than they seem, for the members of the Collège inside the Academy might possibly be 'pulling in' their colleagues from outside, through their votes—a phenomenon reminiscent of what is known in physics as Bose–Einstein Condensation. A statistic which is not subject to this objection is the proportion of College members in the list of foreign awards to French scientists.

The Royal Society has nine French 'Foreign Members', five of whom come from the Collège.

The US National Academy of Sciences has twenty-two French 'Foreign Associates', twelve of whom come from the Collège.

The American Academy of Arts and Sciences has four French mathematicians, two of whom come from the Collège, and four French physicists, two of whom come from the Collège.

Of the four French Nobel laureates, three belong to the Collège.

Of the five French Fields medallists (there is no Nobel Prize for mathematics), two belong to the Collège.

The four French physicists who, in the last ten years, have occupied the prestigious Lorentz Chair in Leyden, were all from the Collège.

I shall stop this anonymous pinning of medals on the lapels of the Collège's scientists here. No doubt more medals could be produced.

I cannot alas provide the same anonymous collection of medals for the *littéraires* of the Collège, for I do not know where *their* medals come from. The alternative is name-dropping, an exercise I do not wish to practice, and so I will ask my English-speaking reader to believe that our *littéraires* are very distinguished scholars indeed, and that he would recognize the names of many of them if I were to cite them.

Perhaps I should explain that the foregoing passage was not part of the French version, and that its only purpose was to give our English-speaking friends some idea of the place that the Collège de France occupies in our country, and to convince them that it is indeed the most prestigious college in France.

Our rulers have recognized the importance of the Collège in various ways. President Giscard d'Estaing honoured it with a visit in 1980 for the 450th anniversary of its foundation. The *Administrateur* had detailed a few of us to explain to the President, in five minutes each, what the main directions were of the studies that we were pursuing. I was not one of the chosen, but it will appear later in this book that more was in store for me. The President approved our teachings, but deplored that they were aimed at such a small minority. He suggested that our proud motto: *Docet Omnia*, be changed to *Docet Omnia Omnibus*, or 'Teaches all things to all people'. I was not displeased with myself for having been the only one to notice and to point out to my *littéraires* colleagues that the presidential *Omnibus* was going into the wrong direction: the correct formulation of the motto that he had suggested should have been *Docet Omnia Omnes*, in accordance with the immortal *Doceo pueros grammaticam*. We debated whether one should consult the presidential aides before correcting the typescript of the presidential talk, and concluded that it would be better policy to do so without making a fuss.

His successor, President Francois Mitterrand, also visited us in the eighties, and entrusted us with the task of preparing an ambitious document called *L'Enseignement du Futur*. My contribution to it was putting on the brakes in a few places. Thus I insisted on the fact that in elementary schools a minimum of discipline should be enforced—that it was a necessary condition, when assembling some twenty to thirty children in a closed space, for some length of time, and for tasks that required some effort and concentration on their part. Most of my distinguished colleagues had never taught in elementary schools; I pointed out to them that the idea of children keeping quiet with good teachers and being boisterous with boring ones was not confirmed by facts; *my* pupils had behaved themselves, but whether because of the quality of my teaching or of the discipline I enforced, I could not say. There were other ideas, such as the claim that familiarity with computers would be an element of the culture of the future. I claimed that using computers was rapidly coming to the same level as driving a car, if not yet the same as watching television.

What amused me most was the insistence of my colleagues on the necessity of an unceasing fight against the Hydra of Elitism. I may have contributed to making this document a little less unrealistic than its first draft, but anyway, where is this document now, four years later?

When I left the College in October 1985, I was leaving four physicists behind: Pierre-Gilles de Gennes, Claude Cohen-Tannoudji, Philippe Nozières, and Marcel Froissart. I had been instrumental in the election of all of them and the actual *rapporteur* for two. I would like to say a few words about them.

All four are in their fifties, the first three are *Normaliens*, the fourth *Polytechnicien*, all four have impressive records.

I cannot conceal that for me, Pierre-Gilles is *primus inter pares* in this quartet. It is out of the question here to summarize the long reports which I devoted to his work on behalf of the Collège and of the Académie des Sciences. He holds the Chair of Condensed Matter, but he is a conqueror who does not dally over his conquests. During the last thirty years there are few fields of condensed matter physics which he has not tackled, renewed, and then left for a group of disciples, experimentalists or theoreticians, to plough more deeply the furrow which he had traced. An American physicist wrote once that de Gennes is our best present-day approximation to Landau. I would add: without the prickles, and with the ability to talk to experimentalists. The clarity of his lectures is sometimes deceptive: 'intuitive' approximations are often the product of profound and subtle reflections and far less obvious than he would have his audiences believe. To carry on his multiple activities this strenuous worker long ago jettisoned all 'unessential' obligations: attendance at the Collège assemblies is one.

Claude Cohen-Tannoudji originated in the talent breeding-ground of the Brossel laboratory, where he is still working. The report for his chair was the one which gave me most work. One would have expected the opposite: the subject I had proposed on his behalf: 'Atomic and Molecular Physics', was exactly the title of the chair vacated by his predecessor, Francis Perrin. The problem was to show that there was in fact a complete turn-around. Perrin's laboratory had become a nebula, with particle physics its main theme, and atomic and molecular physics fallen into neglect. I had to show that the 'new' atomic and molecular physics, born from the work of Kastler and Brossel, and modified in depth through the ideas and the experiments of Claude, had nothing to do with its moribund predecessor. I liked my presentation so much that I included it in my *Reflections*. Claude Cohen-Tannoudji is not only a brilliant physicist whose work on 'dressed' atoms is known all over the world; he is also a marvellous teacher. He scorns the ingenious conjuring tricks that Pierre-Gilles sometimes indulges in, plays fair with his students, and offers them a firm and helpful hand whenever it is needed.

I know Philippe Nozières a little less than the other two because for many years he was a professor in Grenoble. I had tried to attract him to the College some ten years earlier, but at the time did not find sufficient support for it among some of my colleagues. In fact his Chair of Statistical Mechanics was created in 1983, in anticipation of my departure, which was to take place two years later.

Marcel Froissart succeeded Leprince-Ringuet in 1973. I sincerely believe that Froissart had genius, a word I don't use lightly, perhaps more of it than the other three—to the extent that such things can be quantified. In the Service de Physique Théorique at Saclay, where he made his start before coming to the Collège, exceptionally gifted people were no exception; but no one was of the calibre of Froissart. After his early publications, which made him known the world over, one thought of him as another Dyson or another Schwinger; but he seems to have lost interest in that kind of work. Nowadays, from what I hear, Froissart seems to be content to govern, with great competence, the large laboratory which he inherited from Leprince-Ringuet.

I would now like to say a few words about the four *Administrateurs* I have known at the Collège.

The first, whom I found upon my arrival and who 'reigned' from 1955 till 1965 was, as I said, the Spanish scholar, Marcel Bataillon. He was a very handsome man; his noble face, crowned with white hair, his bearing, the slightly distant courtesy of his manner, his slow and deliberate delivery, all made me think of a Spanish grandee. He was not devoid of a cool sense of humour, as witnessed by the following incident: in the second vote for the election of the philosopher Jean Hyppolite, his *rapporteur* spoke far more of Hegel than of Hyppolite, and I thought it natural to write Hegel's name on the ballot paper. When Marcel Bataillon saw the paper with Hegel's name, he said gravely: 'I have not been informed within the prescribed time limit by the person whose name is on this ballot of his intention to be a candidate, and the ballot must be regarded as invalid.'

A Spanish grandee, that is also what he was in his relations with the faceless divinity which presided over our destinies—the Ministry of Education. At an assembly, he displayed astonishment that a written request for a subsidy to one of the Collège laboratories had remained unanswered after two months. The *scientifiques*, who knew full well that in order to tear a pound of flesh from the Ministry, one had to go there in person and more than once, and then ring them up again and again, were amused by so much innocence. The helplessness of some *Administrateurs littéraires* faced with requests from the *scientifiques* took various forms. A colleague, the endocrinologist Robert Courrier, told me how, many years ago, the *Administrateur* Joseph Bédier, a famous mediaevalist, had responded to a request for twenty-four thermometers: 'My dear colleague, do you really need them all? Even if you were to put two in each room of your laboratory, you would still have twice as many as you need.'

The embryologist Etienne Wolff, who succeeded him from 1966 till 1974, was not likely to ask such a question. He was a prince of teratology, who created monsters and chimaeras in his laboratory. At first sight he appeared to be a brusque and abrupt authoritarian, but he improved with a closer acquaintance, for behind this stern manner he hid a great kindness and timidity. It was his bad luck to find himself at the helm of the Collège during the student unrest of 1968, and I think that he was very unhappy during this period. I also think that it was the good fortune of the Collège that the pseudo-revolutionaries of the Latin Quarter had probably never heard of its existence.

His successor from 1974 till 1980, the good-natured and clever Alain Horeau, a specialist in the chemistry of hormones, had no equal in the task of solving any delicate problems of laboratory space or staff which might arise between his colleagues, or of negotiating, efficiently and good-humouredly, with the civil servants of the Ministry or the representatives of the Unions. He imparted to me once that one of the goals of his laboratory was to perfect the contraceptive pill. 'How many children do you think I have?' he asked me. 'Six.' 'Not exactly—twelve.' I refrained from asking him whether his motto was: 'Back to the drawing board!' I have forgotten the number of his grandchildren, and it is just as well for it will have changed before I am through with all my stories. As for Mme Horeau, her elegant and slim figure provokes incredulous admiration when she reveals the number of her children.

Our present *Administrateur* since 1980, Yves Laporte, is a distinguished neurophysiologist. Tall, elegant, stern-looking except when a charming smile lights up his face, he is constantly engaged in improving the comfort and the working conditions of his colleagues, including, I hasten to add, the Emeritus ones, as well as those of all the Collège staff; and he is extraordinarily efficient.

Is it because he is the only one of my four *Administrateurs* who came into this world, as well as into the Collège, a few years later than I, rather than earlier, like the other three; is it because we share a liking for Shakespeare; is it for any other reason? I do not know; but always I had the feeling during our assemblies of an understanding, not to say of a certain complicity, with him, which I had not felt to the same degree with his predecessors.

I said at the beginning of this chapter that I had been a candidate for the Collège because I wanted to teach. It is the truth, but it is not the whole truth. I have also said more than once that the CEA was a strongly structured and authoritarian strucutre. 'A day may come,' I thought, 'when I will have to say no to my masters.' A chair at the Collège de France would then be the bulwark from which I would say it. This day did happen, but more than ten years later, and I will speak of it in due course.

I have said nothing so far about my lectures. They cannot be separated from the activity of my laboratory, and even less so from work done elsewhere.

Among physicists—as in other fields, I imagine—some are specialists, who know everything, but about next to nothing; and some are generalists who know next to nothing, but about everything. Of the specialist, one sometimes says that what he does not know about his subject is not worth knowing; and sometimes, that what he *does* know is not worth knowing either. There is also Hans Bethe, who knows just about everything about everything; and there is a fourth category I need not describe. I prefer to speak of a 'horizontal' or 'vertical' physicist, as he would appear on a graph, where the subjects are plotted along the x axis and the extent of his knowledge of them along the y axis. With the possible exception of nuclear magnetism, I consider myself 'horizontal'. For that I see four or five reasons.

To start with, I am a late beginner, who for too many years was reduced to 'educating himself'—that is reading what others had written on many subjects, instead of writing things for others to read on a single subject.

There are also my past responsibilities within the CEA, which became more and more extensive with time. I could not bring myself to exercise my authority over a fellow physicist without attempting to understand what he was doing. Sometimes, with luck, his physics became integrated with mine. I shall come back to this.

There are also my twenty-five years as a professor at the Collège. According to the statutes, a professor is expected to report the results of his researches in his lectures, and his discoveries over the previous year. I think that with respect to discoveries, two lectures would have been ample during the good years; and as for the description of the researches carried out in my lab, a goodly part of my modest audience was made up of my coworkers from this same lab; and I did not feel like expounding to them, *ex cathedra*, things we had already discussed in detail in the lab.

Therefore I also had to lecture on something else, and it was not simple. The main difference between a course at university and at the Collège is that at university the audience changes, while the teaching remains very much the same, whereas at the Collège the audience, to a large extent, remains the same and the course *has* to change. It is a requirement of the statutes, though it would be easy to get around it by changing the title of the course. But you cannot get around the fact that listeners are free to come or not to come, and that if one wishes to keep them, and even more importantly, to keep one's self-respect, the course itself *must* change.

During my first years at the Collège I had plenty of things to say about nuclear magnetism, because of a sizeable backlog, and I far exceeded the yearly limits prescribed by regulations, which for chairs with laboratories, as mine was, are of nine lectures, and nine seminars under the professor's direction. I would advise the university professor who finds this a very light teaching load, to try and give a new course each year for twenty-five years; he would see how much effort it takes. The first year, full of juvenile enthusiasm (after all, I was only forty-five) I gave twenty-seven lectures and supervised some fifteen seminars; but, later on, this flow ran less exuberantly and seldom exceeded the prescribed limits. (I discovered that my scientific colleagues, young or old, did not exceed them either).

I had to look for new subjects—new to me, that is. The specialization which prevails today in science prevents listeners from attending lectures on subjects which are even slightly removed from their own interests. A delicate problem of balance then faces the Collège professor who lectures on a subject which is not part of his own research: it is desirable that his would-be listeners should be acquainted with the subject, and possibly even be working on it themselves, for otherwise they will not bother to come to the lectures; but it is not so desirable that they should know much more of the subject than the professor, for the unfortunate is then in great danger of losing face. The only way for the neophyte (the professor) to interest the specialists (the audience) is through a novel presentation of the subject, to which they are not accustomed. Sometimes I have succeeded in this. Even more importantly, the subject of the course should also be of interest to the professor himself. During the twenty-three courses that I gave at the Collège (I went twice on sabbaticals), hardly more than half have been devoted to nuclear magnetism proper.

I sometimes hear that for the Collège, the obligation to teach is a thing of the past, which interferes with the professor's research; and that he should be freed from this load, as is the case in some other great research institutions. In my opinion, this is utterly wrong: the obligation to maintain a course of teaching which is capable of interesting research workers, be they beginners or senior workers, is the best antidote for ossification and for sloth. It is so easy to do nothing when one has arrived at a certain level of the scientific hierarchy and one is 'guiding' the research of others. The hour of truth comes when facing an audience in a lecture room, watching for yawning mouths or glassy eyes—an unsufferable insult to one's ego.

All this is to say, at some length I am afraid, that my teaching helped to make me 'horizontal'.

Another factor which pushed me towards the same orientation ('horizontal'), was the very nature of nuclear magnetism, which, by itself or through its applications, is in contact with an incredible number of other sciences: all of physics of condensed matter, statistical mechanics, nuclear physics and elementary particles physics, very low temperatures, chemistry, biology and today, through NMR imaging, clinical medicine. All this contributes to turn the specialist in nuclear magnetism into the generalist whom in my maiden lecture I had pompously called 'a Renaissance man, enlightened in everything'.

And last but not least, I have always had—in physics I mean—a taste for pretty things, whether they belonged to me or not.

*Polarized beams and targets

The clearest example of symbiosis between my physics and that of others is the subject of polarized beams and targets. I worked on this in close contact with my 'subordinate', the nuclear physicist Jacques Thirion, and later with CERN, the great international centre for high energy particle physics.

What is the problem? As I explained in a previous chapter, in nuclear physics one shoots accelerated particles at a target, and one studies the collision between an incoming particle and one of the particles of the target. Anyone who has watched a game of billiards, knows that if a spin has been put on the ball with the cue, the result of the collision with the target ball will be changed. A large number of atomic nuclei, protons and deuterons in particular, possess an intrinsic spin; and the result of the collision of one of these particles with the target depends appreciably on the orientation of its spin with respect to the direction of the incoming beam. The particle beams which are currently used are unpolarized, meaning that their spins are oriented at random, and what is observed in the collisions is an average over all the orientations. There is a loss of information in this procedure, and it is desirable to operate on polarized beams, where the spins of the incoming particles all have the same, well-defined orientation.

In the early sixties I had imagined an original method for producing polarized beams, based on concepts which were familiar to me: the use of RF fields and of my old friend, the hyperfine structure. This structure, due to a coupling between the nuclear magnetic moment and a much stronger electronic moment, provides a handle by which one can act on the large electronic moment, thus indirectly on the small nuclear moment. It is the same philosophy, if not the same method, that we saw in DNP in solids, using the 'solid effect', where the polarization of electronic spins is transferred to nuclear spins. As a result of our collaboration, a source of polarized proton beams and later of polarized deuterons had been successfully built by Thirion's physicists.

But to apply this polarized source successfully to nuclear physics, we had to marry it to another device, the polarized target. In a billiard collision it is relatively easy to put a spin on the ball one strikes with the cue, but it seems more difficult to imagine, and billiards rules are silent on this point, how to put a spin on the target ball. In our laboratory we called this second and more difficult part of the experiment, 'the Princess Margaret part', alluding to our friend Arnie's story about the plans of a Jewish matchmaker to wed Princess Margaret to a young orthodox Jew.

Having at last succeeded in convincing the prospective bridegroom and his family to accept the match, he wipes his brow and exclaims: 'Half the job is done!'

We had mastered the principle of the polarized target several years earlier: it was the 'solid effect'. But the difficult technological problem of constructing an 'operational' target remained.

This target had to let low-energy protons (10 to 20 MeV) in and out, and therefore to be extremely thin (0.1 mm of thickness); to be surrounded with an RF coil which measured the proton polarization; and to be irradiated with millimetric microwaves within a microwave cavity, which was cooled to 1 K within a cryostat, itself placed in a magnetic field of two Teslas produced by a large magnet. Without the ingenious gifts of our cryogenic engineer Pierre Roubeau, a former naval officer, and the skill of his assistant Coustham, I do not know how we would have managed. It all worked at last, and in 1962 Thirion's physicists observed the first scattering of polarized protons on a polarized target, a world première; the target was the one built by Roubeau, and beam and target had been polarized by my method.

Anxious to find clients for our product, I proposed our technique of polarized proton targets to several French nuclear physicists. They seemed interested, but they all imagined some twisted, sophisticated experiments which would have been difficult to carry out, even in the absence of the constraints related to the polarization of the target. I summed up their attitude in a little story: in a circus, a tightrope walker walks his rope twenty metres above the ground, carrying a child on his shoulders and a petrol lamp on his head, and simultaneously plays the Kreutzer sonata (the piano remains presumably on the ground). A man in the audience says disdainfully: 'Heifetz he ain't' (I am afraid this is a New York story). Still, these experiments were continued at Saclay and taken up elsewhere, for several years.

From low energy nuclear physics we moved on to polarized targets for high energy particle physics, in which we collaborated closely with the physicists of CERN. The difficulties there were diametrically opposite. Instead of the ultra thin targets we had been producing before, our new 'customers' wanted targets which were as big as possible. They were takers for anything up to a litre, that is of a volume a million times larger than our first target. In a sense it was even easier, provided that the proper equipment, electronic, cryogenic, magnetic, and mechanical, was available—of which CERN provided a fraction. Another tricky problem was a necessary increase in the proportion of 'free' protons, that is, not embedded in other nuclei, which led to a search for the best hydrogeneous target materials. Finally, an increase in the rate of growth of the polarization and in the speed of its reversal, an important requirement, could be reached through a suitable choice of paramagnetic impurities, which were most apt to acquit themselves of 'King Solomon's' duties. From my lab, Michel Borghini, assisted by Charles Ryter, our best specialist in the techniques of ESR, and naturally our cryogenics wizard, Pierre Roubeau, with a little troupe of technicians, were those responsible for our contact with the 'Big Science' of CERN.

At the same time, the theory of dynamic nuclear polarization in solids was undergoing new developments. It appeared that when the ESR lines of the paramagnetic impurities were too broad, the simple-minded theory of the 'solid effect' could not be applied, and a far more sophisticated theory had to be worked out. The pioneers of this theory, which is too complicated to be explained here, were two Soviet physicists, Provotorov and Buishvilli, followed on the Western side by Solomon, Borghini, Maurice Goldman and myself, and many others.

Other effects, which I mention for the sake of completeness, such as the 'phonon bottleneck', well-known in ESR relaxation, were adding more complexity to the theory. In a long monograph published in 1982, which I wrote with Maurice Goldman for the Oxford University Press, we gave a very complete, and, it must be said, rather forbidding description of the theory of DNP.

For some fifteen years high energy physicists, headed by Owen Chamberlain, who had won the Nobel Prize in 1959 for the discovery of the antiproton, showed great interest in polarized targets. Even Carlo Rubbia, who won the 1984 Nobel Prize for the discovery of the bosons W and Z, briefly collaborated with us in the sixties, before moving on towards other horizons.

An active collaboration began between physicists of resonance and low temperatures, and particle physicists. There was everything to separate them from us—first and foremost the fantastic energy gap of *fifteen* orders of magnitude. In spite of that, several international conferences were organized together: at Saclay, Berkeley, Chicago, Harwell, Brookhaven, Geneva, Lausanne, etc. The two themes were: 'Polarized targets: how?' which was our cue, and 'Polarized targets, why?', which was developed by the particle physicists. It was a meeting of two cultures, Big Science and Little Science.

Chamberlain was fond of saying that polarized targets were a tool comparable to the bubble chamber, which had won a Nobel Prize for Donald Glaser in 1960. In the context of such talk, and of such widespread interest in an idea and an achievement which were far more sophisticated than the bubble chamber, although far less important for physics, as it turned out in the end—is it so surprising that I, too, sometimes dreamed of Father Christmas, I mean Father Nobel?

In my dreams, I was not unwilling to share my glory with my colleague and friendly rival, Carson Jeffries from Berkeley, who, through a route different from mine, had also arrived at the idea and the realization of polarized targets. Shall I avow that in these dreams of mine, I may even have entertained sly hopes based on the Berkeley people's well-known drive in propelling their candidate toward the Nobel, which then would have to be shared with me.

(A short parenthesis: when CERN was beginning to take an interest in polarized targets, there was a faction there which favoured importing them from Berkeley. To convince them to use ours, I told them the story of the American soldier, who was stationed in Australia during the war in the Pacific. His girl friend, who heard rumours of his being unfaithful to her, wrote to him: 'These Australian girls, what is it they got that I haven't got?' 'Nothing, darling,' he wrote back, 'but they got it here.')

Nothing came of these dreams of glory, and for a very simple reason. Chamberlain, and other high energy physicists who shared his opinion, were mistaken. Some interesting results did come out of polarized targets, but nothing fundamental, comparable in any way to those of the bubble chamber. At present polarized targets have almost been abandoned, except by a few enthusiasts who fight a rearguard action and announce unexplained results. And anyway, as I have explained in an earlier chapter, interest has now shifted from *all* fixed targets, polarized or not, towards colliding beams. I am the inventor of a cute device which did not sell well, because it turned out that the market did not really need it, that's all. Anyway the hardware and the plumbing connected with the trade of large polarized targets had begun to bore me to death, long before their limited importance for particle physics had clearly appeared. For my beloved daughter, dynamic nuclear polarization in solids, I had other bridegrooms in mind, of whom later.

With respect to the elusive Nobel Prize, I like to tell my colleagues the following little story: 'Mother used to say to me: "Everybody gets the Nobel prize these days; what are you waiting for?" to which I replied: "I am not Jean-Paul Sartre; when I turn down the Nobel Prize, nobody hears about it."' A doubly apocryphal story: those who have read what I have said of my mother in this book will know that such a remark, coming from her, is unthinkable. And also, Sartre had indulged in his highly publicized refusal of the Nobel Prize two years after my mother's death.

It is interesting to note that when Dirac was awarded the Nobel Prize in 1933, he wanted to refuse it because of the publicity which came with it. Rutherford persuaded him to accept by pointing out that a refusal would bring even more publicity. Sartre was not deterred by such thoughts.

Recoilless nuclei

A field of physics in which my role has been very small, but in which I took a great interest at the start, is the recoilless emission and absorption of gamma-rays by nuclei—or as it is usually called, after its discoverer, the Mössbauer effect. This is its principle.

A nucleus A can pass from an excited state $|e\rangle$ to a ground state $|g\rangle$ by emitting a gamma-ray of energy E. A nucleus B in its ground state $|g\rangle$, can in principle absorb this gamma and rise to its excited state $|e\rangle$. This is the phenomenon of resonant absorption, which is well known in optics. There is however a difficulty in the case of nuclei. During the emission, an energy R is taken up by the recoil of the source nucleus, which makes up for the momentum taken up by the emitted gamma. This recoil energy is borrowed from the gamma, which thus carries away a smaller energy: $E'=(E-R)$. The same argument shows that, during the absorption, the target nucleus, in order to be raised to its excited state, will need an energy $E''=(E+R)$. There is a mismatch of 2R between what is needed and what is available for the resonant absorption. Resonant absorption can thus only take place if the levels are sufficiently broad, and the energy of the gamma sufficiently spread out, to take up the mismatch 2R. This is usually the case for optical transitions, but not for nuclei, where the energy levels are far too narrow.

For example, for the nucleus ^{57}Fe, its much studied transition of energy 14.4 keV, has a radiation width Δ of 4.6×10^{-9} eV, whereas the nuclear recoil energy $R \approx 2 \times 10^{-3}$ eV is six orders of magnitude larger.

All this had been known for a long time and nuclear physicists had been trying to broaden the width of the transition artificially by conveying to the nuclei a kinetic energy comparable to 2R. This was done by raising the temperature of the source and/or of the absorber. A British physicist, Philip Moon, even tried to give the source nucleus an extra energy 2R by placing the source at the circumference of a fast rotating wheel, as if he had been launching the gamma with a sling.

In the late fifties, a young German graduate student, Rudolf Mössbauer, who worked with Professor Maier-Leibnitz, did an experiment where he *lowered* the temperature of the source (or of the absorber, I forget which) of a radioactive isotope ^{191}Ir, instead of raising it like everybody else. He saw that the absorption, instead of going down, as was expected, went up. His immense merit was not only to have *observed* the phenomenon, but to have found its *explanation*, which had actually been known, and even published, for a long time. Only the incredible blindness of all concerned had hitherto kept it out of sight.

Everybody was reasoning as if the radioactive atoms were part of a gas and did not interact with their surroundings. But, in a *solid*, if the recoil energy R is not large compared to the vibration energy of the atoms in the solid (measured by its so-called Debye frequency), it is the *whole* sample, rather than a single nucleus, which will recoil to take up the momentum of the outgoing gamma, with an energy R' which is completely negligible. The same argument applies to the absorber. The effect of lowering the temperature in Mössbauer's experiment was to prevent the recoil of the sample from being accompanied by the emission or absorption of quanta of thermal vibrations, or phonons, which could blur an otherwise fantastically sharp, resonant absorption.

The beauty of the thing is that in 1939, nearly twenty years earlier, Willis Lamb had given a complete theory of this effect—not for gammas, it is true, but for neutrons; but the principle was the same. More beautiful yet, Moon, the man with the sling, had consulted Rudolf Peierls on resonant nuclear absorption, and Peierls, who knew of Lamb's paper, had recommended it to Moon. As for Willis Lamb himself, I told him once, to tease him good-humouredly: 'You missed a Nobel there' (he had been awarded one, a few years earlier, for a discovery called the 'Lamb shift', which had been at the origin of the renewal of quantum electrodynamics after the war); but he was rather bitter about it and would not forgive himself for having missed it.

Two American physicists repeated Mössbauer's experiment, confirmed his results, and published it in *Physical Review Letters*, which at last brought Mössbauer's discovery to the attention of all, including myself. The remarkable thing is that, instead of trying it on another nucleus, and there are many for which the effect is far more spectacular than for ^{191}Ir, they repeated it on the *same* nucleus. The reason is simple: they did not believe Mössbauer's results, and wanted to disprove them (*falsify*, as Karl Popper would say).

The incredible narrowness of the Mössbauer lines, as they were thereafter called, has led to an unprecedented method for sweeping through them. It is known that, through what is called the Doppler effect, the frequency of a source moving toward the absorber with a velocity v is *seen* by the absorber as shifted in relative value by (v/c), where c is the velocity of light. The natural width of a Mössbauer line in, say, ^{57}Fe, is $2\Delta \approx 10^{-9}$ eV; and its relative width—$X = (2\Delta/\Omega)$, where $\Omega = 14.4$ keV is the energy of the transition—is: $X \approx 7 \times 10^{-13}$! It follows that the relative source-absorber velocity necessary to sweep through the line is: $v = cX = 3 \times 10^{10} \times 7 \times 10^{-13} \approx 0.02$ cm s^{-1}. In practice, crystal imperfections, spin–spin interactions within the sample, and a finite thickness of both source and absorber will increase the width somewhat, and a figure of, say, 2×10^{-12} for the relative width of a Mössbauer line in ^{57}Fe is more realistic.

Anyway, the new facilities related to the narrowness of the Mössbauer lines brought these studies straight into the realm of what are known as table-top experiments.

As soon as I heard about this effect I started thinking about it, and devoted the first thirteen lectures of my course at the Collège de France to it. I wrote it up, and it was published by an American publisher as a booklet which, I am told, is still occasionally used today.

The many nuclear physicists who had come to my lectures took some time to realize that the Mössbauer spectroscopy was not for them, but for solid state physicists.

In my own laboratory Solomon took a few days, using bits and pieces of equipment borrowed here and there, to put an apparatus together with which he was able to observe the spectra of a certain number of iron compounds. My knowledge of the theory of hyperfine structure helped him in interpreting his results. Independently from anyone else he discovered an overall shift of the spectra between various iron compounds, which I interpreted for him as an isomeric shift, analogous to the isotopic shift observed in atomic spectra, and caused by the difference between the nuclear radii in the ground and the excited states of the nucleus.

Apart from my lectures, my old familiarity with the hyperfine structure of the iron group enabled me to show that the sign attributed in scientific literature to the quadrupole moment of ^{57}Fe, in its first excited state, was incorrect.

Solomon and I soon got tired of a field which looked overcrowded. My main contribution to it was to persuade a young and gifted physicist at Saclay, Pierre Imbert, who was looking for a problem, to work in it. Today his Mössbauer laboratory is one of the best in the world.*

*The red shift

To conclude, I wish briefly to tell the story of the measurement, by means of the Mössbauer effect, of what is known as the 'red shift'. The red shift is a displacement of the frequency of an electromagnetic radiation in a gravitational field; it was predicted by Einstein, and first observed by Eddington during an eclipse of the Sun in 1919. The extraordinary sharpness of the Mössbauer lines provided the first opportunity for observing this effect in a laboratory experiment.

The principle is extremely simple. Imagine an absorber, placed at a height h below the source, in the Earth's gravitation field. To use an oversimple image, the energy of a gamma photon, 'falling' from the source onto the absorber, will be increased in relative value by (gh/c^2) when it reaches the absorber. It is actually a 'blue shift' rather than a red shift; to make it red, the positions of the source and the absorber should be interchanged. For a height of 10 metres, the shift is $\approx 10^{-15}$, that is, at most, *one part in a thousand* of the Mössbauer width in ^{57}Fe.*

Robert Pound, who was the first to propose this very difficult experiment, was also the only one to carry it out successfully. I understand that he has written a detailed story of it, which I hope he will publish.

But I would like to say a few words about a less successful attempt, because I think it makes a good story. I forget who told it to me. I am inclined to think that it was Walter Marshall, Lord Marshall now, but I will not swear to it.

A group from Harwell had published something in *Physical Review Letters*, but also publicized it in the press and on the radio, which was meant to be the first observation of the red shift by means of the Mössbauer effect. The aim of that publicity was to restore the fortunes of Harwell somewhat, as they were under heavy pressure at the time to show results. This gave rise to what I have called the first Josephson effect.

Brian Josephson, a Cambridge undergraduate, heard about this remarkable observation of the red shift, and asked himself a few questions. After discussing it with his tutor, he communicated the result of his cogitations to the Harwell physicists. They were panic-stricken, and with good reason. Josephson had shown by a very simple argument that a difference in temperature of one degree between source and absorber caused a frequency shift comparable to the red shift they claimed to have measured. The unfortunate Harwellians had never thought of it, and had not bothered to control the temperature difference between source and absorber. They rushed to the phone, called Josephson's college, and asked for Dr Josephson. 'There is no Dr Josephson here' said the porter. 'Well, he may not be a doctor.' 'We have an undergraduate by that name.' 'Would you be so kind as to put him on?' 'Sorry, the undergraduates are not allowed to take calls through the Lodge,' and the porter hung up. Harwell physicists and officials piled into official cars and rushed from Harwell to Cambridge, where they were able to interview Josephson. The faces were redder than the shift.

Speaking of piling into cars, if I cannot vouch for Walter Marshall having been my informant on the Josephson–Harwell story, I am positive about another statement he made. It happened in Jerusalem, when five people including him and me were riding in a Volkswagen. I had to sit on his lap, the opposite being unthinkable, as anyone who had seen Walter Marshall would know. Thereupon he said: 'This is the first time that I have had a *full* professor sitting on my lap.'

What about Josephson? He appeared at the Mössbauer conference that I organized in Saclay in 1961, where he was one of the guests of honour— a very young man, who looked almost like a child, and would not say a word. Everyone knows that he soon became famous through his discovery in the field of superconductivity, which brought him a Nobel Prize in 1973. Not everyone knows that his ideas took an unexpected turn toward fields like parapsychology and telekinesis, which grieves his admirers and enchants the cranks and the crooks.

At our Mössbauer conference we saw the Swedish physicist, Ivar Waller, who was for many years the Swedish Academy's roving ambassador, always on the look-out for potential Nobel Prize winners. I had a lengthy interview with him, in which I explained to him why I thought that Mössbauer was one of them. I was certainly not the only one to think so, since Mössbauer got the prize that same year at the age of thirty-two.

I remember hearing someone speak of the 'tragedy of getting the Nobel too young'. 'Let us thank our good fortunes for having been spared this tragedy' I said. However, in spite of its ludicrous character, there is some truth in this remark. Too often, young Nobel laureates dry out, either because they are caught up in the whirlpool of honours and responsibilities, or because they neglect their former research and wear themselves out looking for the 'second' great discovery. Such may have been the case with Josephson. Such was not the case with Mössbauer. His glory did not turn his head. While accepting wider responsibilities (he had been one of the first directors of the ILL, that is the Institute 'Langevin–von Laue', a French, German, and British institution, based on a high-flux reactor in Grenoble), for many years he continued actively and intelligently to study the applications and developments of . . . the Mössbauer effect, before moving recently to other fields.

Let me come back for a moment to his discovery. Mössbauer's *discovery* undoubtedly deserved the Nobel award. That is what it is given for—discoveries. After nearly thirty years I am still convinced of it, which is more than I can say about a few other discoveries. But what had played an essential part in the importance of this discovery was the existence of the particular radioactive isotope ^{57}Fe. Everything in this isotope, from its isotopic abundance, to the remarkable features of its radioactivity, and last but certainly not least, to the fact that it was an *iron* isotope, was made to measure for its becoming a choice tool in chemistry, metallurgy, and magnetism. This isotope was not the one with which Mössbauer had discovered his effect. Its existence had been a remarkable piece of luck. So what? It is sometimes said that the Nobel Prize is a lottery, and in a certain sense it is true. But, as in all lotteries, you cannot win unless you have a ticket; and not so many have one. Mössbauer did.

Two little stories about the ILL to round it off.

Once when I visited the ILL, Mössbauer, wishing to please me, had assembled those of his coworkers who had an interest in magnetic resonance, and had them show me what they were doing. At the end of the visit he asked me whether it had been interesting. I replied with the apocryphal pronouncement of the Lord Chamberlain on the morality of London theatres: 'Why should I go to the theatre to see adultery, rape and incest? I can get it all at home.'

The other story is also about the ILL and about Germans, but without Mössbauer. At the beginnings of the ILL, of which I was one of the Founding Fathers, there was once a meeting of officials and engineers from France and Germany (the British as usual showed up later) with simultaneous translation. An administrative director from the CEA, who found that there were far too many leaders in the German plans for the reactor said: 'What kind of a Mexican army is that?' '*Welche Mexikanische*

Wehrmacht, warum Mexikanische Wehrmacht?' was the outcry heard
from the Germans.

The magic crystal

*In the field of dynamic nuclear polarization there is one amusing little
thing which I discovered during a stay in Oxford in the winter of
1962–1963, which is the method of the 'rotating crystal'. It works as
follows: within a magnetic field, you rapidly rotate a crystal immersed in
liquid helium. After a while you observe that the polarization of the nuclei
present in the crystal, say, protons, has increased by a factor of one
hundred or more with respect to its thermal equilibrium value. Surprising,
isn't it? How does it work? Elementary: the crystal has been doped with
very anisotropic electronic impurities. When the magnetic field is along a
certain crystalline axis A, their resonance frequency Ω is comparable to
that of a free electron, that is three orders of magnitude higher than that
of the proton. Thanks to their fast relaxation, these impurities quickly
acquire a thermal equilibrium polarization, which is also three orders of
magnitude greater than that of the protons. Along a certain axis B,
orthogonal to A, their resonant frequency is zero (in the rare earth group
there are a few paramagnetic ions of that type). If the crystal (or the field)
is rotated from A to B, there will be an intermediate position, actually very
close to B, where the resonance frequency of the impurity matches that of
the proton, and energy conserving flip-flops between their spins can take
place, equalizing their polarizations. If the spins of the electrons and
protons were in equal numbers, a single rotation would polarize the
protons appreciably. However, since the electrons are in a small minority,
they are greatly depolarized and the protons just a little polarized, by one
passage in B. One brings back the crystal to position A, where the electrons
are repolarized, and one starts again. A favourable circumstance is that
the electronic relaxation is very fast in position A, where the electrons are
uncoupled from the protons and get their polarization, and much slower
near the B axis, where they share their polarization with the protons. The
whole thing works like a pump.

Nevile Robinson, a physicist from the Clarendon who is even better
with his hands than Solomon, took a couple of days, using a toy electric
motor, to build a contraption which was capable of testing the principle,
and with which we did observe a proton polarization enhancement by a
few units. We decided to defer publication until a less rustic device could
give a much more important enhancement. But a physicist from Berkeley,
a coworker of my friendly rival Carson Jeffries, was visiting the Clarendon
at the time. When we told him of our gadget (to tell the truth, we spoke
about it in the Clarendon to anyone who was willing to listen), he said
that he had just received a letter from Jeffries, who had had the same idea.

He had not tested it yet, but he had sent a letter describing the principle, to the editor of *Cryogenics*, a low temperatures journal. There was not a minute to lose. Fortunately the editor of *Cryogenics* was the low temperatures specialist, Kurt Mendelssohn, whose office was next door in the Clarendon. I wrote up our letter the same day and took it to Mendelssohn, who published it in the same issue of *Cryogenics* as that of Jeffries.

Later, large proton polarizations (up to 80 per cent) were obtained by a former student of Jeffries, who used a little turbine to rotate the crystal more rapidly. The main advantage of the 'rotating crystal' method over the 'solid effect' was that, not being a resonant method, it did not require a very homogeneous field. This was an advantage in the eyes of high energy physicists who used polarized targets, but it was far outweighed by the impossibility of reversing the polarization at will, as in the 'solid effect'.

The 'rotating crystal' never supplanted the 'solid effect', but, as an example of amusing physics with spins, it is hard to beat.*

One of the reasons for my stay in Oxford was the absence of Bleaney, who was on sabbatical leave. I gave a series of lectures on ESR in semi-conductors, and I was again plunged into the atmosphere of the para-magnetism of transition elements, which I had known so well when I was doing my thesis, and which I had come across again, with the Mössbauer effect. The classic monograph by Van Vleck which dealt with these problems was thirty years old, and had been written long before the discovery of ESR.

I thought it a pity that the immense arsenal of experimental and theoretical results, obtained over nearly twenty years by Bleaney and his coworkers, and on the theoretical side by Pryce, Stevens, Elliott, myself, and others, had not been assembled in a monograph. I spoke of it to Bleaney, who liked the idea of writing one. The result was an enormous treatise of more than 800 pages, on the paramagnetic resonance of transition elements, from the iron group to actinides, with the groups of the rare earths, palladium and platinum, in between.

I did the theory, and he the experimental methods and results; although sometimes he 'muscled' into my territory, to describe parts of the theory in his own language. As could have been expected from a book written in collaboration by two co-authors, who were geographically removed from each other, each with his own culture and his own personality, there is a certain lack of unity in it. A malicious critic (was it me?) said once that it was two books, put together under the same cover; but, on second thoughts, I think that is a wild exaggeration. We had harmonized our notations, established cross-references, and taken good care not to contra-dict each other. The accumulation of data in Bleaney's part, to which I objected a little at the start, (he never told me what he objected to in mine), turned out to be a precious source of information and one of the assets of the book. For my part, I set myself to understanding and explaining the critical points of the theory, which were too often misunderstood.

The book was published by Oxford University Press in 1970, and translated into French by a group of physicists in Grenoble, and into Russian by the same people who had translated my *Principles*. It sold very respectably and was recently reissued as a paperback by Dover. My Israeli colleagues refer to it as 'the New Testament', implying that the *Principles* was the Bible.

In a later chapter, I shall describe a phenomenon to which I have devoted a sizeable part of my life, and which I consider as my main achievement—namely nuclear magnetic ordering—and I shall also speak of the people who took part in its study with me.

At the end of the present chapter I wish to list some of my other coworkers, who passed through the lab over the thirty years of its existence. I cannot list them all and I beg the forgiveness of those I have omitted. I have not forgotten them, but I fear to weary the reader with names which mean more to me than to him.

The lab itself, born in the basement of the Ecole Normale Supérieure in 1954, was moved to Saclay the following year and stayed there till 1968, when it was moved to an annexe of Saclay, called l'Orme des Merisiers—of which I will have more to say in the next chapter.

After the first few years, its workforce did not vary much: some ten physicists, called 'engineers' within the CEA, three to five graduate students working on a thesis, between five and ten technicians, and between two and five foreign visitors. It is a goodly size for Little Science, and a puny one for Big Science.

*Some coworkers

Ionel Solomon, who left me in 1962 to found his own laboratory at the Ecole Polytechnique, has already been mentioned. From the beginning, his new laboratory was a success. Its main theme was the study of semiconductors and its main tool, magnetic resonance. In a long series of experiments of outstanding elegance, using all the resources of magnetic resonance, optics, and electric measurements, he discovered several new phenomena. It was from him that three of my early coworkers, Maurice Goldman, André Landesman, and José Esratty, received their first initiation into the experimental methods and techniques of magnetic resonance.

Jean Combrisson I have already spoken of, and will come back to him in the next chapter, in connection with my term as a director.

Jacques Winter came to me after an excellent thesis with Brossel. His extensive knowledge of most fields of solid state and atomic physics and his well developed critical sense had been most useful to all, and first and foremost to me. I was fond of saying that whenever I had an idea for a new experiment, Winter's objections ran along three lines: 'It is impossible, it is of no interest, it has been done already.' To refute all three of these objections, as I sometimes succeeded in doing, was a stimulating exercise. Winter eventually left the CEA to become a scientific director at the CNRS, and later a director at the ILL, before returning to the CEA as a *Chef de Département* in Grenoble.

José Ezratty was the model coworker, whom everyone wished to work with, and he collaborated with many. His kindness and sense of humour contributed much to making our lab a friendly place to live in. He left to become the Director of the Fondation Bernard Grégory, where his task is to find jobs in industry for young physics graduates.

André Landesman, after working on dynamic polarization in liquids, went to the US for a couple of years and came back as a specialist of solid ^{3}He. He made several interesting contributions to its study, in particular two excellent review articles on the role of exchange. I made great use of it in a monograph I published with Maurice Goldman in 1982.

Charles Ryter was an excellent specialist in ESR when he came to the lab. He constructed an ESR spectrometer of remarkable sensitivity for us, and was the first to observe what is known as the 'Overhauser shift' in metals, which is the displacement of the ESR line caused by the enhanced polarization of the nuclear spins. He is now an astrophysicist.

Michel Borghini was successful in his theoretical and experimental work at the lab, and later at CERN, where he holds a permanent position, on the problem of polarized targets.

Claude Robert, now a professor at the University of Strasbourg, and an excellent experimentalist, was, among other things, the first to observe the NMR of ^{57}Fe in natural iron.

Maurice Guéron, the son of one of the pioneers of the CEA, Jules Guéron, did a good thesis on the resonance of indium antimonide before veering toward biochemical applications of NMR at his lab in the Ecole Polytechnique.

Denis Jéróme did an excellent thesis on the metal-insulator transition in doped silicon. After he left my lab, he made a name for himself in the field of organic superconductors. I am afraid that the recent discovery of high temperature superconductors may have stolen some of his thunder.

Jacqueline Poitrenaud did a good thesis on nuclear relaxation in alkaline metals, and then went to work with F. I. B. Williams on a subject I shall mention in a moment.

Jean-Marc Delrieu did, practically without supervision, an excellent thesis on the study by NMR of vortices in superconductors of the second kind, and then some very original theoretical work on the nature of exchange in solid ^{3}He. His somewhat, shall I say, *independent* character raised a few problems before he finally lost touch with the lab, to work by himself.

Hans Glättli did some very original work in his study of solid methane by NMR, and in particular the study of its first excited states by level crossing with the Zeeman levels of paramagnetic impurities created in the sample by gamma-ray irradiation. I shall come back to Glättli in connection with nuclear magnetic ordering.

F. I. B. Williams spent some time looking for metastable states in solid ^{3}He in accordance with a (demented) idea of my own of using these states as paramagnetic impurities to polarize solid ^{3}He; after which, he studied the behaviour of ions and of free electrons at the surface of liquid helium. These studies were highly successful and earned him an excellent reputation in that field. I encouraged him at an early date to build up his own group, independently of my lab, which he did. Jacqueline Poitrenaud was his first assistant.

Ray Freeman came to us from Oxford. Once, when I was telling him: 'In the midst of the broken English that is heard here, you remain our standard of English,' he replied: 'If I am to serve as a standard, it is high time I was sent home to be recalibrated'.

Warren Proctor has already been mentioned in connection with spin temperature and dynamic nuclear polarizations in solids—two vital contributions of his. I remember that after we had 'blindly' polarized the nuclei of ^{6}Li in LiF for an hour (it turned out later that a couple of minutes was enough), we saw the augmented signal of ^{6}Li floating on the screen of the oscilloscope, and he asked me: 'Anatole, do you see what I see?' Divine surprise!

Walter Hardy, a Canadian from Vancouver, spent two years with us, in the mid-sixties. I had suggested that he do a study of dynamic nuclear polarization in solid deuterated hydrogen HD, with a view to making a polarized target with a high hydrogen content for high energy physicists. (Pure hydrogen H_2 is inconvenient, for reasons too technical to be given here.) Hardy, who is a remarkably skilful and imaginative experimentalist, built from scratch an apparatus which made very pure HD, and made a very thorough NMR study of its properties. The results of his study were twofold: a) as target material, HD was unsuitable, b) for its own sake as a molecular solid, it was most interesting. This was a by no means unique example of an applied research yielding results of a fundamental nature. Hardy is back in Vancouver, where I saw him last in the spring of 1987.

Neil Sullivan, a New Zealander, had been a student of Robert Pound at Harvard. He stayed in the lab for nearly ten years before leaving for the University of Florida. Most of his work was devoted to a very thorough experimental and theoretical study of phase transitions in mixtures of ortho and para hydrogen, and in solid nitrogen with various impurities.

He too is an excellent experimentalist, and one of his tasks was the supervision of the work of two young French physicists.

Daniel Estéve and Michel Devoret are both remarkably gifted, and have made very interesting contributions to the understanding of the properties of molecular solids. They have now left the field of NMR and work on macroscopic-quantum phenomena in Josephson junctions. Bad luck for NMR!

Slava Luchikov, Milan Odehnal and Alexander Malinovski came to us from the East. All three are very good men who spent several years in the lab working on dynamic nuclear polarization. They are all back to their respective countries. Luchikov, a Russian, is in charge of neutron physics in Dubna. Odehnal, a Czech, is a senior physicist in Prague and works with squids, which are superconducting sensitive devices based on the properties of Josephson junctions (in September 1988 I heard of his untimely death). Malinovski, a Bulgarian, works at the University of Sofia and comes for brief periods to collaborate with Glättli.

I am warning the reader again, there will be more name-dropping in the chapter on nuclear magnetic ordering.*

Director of Physics

Keeping the seat warm—Back to school—The word is delegate—All the King's men—The big projects—June '68 and its proper use—The return of Cincinnatus

In 1962 Louis de Broglie reached retirement age, and his chair at the Sorbonne became vacant. Jacques Yvon decided to give up the Direction de la Physique et des Piles Atomiques (DPPA), to take de Broglie's chair. The two heads of the CEA, Pierre Couture, the Administrator General (the same who, as I recounted earlier in this book, had entrusted me with the purchase of a submachine gun in New York) and Francis Perrin, the High Commissioner, decided to take advantage of this departure to split the DPPA, which had grown too big, into two parts. Two new Directions were created: the Direction des Piles Atomiques or (DPA) and the Direction de la Physique or (DPh). To Horowitz they offered the DPA, which he accepted, and to me the DPh, which, after thinking it over, I declined.

My reasons were simple: between my lectures at the Collège de France, the direction of my lab, and my own research—three occupations which were actually inseparable from each other—my hands were full, (not counting my responsibilities as department head, which would have become those of my successor).

The Director's regalia: weekly directors' meetings with the High Commissioner and the Administrator General, followed by a lavish lunch; a personal chauffeur-driven car; frequent meetings with ministerial advisers and occasional meetings with the Minister himself; invitations to formal receptions given by the President of the Republic—none of them was thrilling enough to make me change my mind. Furthermore I was planning a stay of several months in Oxford in the autumn of 1962, and I could not decently go away for such a long period at the same time as starting on a job of such importance.

One outstanding problem remained: who would be the next director: My professional relations with Yvon had been excellent: I had feelings of respect and esteem for him, and I think he had some esteem for me, and above all for what I was trying to achieve in the CEA. I could see no one in or out of the CEA with whom I could have the same relationship. The problem I had faced three years ago, when, rather than serving under someone I could not get along with, I had accepted the responsibilities of a department head, was arising again. I was not keen on being forced upward again for the same reason.

This is why I suggested to Francis Perrin the name of Henri Baïssas, who had taken the position vacated near him by Jean Debiesse. It would be unkind to use the epithet of King Log about a man as urbane and subtle as Henri Baïssas; but yet I must admit that there was something like it in my mind. Francis Perrin accepted both my refusal and my suggestion of the name of Baïssas with an alacrity which might have been interpreted as ungracious to me, but was not so in fact: I will explain why, in a moment. Like Debiesse, Baïssas was an inspector general of public education. Born in 1899, he was due for mandatory retirement at 65, two years hence, and he assured me that he would be delighted to end his career by keeping the seat warm for me for two years.

His former career must have been very much like that of Jean Debiesse, but doubtless involved more tact and subtlety. As for their competence in the field of physics, I really do not know to whom I would have given the crown. Anyway, for three years, I got along well with Baïssas, and that was all I had been asking for. His deputy was Jean Pellerin, a diligent and intelligent young man, who first appeared in the preface to this book, and whose presence at the side of Baïssas did much to smooth over our relations. In 1964 Baïssas reached 65; but in a long tête à tête, he gave me the administrative reasons, they were obscure, but all the more convincing for their obscurity, for his wish to stay on for another year, and asked me whether I objected to it. I was touched that he should consult me on a point where the decision did not belong to me, made no objections, and he stayed on for a third year. Meanwhile I had realized that the responsibilities of a director, although much vaster than those of a department head, were both less absorbing and more interesting, and I did not dislike the idea of succeeding Baïssas in 1965. All the administrative actions concerned with the different services were on the departmental level, and their management was a task for which I had no special aptitude and even less liking. By contrast, the responsibilities of a director, with the possibility of influencing the higher authority in the making of important decisions, seemed far more attractive to me.

In the spring of 1965 I learned that, with the blessing of Francis Perrin, Baïssas fully intended to stay on for yet another year and perhaps more, arguing that in the Corps of Inspectors General of Public Education, to which he belonged, the retirement age was 70 rather than 65. It was too much. I went to see the Administrator General, Robert Hirsch, who had replaced Pierre Couture, and told him that if I was not made Director of Physics in the autumn of 1965, I would not take up the job on any later date—because of the loss of face it would imply to the personnel over whom I would have to exercise my authority.

It worked, and this is how in the autumn of 1965, at the ripe age of fifty, I became Director of Physics of the CEA. The explanation of Francis Perrin's behaviour in this affair was known to me: its name was André Berthelot.

André Berthelot, a *Normalien*, my elder by two years, had been Frédéric Joliot's assistant at the Collège de France, and had done his thesis under him. He had remained strongly attached to Joliot, and, after his forced departure from the CEA, Berthelot had taken a defiant stance towards the *Polytechniciens*, who, with the exception of Francis Perrin, *Normalien* like himself, were running the CEA. I may add that, because of my belonging to the group of the 'Three Musketeers', he lumped me in with the *Polytechniciens* whom he disliked at the CEA (in contrast to my former boss Kowarski, who was inclined to pass me over for not being one). As a result of his defiant behaviour, Pierre Guillaumat, a former Administrator General of the CEA, a ruthless man, had stripped Berthelot of his title of *Chef de Service*. After that he exercised his authority over his laboratory, in a makeshift arrangement, directly under Francis Perrin, which went against the whole administrative organization of the CEA. It had been the task of Baïssas, first as Perrin's Secretary General and then as Director of Physics, to insure a smooth relationship between the prickly Berthelot and the CEA administration. The fact that it had worked for several years is proof enough of the considerable power that Francis Perrin wielded for twenty-odd years within the CEA, till his departure in 1970.

The reason for Perrin's lukewarm attitude to my becoming Director of Physics, and thus above Berthelot in the line of command, was his fear that I might prove less pliant than Baïssas, and would, as he put it, 'torment' Berthelot. The idea of 'tormenting' Berthelot had never crossed my mind, but I could not and did not tolerate any part of my direction having some kind of administrative extraterritoriality and being totally independent of its director.

I obtained the status of a CEA Department from the Administrator General for Berthelot's laboratory, and for its leader, Berthelot, that of a department head. It took Berthelot some time to get rid of the idea that he had a direct line to the High Commissioner, and that he could by-pass me whenever he saw fit to do so. What reconciled us and brought him to reason eventually, was, beside my firm stand, our common liking for physics and the earnest efforts I made to obtain everything that was necessary for his laboratory.

Berthelot, who left us some time ago, was an honourable man, (I wish Mark Antony had not polluted that expression); and I have a great regard for him as a person, and for what he did. He was an excellent teacher and a dynamic leader, one of those whose energy propelled our country to its present rank in the field of particle physics. What he had lacked in the long run was the opportunity to spend a couple of years after the war in a great laboratory abroad, doing research, instead of having a large service thrust upon him, with troops who, at least at the start, were not of the best. I think he was conscious of it himself, and it may have been the reason for his impulsive behaviour.

For a long time I had been anxious to get acquainted with particle physics, and my new responsibilities had turned this yearning into a necessity. A marvellous opportunity presented itself: the Ecole des Houches in the Alps, well known to physicists all over the world, was offering, in its summer session of 1965, a two-month introductory course in that field. I sent in a student's application, was admitted, and went back at fifty to sit among the students, pen in hand, in a school where I had taught twice some years earlier. It was hard for me, very hard, but I stuck it out and absorbed a large part of what I was taught.

It was not a very good period for particle physics. There were many data and many theories, but none quite satisfactory.

Fortunately, considerable progress was to occur a few years later. I shall come back to particle physics in a later chapter, and so will not dwell on it now. Let me just say at this point that I came back from des Houches with enough knowledge of the subject to pass judgements on the initiatives of the Head of the Elementary Particles Department, his funding requirements, and his proposals for the promotion of his coworkers. They in turn appreciated the considerable effort made by their director to understand their field better, and to find a common language with them.

I would now like to say a few words about the Direction of Physics, and first of all to list its contents: the Department of Elementary Particles, already mentioned, headed by Berthelot; the Department of 'Saturne'—in charge of the 3 GeV CEA proton synchrotron, which I had held over its baptismal font, with my Orbit Group back in 1953—headed by Robert Levy-Mandel, who later made a career at CERN; the Department of Nuclear Physics, headed by Albert Messiah—which, besides the cyclotron of Thirion and the Van de Graaff of Cotton, included a new large instrument, a 600 MeV, high energy, high duty cycle, linear electron accelerator; a Department of Controlled Fusion headed by Michel Trocheris; two Autonomous Services: the Solid State Physics Service, which I had removed from the Department of Nuclear Physics, headed by André Herpin, which contained my own lab, and the Theoretical Physics Service headed by Claude Bloch; finally a kind of nebula called the Services of Applied Physics, headed by Stanislas Winter. If one remembers that Jules Horowitz was the Director of Atomic Reactors, one can see that the 'Three Musketeers' had not done too badly for themselves.

The total strength of the Direction in 1966 was nearly 1500 people, of whom 400 were physicists and engineers; and its annual budget was about 150 million francs.

To assist me with the running of this outfit I had two assistants: Jean Combrisson, with whom I had started my lab ten years ago, and Jean

Pellerin, whom I inherited from Baïssas. I got on admirably well with both of them and they got on fairly well with each other, with the help of a few arbitrations from me, now and then, over their respective fields of responsibility. From the start, I had made two decisions: the first was not to give up, under *any circumstances*, the activities of a physicist, rather go; the second, a consequence of the first, was to do *nothing* that could not be delegated either to my assistants or to a department head. It was understood with my two assistants that we met every day in my office from five to seven to deal with current affairs. These hours could be increased in hectic periods, such as annual discussions of budgets and staff promotions.

I wish to illustrate this 'golden rule' by my solution of the 'Goldzahl problem', which became widely know, not to say, famous, in the CEA and outside. Goldzahl was a particle physicist from the CNRS, whom Perrin had accepted at Saclay with his group. During the fat years, the funding of this group came from a special budgetary line at the personal disposal of the High Commissioner. When the lean years came, Francis had to relinquish this line, the Goldzahl group found itself without support, and its problem landed in the lap of the Director of Physics. One possibility would have been to finance Goldzahl from Berthelot's budget, but he would not hear of it, arguing, not without reason, that he saw no point in paying for activities that he had neither suggested nor followed up, and which were pursued by people who were not under his authority nor for that matter of anyone in the CEA. The CNRS, a logical backer, was unwilling to pay for many specious reasons, and a very real one which was: 'Why pay if the CEA does so in the end?' The Goldzahl problem had become something like the Loch Ness monster: week after week Pellerin was bringing it to my office, like a puppy bringing in an old slipper again and again. I think he was beginning to tire of it himself, for to my usual suggestion that this was exactly the type of problem that he could settle by himself, he said with mock solemnity: 'Monsieur le Directeur, we expect clear-cut instructions from you on this problem.' 'Very well,' I said, looking at my watch, 'I shall give you instructions: from this date and hour I forbid that the word "Goldzahl" be pronounced in my office'. It must have worked, since I heard no more of this problem, and some ten years later I saw Goldzahl himself at Saclay, looking reasonably content.

I have told this little story because, more than my philosophy in dealing with directorial problems, it illustrates the quality of human relations between myself and people who worked with me.

Whatever have been, and still are, the weaknesses of an organization as vast as the CEA, I think that its practice of staff promotion was exemplary. There are several reasons for that: absence of promotion for seniority, replaced by an automatic and sizeable seniority bonus, and thorough knowledge by the scientific hierarchy of the personnel proposed for promotion. In that respect, between the CNRS system, where committees make decisions based on the files of the candidates, and the CEA system, where people are appraised by those who see their everyday work, I prefer the latter. I left responsibility for promotions to department heads, limiting myself to harmonizing the promotions from different departments—with the exception of members of the hierarchy themselves, where the final promotion proposal was mine (I am saying 'proposal' rather than 'decision' because the latter was, at least nominally, the privilege of headquarters).

I also tried to understand the physics that was going on in my various departments, to the best of my abilities. That was by far the most exciting part of my job.

Every Monday morning, from 10 a.m. to 1 p.m., there was a meeting of the nine CEA Directors, co-chaired by the High Commissioner and the Administrator General (HC and AG). It took place in the vast office of the HC on the 11th floor of the CEA Headquarters building, and was followed by a lunch in a private dining room on the tenth floor. A veteran of the CEA, I had met all my fellow directors long ago; the reader has met two of them: Bertrand Goldschmidt, in charge of Programmes and External Relations, and my old friend Jules Horowitz who looked after the Atomic Reactors. The director with the greatest weight, that is budget, was Jacques Robert, who was Director of the Military Division. Of all present I was the one who had known the HC, Francis Perrin, for the longest period: since 1936, as I said at the beginning of this book. But few of us knew our new AG, Robert Hirsch, apart from Goldschmidt, who had been a school friend of his.

Everything, except perhaps a certain sense of humour, separated me from this character, whom possibly for this very reason, I found interesting and with whom I got along fairly well. A *Polytechnicien*, naturally, he was however humanized to a certain extent by not having come from the prestigious Corps des Mines, that old school tie of the French scientific establishment, and alma mater of the CEA's seven other AGs between 1945 and now (1988). He was two years older than I, and he too had had a chequered career, but of a completely different kind. When he was appointed AG of the CEA he had been, among other things, a fighter pilot, a *Préfet de Région* (the government's representative for a region), and a director of the *Súréte Nationale* (the Criminal Police). With his bald cranium and his aquiline nose, he had the profile of a Roman Emperor, Vitellius perhaps, though less fleshy; but his eye was lively and his smile roguish. Familiar with all the pitfalls of a senior civil servant's career, he was cynical and mindful of the way the wind was blowing, but he had seen too many ministers come and go, to exhibit any servility to them. In spite of his cynicism and of his natural caution he was humane and devoid of the brutality of one of his predecessors, Pierre Guillaumat, and of his successor, André Giraud.

He was an inexhaustible source of stories about the inner workings of high administration, and about the mores of politicians.

I liked the one about the visit of General de Gaulle to Lille, where Hirsch, the *Préfet de Région*, was his host. Two days earlier the General had miraculously escaped a terrorist attack. The terrorists, posted in a place called Le Petit Clamart, through which de Gaulle's car was passing, had fired a large number of rounds of ammunition at him without touching him. 'What poor marksmanship' had been the General's only comment. After the visit there was lunch at the *Préfecture*, and Hirsch, looking at the menu, saw with horror that the main course was *Pigeonneaux* (Squabs) *à la Clamart*. Fortunately the General, who was hungry, did not bother to look at the menu.

He had a few favourite aphorisms which he was wont to use. 'Do not answer questions that you have not been asked' was one of them. He said once about Horowitz: 'He overdoes it: he does not answer the questions that I *ask* him'. Whenever a request or a protest was made to him, he replied: 'Let me have it in writing.' A little later I will describe how I made use of that. Finally, on the subject of behaviour towards female subordinates, he used to say: 'I abide by the advice of my good friend, the Bishop of . . . : "Never in the Diocese".'

He believed in horoscopes, which gave rise to an amusing incident in 1970, when, in the course of a ceremony he pinned the cross of *Officier de la Légion d'Honneur* on me. A few days earlier his secretary had inquired about the *hour* at which I was born (the date was naturally in my file). I said, at random, eight a.m. On the day of the ceremony, Hirsch showed up with a horoscope especially drawn up for me—born on 15 December 1914 at eight in the morning.

He read it out, insisting on the accuracy of the description it gave of my character. When he finished, I pointed out to him that my birthday had been recorded as 15 December 1914, in accordance with the old Julian calendar, which was in use in Russia at the time; but that, according to our calendar, which was naturally that of the horoscope, my birthday was on the 28th of December.

His funniest remark dealt with the explosion of the life-size model of 'Mirabelle'. Mirabelle was a giant bubble chamber which functioned on 6000 litres of liquid hydrogen, and which was being built in Berthelot's service to be shipped to the USSR upon completion. A life-size model had been constructed and filled with hydrogen, and it was this model which had exploded. The lightweight building which contained it had been specially designed to resist (or rather not to resist) an explosion, nobody was hurt, and the damage was limited.

At the next directors' meeting, my report of this hydrogen explosion followed a report by Jacques Robert on the difficulties he was meeting with in his attempts to ignite a hydrogen bomb. 'Why don't you two exchange jobs?' said Hirsch.

I hope I haven't drawn too idyllic a picture of Hirsch: he was not a little saint, but I rather liked him and I think he liked me.

In the course of my duties as a director I met several ministers (seven in all). They changed more often than the CEA directors. Their names will mean nothing to the English-speaking reader, and I shall mention only two of my ministerial meetings. The first was with Alain Peyrefitte, a right-wing politician, but an intelligent and energetic young man. He wrote several books and became later a member of the Académie Française. He struck me by his ability to listen and to remember a good deal of what he was told—a rare gift for a politician.

Apparently, he had liked what I had been telling him, for, a few days later, Hirsch told me that the minister wished me to accompany him on a voyage across the USSR, which was to take us to several Soviet laboratories, and all the way to the Chinese frontier. My knowledge of Russian was a supplementary asset. I was naturally delighted, but a few days later Hirsch announced to me, with that smile of his, that in view of the importance of the mission, the High Commissioner had decided to sacrifice himself and go in person with the minister. I was a little chagrined, but in no way surprised: I knew that Francis adored travelling.

I had another meeting, attended this time by representatives from the CNRS and the universities, with Alain Peyrefitte, the Minister of Research, and Christian Fouchet, Minister of Education. Big Science, and especially particle physics, came under attack as too costly, and as a representative of the CEA, I was duty bound to defend them.

Peyrefitte said: 'I know that you like Little Science. Why don't you encourage your CEA colleagues to devote more time and effort to it? It is just as interesting and far less costly.' 'Monsieur le Ministre,' I said, 'I know how well-read you are, and I am sure you remember that phrase by our dear Courteline: "Why should I pay fifteen francs for an umbrella when I can have a glass of beer for twenty centimes?"'

My single contact with the summit was an invitation to a reception at the Presidential Palace, in the honour of the Soviet Premier Kosygin. It was a costly chore, renting tails, buying patent shoes, silk socks, a starched penguin's shirt. Incredible crowds, interminable waiting in line, before shaking the august hands—de Gaulle's in great uniform, and Kosygin's in . . . a lounge suit. 'One of our great atomists,' said de Gaulle to Kosygin via the interpreter. Had he recognized me, ten years after having handed me an empty envelope, the prize for my magnetometer? I doubt it; some underling must have whispered these flattering words to him.

In the context of the public relations policy of the CEA I had several contacts with the Press. I wish to cite one of them because it is a nice illustration of some of the pitfalls of such contacts. When the large, 600

MeV, electron accelerator was coming into service, I was asked to give an interview to the representative of a popular science journal, François de Closets, a bright young man, who also knew how to listen. (He later went into economic journalism, writes best-sellers, and has a very popular TV programme.)

In the course of the interview I explained to him the difference between electromagnetic forces, which are mediated through an exchange of massless photons and have an infinite range, and nuclear forces, which are mediated by massive particles called pions and have a short range. I fortunately insisted on seeing his article before it went to press. Intelligent and conscientious as he was, François de Closets did some reading on his own and came up with the following explanation for the finite range of nuclear forces in contrast to the infinite range of the electromagnetic forces. Pions, which mediate nuclear forces, are unstable particles and, when emitted by a nucleon, will disintegrate before reaching another nucleon unless they are very close to the first one. Nothing like that occurs with photons, which are stable and will fly for ever. It seemed a shame to knock down such an ingenious explanation, and I congratulated him warmly on his ingenuity, before doing so.

I am coming now to some of the larger achievements and also non-achievements, to which I have contributed in the course of my duties, taking possibly more pride in the latter than in the former. Among the former, I shall cite: the linear electron accelerator; the transfer of Little Science to a new site, an annex of Saclay, called l'Orme des Merisiers, and the 'Mirabelle' project. Among the latter: the 'non-construction' of a 45 Gev accelerator; the non-construction of a large machine for nuclear fusion called 'Superstator'; the 'non-revolution' of 1968, in striking contrast with the university and the CNRS; and the non-realization of a large magnetohydrodynamics programme. My worst failure was a project of internal mobility within the Direction of Physics, which I described in detail in *Reflections*, and about which I shall say a few words in this chapter.

The 600 MeV, high intensity, high duty cycle, electron accelerator was what one might call a microscope, designed to probe the finer features of atomic nuclei in detail. It is well known that the higher the energy of a particle, say, an electron, the smaller its de Broglie wavelength, and the sharper its resolution of the details of the target nucleus. The high intensity yields naturally better statistics and higher accuracy, whereas the high duty cycle makes it possible to do coincidence experiments between various products of the electron scattering on the nucleus.

I believe that when it was commissioned, that machine was the best of its kind in the world. My main task had been to convince the authorities, at the ministerial level, of the interesting features of the project, and to prepare their decisions about the choice of the constructor and of the site.

The project was brought to completion very nearly within the prescribed funding and time limits. The site chosen, the so-called l'Orme des Merisiers, was situated about two miles outside the Saclay laboratory.

I thought it unwise to leave the physicists of the linear accelerator in an intellectual vacuum, separated from their fellow physicists of the main laboratory, and to keep them company I requested, and obtained, the construction of a building to house the 'Little Science' of Saclay: solid state physics, theoretical physics, a scientific library, plus the headquarters of the Direction of Physics, and a lecture room with a hundred seats. As a bonus—since, unlike Saclay, there were no classified activities on the site of the Orme des Merisiers—it could be opened to visitors from outside and even from abroad. We moved in during the summer of 1968, without a hitch, in spite of the unrest which prevailed in the country.

The 'Mirabelle' project, launched by Berthelot long before I became a director, had received a lot of publicity with the thaw, apparent or real, which was taking place in relations between de Gaulle's France and the Soviet Union. In October 1965 the Russians were completing the construction of an accelerator of 70 GeV, which was to remain for several years the largest in the world, but which never gave birth to a major discovery. It was in the beam of this accelerator, sited near the old Russian city of Serpukhov, that our giant bubble chamber, christened 'Mirabelle', was to be placed. In my view this project has been both a remarkable success and, on another level, a dismal failure. Because its implementation resulted in my taking several trips to the USSR, I shall defer the explanation of this statement to another chapter, devoted to travel and called 'East and West'.

I am coming now to what I shall call 'the 45 GeV Crusade'. In the sixties Berthelot had proposed the construction of a national accelerator, very aptly called 'Jupiter', since its planned energy of 60 GeV dwarfed the 3 GeV of our 'Saturne'. I did not understand at the time, and I still do not understand now, why France should have wanted to build its own accelerator with two and a half times the energy of the European CERN machine; but the project had fired the imaginations of all French particle physicists, CEA or not CEA. Fairly soon, in order to demonstrate the 'realism' which presided over their project, they agreed to lower the energy from 60 GeV to 45, but swore not to yield another GeV. The man who appeared as the leader of the crusade was Professor André Blanc-Lapierre, who was at the time in charge of the Orsay linear electron accelerator—a machine, let me say in passing, which was very different from ours, planned as it was for particle rather than nuclear physics.

Blanc-Lapierre was no more of a particle physicist than I was, perhaps even less, but he was a skilful administrator, well versed in the art of dealing with senior civil servants and ministers. He had the soul of a great builder, and was responsible for the Institute of Nuclear Physics in Algiers, (a French city at the time)—which is widely recognized, I am told, as an architectural success—and for the new campus of my beloved *Supelec*, built within a stone's throw of the Orme des Merisiers. I think it was the 'Great Achievement' aspect of this project which had caught his imagination, and if anyone could carry off its funding, it was he. I was in an embarrassing position. As guardian, via Berthelot, of the Saclay particle physicists, I could not afford to appear to be lacking in ardour with respect to a project they felt so strongly about; especially when the physicists from the CEA and the CNRS, brothers who usually bickered, had for once joined in the same clamour: 'We want the 45 GeV.' At the same time, deep down inside, I found this project little short of insane. This is why, while clamouring with my troops: 'Onward, Particle Soldiers', I was dragging my feet as best I could.

Fortunately I found an unexpected ally in Francis Perrin. He feared, not without reason, that if this project succeeded it would be detrimental to the development of CERN, to which he was greatly attached; so he was putting on the brakes from his side, surreptitiously but efficiently. Finally the Minister decided to form a commission, called the Panier (basket) commission, after the name of the very senior but retired civil servant who was to chair it. The partisans of the 45 GeV were expected to convince M. Panier, and through him the government, of the importance of this project for the prosperity and the renown of our country. I have forgotten how many times this commission, on which I sat, assisted by Pellerin, met, but it lasted a long time. Under the chairmanship of M. Panier we proceeded to a careful examination of the past of particle physics, and to a prospective study of its future. M. Panier, who had little else to do, took a great interest in the proceedings, and would have willingly, I think, made his commission into a permanent organization. All the other members were beginning to get tired of it, and one day I told M. Panier: 'Monsieur le Président, I think we have been sitting on this commission long enough. I had a thin dark moustache when we started, I have a thick grey one now—enough is enough'. (I had shifted to an electric razor, ill-suited to the cultivation of a thin moustache.) The decision not to build the 45 GeV was never taken; it did not have to be since no funding had ever been officially considered for it.

It was different with the project for a large machine for controlled thermonuclear fusion, called 'Superstator', which was put forward by the department, before it had become part of my responsibilities. I shall not dwell on the principle of this machine, which was entirely funded in 1968, at a cost of 40 million francs, and whose construction was due to begin shortly. I was naturally not competent to make a technical appraisal of the project (although its principle seemed far-fetched to me), but it was the result of years of work by the best French specialists, the train was on the rails, and nothing seemed to be able to stop its progress. Francis Perrin had even told me, when the funding had come under discussion, that he was ready to fight for it, if necessary.

It was then that I heard, in a roundabout way, of deep differences within the department on the relative value of the 'Superstator' and another type of machine, born in Russia and called the 'Tokamak'. (Incidentally, as I learned later, the man at the origin of the Tokamak principle was Andrei Sakharov.) I called a meeting of all those concerned with this project and asked to come out in the open with what they thought of 'Superstator', to the best of their knowledge and belief. 'There is still time to speak out—tomorrow it will be too late', I told them. After a long and passionate discussion, followed by a vote (a most unusual procedure, but May '68 had passed by), there was almost unanimous agreement not to build 'Superstator'. I informed the financial director of this change of plans, and he was strongly displeased at seeing his budget, which had been all sewn up, put out of joint at the last minute.

This brings me to the events of May 1968 into which, as a director, I crashed headlong. Books and television shows come out in droves these days to mark their twentieth anniversary. I shall not attempt to compete with their authors, and will assume that my English-speaking reader has heard of what went on: student unrest, rioting in the streets of Paris, the burning of buses, the throwing of paving stones at the police, an occupation of the Sorbonne, and, to crown it all, a general strike and the coming to a standstill of all activity in the country.

To this day I have not understood how the instigator of these events, Daniel Cohn-Bendit—a little, grinning, clever, plump, and, on the whole, rather likeable Franco-German Jew—had managed to make the Gaullian State tremble on its foundations, and, in the long term, cause the departure of its august head. I have refrained from reading the numerous 'explanations', which are at best 'descriptions' of what went on; I do not need them, having lived in the middle of it myself. I am not far from thinking that the best description was mine: 'Water boiling at room pressure and temperature'. Perhaps the best *prediction* of these events was made by a great French journalist, Pierre Viansson-Ponté, who did not live to see May '68, but had written in a famous article: 'France is bored' (*La France s'ennuie*).

I have nothing of interest to say about the unions, who climbed on the students' bandwagon and wrested massive salary increases from their employers, or about the economical consequences thereof; what I was able to observe at close range was the behaviour of the 'Intellectual Leaders' in the university and in research.

Perhaps one should stress the rather good-natured character of this 'revolution'. In spite of a lot of spectacular street violence, no one was killed, for which one should be grateful to the intelligence and humanity of the man then responsible for law and order, the Préfet de Police M. Grimaud (and also to the self-control of some student leaders).

Language was a different matter, with exaggeration lapsing into verbal shamelessness, and the appearance of expressions like CRS-SS. (The CRS is the French riot police. Later, in conflicts between the CEA and the CNRS, CNRS-SS became my private little joke.) Even people for whom I had the greatest regard, like Alfred Kastler, Laurent Schwartz, and Jacques Monod, had lost their bearings, going so far as to speak of 'the slaughtering of students'. Among professors, sham protest resignations were raining. As for the junior staff, the so-called, *Assistants de Faculté*, who were far more virulent than the students, their motto could have been: 'World Revolution and Tenure for all'. The best (or the worst if you prefer) were some professors of mathematics, who had been systematically flunking all their candidates before May '68, and passed them all systematically after May '68—exhibiting the same contempt for their students in either case. I shall not describe any further ridiculous behaviour which took place, even in good scientific faculties like Orsay or Paris VII.

Naturally the ageing Jean-Paul Sartre could not resist the attraction of this Fountain of Youth, and one saw him everywhere in student assemblies outdoing the young in contests of absurdity. In an article where he violently attacked his former schoolmate, Raymond Aron, he drew a picture of the ideal university as he saw it. Although opposed on all points to the one I knew and hated in my youth, it was, if anything, worse. I wrote him a long letter, to which I did not expect and did not get an answer. When, fifteen years later, Raymond Aron mentioned Sartre's article, which apparently had hurt him, in his memoirs, I sent him a copy of my letter to Sartre. He replied, shortly before his death: 'I liked the lesson you gave him; he deserved it.' I have removed that longish letter from the English version, for fear of boring my English-speaking readers with our *querelles Franco-Françaises*.

A last remark about the general features of May '68, before passing on to its consequences for the CEA and the DPh. What struck me most painfully was the extreme fragility of the national structures and the almost instantaneous disintegration of all powers. I had seen it happen in 1940 under the pressure of the German advance: one day there were the army, the police, the ministries, and public transportation, and the following day . . . nothing. It was the same in 1968 until someone in charge remembered to reopen the gas-stations, which had been closed because of strikes, and the Parisians ran out in all directions, bound for their holidays.

What happened at the DPh? Well, next to nothing. The contrast with the university, and even with some industrial research laboratories, was striking. My people went on working and the number of hours lost was remarkably small. We had a few general assemblies, with the usual shouting and voting by show of hands, but it amounted to very little. The most 'revolutionary' of all have not bee the slowest in later becoming members of the CEA establishment. A couple of unfortunates lost their sense of reality permanently, but it would probably have happened to them anyway, sooner or later.

A few of the *Chefs de Service* agreed to stand for election for their job. All were re-elected except one, who took up his job again a few weeks later. I called a meeting of my lab, and asked for grievances and suggestions. There were very few of each, and on minor points only. There was, however, one innovation from the personnel which I approved of heartily. It was the creation of unit councils at the level of the services, departments and directions, chaired by the unit's head but with members elected by the personnel. These councils were different from the unions, insofar as they were not concerned with the defence of the personnel's interests, such as salaries, promotions, working hours, holidays, etc. These were in the jurisdiction of the unions. The councils were only concerned with improving the scientific and technical work within the unit.

I was able to enlist the support of the units in solving a ticklish problem, which had been crying out for a solution for a long time—the activities of the Services de Physique Appliquée (abbreviated to SPA). Part of the programme of that unit was the study of magnetohydrodynamics, which cost in the order of 11 million francs a year, but, it was claimed, was of paramount interest to the National Electricity Board. I arranged for a lunch with the head of the Board's Research Department, in the course of which he affirmed to me his great interest in the technological research in magnetohydrodynamics which was being pursued at Saclay. 'I am delighted to hear it,' I said. 'How shall we split the expenses: does fifty–fifty look fair to you?' 'Very amusing,' he said. 'No, but seriously, how much are you prepared to pay?' 'But Monsieur Abragam, magneto-hydrodynamics is a budget line which we closed some time ago; I cannot pay you anything.' There was nothing left for me but to close *our* budget line on the subject.

Besides magnetohydrodynamics, which turned out to be a dead-end, since our only potential customer was unwilling to spend one penny on it, there was another problem with the SPA. They pursued researches on controlled nuclear fusion, duplicating those of the department whose responsibility it was. I came to the painful conclusion that the existence of the SPA should come to an end, and that its personnel should be redistributed among the other units of the DPh. It was a complicated operation, which would have been very painful without the assent and the assistance of the unit councils. I had put Combrisson in charge, and he acquitted himself of the reshuffling of the personnel with patience, intelligence, and humanity. Everyone had an individual interview, at which representatives of the unit councils were present. For once, May '68 had been good for something.

On the other hand the unions had been very hostile from the beginning towards the unit councils, in which they saw rivals for their influence, and did what they could to reduce their role. They succeeded eventually: the councils were never suppressed, but slowly lapsed into nothingness.

It was at the end of September 1970, a few months before abandoning my director's duties, though I did not know it yet, that I conceived a plan for internal mobility within the DPh, and expounded it in a letter to all its unit heads. I published it in *Reflections*, and shall only summarize it here. The gist of it was to create conditions under which every physicist who wished to change his field could do so in the safest and most efficient way. I proposed to create a welcoming structure in each unit, where a candidate for change would find information on the new activities which had tempted him. This information was to be on several levels, succinct at first, then more and more detailed as the candidate persisted in his plans. It was to be followed by a phase of initiation, in which a 'godfather' would be assigned to each newcomer. During a trial period of up to a year, this newcomer was able to return at any time to the unit he came from, without any prejudice to his career, and his final transfer would be pronounced after a year (unless he requested it earlier).

I wished to provoke a vast debate within the DPh on this idea: the main point being that the internal structure of the DPh was, I thought, admirably suited for the success of this operation. Unfortunately at the beginning of October, I left for the US to give the Loeb and Leigh Page lectures at Harvard and Yale. When I came back, an entirely new situation had been created at the top of the CEA. The AG, Robert Hirsch, and the HC, Francis Perrin, had both been replaced by a newcomer, André Giraud, as the new AG, and by Jacques Yvon, who was giving up his Sorbonne chair after eight years, as HC. Furthermore there had been a complete change in the balance of power, since practically all power was now in the hands of the AG. This was the result of a new definition of their respective roles by the government, but also of a loss in the personal prestige of the HC, related to the departure of Francis Perrin, who had wielded considerable power for nearly twenty years.

I had been thinking for some time of leaving my director's position. Inexorably, my duties were becoming more and more time-consuming, and what's worse, more and more budgetary and less and less scientific. One day, feeling low, I told my good friends Combrisson and Pellerin: 'If I'm going to bicker about cash all day long, I'd be better off in banking than physics.'

I also had less and less time to devote to my lab and to my lectures at the Collège de France. I was haunted by sorry memories of the lectures of Joliot and Perrin. Should I have given up earlier? A decision like that is never easy. I was fifty-five. Would I still have the capacity to work in science full time, without the excuse of heavy administrative responsibilities? To put it in a lighter vein—now I was in my fifties and able to devote all my time to my beloved mistress, Science, would I still be able to satisfy her? I thought that before leaving I should at least take the time to push through my project on internal mobility. The arrival of Giraud put an end to my hesitations, in spite of the fact that I was one of those who received the best treatment from the new master of the CEA.

I do not think that André Giraud would have disagreed with this description of him: intelligent, energetic, brutal. He had his plan for reorganizing the CEA and, as soon as he arrived, the reshuffling of some directors and firing of others began. In his plan there was to be a division at the top into what he called: 'staff' and 'line,' that is between the so-called 'delegates' in charge of the programmes and the budgets, and the 'directors' responsible for the running of the larger units. He offered me the job of Delegate to Fundamental Research, which besides physics, included chemistry and biology. I could instead, if I wished, keep my job of Director of Physics, but with reduced powers, since a delegate would be responsible for the decisions on the programmes and the budget. I asked for a delay of a few days to think it over, but one was enough. I did not want to supervise fields like chemistry and biology, of which I knew nothing. To keep the Direction of Physics without the responsibility for its budget did not tempt me either: I knew the proverb about the piper and the tune. But there was another, more cogent reason. I had seen how Giraud was treating some of my fellow directors, and I knew that I would not stand for it. Rather than face it another day, I decided to give up the power while the going was good. During the night I wrote a letter of resignation, in which I carefully weighed every word and asked him for an appointment. After he had greeted me very courteously, I said to him: 'Your predecessor always told me: "Let me have it in writing"—here it is', and I put my letter on his desk. I think he was surprised, because after reading it he asked me: 'But what exactly do you want?' 'What it says in the letter, Monsieur l'Administrateur Général'.

He asked me to stay on the job for a few more months, and to suggest the name of a successor to him. Claude Bloch was an obvious choice, and I told him so straightaway. I am not sure that it made Albert Messiah very happy: he would not have disliked the job.

Claude Bloch did not have the time to give the full measure of his great abilities in his new position, for a heart attack took him away a few months later; and Messiah did get the job after all. The way fundamental research has been run at the CEA since then is outside the scope of this book.

A few years later, when Yvon retired, Giraud asked me whether I would like the job of HC, which had become purely honorary, except for one or two points. I told Giraud: 'Our relations are non-existent and, as a consequence, excellent. I would like them to stay that way.' He took it in good part and contact between us, while not non-existent, has not been unpleasant. He created the position of 'Director of Research' for me, which, later, was given to other worthies upon relinquishing their responsibilities. My colleagues from abroad mistook my new title for an increase in responsibilities: after having been Director of Research in physics, they thought I was now in charge of the whole of research.

1971 was the last year when I could get an overall view of fundamental research in physics at the CEA and form a general impression. This impression was good.

Thanks to an initiative taken by Kowarski and followed up by Francis Perrin, many young men were able to get a training abroad, and later to keep up a flow of exchanges and collaborations with foreign scientists. Apart from a few notable exceptions such as Aigrain, Brossel, and Friedel, the CNRS and the university were slow in following suit. The fact that, in the CEA, the checking and approval of expenses took place *after* the act rather than before, as in the university and the CNRS, made for far greater efficiency. Slightly higher salaries for technicians, and hiring procedures which were much faster than in the university, had the same effect. I have already spoken of the fact that the staff were far better known by those on whom their promotion depended. Above all, the members of staff indiscriminately called *Agents CEA* had an *esprit de corps* which speeded up large projects as well as small experiments.

It has often been said that the CEA's scientific projects were more costly than those of its competitors, but I do not agree. Someone (I think it was Pierre Aigrain) had invented the concept of the 'cost per research worker' which was the budget, salaries excluded, divided by the number of research workers. This concept had been proposed to the ministries as a means of sizing up the efficiency of a laboratory, but it suffered from two defects which I vehemently denounced. In the university it led to 'dressing up' people like teaching assistants, or old professors, as research workers, who did not do any research; and furthermore it amounted to saying that an experiment had been done more efficiently if, say, ten people, took part in it, instead of five. I did my best to make CEA physics better known and appreciated in France and abroad, and to obtain various prizes or medals for its workers. If I succeeded in it more often than some of our competitors, it may have been because I had good cases to plead for.

The great merit of Francis Perrin, with whom I have been severe more than once in the course of this narrative, is to have systematically encouraged and protected fundamental research within the CEA despite opposition from inside, from the successive AGs, and from outside, from other agencies competing for funds. He put behind this task his scientific prestige, which was great among the general public, and his considerable tactical skill.

Was I a good Director? When I left in early 1971, it was very discreetly: my voluntary departure was hardly noticed in the CEA, among the many not voluntary ones, and there were no speeches to celebrate my merits, real or imaginary. One little sign, though: after Claude Bloch's untimely death, a delegation of physicists came to ask me, very insistently, to take up the job again.

Looking back, if I try to form a judgement about myself, there is no getting away from the fact that I was at best a half-time director, combining my duties with those of a professor and of the leader of a small laboratory; and I never had the time to follow up problems in detail. From the beginning, I had to delegate a lot to my assistants and also to the department heads. I am not sure, though, that this situation was entirely a bad thing. My authority, exerted less often and on important points only, was perhaps better accepted by my Vassal Lords whose Sovereign, that is me, maintained a certain distance with respect to daily and even weekly events.

In conclusion, and on the basis of my past experience, I would say that authority starts when one is able to say no, and stops when one takes pleasure in saying no.

For the next ten years, I was able to devote myself entirely to my teaching and my research, and I think that both profited from it. The fact that my title of Director of Research carried no administrative duties but also no authority, beyond personal prestige, did give rise once to a problem with the *Chef de Service* who was the nominal head of my laboratory; but I was able to nip it in the bud.

A more serious problem was looming ahead as I approached sixty-five, the mandatory retirement age in the CEA. At the Collège the retirement age is seventy, and my chair without my lab did not make much sense. I was looking for an amicable arrangement within the DPh, when in 1979 a statement from this organism put an end to my hopes. The statement proclaimed: 'We are confronted more and more often by the problem of worthies (*notables*), due for retirement, who wish to keep some kind of activity or presence in our laboratories. The policy is that whatever the respectability of the persons concerned, there can be no official link between these persons and the CEA. In consequence these persons will have to surrender their service card; if they wish to come back from time to time, it can only be as visitors.'

Apart from the word '*notables*' which, I admit, made me gnash my teeth, there was nothing in this statement but an authentic expression of the CEA's official policy, and a refusal in advance to enter into any kind of amicable arrangement within the framework of the DPh. A third party later told me that the statement was not aimed at me; but, in truth, who inside the DPh could have been more '*notable*' and more 'respectable' than I?

Since there was no possible arrangement to be had inside the DPh, I had to look for it outside, and for that I had to go to the top. I knew that the administration would be hostile to any individual arrangement which might serve as a precedent. I went to see Michel Pecqueur, the new AG (Giraud had become Minister of Industry) and proposed to him an association convention between two organizations—the Collège de France and the CEA—for a joint study of nuclear magnetism.

The Collège de France was offering the services of two eminent personalities: Professor Anatole Abragam, incumbent of the Chair of Nuclear Magnetism, and Dr Maurice Goldman, Deputy Director of the Chair (I had obtained this position for him from the Collège de France some time ago), and a symbolic amount of money: 25,000 francs. I had naturally obtained the agreement of Alain Horeau, the *Administrateur* of the Collège, to the signing of the convention. The CEA was offering a laboratory sited at the Orme des Merisiers, with its staff, its equipment, and its budget. This convention was not unlike the recipe for partridge pâté: one partridge, one horse. (It may be granted that I was a plump partridge.) The convention was signed by both parties, and gave me five active and happy years from 1980 to 1985.

Shall I confess that I cannot reread this chapter without a feeling of annoyance. All through it I come out as the smartest, the one who always has the last word and makes the right decision, and I cannot help asking myself: was it really like that? Haven't I kept silent about circumstances where, in exercising my directorial activities, I made crude mistakes, where I had to back down, or made a fool of myself as I did more than once in my youth?

Digging in my memory, I don't have that impression, but what does it prove? In the course of a fairly long life, the mind ends up learning how to filter memories, in order to preserve one's emotional and intellectual balance, and to reject what might upset it. Perhaps on a psychoanalyst's couch, or in a shrewd lawyer's office, I would appear as a director who did lots of stupid things. Perhaps. But to me, my dear memory, obedient and well-disciplined, repeats only what I wrote in this chapter.

Nuclear magnetic order

The Conquerors of the Useless
Lionel Terray

*What I did not do—*Order External and Order Internal—Vatican and London—*The keys to the problem—**The lamp in the refrigerator and the rotating frame—The send-off—*First steps and first results—**Microscopic probes—**Calling up neutrons—*Interdisciplinarity—*Taking the bull by the horns—**Ordered rotating phases—**Nuclear pseudomagnetism—*Pseudonuclear magnetism—Dramatis personae—*The drones—*μSR, a late child*

During the thirty odd years I spent in my nuclear magnetism laboratory at Saclay, we naturally tackled a good many problems. We selected them and handled them with a certain penchant for elegance, which, unlike the great Ludwig Boltzman, we did not view as something to be left to the tailors.

My own tastes have always pushed me towards so-called 'crucial' experiments which yield a 'yes or no' answer, towards husbandry of means, towards the search for original and specific methods which appeal to the imagination, but which, all too often, are limited to the purpose for which they have been devised. I had little patience with long, painstaking and accurate studies (fortunately, some of my coworkers did have that patience). I could have been accused, with good reason, of lacking in perseverance—were it not that the study which has given its title to this chapter and which, with ups and downs, extended over nearly two decades, offers striking evidence to the contrary.

Before getting to it, it would be disingenuous not to mention two domains of nuclear magnetic resonance (NMR), to which the efforts of more than 90 per cent of the users and nearly 100 per cent of the designers of NMR equipment are now devoted—and in which my laboratory took no part.

The first of these is the so-called high resolution NMR, which is devoted to the observation and interpretation of the very complicated spectra of organic and biological molecules. Sophisticated (and costly) equipment, using extremely ingenious and continually renewed methods which rely massively on computers, offer deep insights into the structure of biological molecules. It is, no doubt, a fascinating domain, and one may well ask why my lab has stood outside these studies, which are as beautiful as meaningful. The answer is simple: a physicist specializing in NMR, who offers his assistance to biochemistry or biology, with his specialized knowledge of NMR as his only asset, will never be more than a high level technician—unless he decides to make a radical change and to become half (and perhaps all) biochemist or biologist. If I had known a first class specialist in these fields, capable of carrying me along in that direction, I might have made the move, for I have long kept some flexibility and capacity for change; but it just did not happen.

The second field, which is probably the most familiar one to the layman today, is NMR imaging. This technique, which has developed considerably during the last decade, makes it possible to observe human organs with a resolution superior to that afforded by X-ray scanners. There again my lab has remained by the side of the road, but for a different reason. In this method, every little fragment of the organ under study offers in turn an NMR signal from the protons it contains. By means of appropriate techniques, the signals relative to these fragments are observed and recorded one after the other, and a computer algorithm transforms the time sequence of these signals into a map of the spatial density of the organ's protons, just as the X-ray scanner offers a spatial map of its electronic density. The contrast can be further improved by using local variations in the relaxation times.

Ninety-five per cent of NMR imaging is a matter of computers, and what brought it to the forefront are the fantastic advances made in that field during the last fifteen years. One should admire, no doubt, the foresight and the perseverance of the pioneers, who, in the early seventies, undertook these studies with rather primitive techniques of signal processing; but it should be recognized that, without the computer explosion which took place in the last two decades, they would hardly have succeeded.

The progress of NMR imaging is sometimes a source of embarrassment to me. Because of the success of my book *The Principles of Nuclear Magnetism*, many imagine that I am one of the fathers of this method, and some medical radiologists buy a copy, in the hope, rapidly disappointed, of finding there some enlightenment relative to the problems of their trade. This embarrassment became acute when, a couple of years ago, the French Society of Radiology decided to award me a medal for eminent services to the imaging of the human body. I tried to explain that not only did I not contribute anything of interest to imaging but, even worse, I did not even believe at the beginning that it would work. They said that Rutherford had never believed in the possibility of getting energy out of atomic nuclei. The fact that Rutherford had discovered the atomic nucleus, whereas it was not I who discovered NMR, did not seem to bother them.

But enough about things I did not do, and let us move on to the subject of this chapter.

Order External and Order Internal

*I believe it was in 1950, when I first met Ed Purcell at the Amsterdam conference, that I heard him mention nuclear ferromagnetism as a very interesting phenomenon, but inaccessible in the present state of cryogenic techniques. Since then I had been thinking about it from time to time, but it was only after I discovered dynamic nuclear polarization (DNP) in solids that I had an inkling of the key to the problem.

To understand what nuclear ferromagnetism, or, more generally, any long range nuclear order is like, one should first recall the nature of the external order introduced in a system of nuclear spins by an external magnetic field—the so-called Zeeman order. This is the kind of order which exists in all NMR experiments. A nuclear spin placed in a magnetic field tends to align the magnetic moment it carries along that field, that is, into a position of lowest energy. However, when embedded in a piece of bulk matter, the nuclear spins are continually disoriented through thermal agitation. Between the orientation originating in the magnetic field and the disorientation caused by thermal agitation, a compromise is reached, where the nuclear polarization is of the order of the ratio $(\mu H/kT)$ of magnetic energy of a nuclear moment μ, to thermal energy kT. We saw in an earlier chapter that, for protons at room temperature, this ratio is of the order of a few parts in a million in a field of one Tesla, and of the order of one part in a billion in the Earth's magnetic field. But we also saw that at the temperature of liquid helium it was possible, using DNP, to reach polarizations close to unity.

If there is no external field, what are the conditions for the existence of a long range order—say, ferromagnetic—of nuclear spins? It should occur when the energy of a single spin, resulting from its interaction with the surrounding spins, is not small compared to the thermal energy kT. A crude estimate can be made as follows: at the site of each nucleus exists a local magnetic field H_L, produced by its neighbours. It is of the order of a few gauss for protons, and smaller for other nuclear species. One can guess that for a long range order to exist, the ratio $(\mu H_L/kT)$ of the magnetic energy of each spin in the local field H_L to the thermal energy kT, should be at least of order unity. With a local field H_L of a few gauss and the μ of the proton, this yields temperatures below one microkelvin. No wonder that Purcell had considered it to be beyond the cryogenic possibilities of the day.*

Before discussing the means for reaching this goal, I would like to illustrate the difference between a Zeeman order—induced by an *external* field—and an *internal* order—induced by interactions between the spins—through an image suggested perhaps by my belonging to both the Pontifical Academy and, as a foreign member, to the Royal Society of London.

Imagine a Roman crowd massed in St Peter's Square, being addressed by the Supreme Pontiff from a window of the Vatican. All the eyes in this crowd are turned towards that window; and also, inevitably, all the noses, which we shall choose as vector models of the spins. All the noses are therefore parallel to each other, (neglecting the small effect of parallax). We have here a Zeeman order of noses, induced by external 'Pontifical field', which is the Pontifical presence.

Now imagine the same Roman crowd, already massed in the square half an hour before the Pope is due to appear at his window. They have no particular reason to look towards a window where the Pope will not appear for another half hour, and one might think that their noses are oriented entirely at random. To see how an internal order of the noses may conceivably appear, we have to make a few plausible assumptions about interactions. We shall assume (not an unrealistic assumption), that these Romans are fond of eating garlic, which they consume in large quantities, but that they relish the taste of garlic in their own mouths more than its smell on their neighbour's breath. There will be, for each Roman nose, a trend toward avoiding his neighbour's face and turning preferentially toward his back, which makes his nose parallel to this neighbour's nose. There is a 'ferromagnetic' coupling between their orientations. Does it mean that all the noses in the square will be parallel to each other? Not quite.

This, as I said, is a Roman crowd, warm and lively. They exchange jokes and comments, they fidget, they jostle each other, and no nose keeps the same orientation for any length of time. Furthermore their dislike of the smell of garlic exhaled by their neighbours is slight. It is a case of weak interaction and high temperature. There will be a short range order where two neighbouring noses tend to be parallel, but this order will not spread over a large distance, and there will be no correlation between two noses, say, twenty feet apart.

Now picture a crowd of English gentlemen (an endangered species, I am told) *unacquainted with each other*, who naturally would not dream of eating garlic. They are, however, mortally afraid of being spoken to by people to whom they have not been introduced. There will be a strong incentive for each of them to stare at a neighbouring back, with again a ferromagnetic arrangement of the noses, caused by a ferromagnetic interaction which is much stronger than with my Romans. Furthermore, this is a *cold* crowd. They don't fidget and jostle each other, and every English nose keeps the same orientation for a long time. Strong interaction and low temperature: there will be a long range order, and two English noses many yards apart will be parallel to each other.

The ferromagnetic order of spins is not the only one which exists in nature: with electronic spins, an *antiferromagnetic* order was observed more than half a century ago; this is where the two nearest neighbours are antiparallel. (The reader may, if he so wishes, imagine for himself what kind of food would induce an antiferromagnetic arrangement in the model of the Roman crowd.)

The frivolous analogy between an assembly of spins and the Roman crowd can be pushed a little further. The external 'Pontifical field' acts on the *eyes* rather than on the *noses* of the Romans, and, if it orients the noses, it is indirectly because they are anatomically parallel to the direction of the eyes. On the other hand, in the internal order, it is the noses themselves which are responsible for their orientation in the 'garlic' model. The same thing happens in ferromagnetic ordering of electronic spins. Each spin carries a magnetic moment collinear with it, which is the analogue of the parallelism between the eyes and the noses of the Romans. An external magnetic field applied to a ferromagnetic substance will act on the *magnetic moments* rather than on the spins, and the spins will follow because they are collinear with the moments. On the other hand, it is the spins themselves which are responsible for the ferromagnetic ordering through a non-magnetic quantum-mechanical exchange coupling, as explained in an earlier chapter, and it is the magnetic moments which follow suit.

In nuclear ordering the exchange coupling between spins does not exist (with the exception of ^{3}He, to which I shall return). There is no other coupling between nuclear spins but magnetic, and at least for light nuclei it has a well-defined mathematical form—the so-called dipolar form—and a magnitude which is entirely determined from the values of the magnetic moments and the interatomic distances: all of which is very well known. Everything in nuclear dipolar order can thus be calculated entirely, at least in principle, if not in practice; it is a 'clean' problem. It was these twin aspects, the cleanliness and the arduousness (something like the snowy purity of a Himalayan summit), which for nearly twenty years attracted me to nuclear magnetic order, along with those who had been willing to accompany me in this quest.

All right; but 'How and Where and Who?' says Kipling.

'That is the question', says someone else.

The keys to the problem

*The two keys were in my hands: their names were 'dynamic nuclear polarization' (DNP) and 'spin temperature.'

The first produced an almost perfect Zeeman order of the spins; the second a 'cooling' of the nuclear spins down to the temperatures required for the production of a long-range order—a microkelvin or less—replacing the 'external' Zeeman order by an 'internal' dipolar order.

In fact, the concept of spin temperature can advantageously be replaced by that of entropy, of which it is enough to remember here that is is a quantitative measure of the order existing within a system. The entropy is zero if the order is perfect and has its maximum value in a situation of complete chaos. By producing an almost perfect Zeeman order, one reduces the system's entropy to nearly zero; or at least to a value lower than the critical entropy, which is the value below which an internal long-range order appears. The next step is to suppress the applied field very slowly and reversibly, (adiabatically is the technical term), taking care to introduce as little new disorder as possible in the process, i.e. an increase in entropy which is as small as possible. During this 'adiabatic demagnetization', as it is called, the external Zeeman order turns progressively into an internal dipolar order. (The Roman analogue of an adiabatic demagnetization would be a disappearance of the Pope from his window, very gradually and very slowly, something like the Cheshire Cat.)

In 1960 I wrote down my ideas on nuclear magnetic order, with a few details on their possible implementation, in a letter to the *Physical Review*, under the title 'On the possibility of observing cooperative phenomena in nuclear magnetism'. It was returned to me with two comments from the referee, one rather flattering, the other less so. In the first, the referee said that, since the author was the leader of a laboratory, the very high quality of which was recognized by all, why didn't he do the experiment first and talk about it then? The other comment was that the idea had occurred to many physicists. There was indeed some good sense in the first comment; but, as for the second, one may well ask why none of all those physicists, who were said to have thought about it, didn't do anything about it. Be it as it may, I published my cogitations in the *Comptes Rendus de l'Académie des Sciences*, a publication which is both hospitable and not much read abroad—which makes it possible to publish interim results without catching the eye of the competition.

On the experimental side there was one difficulty which had not escaped me. Considering the weakness of nuclear magnetic moments, NMR was, and still is to a large extent, the only method for observing their behaviour. But NMR is only observable in a high magnetic field. By reducing this field to zero in an adiabatic demagnetization, one was perhaps creating an ordered state of the spins, but in the same move one deprived oneself of the possibility of making sure of its existence. It is not unlike trying to find out whether the lamp in a refrigerator goes off when one closes the door. I had this difficulty on my mind when, in 1962, I published a short note in the *Comptes Rendus* with the title 'Nuclear ferromagnetism in the rotating frame'. I am now going to open a parenthesis to explain the nature of the rotating frame, a concept familiar to NMR users, and how it may solve what I call the problem of the 'refrigerator lamp.'

**The rotating frame and the refrigerator lamp

Use of the 'rotating frame' makes it possible to 'have your cake and eat it', that is to transfer the Zeeman order which has been created by DNP in a high field H to the dipolar spin-spin interactions, while keeping on, that high field for observing the state of the spins by NMR.

The difficulty resides in the fact that the Zeeman spin energy is quantized in quanta of the order of, say, a hundred megahertz, whereas the energy spectrum of the dipolar interactions does not extend beyond some hundred kilohertz. In high field the two systems are not on 'speaking terms'. It is, however, possible to ensure a flow of energy, and thus also of entropy, between them, by providing the dipolar system with the energy it lacks to 'speak' to the Zeeman system, in the form of radiofrequency quanta, which are brought in by an RF field, rotating at a frequency Ω, near the Zeeman frequency Ω_0.

One of the two frequencies (the Zeeman frequency Ω_0, in general) is swept slowly (adiabatically), from a value distant from Ω, all the way to Ω—that is to resonance. At resonance, most of the entropy contained in the disordered dipolar system passes on into the Zeeman system, or, in other words, most of the Zeeman order passes on into the dipolar system. Then, after the RF field is cut off, the two systems are again isolated from each other, and one might think that the presence of the high magnetic field can be forgotten. Not quite. Although the cutting off of the RF field suppresses the flow of energy (and entropy) between the Zeeman and the dipolar systems, it can be shown that, simply by being present, the high applied magnetic field forces a splitting of the dipolar interaction into two parts. Only one of them, the so-called 'truncated' dipolar interaction, is effective in the presence of the high applied field. This 'truncation' is due to the fact that in high field some parts of the dipolar interaction, which precess at the Zeeman frequency Ω_0 (or at twice that frequency), have no influence on the dipolar order and should be dropped. The form of the remaining, 'truncated' part depends on the orientation of the applied magnetic field with respect to the crystalline axes of the sample—which is a very essential fact.

The above presentation can be put on a more quantitative basis by introducing the concept of the 'rotating frame'. To describe the behaviour of the spins in the presence of a rotating field, it is convenient to choose as a frame of reference one which rotates with the velocity Ω of the field; this is the 'rotating frame'. In that frame the rotating field, of amplitude H_1, orthogonal to the applied field H, appears as a *static* field of amplitude H_1 which is much simpler. On the other hand, since the new frame is *rotating*, it is not an inertial frame any more, and a force of inertia must be brought in. It can be shown that this is equivalent to replacing the large applied field H by a fictitious field $\Delta H = (H - H^*)$—where H^* is the value of H at exact resonance—when the Zeeman frequency Ω_0 has been made equal to Ω. In the rotating frame the nuclear spins 'think' that they 'feel' an effective field H_e, which is the geometrical sum of the two *static* fields, ΔH and H_1, orthogonal to each other.

The opening of the flow of entropy between the Zeeman and the dipolar systems is called adiabatic demagnetization in the rotating frame (ADRF). Far from resonance, the effective field H_e is practically parallel to the applied field H, and thus also to the equilibrium nuclear magnetization M. In the course of the ADRF this magnetization 'follows' the effective field which moves more and more away from the direction of H, until, at exact resonance, where ΔH vanishes, H_e reduces to the RF field H_1. The ADRF is then brought to an end by removing the field H_1. If the initial polarization was high enough, a long range dipolar order of the spins will appear.

One should notice that if the ADRF is started from the end of the resonance where $\Delta H = (H - H^*)$ is *antiparallel* to H, one starts from a situation where the equilibrium magnetization M is *antiparallel* to the effective field, that is from a state of *negative* temperature. This sign does not change as the ADRF proceeds and leads to a dipolar state of negative temperature.

Besides solving the problem of the 'refrigerator lamp', ADRF brings many new and fascinating variations on the conventional theme of dipolar order. Two different orientations of the applied field with respect to the crystalline axes correspond to two different ways of truncating the dipolar interaction and two, qualitatively different, ordered structures. Furthermore. for a given orientation of the field, the two signs of the spin temperature must correspond to quite different structures, since at negative temperature a stable structure of the spins is the one which *maximizes* the energy.

Naturally the lifetime of a state where the spins are at a positive or negative temperature, whose absolute value is millions of times lower than the lattice temperature, is limited by the spin–lattice relaxation time T_d of the dipolar energy, which, for reasons that it would be too long to discuss here, is shorter by several orders of magnitude than the Zeeman relaxation time T_1. Yet these times T_d may sometimes reach values of the order of one hour, making the study of such ordered states possible.**

The send-off

I seem to remember that most of these ideas were present in my mind, at least qualitatively, in 1965, when, despite the objections of my usual 'acid test', Jacques Winter, I suggested that two of my best coworkers—the two Maurices, Maurice Chapellier and Maurice Goldman—tackle this problem with me, head on, in the framework of the ideas I have just outlined.

In 1965 Chapellier was twenty-seven, Goldman thirty-two, and I fifty. No one in our trio was a *Polytechnicien* or a *Normalien*; Chapellier had come from the Ecole Supérieure des Télécommunications or *Telecom*, Goldman from the Ecole de Physique et Chimie or PC; and the reader remembers, I hope, that I am a graduate of *Supelec*. Nothing very prestigious by French standards.

The contribution made by Chapellier and Goldman was vital, and it was only fair that, a few years later, they should share the largest prize of our Academie des Sciences with me. Over the years our little team was enriched with more participants, whom I shall mention as I go along. Chapellier drifted away from us in the early seventies, to work on problems of his choice in the field of very low temperatures, after being the main actor in the first experimental observation of nuclear magnetic order.

Goldman's activity remained closely associated with my own until my final retirement in 1985. For fourteen years he was deputy director of my chair at the Collège, a position he gave up to return to the CEA full time, two or three years before my retirement. His contribution to the theory of nuclear magnetic ordering was invaluable: there are few points there for which he was not responsible. We wrote a comprehensive monograph together, published by Oxford University Press in 1982 under the title: *Nuclear Magnetism, Order and Disorder* (a title suggested by Bleaney), in which we reviewed all the matters which had caught our imagination since the publication of my *Principles*. I have made it clear in advance, at the start of this chapter, why there is nothing in it on the biochemical and medical applications of NMR. Spin temperature, dynamic nuclear polarization, and nuclear magnetic order, (henceforth sometimes abridged to NMO), take the lion's share. A large part of the last chapter is devoted to the theory of NMO, a theory which was slanted towards rigour by Goldman, and towards pedagogy by me. In 1976 Goldman was awarded the Holweck Prize (some twenty years after me and five years after Solomon), and in 1986 he was elected as *correspondant* (the equivalent of junior member) of our Academy. Both gave me great pleasure. Among the physicists of his generation, Goldman holds a special place. His excellent physical intuition, backed by great computing ability, his constant search for rigour, our common tastes and interests, as well as the significant differences in our approach to problems—all of it made him an ideal companion for my long journey through nuclear magnetism. With time he got rid of a certain trend for complication, and of some diffident and oversensitive traits of his character. I learned a lot by his side, and I like to think that he picked up a few things from me. My wish would have been to see him continue the good work as a professor at the Collège, something in which the Collège tradition left me no say whatsoever. My colleagues preferred a clean break, not only with nuclear magnetism but the physics at large, since, as I said in an earlier chapter, my successor's chair is devoted to geodynamics.

*First steps and first results

I wish now to retrace the main steps of our work. First of all, there was the choice of the substance in which NMO could be produced and observed. In 1965 we knew how to polarize the hydrogeneous substances we used as polarized targets material, but we discarded them from the start because their structure was so complicated and so poorly known that, even if we had been able to produce an NMO in them, we could not have recognized it by NMR methods. Instead we chose a single crystal of calcium fluoride CaF_2 where the nuclei of ^{19}F, which have a spin (1/2), form a simple cubic lattice, and the calcium nuclei, apart from a rare isotope, have zero spin Since the ordered structures depend on the orientation of the magnetic field with respect to the crystalline axes, it was imperative to use single crystals. Goldman calculated the structures to be expected, and the critical polarizations required for various orientations of the magnetic field and for both signs of the temperature, using methods derived from the theory of the so-called Weiss mean field. Next there was the choice of the doping paramagnetic impurities which would perform King Solomon's duties in our crystal. Then followed a long period of trials with trivalent uranium as the paramagnetic impurity, in which fluorine polarizations of 35 per cent were reached in 1966, and 50 per cent in 1967. A decisive step was the replacement of trivalent uranium by divalent thulium, and even more important was the lowering of the lattice temperature down to 0.3 K. This was achieved with a liquid ^3He cryostat that Chapellier boldly improvised from scratch in six months, with a lot of dash and a pinch of luck. A third innovation was the doubling of the microwave DNP frequency, its wavelength passing from 4 mm to 2 mm. The nuclear polarization exceeded 60 per cent (and later 90 per cent) and, following the ADRF of the fluorine spins, we observed a characteristic plateau in the dependence of the transverse susceptibility as a function of the spin dipolar energy—an unmistakable sign of a nuclear antiferromagnetic state, in accordance with the predictions made by Goldman.

It was in 1969, nearly four years after the team was formed, that Chapellier, Goldman, Vu-Hoang-Chau (a graduate student), and I published a description of something that no one had seen before, the production and observation of an antiferrogmagnetic nuclear state.

The significant steps of the next five years, were the following (not necessarily listed in strict chronological order). NMO was looked for and observed in another crystal, LiF the lithium fluoride. For paramagnetic impurities we used colour centres, the so-called F-centres, produced by the irradiation of the crystal with gamma-rays. Some interesting phenomena were observed relative to the couplings between the spins of the two different nuclear species, ^7Li and ^{19}F, but nothing fundamentally new in the NMO proper. One should simply note that for the ADRF of the two nuclear spin species, two RF fields of different frequencies must be used simultaneously.

In calcium fluoride, where fluorine polarization had meanwhile gone up to 90 per cent, we discovered a ferromagnetic domain structure, predicted by theory for a negative temperature and a field applied along a threefold axis of the cube. This observation raised the crucial problem of finding 'microscopic probes' capable of discriminating between antiferromagnetism and domain ferromagnetism.

In the antiferromagnetic structure, the nuclear spins of successive atomic planes are alternately parallel and antiparallel to the field, which is applied along a fourfold axis of the cube. It is the Néel's two sublattices model. The spins parallel to the field provide a positive signal, while those antiparallel provide a negative signal equal to the former but opposite in sign; the two do not cancel, however, because they are shifted in opposite directions by the internal fields of opposite signs which each sublattice exerts on the other one.

The ferromagnetic structure is made of ferromagnetic domains, which are slabs perpendicular to the applied field, each some hundred atomic planes thick, whose magnetization is alternately parallel and antiparallel to the field. It is easy to see, with the same arguments as for the antiferromagnetic structure, that its NMR signal has qualitatively the same shape. Theory does predict a small difference in the distance between the two peaks, positive and negative, of the NMR line, but it is impossible to observe in practice. This is a general weakness of NMR, whose RF fields are homogeneous over a small sample (ours was a sphere of 1.3 mm in diameter) and ill-suited to this problem.

** Microscopic probes

The problem of discriminating between the two structures was solved thanks to the existence of ^{43}Ca, a rare (0.13 per cent) isotope of calcium, with a small magnetic moment. It turns out that in the antiferromagnetic structure of the fluorines, all the positions of a calcium nucleus are equivalent, and all the spins of ^{43}Ca 'see' the same mean field produced by the fluorines, whereas in the ferromagnetic domain structure, spins of ^{43}Ca situated in domains of opposite signs, 'see' opposite mean fluorine fields. The Zeeman NMR signal of ^{43}Ca is thus a single line in the antiferromagnetic structure, and a double line in the ferromagnetic case: an introconvertible experimental evidence of the difference between the two structures. I rather like that experiment.

In view of its rarity and of its small magnetic moment, it had been necessary to polarize ^{43}Ca to nearly 100 per cent, in order to get a signal of acceptable magnitude. Because of this isotopic rarity it could not be polarized from paramagnetic impurities in a straightforward manner by the King Solomon method, and had to get its polarization from the polarized fluorines in the following manner (called the Hahn and Hartmann method after its inventors). Two RF fields are applied in the neighbourhoods of the resonance frequencies of both ^{19}F and ^{43}Ca in such a way that the Larmor frequencies of the two species, each in its own effective field, are made equal. The two spin species are then on speaking terms, and the polarization of ^{43}Ca can be made equal to the high polarization of ^{19}F. It took some time but was made to work eventually.

Presenting this observation of the ferromagnetic structure for the first time at an international conference in 1973, I remarked: 'Four years separate this presentation from the publication of an antiferromagnetic structure, where the field was applied along a fourfold axis of the cube, instead of the threefold axis as in the present experiment. Taking four years to rotate a magnetic field from one axis of the crystal to the other, should be rated as one of the slowest rotations in the history of physics.' I shall speak later of another crucial experiment where the spin of ^{43}Ca acted as a probe; but I shall pass on now to another type of probe, the spin of the neutron, whose role has been vital.* *

* * Calling up neutrons

For over twenty years neutron diffraction has been a choice tool in studies of *electronic* antiferromagnetism. Let me explain how, beginning with X-ray diffraction. When an X-ray beam impinges on a crystal, for certain orientations of the beam with respect to its atomic planes, there is constructive interference between the X-photons scattered by the different atoms of the crystal, and sharp maxima of diffracted radiation, called Bragg peaks, are observed in certain well-defined directions. If the crystal is antiferromagnetic, the magnetic moments of its atoms will have opposite orientations in two neighbouring atomic planes. The scattering amplitude of an X-photon on a magnetic atom is (practically) independent of the orientation of the atomic moment, and the X-photon is unable to 'distinguish between' two such planes, which appear identical to it. On the contrary, the neutron which carries a magnetic moment itself, will have different scattering amplitudes on two magnetic atoms with opposite moments. It will 'see' two neighbouring atomic planes of an antiferro-magnet as being different, and the lattice period will appear twice as large to it as to an X-ray beam. The Bragg condition applied to this new period will give rise to new Bragg peaks when an antiferromagnetic state sets in. Their observation, in 1949, was the first direct evidence of the correctness of the two sublattices model, which Néel had proposed some fifteen years earlier.

Well then, why not seek the same tangible evidence from neutrons for the existence of *nuclear* antiferromagnetism—which, I regret to say, had met with considerable misgivings from specialists in electronic magnetism. (In 1969 when I presented the first nuclear antiferromagnetic structure at an international magnetism conference, it was pointed out to me that such a structure could not possibly exist because it *maximized* the energy of the spin system; and my answer—that this is exactly the kind of state that spins at a negative temperature were hankering for—did not convince everybody.)

There was just one little difficulty, which specialists in neutron diffraction were not slow in pointing out to me: namely, that scattering amplitudes of the neutron magnetic moment by nuclear magnetic moments were thousands of time smaller than for *atomic* moments, and that what had worked for atomic antiferromagnetism, would not work for the nuclear version. True, but there was a way out. The scattering of a neutron by a nucleus is due to a *nuclear* force, and, as I explained in connection with polarized targets, its amplitude depends on the relative orientation of the spin of the neutron and the spin of the nucleus. This scattering amplitude will be different for two nuclei with opposite spins. The neutron spin is thus capable of distinguishing between two nuclear spins with opposite orientation, not through a *magnetic* interaction with their magnetic moments but through a *nuclear* interaction with their spins. But— '*Qu'importe le flacon pourvu qu'on ait l'ivresse*'—the main thing is that the neutron is capable of rcognizing the difference between two planes which carry opposite nuclear magnetizations.

It is convenient to pretend that this 'recognition' is of a *magnetic* nature by assigning each nuclear species with a fictitious magnetic moment, which I called its 'pseudomagnetic' moment and represented by the symbol μ^*. By definition, this pseudomagnetic moment is equal to the magnetic moment a nucleus should possess in order that its *magnetic* coupling with the *magnetic* moment of the neutron be equal in strength to the *actual nuclear* coupling, which exists between the spin of the neutron and that of the nucleus.

Nuclear forces are much stronger than magnetic forces, and there was reason to hope that a nuclear pseudomagnetic moment might be much larger than its true magnetic moment, and even be comparable to atomic magnetic moments which had made possible the observation of electronic antiferromagnetism by neutron diffraction. It was certainly true for the proton, about which it had been known for a long time that its scattering of neutrons was strongly spin-dependent. Translated into pseudomagnetic language, its pseudomagnetic moment μ^* (^{1}H) was equal to 3500 times (!) its real magnetic moment.

What was it likc with ^{19}F, thc only nucleus whose NMO we had observed so far? I rushed towards tables of nuclear data and was chagrined to find there the pseudomagnetic moments (presented naturally in a different language) of only four nuclei: proton, deuteron, cobalt and vanadium. The reason for this dearth was that in a neutron scattering on an *unpolarized* target, as were all the scatterings reported in scientific literature, μ^* appears squared and is measurable only if it is relatively large.

This was the case for the four nuclei in the table. With respect to ^{19}F, the table only gave for μ^* (^{19}F) an upper limit of 200 times its true magnetic moment $\mu(^{19}F)$, with the sign unknown. It followed that the observation of nuclear antiferromagnetism in CaF_2 was not ruled out *a priori*. To be certain, it was crucial to do a Bragg diffraction of *polarized* neutrons on a *polarized* target, for only then is the result linearly dependent on the product of μ^* times the target polarization.**

*Interdisciplinarity

There was a research reactor at Saclay, and a group of neutron physicists were busily studying antiferromagnetic structures—electronic naturally— using neutron diffraction. My problem was to persuade them to drop whatever they were doing, and to launch themselves, with the assistance of my lab, into an experiment of neutron diffraction on a polarized fluorine target. This was not the simplest thing in the world at the time. I was not surprised by their lack of enthusiasm: they had to be talked into it. I am going to describe, at some length, I am afraid, how I went about it. I explained to them how important it was to demonstrate, resoundingly and beyond all doubt, the physical reality of nuclear antiferromagnetism, using neutron diffraction, which was after all their own province. Before starting on that experiment, which would no doubt prove lengthy and difficult, it was important, I said, to do a quick preliminary experiment, and make sure that the μ^* of the fluorine was large enough to attempt it. Unconvinced by my 'quick', they asked me the following question, which was indeed far from unreasonable: 'If, after doing with you the preliminary experiment you propose, which does not look all that "quick" to us, it turns out that the μ^* of fluorine *is* too small to attempt the observation of nuclear antiferromagnetism, will our efforts have been completely wasted; or will the knowledge of μ^* (^{19}F) be at least of some use to theorists of nuclear structure?' 'I don't know,' I answered honestly, 'but I shall find out.'

I went to see the leader of the nuclear theorists, a fanatic of nuclear wave functions, and asked him whether the problem of the μ^* of fluorine, or more generally of the μ^* of nuclei at large, was of some interest to his group. 'Not really,' he said. 'We cannot compute these things to anything better than 20 per cent accuracy, which is not good enough to discriminate between the various nuclear models at our disposal.' 'What a pity,' said the honest go-between. 'The neutronists are all set to do the measurement, and naturally they would like to compare their result with theoretical predictions.' 'That changes everything,' he said. 'If they are really doing the experiment I shall give the calculation as a thesis subject to one of our graduate students.' I went back to the neutronists, and informed them that the theoreticians were tickled to death by the prospect of their measurement, and were even putting a man on the subject, full time. 'That changes everything,' they said. 'We shall start on it straightaway.'

The reader can draw his own conclusion from this little true story. Mine is that interdisciplinarity is a beautiful thing if the interdisciplinary contacts are carried out in an intelligent manner.

A word about the results. The theoretical prediction was: $\mu^*(^{19}\text{F}) \approx -140\mu(^{19}\text{F})$. The neutronists measured $\mu^*(^{19}\text{F}) \approx -15\mu(^{19}\text{F})$, much too small to attempt a study of fluorine nuclear antiferromagnetism with neutrons. The enormous overestimate of the theoretical calculation (where was the promised 20 per cent?) was in a way a boon, for if they had predicted the order of magnitude correctly, we would have probably not dared to attempt the experiment, which gave us a most useful experience with polarized neutrons and polarized targets. It was the start of a long, friendly, and fruitful collaboration with our neutronists. More of that later. By the same method we measured $\mu^*(^{7}\text{Li})$, and would have attempted other nuclei if I had not invented a different and much better method, which I shall describe later in this chapter.*

*The bull by the horns

It was in 1974 that we decided to polarize the nuclei of hydrogen and lithium in lithium hydride LiH, in order to produce an NMO which was observable with neutrons. It took four years (!), since it was only in the spring of 1978 that we saw the first antiferromagnetic Bragg peak. I do not wish to describe the innumerable difficulties we had to face in detail: obtaining single crystals of LiH; creating the paramagnetic impurities necessary for DNP in the crystal by bombarding it with fast electrons from an electron accelerator; empirically determining the optimal conditions for this irradiation (energy of the electrons and temperature of the target). We also had to design and construct a superconducting solenoid which produced a magnetic field of 5.5 Teslas and a dilution cryostat which went down in temperature below 0.1 K—both of them permitting the passage of incoming and outgoing neutron beams without depolarizing them; a sample holder permitting the orientation of the crystal *in situ*; a horn permitting the irradiation of the sample with polarizing microwaves; an RF electronics permitting the simultaneous ADRF of both nuclear species ^{7}Li and ^{1}H, and the automated measurement of their polarizations. It was far from being Big Science yet, but it was already far from being table-top physics. I should add that polarization times were of the order of forty-eight hours, that is two days and two nights, whereas the lifetime of the ordered nuclear state, which was observable after the ADRF, was an hour at best.

But, as was proclaimed in the motto printed on the back of my school exercise books: '*Labor improbus omnia vincit*', and one day in the spring of 1978 we did the following experiment.

The neutron counter for diffracted neutrons had been placed in the position where the antiferromagnetic Bragg peak was expected, and the nuclei of the sample of LiH were duly polarized to 90 per cent for ^{1}H, and 65 per cent for ^{7}Li. The counter started to count background neutrons. Nothing else was expected since the sample was *not antiferromagnetic yet*. Then the ADRF was performed. The counting rate made a jump which corresponded to the expected antiferromagnetic peak, and then decreased slowly with a time constant of the order of an hour, while the entropy of the nuclear spins slowly grew as a result of relaxation, until it reached the critical value above which the antiferromagnetic nuclear order disappears. I remember that we were gathered silently around the apparatus which recorded the counting rate, while the physicist entrusted with the final thrust of the ADRF was officiating; then the jump in the counting rate appeared, crowning four years of efforts—'divine surprise of seeing the predicted phenomenon where it was expected and such as expected.'

Need I add that diffraction experiments with LiH were pursued, improved, amplified, compared to theoretical predictions, and reported at numerous international conferences. I will say no more for fear of exhausting the patience of those of my readers whom I have not already lost long ago.

A last remark about the studies of NMO with neutrons. There is in that respect an amusing symmetry, or rather antisymmetry, between electronic and nuclear magnetic order. I have insisted at various places in this book on the fact that electronic antiferromagnetism was caused by so-called exchange interactions between *spins*, which were *non-magnetic* in nature. On the other hand its observation by neutron diffraction rests on the existence of *magnetic* interactions between the *magnetic* moments of the neutrons and the electrons. To sum up, it is a *non-magnetic* phenomenon, detected by *magnetic* means.

On the other hand, nuclear antiferromagnetism is a purely *magnetic* phenomonon due to *magnetic* interactions between nuclear *magnetic* moments. But its detection with neutrons rests on a nuclear, and therefore non-magnetic, interaction (termed for that reason pseudomagnetic) between nuclear spins and neutron spins. A purely magnetic phenomenon, detected by non-magnetic means. 'So what?' I may be asked. 'So nothing; it's amusing, that's all.'*

At the risk of completely discouraging my patient reader, I want to speak briefly of three more phenomena: ordered rotating phases, nuclear pseudomagnetism, and a phenomenon I beg him not to confuse with it, namely pseudonuclear magnetism.

In all the nuclear structures, ordered in the rotating frame, which we had observed before 1980, the spins were always aligned parallel or antiparallel to the large applied field H. Since the axis of rotation of the rotating frame is precisely that same magnetic field, these structures appeared as identical in the rotating frame and in the laboratory frame. In order not to scare specialists in electronic magnetism away, in conferences at least, I even spoke of 'nuclear order in high field', rather than of 'nuclear order in the rotating frame', since for longitudinal structures the two languages were equivalent. However, Goldman's theory predicted the possibility of *transverse* structures, which, although static in the rotating frame, had to appear as rotating in the laboratory frame—which is after all the one where we live and our detectors stand. Such structures, stable at the time scale of the dipolar relaxation time T_d, and yet rotating at a hundred million turns per second, looked improbable, to say the least.

Their seeming extravagance was tempered to some extent by the fact that after an ADRF, there is no transverse nuclear magnetization left, and no electromotive force could be produced by such rotating structures in any macroscopic coil. This was just as well, because the loss of energy by radiation, known in scientific literature, (somewhat improperly), as 'radiation damping', would have put an end to the existence of such a structure in a time much shorter than T_d.

A theory of Goldman's, more refined than the simple mean field theory, predicted that in calcium fluoride, with the field along a threefold axis and at *positive* temperature (remember that at *negative* temperature the structure for this orientation of the field was a longitudinal domain ferromagnet), the spins should be arranged in a transverse helical structure. Goldman had thought up an extremely elegant experiment to demonstrate its existence, and I am going to try to explain its principle.

Let's return to the Hahn and Hartman method, which we used to polarize the spins of ^{43}Ca from those of ^{19}F. A resonant transfer of polarization from one species to the other did occur when the Larmor frequencies of the two species, each in its own rotating effective field, were equal. Such a resonant transfer of polarization was indeed observed in the would-be helical phase, but *without any rotating field being applied to the fluorines*. The explanation was staring us in the face: the local mean field—the so-called Weiss field, 'seen' by each fluorine spin and produced by all the other fluorine spins—was *rotating*, which was only possible if the whole fluorine structure was rotating also. Naturally, the phases of the rotating Weiss fields were distributed in the interval $0, 2\pi$, across the sample, which made them unobservable on a macroscopic scale, but accessible to ^{43}Ca, our microscopic probe. Needless to say, the foregoing

had been expanded and made quantitative, experimentally and theoretically. I like to keep this crucial experiment in my personal little Museum
of Science.

**Nuclear pseudomagnetism

Having assigned each nuclear spin with a pseudomagnetic moment μ^*, it
was tempting to extend it further and to introduce also a nuclear pseudomagnetization $M^*=NP\mu^*$, where N is the number of nuclei per unit
volume and P their polarization, and then a pseudo-induction defined as:
$B^*=H+4\pi N\mu^*$. If one remembered that, inside a magnetic substance,
what the neutron 'sees' is the magnetic induction B rather than the field
H, (the subject of a controversy between Felix Bloch and Dirac before the
war), it was tempting to speculate by analogy that, inside a nuclear
polarized target, the Larmor frequency Ω_n of the neutron is proportional
to the pseudomagnetic induction: $B^*=(H+4\pi M^*) = (H+H^*)$, where
$H^*=4\pi M^* = 4\pi N\mu^* P$ is the pseudomagnetic field 'seen' by the neutron.
The neutron Larmor frequency Ω_n is then displaced with respect to its
vacuum value by: $\Delta\Omega_n=\gamma_n H^*$, where γ_n is the gyromagnetic factor of the
neutron.

I did not 'speculate' on it for a long time, for it turned out to be quite
easy to prove from a very simple concept—the pseudopotential introduced
by Fermi many years ago (everything was pseudo but none the less very
real in that affair). All that remained was to demonstrate experimentally
the existence of this pseudomagnetic field which nobody had seen yet.

For a polarized proton target it looked easy. The pseudomagnetic
moment $\mu^*({}^1H)$ of the proton is enormous, and the pseudomagnetic field
H^* inside a polarized hydrogeneous target would be of the order of two
to three Teslas (!) for a 100 per cent proton polarization.

The proposed experiment was a standard one. A 100 per cent polarized
neutron beam crossed a polarized proton target in an applied field H. The
transmitted beam went to a neutron polarization analyser, which was set
to supply a neutron counter only with neutrons of a polarization *opposite*
to that of the incoming beam—which resulted in a very low counting rate.
An RF coil, surrounding the sample, produced inside it a rotating field H_1.
When the frequency of the RF field was equal to the Larmor frequency of
the neutron *inside* the target, the neutron spins were flipped and more of
them were sent by the analyser toward the counter, whence a resonant
increase of the counting rate. From the resonant frequency, the Larmor
frequency shift $\Delta\Omega_n$ and the pseudomagnetic field H^* could be measured.

An experimental difficulty appeared—a blessed one, for the way in
which we overcame it made the experiment far less standard and far more
beautiful. To flip the spin of the neutron within one microsecond, for such
was its time of flight within the target, we required a rotating field with an

amplitude of the order of 100 gauss, which was not feasible with a coil wound around a sample cooled to 1 K. I shall now describe how we got out of this quandary, which is not the easiest thing in the world to explain with words alone.

We applied a rotating field H_1, with an amplitude of 1 gauss (and not the 100 that were needed), shifted in frequency with respect to the *proton* resonant frequency (I repeat 'proton', not 'neutron') by a distance Δ of the order of 100 gauss. The effective field H_e 'seen' by the protons is tilted with respect to the main field H through a small angle $\beta = (H_1/\Delta) \approx (1/100)$. It is along this effective field H_e that the nuclear magnetization M will align itself, and thus also its pseudomagnetization M^*, and also the pseudomagnetic field $H^* = 4\pi M^*$, which in our experiment was of the order of 10,000 gauss! Because of the smallness of the angle β, the longitudinal component of H^* remains practically unchanged, but H^* will acquire a transverse component: $H_1{}^* \approx \beta H^* \approx (1/100) \times 10{,}000 \approx 100$ gauss, which is of the required magnitude. We have thus given to the pseudomagnetic field a rotating component $H_1{}^*$, a hundred times larger than the applied rotating field H_1. Are we out of the wood? Not quite yet! We have indeed created a rotating pseudomagnetic field $H_1{}^*$, with an amplitude of 100 gauss, but it rotates at the *wrong* frequency, nearly that of the protons ('nearly' because of the small detuning Δ of 100 gauss), which differs frm the *vacuum* Larmor frequency of the neutron by a factor of nearly $-(3/2)$. What can we do about it? 'Vacuum' is the key word. The proton (and any other nucleus of the sample), 'sees' the applied field H only, but the neutron 'sees' also the longitudinal component H^* of the pseudomagnetic field. Remember Macbeth, the only one to see Banquo at the feast. It is easy to adjust the applied field H so that the Larmor frequency of the proton $\Omega_p = \gamma_p H$ be equal to the Larmor frequency of the neutron inside the sample $\Omega_n = \gamma_n(H + H^*)$. And it works! The neutron spin is made to flip like a good boy by a rotating pseudomagnetic field $H_1{}^*$ with an amplitude of 100 gauss. The physical reality of the pseudomagnetic field had been displayed in a spectacular manner. I shall add that, to my knowledge, this is the only example of a *nuclear* field, made to vary in time in a coherent manner. Amusing, what?

Besides being a striking demonstration of the physical reality of the pseudomagnetic field, the somewhat acrobatic experiment that I have just described provided a resonant measurement of the μ^* of the proton. That part of it was of little interest, to tell the truth, because μ^* (^1H) was already known. Also, as what had made the experiment possible was its very large numerical value, it could not be extended easily to other nuclear species.

I imagined a variant of it, inspired by the method invented by Norman Ramsey for molecular beams, which I mentioned in an earlier chapter in connection with Harvard. It made possible the measurement of μ^*s as small as 1 per cent of that of the proton. This is the principle.

Two RF coils of the same frequency, separated by some ten centimetres, and tuned to the vacuum neutron Larmor frequency, are placed in a large magnetic field extending over a polarized neutron beam which crosses the two coils. Without going into details, the effect of the RF coils is to induce a change in the neutron polarization, which is detected by an analyser. If a nuclear polarized target is inserted into the beam between the two coils, the pseudomagnetic field due to the nuclear spins of the target causes a pseudomagnetic precession of the neutrons inside the target and a change in their phase. This in turn produced a measurable change in the polarization of the outgoing beam, related to this change of phase, and in the last resort to the pseudomagnetic moments of the polarized target nuclei.

With respect to the earlier demonstration experiment, which is spectacular but difficult to generalize, the present one offers the following advantages: a) the RF coils are outside the cryostat which contains the target, and therefore at room temperature; b) what is measured is a change in phase rather than a change in frequency, which is far more sensitive and makes feasible the measurement of much smaller μ^* with much lower sample polarizations. This was an experiment, or rather a systematic series of experiments, which over the years filled the neutron data tables with values of μ^*—or to use a language that all neutron physicists recognize, with 'spin-dependent scattering lengths' of some hundred nuclear species— a programme which remains a monopoly of our lab.**

To finish off with nuclear pseudomagnetism, I must reveal that some time after doing our demonstration experiment with the rotating pseudomagnetic field, I discovered, not without displeasure (three negatives, as in German) that, a few years earlier, two theoreticians from the Soviet laboratory of Dubna, had done a calculation predicting a neutron precession in a polarized nuclear target. They had arrived at it through an approach which was quite different from mine. Although Dubna had at the time the best neutron beams in the USSR and a large group working on polarized targets, the paper did not contain any reasonable suggestion on the manner in which this precession could be observed, and no experiment was attempted. It says a lot about the quality of contacts between theoreticians and experimentalists in that country.

More generally, Soviet theorists, who are among the best in the world, have the regrettable habit of predicting an incredible quantity of phenomena in their calculations, without worrying much about their order of magnitude, and even less about the method of observing them. When, years later, somebody who has never heard of their calculations does observe one of these phenomena, they come forward and claim priority. Each of their publications is, in this way, a bet on the future.

I had once compared such behaviour to that of 'Hot Horse Herbie', a character created by the American humorist Damon Runyon. Hot Horse Herbie is a race-track tout who offers sensational betting tips to anyone willing to let him have a fraction of the proceeds of the bet. If the horse wins, Hot Horse Herbie claims his due. If he loses, Herbie just keeps out of sight.

A watchful reader could tell me that I had done the same in my first publication of 1960 on nuclear magnetic order. He may have something there.

*Pseudonuclear magnetism

This is what I call the following phenomenon. Some ions, especially some rare earth ions, have no electronic magnetism in their ground state, the only one to be populated at low temperatures. However, they may have a large magnetic polarizability, which means that in the presence of a magnetic field they may acquire a sizeable magnetic moment. The polarizing field may either be an applied field, or, as is our concern here, the magnetic field produced by the magnetic monent μ of the nucleus of the ion. Under the action of that field the electronic shells of the ion themselves acquire an induced magnetic moment μ'', often much larger the μ. What is then observed in an NMR experiment is the geometric sum: $\mu' = (\mu + \mu'')$

Each component of μ' along a principal axis of a crystalline sample is proportional to the component along the same axis of the nuclear moment μ which gave rise to μ'', but the proportionality coefficients are in general different for the three principal axes of the crystal. The relation between μ' and μ, and thus also between μ' and the nuclear spin I, is an anisotropic, or so-called 'tensor', relation, which can be written: $\mu' = \mathrm{T}I$.

This anisotropy is sometimes very pronounced. Thus in thulium phosphate, a crystal of tetragonal symmetry, the ratio of the transverse components of the tensor T to the longitudinal one is of the order of 25. The coupling between the transverse components of the spins I of two nuclei of ^{169}Tm, which results from the magnetic coupling between the μ' moments, is even more anisotropic, with a ratio $(25)^2$, between the longitudinal and transverse couplings. It follows that in an external magnetic field applied along the longitudinal axis—if the entropy of the nuclear spins, after ADRF, is sufficiently low to permit the appearance of a long range dipolar order—it is certain *a priori* that this order *must* be transverse, that is rotating. This is what attracted me in thulium phosphate, a compound I met with in Bleaney's laboratory, during a lengthy stay there in 1981. I brought home several samples, as well as Bleaney's best graduate student, who for a time became a member of our team. The experiment, which was supposed to last two months, lasted two years for various reasons, some quite predictable, others less so; but ended up with a result in accordance with my *a priori* prediction of an ordered transverse structure.

One may ask why I call it pseudonuclear magnetism. The answer is that the moment μ'' induced by the nuclear moment μ is not nuclear but *electronic*. It is not a philosophical distinction: the *magnetic density* which corresponds to it is distributed all over the ion instead of being concentrated at the nucleus, as for the *true* nuclear moment u. In theory, if not in practice it could be possible, in the sum $\mu'=(\mu+\mu'')$, to separate the distributed part μ'' from the point-like part μ by neutron diffraction.

The moment μ'' is definitely *magnetic*, but it is not *nuclear*. This is why I am splitting hairs in speaking of *pseudonuclear magnetism*. Earlier, particularly in relation to protons, we had met with *nuclear pseudo-magnetism*, a phenomenon which is *nuclear but non-magnetic*.

There is another type of order of the nuclear spins, which is sometimes called magnetic—quite improperly, for there is nothing magnetic about it. It is the order which was observed in the seventies, in solid ^{3}He. The coupling between the nuclear spins which prevails in ^{3}He is of a different nature; it is a quantum-mechanical exchange coupling. I do not propose to talk about it here, beyond the following remark. Its strength is greater, by three to four orders of magnitude, than that of the nuclear dipolar magnetic couplings which are the subject of this chapter, and the transition temperature of ^{3}He is higher by the same amount. This temperature of 1 or 2 millikelvins (not microkelvins or fractions thereof) can be reached directly in a dilution cryostat, without going through the process of nuclear polarization followed by adiabatic demagnetization.*

Dramatis personae

'*How and Where and Who?*' said Kipling.

How I have described at some length in the previous pages.

Where is quickly said: at the annex of Saclay called the Orme des Merisiers, to which we moved in the summer of 1968; with the exception of the neutron diffraction experiments, which were done on the research reactor in the main Saclay laboratory.

Who is a list of the *dramatis personae* who acted for so long in our play. I have already spoken of the two pioneers, the two Maurices, Goldman and Chapellier, and I remember giving a few details about Anatole Abragam. Here are some more actors.

Yves Roinel came from *Supelec* and began with a study of lithium fluoride, in which he replaced Steve Cox, of whom later. Roinel teamed up with Vincent Bouffard, a graduate of the 'National Higher School of Petroleum and of Engines of Internal Combustion' (*sic*, and phew!). The role of that team was absolutely essential. Except for calcium fluoride, on which they did not work, they were a part of everything else. The solidity and reliability of Vincent, and the brilliance and ingenuity of Yves were an excellent combination. The nuclear order in lithium hydride, the only one to have been observed by neutron diffraction in our lab, was their work from A to Z: the doping of the samples by fast electron irradiation, the interminable dynamic polarizations, the selection of the best samples, and finally the transfer to neutrons. It was Yves who gave the triumphant final thrust to the spins of LiH in the neutron beam, in the maiden experiment I spoke about.

Jacques-Francois Jacquinot, a graduate of the Ecole Normale Supérieure de Saint-Cloud (not to be confused with the prestigious one of the Rue d'Ulm), was the calcium fluoride man after Chapellier, who taught him to experiment, and Goldman, who taught him to theorize. He had a gift for saying things which were true and profound in a confusing and muddled way. He in turn taught Christian Urbina, a young Chilean, who was intelligent and likeable (but they were all likeable in that crowd!).

Hans Glättli, a graduate of the Ecole Polytechnique (the one in Zurich, of course!), is an outstanding experimentalist, full of ideas and as clever with his hands as a Swiss watchmaker. His only weakness is his good nature. He somehow manages to attract a very large proportion of lame ducks among his students, whom he drags by the ears (mixed metaphor) toward their degrees, mainly by doing their work himself. He's the man for pseudomagnetism and the enormous programme of measuring the nuclear μ^*.

Claude Fermon, a young true *Normalien* (at last) has taken up the torch left by Yves Roinel, who went on to other things. He twigs before you are through telling him, and should go far—but without me now.

Three talented foreigners have played various parts in the play.

Steve Cox—British, slim, tall, bearded, refined, clever with his hands (and his head)—spent two years in the lab, and he and Vincent Bouffard imposed law and order on the nuclear spins of lithium fluoride. He is now at the Rutherford laboratory where, after a bout with polarized targets, he is a great success in μSR, a pastime of which I shall say a few words presently.

Tom Wenckebach—a Dutchman, whiskered, subtle, and profound—spent only one year in the lab, but it was well filled. He was one of the pioneers in the use of the spin of ^{43}Ca as a microscopic probe, which I have mentioned. He came to us with some beautiful work behind him on spin temperature and dynamic polarization. On his return to Leyden, where he is a professor now, he pursued studies in nuclear magnetic order, an order he produced and observed in calcium hydroxyde: $Ca(OH)_2$.

John Gregg, the one I brought in my luggage from the Clarendon with the samples of thulium phosphate, is an Irishman from Dublin—a protestant (!), but with that grain of mad humour without which Ireland would not be Ireland. Before he left I showed him a rather laudatory letter of recommendation, which I had written for the jury of a fellowship he had applied for. He read it and asked gravely: 'Who's this chap? I would like to meet him.'

I have already spoken, in connection with polarized targets, of our cryogenist Pierre Roubeau, the sailor who came in from the cold; he was irreplaceable, and, alas, was not replaced after his retirement.

I do not wish to forget our technicians, Pasquette and Eisenkramer, who took the same interest in our work as the physicists, and the young Gérard Fournier, who was so gifted and so conscientious, and who tragically left us.

This gallery of portraits would not be complete without our three neutronists: Pierre Mériel, Gian Bacchella, and Marcel Pinot.

Pierre Mériel, the head of their team, a true *Normalien* he, whose sharp and subtle mind contrasted with his huge bulk; Gian Bachella, an Italian, bearded, cultured, delicate, always indignant about some injustice or brutality; and Marcel Pinot, the mainspring, everywhere at once in the course of an experiment, ready to meet fresh disasters head on. Thinking back, I wonder whether Mériel had ever really been my dupe while I was shuttling between their group and the nuclear theorists; or whether, having decided from the beginning to do the experiment, he was amused by my comings and goings. He says no, but I don't quite believe him.

The reader who has browsed through the previous chapters, which have not always been overflowing with the milk of human kindness, may well wonder what miracle has caused the current mood, that '*tout le monde il est beau, tout le monde est gentil*' (the title of a French film).

Well, it was long, it was hard, it was not particularly fashionable (I shall come back to that), and one had to stick at it, and to stick together. The first to drop out was Maurice Chapellier. When he left us, I asked him for a laugh: 'Are you trying to kill the father?' 'It's a bit like that,' he said. Those who stuck it out were sticking together; or perhaps it was those who felt like sticking together who stuck it out.

What future for nuclear magnetic order? I have just said that it is not very fashionable. It is not always easy to analyse the reasons why a subject does or does not take off in the laboratories.

The reason for our isolation has not been a lack of interest in our research, far from it: the innumerable invitations, for my coworkers and myself, to speak at conferences—generally at the main sessions; the interest aroused by our talks; finally, why hide it, the prizes awarded to my coworkers, and the various academic 'honours', French or foreign, which have been my lot, would have demonstrated, if need be, that what we were doing was worth doing. At the risk of passing for a megalomaniac, I shall say that we remained isolated because we were too far ahead: it discouraged newcomers.

In a conference at which my talk had been particularly well received, I recall that, to express my regret at not having instigated more vocations, I told this little story about the First World War: leading an attack, an Italian colonel rushes out of the trench with sword bared, roaring: '*Avanti!*' His men, deeply moved by the bravery of their chief, burst into applause from the bottom of their trench, and shout: *bravo, bravissimo!*'

It seems only fair at this point to mention a recent (1988) publication, relating the observation at the Risö reactor of nuclear antiferromagnetic order in copper by neutron diffraction. I shall quote only its first two lines (the italics are mine).

'In this letter we report the *first* observation of *spontaneous* nuclear order in an *elemental metal* by neutron diffraction.'

Why not add: 'Made as far North as Risør'?

*The drones

The main weakness of our method of ordering nuclear spins is the inevitable presence of paramagnetic impurities, which are introduced purposefully for the sake of DNP. The local fields produced by these impurities slightly spoil the 'cleanliness' of nuclear magnetic order, which is so dear to my heart. A possible way out, to use a 'metaphor drawn from the bees', (Canon Chasuble in *The Importance of Being Earnest*) would be to turn all the males (the Kings Solomon), out in the cold once they have served their purpose of impregnating, sorry, polarizing, the nuclei.

In that scheme, the paramagnetic impurities are produced by shining light on a molecular crystal, thus creating excited paramagnetic states. Once they have served their purpose of polarizing the nuclei, the light is turned off, the excited molecules return to their ground diamagnetic state, and the impurities disappear (at least the magnetic ones, the only ones which are bothersome).

The idea is very simple, but it is easier said than done. It is a matter of superimposing the sophisticated equipment involved in the study of excited triplet states in molecular crystals on the hardware of nuclear magnetic order which I outlined earlier.

I was fortunate in getting the interest of Professor Wenckebach and his colleague, Professor Schmidt, in Leyden. Some time ago, using this method, they obtained a 40 per cent proton polarization.*

*μSR: a late child

What attracts me in the story I am about to tell, which has no connection with the rest of this chapter, is its anecdotal aspect, far more than its scientific interest. It was my last scientific publication (1984); and my first, and no doubt last, contribution to μSR, a field into which I backed up, so to speak. And to start with, what is μSR?

It has been known for a long time that the electron has a big brother, called a *muon*, which differs from it by a mass which is some two hundred times larger, and—according to the laws of quantum electrodynamics, which it obeys slavishly—by a magnetic moment, which is smaller in the same ratio. The muon is an unstable particle with a lifetime of 2.2 microseconds, which disintegrates into an electron (or a positron, for its charge can have either sign) and two neutral particles, the neutrino and the antineutrino. The principle of μSR or muon spin rotation (or resonance) rests on two facts: a) positive muons produced in accelerators are 100 per cent polarized when they are stopped by a target; b) there is a strong correlation between the direction of the spin of the muon and the direction of the positron which it emits. These two facts permit one to follow up any precession or disorientation of the muon spin inside matter, caused by internal local fields, by counting the positrons emitted in a given direction as a function of time (corrected naturally for the exponential decay due to the muon's lifetime).

The muon spin thus becomes, like the spin of the neutron (and as we saw, the spin of ^{43}Ca), a microscopic probe of the magnetic properties of bulk matter. The fact that the muon carries an electric charge, and for that reason cannot wander unobstructed in the midst of matter, does not go without consequences, which are good or bad, depending on the problem. Let's add also that the positive muon can capture an electron and become a hydrogen-like atom called *muonium*, which extends its possibilities still further as a microscopic magnetic probe.

In 1984 half a thousand physicists across the world were doing μSR, and I decided to educate myself in that field. As everybody knows by now, the best way to learn a subject is to teach it, which I did by choosing μSR as the subject of my 1984 course.

One fact attracted my attention. In the absence of a magnetic field, a muon at rest is rapidly depolarized through flip-flops (or flip-flips) with neighbouring nuclear spins, unless a field much stronger than the local fields, called the *holding field*, is applied along the direction of the muon polarization. The muon, whose Larmor frequency in the holding field is very different (much higher in fact) than that of any other nucleus, cannot flip anymore with neighbouring nuclei, for it would not conserve energy, and the muon spin remains polarized. All of this was naturally well-known.

If, on the other hand, and this was my idea, a zero field splitting exists within the sample, due for instance to a quadrupole coupling, (or a field-independent splitting, such as a hyperfine splitting of a free radical), it is possible to make this splitting equal to the Zeeman splitting of the muon in the holding field. When this happens, flips of the muon spin with the nucleus concerned become possible, and an easily detectable resonant depolarization of the muon should occur. It is straightforward to generalize to the case where the muon has formed a muonium. This method is well known in NMR, where it is called *level-crossing*.

It seemed to me that there was a possibility here for a new type of μSR spectroscopy. The idea was so simple and so obvious that I could not help thinking that it must have been tried and rejected, for a reason which escaped me.

To be certain I asked our librarian, Madeleine Porneuf, to make a computer search for articles containing both of the key-words *muon* and *level-crossing*. She found thousands with *muon*, hundreds with *level-crossing* but none with both! This made up my mind for me. I wrote in one day a brief note to the *Comptes Rendus de l'Académie des Sciences*, and sent out preprints to the main μSR laboratories.

It got fast results. Nobody had thought of it, and the technique spread like wildfire. In 1986 it got me an invitation to an international conference in Sweden, where a good third of the papers were based on the use of that technique, and where it was rated as the most important step since the last conference three years ago.

This little story shows once more that the kibitzer (my dictionary says that there is such a word) can sometimes see better than the players.

In any case, this was the first and probably the last time in my life that I cooperated with a computer (unless typing this on a word processor falls into that category).*

East and West

Oh, East is East and West is West and never the twain shall meet

OXFORD: *High table—Living dangerously—There are doctors and
doctors, Fellows and Fellows,*
USSR: *The invisible Popov—Georgian hospitality—the Tartar
metropolis—Mirabelle—* A thermodynamic model—books, Scythians,
and henchmen—The silenced poetess—Brave New World—A man—A
brief friendship—Irreversible?*
UNITED STATES: *Bucolic conferences—Which Washington?—*
* Electro-weak optics.*
FAR EAST: *A long journey—Surviving in India—Dressing in Hong
Kong—Amusing the Japanese*
GENEVA: *Rocking the boat*
THE NETHERLANDS, ISRAEL
Two stories: Belgian and Bulgarian

I had never crossed the borders of France, outward-bound, before 1947
(nor inward-bound before 1925, as I have recounted in considerable
detail). With the exception of a journey of eight weeks across some Asian
countries in 1964, all my travels and sojourns have been limited to Europe
and North America. (Correction, in 1987 I spent a week in Novosibirsk in
the USSR, which counts as Asia.)

Nowadays, as chartered flights take tourists in droves to Sri Lanka or
Tahiti, and the whole of Japan has become an industrial suburb, I can
hardly hope to impress my readers with exotic descriptions of faraway
countries. (These days I am one of the few unfortunates who have never
been to China!). Of my travels and stays abroad, of various lengths, the
following are those I feel like recollecting. I have already described those
earlier than 1960, and will not return to them.

Oxford

Untruthful! Impossible, he's an Oxonian.
Lady Bracknell

After my two years in Oxford, from 1948 to 1950, I came back for four
months, from October '62 to January '63, in what was a terribly cold
winter. I have just said that I had little hope of impressing my reader with

'exotic descriptions of faraway countries'. On second thoughts, I am not so sure; during the winter of 1962, and although I had been already hardened by my former stay, Oxford did appear to me as 'an exotic and faraway country'.

A 'Visiting Fellow' at Merton, I had changed sides, and it was from the High Table and the Senior Common Room that I was now contemplating the landscape. It looked very different from the way it had seemed to the 'advanced student' which I had been fourteen years earlier.

And first the fare: lunch was served buffet-style, from sideboards on two sides of a long, low-ceilinged room, the Savile room—cold lunch on one side, hot on the other, fairly decent both. But the dinners! The Fellows, gowned during term, gathered, with their guests, in an anteroom leading to the great hall where the meals were taken. One helped oneself to sherry, for which one signed. Then, after a few minutes of silent conversation, so to speak, the butler announced to the president, the Warden if he was dining in hall that evening, or the most senior Fellow present, that dinner was ready, and the president led the procession to the High Table. Around this large table of solid oak, the guests took place in an order determined by seniority—the novices, of whom I was one, taking their places last. Everybody remained standing until the president gave a resounding knock on the table with a mallet, and an undergraduate, the senior scholar, read a shortish prayer in a Latin which to my ears sounded like double Dutch. (I should at this stage warn my reader that I am probably offering him a mish-mash of the customs of several other colleges beside Merton, where I had had the privilege of dining at the high table at one time or another— Jesus naturally, but also Brasenose, Wadham, New College, and a few others.) Then everybody sat down and the servants offered the dishes to the guests. Whilst the food was plentiful, but not much more than that (except on special occasions two or three times per term), the wines were excellent. The Merton bursar, the fellow whose duty it was to see to the well-being of his colleagues (a mathematician, I seem to remember) spent a fortnight every year in the Bordeaux region, touring the châteaux and selecting the vintages which would lie in the college cellars for a decade and sometimes much longer, before charming the palates of the fellows.

The meal did not end up with the pudding, but was followed by something called the savoury. This was a kind of salty, spicy hors d'oeuvre with a core of strong cheese, mushrooms or sardines, and was sometimes even more exotic (for a French palate)—for example, baked oysters (!) on toast, with the grand name of 'Angels on horseback'. The explanation for this strange order, where salt follows sugar—so contrary to our (French) customs—rests, I was told, on the following assumption: these salty foods, which are strong and sometimes odoriferous, could have proved offensive to the sense of taste and smell of the ladies (nothing if not delicate) and they were given the choice of retiring to the drawing room after the pudding, leaving the gentlemen to their coarse delights. I do not know what this explanation is worth; in any case it could hardly have applied to Merton, where it was not before the seventies that the ladies began timidly to show up.

The sweet would have been excellent if the chef had not had an immoderate taste for jelly. (One remembers the story of the Frenchman who is served some, and, seeing it shivering in his plate, addresses it thus: 'Do not be afraid, little thing, I am not going to eat you'.)

On a typical evening, when dinner is over, the president gets up, gives another little knock with his mallet, says another bit of a prayer, and leads the procession out of hall. (The undergraduates have disappeared long ago.) Everyone has picked up his linen napkin, and the procession moves to another room; the evening is still young!

There, another long table, but of mahogany this time, lit by candles whose trembling lights are reflected in the varnish of the table and in the portraits of the worthies (wearing wigs or wing-collars, according to their period) whom for some reason or other the college has decided to honour. At Jesus, I remember portraits of Queen Elizabeth, founder of the college, of Lawrence of Arabia, and of Harold Wilson, former Prime Minister and Honorary Fellow. At Merton I can only remember the portrait of my very good friend Sir Rex Richards, a star of high resolution NMR, who owes his place on the walls of the college to having served with great distinction as Warden of Merton and then as Vice-Chancellor of the university. The Vice-Chancellor is the real President of the university; the title of Chancellor (which was held for many years by the former Prime Minister Harold Macmillan), who appears once or twice a year, at great ceremonies, is purely honorary. (Macmillan once explained the importance of his position as follows: 'Without a Chancellor, there can be no Vice-Chancellor, and without a Vice-Chancellor, where would you be?') But let us return to our *soirée*.

Fellows disrobe with a flourish, everyone takes their place around the table, after looking for a change of neighbours, and the feast resumes. On the table there are nuts, dates, raisins, dry figs, fresh fruit (usually uneatable), chocolate mints etc. In front of the senior Fellow, who sits at the head of the table here, there are two decanters with port (a port stronger and sweeter than the French are used to) and Madeira. Sauterne, which is not decanted but served in its bottle, has since joined its two elders. The decanters move around the table clockwise. If the senior Fellow finds that they are moving too fast, he can keep them in front of him for some time. After the third, and usually last, round, the butler offers the cigars round, and the junior Fellow the silver snuff box. Only then is smoking acceptable. The senior Fellow rises and takes his troop to a third room, furnished with sofas and armchairs, where one helps oneself to coffee. In a fourth (!) and last room, there are drinks, alcoholic—cognac, whisky, beer—or not—Schweppes, Canada Dry, etc. My good friend Erwin Hahn, who adores Oxford and goes there as often as he can, had very aptly called these various steps: 'decompression chambers'.

I soon discovered the necessity of acquiring what the English call a 'dinner jacket', or 'black tie', and the Americans 'tuxedo', the French word being 'smoking'.

Having been forced to decline two or three invitations which mentioned 'black tie', I resigned myself to the inevitable investment. It is still hanging in my wardrobe, in excellent condition after more than a quarter of a century. I last wore it in June 1988, to a 'Gaudy' (a feast) at Jesus.

The second piece of exoticism was what in retrospect I call 'Operation Survival'; this took place in an English house of which we were the only tenants. This lovely little house, situated at the northern limit of Oxford, belonged to two old ladies, who used to move to a warmer climate during the wintry season (never had they been better inspired to do so than that year), and who were not in the habit of accepting tenants without a careful screening. To qualify, you had to be over forty, childless, and a member of Oxford University; to employ their two charwomen, both fairly ancient, for three days each; to feed the birds daily—they were accustomed to alight on a roost specially provided for them in the garden; and, last but not least, to be introduced to them by their delightful friends, the Kurtis. He is a physicist of Hungarian origin but the most Oxonian of Oxonians, of whom I have already spoken more than once; she, a daughter of an English general, spoke the kind of English one only hears, I think, in British films in which white feathers are handed to cowards.

The house was a litle bijou, to use an English expression, and harboured treasures: Axminster carpets, Chippendale furniture, Royal Worcester and Crown Derby china, sterling silverware, hand-embroidered tablecloths and napkins. Suzanne locked everything up immediately and we never used any of it (except perforce the carpets and the furniture). What was wrong was the heating and the plumbing.

Only through unremitting vigilance did we manage to escape the catastrophes which during this winter befell most of our neighbours. One should know that the English like to place their drains against outside walls, without cover, arguing that, if frozen, they are easily accessible to the repairman in this location. The fact that, placed differently, they might not freeze at all, is not part of the rules of the game. Every night, to prevent frost, we put salt in all the waste outlets. It is bad for the pipes but not as bad as bursting. (When Suzanne asked me every night, before going to bed: 'Did you salt the bathtub?', I was reminded of the old joke about the Russian sugar which dissolves very slowly: 'Did you put the sugar to soak for tomorrow?') The absence of heating in the bathroom forced me to wear an overcoat and a muffler while shaving, which is inconvenient, to say the least. In the morning the frozen milk used to emerge from the bottle as a little white rod. I had planned a few visits to other cities, but gave them up: one did not know if or when one would be able to leave, or to come back, and if one did, in what state one would find the house.

Two features of the English character appeared clearly to me during this period: a complete lack of foresight and preparedness in the face of the rigours of this winter, which was admittedly very exceptional; but also a patience, a capacity to bear, with a stiff upper lip, all the slings and arrows of outrageous fortune, which forced my admiration. To quote my good friend Viki Weisskopf: 'The English are like other people, only less so.'

I have not kept track of the number of visits I made to Oxford from 1950 on, but it is probably more than twenty; and, apart from my own lab at Saclay, no single lab is, or at least was until a few years ago, more fmailiar to me than the Clarendon.

For many years they had been using liquid hydrogen to cool their cryostats, to the dismay of their American visitors, who consider, with good reason, that it is a dangerous practice. (Since the accident with 'Mirabelle', I had excellent reasons to share their opinion.) The door of every other room at the Clarendon carried the warning: 'HYDROGEN, NO SMOKING', which led me to put on mine: 'SMOKING, NO HYDROGEN'.

The pioneers of the practice of using liquid hydrogen, which went back to their work in Berlin, were Simon and Kurti, his coworker at the time, who told me the following story about what happened in their Berlin laboratory. (Nothing could be easier for me than to check with Kurti what exactly had happened, and how. I have no intention of doing so; I like the story the way I remember it, and this is how I am going to tell it.)

One morning, when Simon was not in the lab, an explosion occurred, which blasted the roof, demolished the equipment, and nearly killed the unfortunate Kurti. He rushed to the phone to inform Simon of what had happened. Simon took the news very calmly: 'These things will happen, don't get excited about it; and anyway I am too busy to come to the lab this morning'. 'What do you mean "don't get excited"? The equipment destroyed, and myself nearly killed, is that not enough!' 'You always exaggerate everything, Nicholas, calm down'. Finally, in the face of Kurti's indignation, Simon said: 'Look here, you should not work it to death. I have a calendar in front of me and I can read April 1st, as well as the next man'. 'But it is not a joke, there really has been an explosion!' 'What!' screamed Simon, before rushing to the lab.

Besides my visits to the Clarendon, I usually take advantage of my time in Oxford to walk to the bank where the Oxford University Press deposits my royalties, then across the street to a shop where I find the kind of flannel trousers which agree with my build, then to Blackwell's, the greatest bookshop in the world, where I find the books I like. They have an annexe where I find my cassettes of Shakespeare. After that, sometimes I return to the bank.

Of my visits to Oxford, the following still remain in my memory today. In 1968 I gave the Cherwell–Simon lecture, an annual conference in honour of these two great figures of the Clarendon. It is aimed at a lay audience, and was started a few years after Simon's death in 1957. Among my predecessors one finds Casimir and Van Vleck, and among those who followed me, Steven Weinberg and Michael Fisher, brilliant specialists in particle physics and phase transitions respectively. The lecture is given in May, but I was able to give mine only in October, because of the strikes of May 1968. I had chosen for my title: 'Big Science versus Little Science', drawing widely on my experience as a director of physics, acquired during the previous three years. I honestly think that the audience liked my lecture. In any case I liked it sufficiently myself to include its text, after translating it into French, in a collection of various talks and lectures, gathered in my *Réflexions d'un Physicien*, which was published in 1983. Two years later, this book of *Reflections* was published in English by the Oxford University Press in a translation by Ray Freeman: I remembered at the last moment to warn Ray not to translate this particular lecture back into English. I regret a little having done so; it would have been interesting to compare the two English versions.

1976 was a year, when honours rained on my shoulders.

I received a letter from Oxford University, informing me that they would be very pleased to make me a doctor *honoris causa*, if I would see fit to accept this mark of esteem. I hastened to reassure the timid Oxford University on this point, wondering all the while how they would go about it. I had been an Oxford doctor for the last twenty-five years, and I innocently thought that the condition for becoming one, like all other virginities, was valid only once. It was a gross underestimation of my Alma Mater. In 1950, I had been made a Doctor of Philosophy or D.Phil., whereas now I was going to be made, *honoris causa*, a Doctor of Science or D.Sc. The first wears a gown that is red and blue, whereas the second is entitled to a red and silver gown; it is obviously very different.

Is this the only difference between D.Phil. and D.Sc? Not quite. I was told that every D.Phil. could obtain 'leave to supplicate' for a D.Sc. if he kept his name on the books of his college long enough, by paying the appropriate dues. Now the university was offering it to me, *honoris causa*, that is for free, and what is more, in the course of a splendid ceremony.

A magnificent pageant, led by the Chancellor, his heavy train carried by two pages, followed by the dignitaries of the university, took the *honorands*, wearing their robes and mortar-boards (when I first heard the word in 1948, I thought it was 'motorboats', a very strange name, I thought, but everything had seemed so strange then) into the Sheldonian theatre. There, the *public orator*, my good friend John Griffith, extolled in Latin the merits of each doctorand, before pushing him toward the Chancellor, who also mumbled a little Latin, and handed the doctorand, now a doctor, the precious diploma encased in a cardboard cylinder.

'*Mihi summo est gaudio vobis praesentare Anatolium Abragam, Academiae Franco-Gallicae sodalem, ut admittatur ad gradum Doctoris in Scientia honoris causa*'. Thus spake John Griffith to the Chancellor.

'*Arcanorum naturae investigator sollertissime, qui in "campis magneticis" tam scienter decurrere, ego auctoritate mea et totius Universitatis admitto te ad gradum Doctoris in Scientia honoris causa*'. Thus spake the Chancellor.†

The ceremony was followed by lunch in the magnificent library of All Souls, and dinner in full evening dress at Christ Church, with 'black tie' mercifully tolerated for the *honorands*.

In the same year, 1976, two other honours, which were completely unexpected and indeed quite exceptional, fell upon me: my two former colleges, Jesus, where I had been an advanced student from 1948 to 1950, and Merton, where I was a Visiting Fellow in the winter of 1962, saw fit to make me an Honorary Fellow. I learned on that occasion that electing someone as an honorary fellow is the greatest honour that a college can bestow on him. Why my two former colleges should have *both* decided to elect me, and at exactly the same time, since the two letters announcing my election reached me on the same day, was as puzzling as it was delightful.

The privileges attached to the title of Honorary Fellow are rather exorbitant, since, in principle, its happy recipient is entitled, among other rights, to free lunch and dinner in college for the rest of his life. Malicious gossips say that if an Honorary Fellow were reckless enough to make full use of his privileges, an appropriate addition to his food could put a premature end to that use. I was too well aware of prevailing customs and usages, to take such risks. As early as 1962, when I was only a humble Visiting Fellow at Merton, word got to me that my manners had been found excellent, because I practically never went near the place. And anyway, the colleges, in their great wisdom, avoid bestowing the title of Honorary Fellow on a permanent resident of Oxford. I had known one exception, a fearless individual, who, although an Honorary Fellow of Merton, lunched there next to me for several months and, I was told, had been lunching there for several years. He was Sir Basil Blackwell, the son of the founder of B. H. Blackwell, an amiable nonagenarian, and the owner of a red Rolls-Royce which could often be seen in Broad Street. His

---

† This is probably the only place in my book where I have *willingly* departed from the truth. It was not the Chancellor (absent because of ill-health) but the Vice-Chancellor, my very good friend Sir Rex Richards, who gave me my degree. If I have replaced him, by the Chancellor it was because the youthful visage and the slim athletic figure of Sir Rex, a man of his time, lacked the archaic flavour embodied in the Chancellor, Harold Macmillan, that I was trying to convey.

great age, and even more importantly, the rare books that from time to time he donated to the Merton Library, no doubt sheltered him from any alimentary mishap.

'And you sir', I might be asked, 'what sheltered you?' It was an additional fellowship, the *Sir Henry Savile Fellowship*, this one a *working fellowship*, which had been granted to me for eight months in 1981, and whose temporary character could not alarm my hosts. It was as a result of that stay at the Clarendon, that I started in my lab the studies on pseudonuclear magnetism, which I described in the previous chapter.

I wished to know whether the fellows' privilege of walking on the grass in the quads extended to Honorary Fellows. The principal of Jesus replied to me that all the Fellows' privileges extended as a matter of course to Honorary Fellows, but with respect to that of walking on the grass in the quads, I would be disappointed. A few years ago, following a gentleman's agreement between Fellows and undergraduates, the Fellows agreed to give up their age-old privilege of walking on the grass, provided the undergraduates undertook to refrain henceforth from the unseemly practice of trampling on the same grass. Alas, the Fellows are the only ones to respect the terms of the agreement, and the undergraduates the only ones to be seen walking on the grass (or *lying* on it, as I was able to observe in June 1988). In this problem of walking on grass, there is a class prejudice firmly anchored in the conscience (or the subconscious) of the British: on the lawns surrounding King's Chapel, an architectural jewel in Cambridge which attracts many tourists, notices in several languages touch on the problem of walking, or rather not walking, on the grass. The notice in French is blunt: *Il est interdit de marcher sur les pelouses*. The English notice is more discriminating: *Members of the public are requested to refrain from walking on the grass, unless accompanied by a Senior Member of the University*.

As an Honorary Fellow of Jesus, every June I get an invitation to attend a 'Gaudy', that is a dinner for college old-timers (black tie, needless to say). I have so far attended it twice, in 1976 and in 1988. The first time I had the interesting experience of being seated next to the former Prime Minister, Sir Harold Wilson. Reminiscing about his career, he told me that after a dinner offered to him by General de Gaulle at the *Grand Trianon* in Versailles, de Gaulle and he went for a drive in the park with de Gaulle's personal interpreter. The car was surprisingly small and the chin of the General, who was a very tall man, rested on his knees. Wilson wished to know whether, once Britain had made all the concessions requested by the General before accepting its admission to the Common Market, the General would not try to impose new conditions. The General replied by making a face, which Wilson mimicked for me. The interpreter translated: 'The General considers this contingency as highly improbable'. Another memory of that dinner has to do with drinks. Excellent wines were served, but Wilson called for a tankard of beer. 'Demagogue', I thought to myself, 'the gentleman tries to appear working-class'; but with each new course Wilson called for more beer, which he consumed with disconcerting ease. 'Well, maybe he really *likes* beer', I thought.

During another visit to Oxford, which took place in September 1982, I had a most unpleasant surprise—an intestinal blockage, accompanied by high fever and terrible pains. (Frankly, I do not think one should see this as an attempt by one of my colleges to make room for new Honorary Fellows.) Thanks to Bleaney's prompt and efficient assistance, I was immediately taken to the surgery department of an Oxford hospital, where I was apparently considered to be a VIP, and put into the care of several eminent surgeons, remaining under surveillance for nearly a fortnight. Their competent treatment made it possible to avoid an emergency operation. (Back to normal, I had a safe operation in France, in January 1983.) Three of my British doctors were members of the Royal College of Surgeons who, as I knew well, were to be addressed as 'Mister' rather than 'Doctor'. But 'Mister' who? You can't just say 'Is it serious, Mister?' or 'Thank you, Mister'. And so, lying there, nauseous and in great pain, I was trying to recollect the names of the guardian angels leaning over my bed. My condition forbade the absorption of any drugs through the mouth, and suppositories had to be used, which is fairly common in France, but not in Britain, it seems. The charming nurses who took care of me considered it part of their duty to reassure me, by explaining that it was neither dangerous nor painful: 'Turn over, love, it won't hurt'.

In the autumn of 1983, to celebrate the thirty-fifth anniversary of my arrival in Oxford, I had a private party in Merton, to which I invited some old friends with their wives: Bleaney, Kurti, Peierls, Richards, Berlin, and a few more. Isaiah Berlin is a philosopher, quite famous in Britain (and elsewhere). He is also an adorable man, a highly literate scholar, and a connoisseur of Russian literature (like myself he was born in Russia, but a few years earlier). He is also that *rara avis*, a man of infinite wit, but quite devoid of malice, belying Lady Sneerwell's: 'The malice of a good thing is the barb that makes it stick'.

For this party Merton had offered, free of charge, the service and the beautiful setting of its Senior Common Room; and at cost price, that is practically free, the nectar—prestigious wines from its cellars—and the ambrosia, which was more than adequate. Still, I considered that I was paying the piper, however moderate the cost, and called the tune: in other words, I had cheese served *before* the pudding, and proscribed the savoury.

These memories of Oxford will no doubt be deemed an exercise in levity and frivolity. This is how I see them myself. But had I not promised to my reader a little exoticism, an exoticism which is rapidly fading away?

The Oxford *honoris causa* degree in 1976 was not my first in Britain. In

1967, the young University of Kent, sheltered by the prestigious cathedral of Canterbury, had given me a foretaste of the thing. The ceremony, built perforce from scratch, had a prefabricated archaism which rivalled the age—honoured traditions of Oxford. As a sole concession to modernity, the public orator spoke in English. The university had chosen well: the two other doctorands were the poet W. H. Auden, and the great crystallographer and Nobel winner, Dorothy Hodgkin. The Chancellor was Princess Marina, former Duchess of Kent, a lady who impressed me, not only by her elegance and *allure*—far more regal, I thought, than that of her royal relation, Queen Elizabeth—but also by her extraordinary kindness. The ceremony required that she should hold me by the hand while pronouncing the few sentences which made me Doctor *honoris causa* of the University of Kent. Marina is no more, but, to this day, I keep the memory of her frank and friendly hand in mine.

I have not often been to London, a town which I hardly know. In the next chapter I shall describe two trips there, in 1983 and 1986.

A last word about this country. What is happening today to my beloved England—a country I had admired long before she stood up alone to face Barbary in 1940, and loved so much, when I learned to know her better? Philistines rule over its scientific research, shortsightedly restricting fundamental research a little more every day. May this great country come to its senses before it is too late. But more of that later in this chapter.

Russia

This is a country with which I have a love—hate relationship. I cannot forget its language, its literature, or its poetry, the only poetry which moves me. I cannot forget my childhood. I cannot forget that between 1941 and 1945, this country—as much as England, if not more so—had been at the heart of my thoughts. I cannot forget the attraction it still exerts on me, in spite of the disappointment and the disgust which have slowly penetrated the wall of deception erected by a large fraction of the French Left.

Thank God there is no lack of competent Sovietologists and Kremlinologists in our country, and I do not plan to add my voice to theirs. I shall be content to tell a few personal stories concerning Russia, to be added to those of the chapter called 'Looking Back'. What will come out of it will not so much be the abominable—others who have personally suffered from it, are better qualified to speak of that—but the absurd, which I have noticed at every contact. In fact, if I had one single adjective at my disposal to describe my experience of the Soviet regime, 'absurd' is the one I would use.

After my voyage of 1956, I returned to Russia for the first time in 1961, on the occasion of a French exhibition which was taking place in Moscow.

I gave two lectures on my lab's work on dynamic polarization, which interested a young audience who were delighted to hear a Western speaker who spoke and understood Russian—a unique experience for them. After my talk, a young man, who did not introduce himself, came up to me and handed me a few typewritten pages. It was a barely legible carbon copy, covered with equations, dealing, it seemed to me, with the problem of spin temperature. In my hotel room that night, after a few unsuccessful attempts at understanding it, I put it into my briefcase and forgot about it. In fact, I was then the first Western physicist to have been exposed to the Provotorov theory, one of the most important contributions to the theory of NMR during that decade. In my defence, I can say that, even when I realized, a year or two later, the importance of this theory, I still had great difficulty in understanding it, so sibylline were its author's explanations. In Goldman's book on spin temperature, published in 1970, then in *Nuclear Magnetism, Order and Disorder*, the book we published together in 1982, Provotorov's theory is explained in a way which is accessible to ordinary mortals.

I visited the gigantic Lebedev Institute, where I saw physicists I had met in Paris or England, like Prokhorov, who was later to share Nobel prize with his compatriot Basov and the American Townes, for discovering the laser; and I met a number of physicists, most of them very pleasant. A few years later, after their Nobel for the laser, I had dinner in Moscow with Basov and Prokhorov and their spouses. They had not yet become engaged in that fierce power struggle, which was to end with the directorship of the Lebedev Institute going to Basov, and some regrettable choices in the behaviour of Prokhorov, whom I had rather liked. The Nobel Committee had awarded half of the prize to Townes and a quarter to each of the Russians. At dinner, the ladies deprecated in strong terms the way in which the Nobel Committee had cut the cake. It is only fair to add that, in the US, Mrs Townes had said candidly on the radio that the Russians had stolen her husband's discovery.

I had another contact with the Russians during the same year, 1961; the occasion, this time, was a Soviet exhibition which took place in Paris. This is where what I call the Popov incident (I have changed the name) took place, as I am now going to narrate in great detail (not too great, I hope). That year I had organized an international conference on the Mössbauer effect. I received a letter and two telegrams in quick succession from the USSR, asking me to accept the participation of the Soviet physicist Popov in the conference. I replied to each of these messages that Popov would be welcome. A last message informed me that Popov would be taking advantage of the coincidence in time between my conference and the Soviet exhibition in Paris, of which he was going to be one of the organizers. Everything was flowing smoothly, it seemed. The conference came and went without Popov showing up. Slightly irksome, but hardly surprising.

The day after the conference ended, I went for the first time to visit the Soviet exhibition, which was still going on. I addressed—in French, for I knew that the use of Russian by a foreigner arouses the suspicions of Soviet citizens abroad—an imposing lady seated behind a desk. I introduced myself: 'Professor so-and-so at the Collège de France . . . organizer of an international conference . . . participation of Popov . . . organizer at your exhibition . . . promised and expected . . . no Popov . . . why?' The lady turned towards a man seated behind her and addressed him in Russian (I transcribe in italics the Russian part of the dialogues): '*He says he is Professor so-and-so, that they had a conference, that they expected Popov who did not show up*'. '*Ask him when his conference ended*'. The lady turned towards me: 'When did your conference end?' 'It ended on the 15th.' '*He says that it ended on the 15th*'. '*Tell him that Popov left for Moscow on the 15th, having accomplished his mission.*' The lady turned back toward me: 'Popov left for Moscow on the 15th, having accomplished his mission.' 'But why?' I bleated. 'Such were his instructions'. End of dialogue. True to form, but no more. I continued my walk through the exhibition towards the display of scientific instruments, where a pleasant-looking young man was tinkering with some apparatus. I addressed him, in Russian this time, to deplore the absence of the elusive Popov. '*I am Popov.*' '*But, then, why?*' The young man spread his hands in a fatalistic gesture: '*Well, you know . . .*' A good scene from the Theatre of the Absurd.

In 1970, I am at an international conference on magnetism, organized in Grenoble by Louis Néel. We are expecting Borovik-Romanov, a distinguished specialist in magnetism from the USSR. On Monday, the absence of Borovik-Romanov is, according to his colleagues, due to ill-health. On Tuesday, there is a new explanation: Borovik-Romanov is having a vacation somewhere near Lake Baïkal. On Wednesday, Borovik-Romanov is in Grenoble . . .

In the winter of 1968, a sizeable group of French physicists, including myself, who were working in the fields of low temperatures and condensed matter, went to Moscow and from there to Bakuriani, a Georgian ski resort where conferences often take place. Our hosts were three leading Soviet theoreticians, Migdal, Abrikosov, and Khalatnikov, surrounded by some of the best representatives of the school of Landau; and also the Pope, or rather the Ayatollah, of Georgian physics, Eleuther Andronikash-vili, who is well known for his pioneering experiments on the superfluidity of liquid helium, and is the director of the Institute of Physics at Tbilisi. The Russian version of his name is Andronikov. This name was used by his brother, a well-known literary critic, Heracles Andronikov (and why shouldn't Eleuther's brother be christened Heracles?), and also by de

Gaulle's personal interpreter, a remote cousin of the family. On the way to Bakuriani there was a stopover in the Georgian capital of Tbilisi, and a Georgian dinner, with food galore and drink far more. I recall two diabolical Georgian inventions designed to drink the guests under the table. The first is the custom of toasts: after drinking to France, to the Soviet Union, to Georgia, to peace, to French physics, to Soviet physics, to Georgian physics, to French women, to Georgian women, etc., when all the excuses for drinking seem to be exhausted, each half of the table drinks in turn to the health of the other half. But there is worse. They hand you a horn, and if you innocently let them fill it with drink, you have to down it nonstop, because there is no way of standing it on the table, without spilling the contents.

There was a significant incident on the return flight from Tbilisi to Moscow. Usually the passengers in the care of Intourist go aboard first, and take the seats reserved for them before the *vulgum pecus* boards the plane. This time somebody had made a gaffe, and when we arrived at the plane's steps, the ordinary passengers were already seated. After some consultation between our guides an announcement was heard: 'Boarding for flight . . . will take place at the far right of the airfield.' I picked up my bag and prepared to proceed there, but our guide told me to wait. Little by little we saw the Soviet travellers, filing out of the plane with their bags, rucksacks and other bundles, and trundling in the snow to the far end of the field. After a while, with the plane emptied of its occupants, who were now at a fair distance from the plane, the guides made us board it, and take the seats assigned to us. A quarter of an hour later we saw our Soviet fellow-travellers climb into the plane again. They gave us some unfriendly looks, but said nothing . . . A little touch of the Soviet life.

In Moscow, during a memorable dinner washed down with plenty of vodka and Armenian n-star brandy, I saw, for the first time since his disappearance, Bruno Pontecorvo, the defector. He was a Soviet Academician now, apparently still bubbling with mirth, but the sparkle had gone out of his eye. I was interpreting between my French colleagues and some of the Russian guests, when a Russian lady asked me: 'Where did you learn to speak French so well?'

Mrs Khalatnikova, whose husband is a big shot, and who, being the daughter of a hero of the Revolution, is an even bigger shot herself, took me in her car to see the house I grew up in. It was even more decrepit than it had been twelve years before, but this time I decided to go beyond the gate and to penetrate into the yard where I had played in my childhood. A little old crone came up to us and asked, not too kindly, what we wanted. I told her that I had lived here before 1925, that my name was Abragam, and that I had wanted to have a look at my old house. 'Tolya, my little boy, is that you?' exclaimed the old girl. I took a better look at her, saw that she was not all that old, and suddenly recognized Nyura, a pretty young girl of some fifteen or sixteen years, whom I had known on another planet a thousand years ago. So many changes, upheavals, new countries, and new experiences for me, and all this time Nyura had stayed in this little yard, getting old before her time. Mrs Khalatnikova had to leave soon because of an appointment, and I did not feel like conversing any further in her presence.

In 1969 there was a great international conference in Kazan to celebrate the twenty-fifth anniversary of the discovery of ESR, made in this city by Zavoysky. This was after the Soviet tanks had invaded Prague, and I had already made up my mind to sever all official contacts with the USSR, but Kazan presented me with a problem of conscience. The conference was organized by Altschuler, the best ESR theoretician in the Soviet Union, and someone for whom I had great respect, as a scientist and as a man. In 1941, when the war with Germany started, all his colleagues had scientific jobs in the rear, but he enrolled in a fighting unit and fought the Germans for four years. Being a Jew, he did not want it said that his kind were shirkers. When he came back in 1945, he discovered that the best jobs were taken. He had to start from scratch, something with which I could sympathize, and achieved his position in Kazan through talent and strenuous work. For years, obstacles were put in the way of his candidacy to be a corresponding member of the Soviet Academy, and much depended on the success of this conference, for which he was responsible. I decided to attend the conference and even to publicize it around me. It was the only time that I departed from my position of boycott, which has been strengthened since then by the imprisonment of Orlov, the sequestration of Sakharov, and the harassment of refuseniks. In line with this stand, in 1980 I resigned from my position as a Vice-President of IUPAP (International Union of Pure and Applied Physics), which seemed to me to be incompatible with my personal policy of boycott of the USSR.

Kazan is a Tartar metropolis, a few hundred kilometres from Moscow, which had just been opened to foreigners—foreigners arriving by plane, I hasten to add, for access by land, train or car, remained strictly forbidden. The same absurd situation prevails for the Institute for Theoretical Physics in Chernogolovka, a suburb of Moscow. The Institute is nominally open to foreigners, but the roads to it are closed, and in that case you cannot go by plane. Kazan has one of the oldest universities in the USSR, which takes pride in counting the great Lobachevski among its former students.

My talk was a resounding success with the Russian audience, even if I say so myself. They knew my work in ESR and NMR, and my *Principles* had been translated into Russian (I'll come back to that). Furthermore, like all my Russian audiences, they were surprised and delighted to hear a Western speaker express himself fluently and without an accent in their language—not to forget my talent as a lecturer, for which my reader cannot accuse me of hiding my own regard.

One last detail about Kazan. We were taken to a concert, at which we heard Tchaïkovsky's Piano Concerto, not my favourite piece, I must admit, but played by an excellent orchestra, which was led by a remarkable conductor. 'We are lucky to have him in Kazan,' said one of the physicists who were acting as our guides. 'You bet your life that he would have been conducting in Moscow or Leningrad long ago if he were not a Jew.'

During one of my trips to Moscow in the sixties, I forget which, I requested and obtained permission to visit the Institute for Physical Problems and to have an interview with its founder and director, Kapitza. Unfortunately our conversation was completely spoilt by the following circumstance. Kapitza, who had spent 13 years in Cambridge and had been a close friend of Rutherford and a Fellow of Trinity College, also speaks very passable French, as I discovered during a visit he made to Paris in the seventies. I myself am reasonably fluent in English. All this, not counting our common mother tongue, Russian. Well, they still gave us an interpreter.

He came with me into Kapitza's office and asked him if he was in the way. Kapitza did not answer, and he stayed. After half an hour of trivial conversation, I took my leave.

Mirabelle

In October 1965, freshly promoted Director of Physics, I flew to Moscow for a first contact with the Soviet authorities, to deal with the installation of our large bubble chamber 'Mirabelle', in the future beam of the nearly completed 70 GeV accelerator, which was then the largest in the world, and which the Russians had been building near the old Russian city of Serpukhov. My companions for this trip were André Berthelot, two of his assistants, Prugne, the head engineer responsible for the construction of Mirabelle, and my faithful deputy Jean Pellerin; and from the other side, a Russian lady from the Soviet State Committee, a blonde of uncertain age—a physicist, an interpreter, and perhaps something else.

I had two trump cards: my title of Director, which, in the eyes of my Soviet interlocutors, was a guarantee of competence, and my knowledge of Russian, which gave me a direct contact with them, faster and more faithfully than through an interpreter.

At the start I had two preconceived ideas about this project, one of which unfortunately turned out to be correct, and the second unfortunately proved wrong. I did not harbour great hopes about the scientific outcome of the Mirabelle–Serpukhov combination. In 1965 I thought that the importance of large hydrogen bubble chambers as particle detectors, which had served particle physics magnificently during the previous decade, was going to decline; and what I had learned during my two month session at

Les Houches that summer had fortified me in that opinion. On the level of pure physics, I think that in the end my premonition turned out to be right, and I shall say no more about it. On the technical level, I must pay homage to Pierre Prugne, who was responsible for the project. The immense task of the design, construction, trials, dismantling, and shipping of this giant machine to Serpukhov, then re-assembling it and ensuring its satisfactory functioning for many years, is to the credit of Prugne and of his construction team.

On the other hand, the Mirabelle project appeared to me of great human interest. The idea that some forty French technicians and engineers, who were in charge of the functioning and maintenance of Mirabelle, would reside for several years in the heart of Russia with their families, that French physicists would come for frequent and extended visits, leading up, I hoped, to symmetrical visits by Soviet scientists to our country—all this, to my innocent mind, would contribute to an open relationship, to peaceful coexistence, to friendship between our two peoples, etc. . . . The considerable publicity from which the Mirabelle venture benefited in the press, ours and theirs, presented it as one of the aspects of the Gaullian policy of an open Europe 'from the Atlantic to the Urals, and could have led even less innocent people than myself to hope for its successful outcome as a human venture.

I made in all three trips to Russia connected with the Mirabelle project. In the first, talks at the headquarters of the Soviet State Committee in Moscow were followed by visits and discussions in Serpukhov.

In the second I was accompanied by three other CEA directors, for external relations, finance and administration. We established the terms of an agreement which was to be followed by the signing of a convention at a higher level. The convention was signed during my third trip, by our Administrator General, Robert Hirsch, and by Andronik Petrosyants, the president of Soviet Atomic Energy. Our minister, Alain Peyrefitte, had also made the voyage to mark the importance that our government attached to this convention by his presence.

Three main points constituted the subject of our discussions.
a) Who would pay for what: the construction of Mirabelle, its transport, its installation at Serpukhov, the electric energy it consumed (a lot because of the large electro-magnet which surrounded it), the film for the trajectory photographs it would take, the travelling and living expenses on both sides, etc.? In spite of much haggling, these were not the most difficult points.
b) How would the scientific results be published, and how would scientific conflicts be arbitrated? Also, what would become of Mirabelle after five years, when the convention expired?
c) What would be the living conditions for the French residing in Serpukhov—lodgings, food, schooling for the children, possibility of importing cars, and, above all, freedom of movement on Soviet territory?

It was on this last point that my discussions with the Soviet representatives fell down. I had set down a condition, *sine qua non*, that the French could go freely to Moscow at the week-ends. 'Naturally,' they said. 'All they have to do is ask for permission, which will be granted very liberally.'

I replied forcefully that this was not what *we* called freedom of movement, and that under such conditions I feared to be unable to find volunteers to work at Serpukhov. The Russians offered a compromise: it was enough for the French going to Moscow for week-ends to give advance notice of their intent. This did not seem unreasonable to me: the Russians would know of any such trip anyway. When I read the minutes of our discussions I saw that freedom of movement was not mentioned there. In spite of my insistence, the Russians remained unshakeable. Petrosyants personally solemnly promised to me that they would keep to the agreement, but we would have to trust them; they would not put it in writing. This rigid attitude, contrasting with their willingness to compromise on other points, was puzzling. Someone who was well informed on Soviet legislation and habits offered me the following explanation: the Soviet Constitution guarantees the freedom of movement over the entire Soviet territory to all, citizens and foreigners. It would not be desirable to write something into an international convention which might appear as a restriction on the fundamental freedoms granted by the Soviet Constitution. *Se non é vero . . .*

In the course of the ceremony for the signing of the convention, Hirsch and Petrosyants, to whom I acted as interpreter, found that they had a lot in common and swapped jokes. Hirsch told a story to illustrate scientists' perpetual requests for money: 'My wife is hard to please. She keeps asking for money: she asks for it on Monday, and then again on Tuesday and Wednesday; she still wants some on Thursday and Friday, and again on Saturday.' 'But what does she do with all that money?' 'I don't know, I never give her any.'

Petrosyants told stories bearing on the rivalry between Georgia and Armenia; for example: 'Armenia wants a Ministry of the Navy.' 'What for? They have no ships.' 'Doesn't Georgia have a Ministry of Culture?' He also cited d'Artagnan as one of the great Armenians of the past, and suggested that Armagnac should be the correct name for the Armenian cognac of which the Armenians are very proud. I do not know how old Petrosyants is; he looked like a brisk sexagenarian in 1965. I spotted him on television after the Chernobyl disaster, still president of Soviet Atomic Energy, looking pleased with himself, a living example of the famous rule for Soviet high officials: 'From the desk into the grave'.

The signing of the convention put an end to my diplomatic concern with Mirabelle, which I henceforth delegated to Jean Pellerin. It was through him that I learned of the Soviet policy of isolating the French who lived in Serpukhov in a ghetto, and of sabotaging all attempts at friendly contact between the two communities, which might arise from either side—even resorting to elaborate police provocations. I eventually lost all interest in the Mirabelle project, which I had done my best to promote, and whose failure on the only level which had seemed promising to me, had left me with a bitter taste.

* A thermodynamic model

While I am unable to provide a rational explanation for behaviour as unreasonable as that of the Soviet regime, which clearly goes against the best interests of its own country, I can propose a *thermodynamic model* for it, where I make the assumption that the Soviet Union is a *system at a negative temperature*.

One should remember that what physicists call a model does not claim to provide a realistic picture of the system that it models, nor to *understand* what goes on inside it. All that is required from the model is to be as simple as possible and to reproduce the essential features of the system.

Let us recapitulate those of a system at a negative temperature, such as a spin system, as outlined in an earlier chapter.

a) As long as it is isolated, it is as stable as a system at a positive temperature, but, like all systems whose temperature, positive or negative, is not zero, it exhibits internal fluctuations, which do not affect its stability.

b) On the other hand, any contact with a 'normal' system—whose energy spectrum does not have an upper bound, and which therefore is necessarily at a positive temperature (such as the system of elastic vibrations of a crystal, or 'phonons', or the system of electromagnetic radiations, or 'photons')—is catastrophic for a system at a negative temperature, in that it cannot come to thermodynamic equilibrium with a 'normal' system without passing through a state of infinite temperature, which is complete chaos. The foregoing is just physics, and is not controversial. *

Let us now try such a system at a negative temperature as a model for the Soviet Union, surrounded by 'normal' systems serving as a model of its capitalist environment, and let us see what conclusions can be drawn from these assumptions.

a) The Soviet regime is stable, as proven by its having been in existence for seventy years.

b) No contacts with the environment can be tolerated by its rulers, even though the isolation causes serious harm to the country, of which these rulers are well aware. It is not paranoid behaviour, but rather a lucid realization of the threat of chaos such contacts would produce in the long term.

c) One should remember Stalin's systematic assassination of foreign communists who had found refuge in the Soviet Union during the war, and the systematic deportation to the gulag of all war prisoners repatriated from the West. Both had been contaminated by the West, and were dangerous as a source of chaos.

d) Why is there a policy of international tension, maintained by the USSR through localized conflicts in many places in the world, at great cost and no profit to itself? What is Cuba to them, or they to Cuba?

It is because you cannot permanently quarantine a great people unless you persuade it that its safety is threatened. The Soviet policy of international tension is not imperialistic, it is for inner use: it is not a matter of conquests, which are more burdensome and costly than useful; it is a matter of convincing the people that the fatherland is in danger, that its frontiers are threatened and must remain impenetrable. It is enough to see the reverence which surrounds the special troops with their green peaked caps, who are responsible for guarding the frontiers of the country—far greater than for any other parts of the armed forces.

e) In following contemporary Soviet literature, one is impressed by certain descriptions of everyday life, which paint such a dark and hopeless picture of it that one is surprised at their not being stopped by censorship. The explanation is that these fluctuations are *internal* to the system, and do not affect its inherent stability. They are unpleasant, but not dangerous for the State, and can be tolerated.

f) What are the predictions of the model?

Détente, in the sense of contacts with the West, where Soviet citizens would freely travel abroad, and foreign tourists, even well disposed toward the USSR, would freely associate with Soviet citizens, is impossible.

The sources of international tension are there to stay. They are part of the model. At most, extra care will be applied to prevent them from degenerating into more serious conflicts, which is not their purpose.

A peaceful transition to a state of positive temperature—that is, to normality—can only occur through a period of chaos.

I hope the reader realizes that the above has been written with tongue in cheek and must not be taken too seriously. Also, it was written a couple of years ago and takes no account of what is now happening in the USSR. I will come back to it in a while.

Books

My three books: the *Principles*, the ESR book written with Bleaney, and *Order and Disorder*, written with Goldman, have all been translated into Russian. (The *Reflections of a Physicist* might have been translated had it not contained an offensive passage about Orlov and Sakharov.)

This gave me an opportunity to find out about the workings of the Soviet publishing system, at least for books on science. There is an excellent principle, which is the extremely low price of such books, sold well below cost. This generous policy is unfortunately offset by stupidity: the number of printed copies is fixed by the plan, in advance and for ever, *independently of demand*.

My *Principles* have now been out of print for nearly twenty-five years, and the students can only acquire it on the black market. Somebody told me that it had been exchanged once against a copy of *Playboy*!

I was told by the late Eugene Livshits that the royalties are independent of the number of copies sold, and are calculated on the volume of the book (and perhaps also on the 'volume' of the author). Before the Soviets signed the international convention on royalties, they translated what they pleased and paid when they pleased, and almost exclusively in roubles.

For the *Principles* they were rather generous: I was able to bring home with me a little sable fur collar for Suzanne and two kilos of caviare for me, and to put the balance into a savings account in Moscow. The translator had omitted all the epigraphs in the *Principles*, claiming that they would confuse (?) the Soviet reader.

For the book I did with Bleaney, we did not get any royalties. The publisher informed me that a prerequisite for their payment was my writing a special preface for the Russian version. After the invasion of Prague I was not in the mood, and told him what he could do with his royalties.

For *Order and Disorder* the Soviets had by then signed the international convention, and we were paid in pounds through the Oxford University Press.

The translator, the same one who had suppressed the epigraphs from the *Principles*, decided to make up for it by translating those in *Order and Disorder*, but had to ask for my assistance because, as he put it 'some of the epigraphs were *not* unambiguous'. One of them, from George Orwell: 'Big Brother is watching you' was *quite* unambiguous, and I could see why he was embarrassed. I selected lines from *Eugene Onegin* (the poem by Pushkin, mentioned in the Introduction to this book) each of which had some bearing on the chapter it headed, which made him exceedingly happy. Some time later he informed me that he had shown a Russian copy of *Order and Disorder* to the director of the Pushkin Museum, a friend of his, who requested two copies to be placed in the museum as Pushkin *memorabilia*, which amused *me* exceedingly.

I made two more trips to Russia (correction, I made a third one in September 1987, to which I shall return in a while): the first in January 1972, and the second in June 1986, but both times as a tourist. I was able to see for myself that the reception of tourists by the police and customs officers had nothing in common with that reserved for the official visitor that I had been on previous trips.

The 1972 trip, on which Suzanne came with me, was after a series of lectures I had given in Helsinki in January. We had decided to go by train from Helsinki to Leningrad, and to spend two days there before flying to Moscow for three more days. I had booked our Russian stay with Intourist, first class, but because of the shortage of tourists in January, they spontaneously promoted us into the 'de luxe' category at no extra charge. This entitled us to a personal French-speaking guide, and to a chauffeur-driven car for three hours a day.

The journey by train proved colourful. In Helsinki we were put into a compartment of a Russian sleeping-car (the final destination of the train was Moscow), and before the departure, the doors of the carriage were locked at both ends. This prevented us from access to the dining-car, but the Russian attendant brought us tea from his samovar and some biscuits. Suzanne was struck by a Russian habit that I knew well: the sounds of conversation which came from the next compartment—a discussion of a football game, I told her—suddenly became inaudible for a few minutes, before being heard again on another, equally harmless subject.

At the frontier the train stopped for three hours. An army man, wearing the famous green peaked cap, made his appearance, lay on the floor to look under the seats, inspected the toilet which we shared with the neighbouring compartment, and disappeared. Another collected our passports and disappeared also. At last came the customs cops. They scrutinized the list on which we had written out all our currency, travellers cheques, jewellery, gold coins, firearms, and ammunition. One of them exhorted me to re-count my currency carefully. 'When one is old,' he said (poor me! At fifty-seven I thought I looked younger than my age) 'one forgets things and then one is sorry'. He asked me whether I was carrying any religious literature, and then went in earnest through our luggage. Having passed his arm into the sleeve of my jacket he felt some paper, and his eyes shone. He pulled and pulled on the paper, dragging out an incredible length of tissue paper, with which my dear Suzanne likes to stuff our clothes when she packs, in order to prevent them from getting wrinkled. 'What the hell is that?' he asked angrily, unable to hide his disappointment. I explained.

In Leningrad we were met at the railway station and taken to the Astoria, the most attractive hotel in the USSR, which was less than half-full at that season.

We had a three-room apartment, with fake *Louis Quinze* furniture, a piano, and a gigantic television set and refrigerator, neither of which worked. The little old woman who was in charge on our floor, was so impressed by the long and ample sheepskin coat which I had purchased for this voyage (I never wear it in Paris because it is never cold enough, but here it was a blessing) that, when she had opened our door for us with an enormous gilded key, she invited us to enter our apartment with an ample gesture of welcome. The following morning our lady guide arrived. She was a beautiful young woman, elegant, refined, and cultivated, and delighted to be able to chat in Russian with me. Alas, a few minutes later, the remark I dreaded came up: I must have some relatives left in Moscow, what a pleasure it would be for them to see me! 'I have no relatives left in the USSR', I said curtly, and she did not insist.

We left for the Hermitage, where I asked to see the Scythian golden treasure, a fraction of which had been shown in the West at various times, but which I had always missed. I do not wish to describe these treasures here, relics of an art and a civilization which flourished more than two thousand years ago, leaving no other trace than these golden jewels chiselled with incredible artistry and skill. A problem arose: the visit required a special guide and only 'excursions' were admitted. Our visit seemed to be in jeopardy when I had an idea. 'How many people to an excursion?' 'Thirty-six minimum.' 'And what is the charge per person?' 'Twenty kopecks.' 'If I pay seven roubles and twenty kopecks would you be willing to consider my wife and me as an excursion?' After some consultation, my proposal was accepted and our 'excursion', namely Suzanne and myself, our guide from Intourist, and a specialized guide from the Hermitage were able to make the visit in incomparable comfort.

The following day we took leave of our beautiful companion. She apparently shared the ideas of our friend, the customs cop, about the poor memory of old codgers (she probably also shared his duties), because she asked me again if I would be pleased to see members of my family in Moscow. 'You are very persistent, Miss; I have no relatives in Moscow,' I said with a heavy heart, for she really was very beautiful (de luxe, remember).

The outside temperature was −20°C when we landed in Moscow. An employee from Intourist fetched us from the plane, took us to a warm car, and returned for our luggage. 'De luxe' again. During that time the Soviet travellers were waiting in the *open air* for their luggage to be unloaded from the plane!!

We were put up in an hotel, which was brand new, but lacking the spacious old-fashioned charm of the Leningrad Astoria, and taken to visit the Kremlin, with its huge bell, its huge gun, and the treasures of its museums. The celebrated works of *Fabergé*, the tsar's famous court jeweller, looked to me heavy, over-ornate, and to be blunt, of poor taste, after the marvels of the Scythian treasure which we had admired two days earlier.

For forty dollars each, we were able to visit the glorious Zagorsk monastery and hear a service, beautifully sung by the faithful—an excursion 'quite worth the detour', to quote the Michelin guide. I drew some money from my savings account in a bootless attempt to buy some caviare with roubles. My friend Migdal took us to a typically Russian restaurant on the outskirts of Moscow and, yielding to my prayers, let me pay with what I called 'hay', my useless roubles.

We saw a ballet in the immense Conference Palace at the Kremlin. We had arrived early and were able to admire a gigantic buffet overloaded with victuals. 'We shall eat something in the intermission,' said my naïve Suzanne. When we returned, a flight of locusts had passed: only tea and some biscuits were left. As I was standing in line for tea, a man came up to me and asked me to let him in front of me, because, he said, he was with two foreign tourists. I shook my head. 'You don't understand, comrade, these tourists are our guests and we must show them consideration.' 'Well, I am your guest too, show *me* some consideration by leaving me alone.' The cut of my clothes must have shown him that I was from the West, for he did not insist.

My last (but one), visit to the USSR, took place in June 1986. It was a forty-eight hour excursion, following the μSR conference in Sweden which I spoke of at the end of the last chapter. As in my visit of 1972, we (by *we* I mean some thirty participants in the μSR conference, of all nationalities) arrived by train from Helsinki to Leningrad. During my 1972 visit, I had attributed the suspicious behaviour of the Soviet gendarmes to the unusual character of my visit: an individual, speaking Russian like a Russian, chooses to arrive by train in the middle of winter, when there are no tourists to speak of; strange isn't it?

I was mistaken. This time, in glorious summer, as soon as the train stopped, six uniformed henchmen of the regime, four men and two women (sorry, four henchmen and two henchwomen) erupted into the carriage. They grabbed all the passports and customs declarations, and started a thorough search. Each compartment in turn was emptied of its occupants, and these ladies and gentlemen closeted themselves in it for God knows what task. I forgot to say that they were armed with electromagnetic detectors, with which they did not seem to be fully familiar. After their little private ceremony in each compartment, the travellers were summoned and requested to open their bags, which were carefully searched.

A little incident enlivened these lamentable proceedings. A Japanese lady, a participant in the conference, overcome by the heat, and perhaps perturbed by the behaviour of our Soviet hosts, suddenly felt faint. The valiant guardians of the Soviet frontier lost their heads. Not one of them spoke a foreign language, and having noticed that I spoke Russian, they asked me to interpret between the Japanese lady and a lady doctor and a nurse whom they had produced in great haste—from some museum, if one went by their appearance. My problem was the Japanese participant in the dialogue, whose English I understood but faintly. We solved the problem by introducing a second Japanese lady into the circuit, whose English was more accessible to me. This, at the cost of some slowing down in the exchanges, informed our hosts that the Japanese lady had suffered much from the heat, for the train had been standing in the sun for two hours now, and that she felt nauseated. Across the Russo-Anglo-Japanese chain she was informed that she would be transferred at no extra cost (they were very insistent on this point) into a first class air-conditioned carriage, which was immediately performed. Alas, the air-conditioning only worked when the train was moving, but this is a detail. The lady doctor took the temperature and blood pressure of her patient, gave her a pill for her nausea, and all the medical and military personnel withdrew, not without covering me with quite disproportionate thanks, to which the two Japanese ladies added theirs—to the extent of embracing me.

In Leningrad I scorned the collective visit to the Hermitage and the tour of the city by bus, proposed by Intourist, in favour of my own project to see my beloved Scythians once more, and, something that I had never done before, to walk the length of the Nevsky Prospekt, which is the *Champs-Elysées* of Leningrad. For the Scythians, as in 1972, I was considered as an 'excursion', but payable in dollars this time. I had two companions, someone from the Bangladesh embassy and his two young sons, who had certainly not paid anything, and who were all bored to death. I devoted my walk on the Nevsky Prospekt to watching the people strolling towards me. It was not very cheerful. We were in the wrong mood, the crowd, or I, or both. I mainly saw sullen faces, shabbily dressed women, and elderly people, men and women, looking limp and tired. The pretty women one encountered every now and then seemed harsh and arrogant to me, carrying their prettiness like capital which they wanted to hold onto. I could not help remembering the Swedish girls, whom I had seen a few days earlier, who, if not all beautiful, had all looked cheerful, friendly, and happy.

I had noticed long ago that in winter Russian girls—cheeks pink with the frost, clad and bonneted with furs—look far more pleasant. Winter is the right season to appreciate the Russians.

And now, before I leave Leningrad, a few words about the great lady of Russian poetry, the greatest I think, who lived there most of her life and loved this city more than any place in the world—Anna Akhmatova (1889–1966). Her first husband, the poet Gumilev, was shot in the early twenties, and her son Lev was arrested and sent to a camp during the nightmarish Stalinist terror of the years 1937–8, when, as Akhmatova wrote: 'Like a useless trinket, Leningrad was dangling around its prisons'. In 1946 she fell into disgrace, and the official ideologist, Zhdanov, denounced her publicly as 'half harlot, half nun'. None of her work could be published, and she eked out a living by translating foreign poets. After Stalin's death she slowly came back to normal, if not into favour. In 1965, she got permission to travel to Oxford to be awarded a doctorate, *honoris causa*, eleven years before me. (If only I could have belonged to her batch of doctorands!) In 1966 she died, mourned by all and honoured by the officials. It was during the terrible years that she wrote her most beautiful poem, *Requiem*, in which the unspeakable sufferings of the mothers and wives burst forth.

'Wrote her poem' is not quite right. Seven or eight of her friends, of whom not one knew who the others were, had all in turn heard fragments of the *Requiem*, recited by Akhmatova until it was etched in their memories. It is thus that the *Requiem* had been collectively 'carried' through the terrible years, until it became possible to transcribe it. Akhmatova's works were published in Paris in the seventies; I bought a copy, and out of piety, and for my pleasure, I too learned the *Requiem* by heart.

All right, but why tell this story now, when it goes back to the 'cult of the personality', its 'errors' and its 'departures from socialist legality', which were all happily put right long ago? I'll tell you why. In 1985, that's not so long ago, a young Soviet scientist came to work in Paris for a few months. Having heard me quote the line on Leningrad and its prisons, he asked me to lend him a copy of the *Requiem* which was still unavailable in the USSR. When, a few days later, he returned the book to me, I asked him if he would like me to make a Xerox copy of the poem for him. 'Thank you, no,' he said, 'it's here,' pointing to his forehead.

Brave New World

In September 1987 I visited the USSR again, but, for the first time since 1969, this time it was on official business: I had had an invitation from a scientific Soviet institution, or rather two of them: the Institute for Physical Problems in Moscow, where Borovik-Romanov had succeeded Kapitza, and the Institute for Chemical Kinetics at Novosibirsk. The man responsible for this visit, although he was unaware of it, was the Secretary General, Mr Mikhaïl Gorbachev.

In the early seventies, in line with my stand on human rights, I had declined an invitation from Borovik-Romanov to give an invited paper at the international conference on magnetism in Moscow, and in 1978 another one, at a conference on magnetic resonance in Tallin. During a visit to Paris a few years later, Borovik-Romanov asked me when they would see me in Moscow, and I said that I should be very glad to come when Andreï Sakharov was back in Moscow. Neither he nor I knew if or when this would ever happen. This is why, when I received an invitation to give an invited paper at a conference in Novosibirsk in September 1987, I not only accepted it but also wrote to Borovik-Romanov to remind him of his past invitation.

So much has been written in the press about the changes which have been taking place in the USSR since the advent of Mikhaïl Gorbachev, that I do not feel like adding any detailed description to what the journalists have said and go on saying. Anyway, I could only testify to the reactions of the scientific class, which are far from representative of the general population.

The most striking thing that I was able to observe was that the *fear* had gone. In the conversations which took place during the intermissions at the conference in Novosibirsk (in Akademgorodok, to be more accurate), for the first time people did not look behind them or lower their voices when they broached a subject which was not absolutely trivial—a habit which had impressed Suzanne so much during our visit in 1972.

One little incident provided me with striking evidence of the new spirit. I had been watching on television a long speech that Mr Gorbachev had been making at a meeting in Murmansk. The following day, when the young physicist who served as my guide during my stay, rang me up at my hotel in Moscow to discuss the programme of the day, I told him, quite sincerely, how refreshing I had found Gorbachev's speech. 'Yes,' he said, 'but I have some reservations about some of the things he said.' 'Do you realize what you are saying?' I told him. 'You are telling me, a foreigner, on the phone, that you have reservations about things the Secretary General has said!' 'I hadn't thought of that,' he said, naïvely, without seeming particularly perturbed, however. That kind of thing would have been unthinkable before Gorbachev.

This newly-found absence of fear did not prevent nearly all of my fellow scientists from being very sceptical about the chances of success for the economic reforms that Gorbachev was trying to promote, and I cannot say that the new laws on alcoholic beverages met with more than lip service within their circle.

The other striking change was in the Soviet press. Reading in *Pravda*, that a male's life expectancy is 65 in the USSR and 74 in the US, and that child mortality in the USSR is increasing, or in *Izvestia*, that unless people see some financial advantage in working more, they will *not* work, was a novel experience, to say the least. As everybody knows, the regime has since gone much farther in its denunciation of its past.

In the little things of everyday life, on the other hand, the usual absurdities showed no sign of abating. At the guesthouse cafeteria in Akademgorodok, no trays were provided, and the guests had to balance the components of their breakfast perilously in both hands.

Coming back from Novosibirsk to my room in the Academy Hotel on 30 September, I asked the floor attendant for some toilet paper. 'Well, this is the last day of the month, you know; couldn't you wait till tomorrow?' she said. 'I most certainly couldn't.' Grumbling, she went to fetch some for me, from what must have been her personal reserve. In one of the buffets which function on some floors of the hotel and provide plentiful food at ridiculously low prices, I saw a waitress seated at a table, cutting paper napkins in two with scissors, when they were already the size of a handkerchief. For a Russian it is still next to impossible to get into a restaurant unless he tips the doorman lavishly, or is able to pull rank on him, and at dinner no conversation is possible because ghastly 'music' is blaring at you from all sides. But, as I said, these are little things.

At the Institute for Physical Problems, at the gate between the hall and the corridor which leads to the laboratories, there stands a strapping chap in a dark suit, to whom the people who work in the Institute have to show their credentials each time—although he knows them all by sight, although they pass in front of him several times a day, although there is no classified work of any kind beyond that gate, as I was able to see for myself.

I finally asked: 'Do you have to keep this man in here—what use is he?' 'Well, we must have someone here, if only to see that nothing is stolen.' 'All right, but couldn't you just have some retired *baboushka* for that?' (That's what Kapitza had.) 'A *baboushka* we would have to pay, however little; this man is from the Ministry of the Interior and *they* pay his salary. Besides, it never hurts to have people at the top think that our work is important enough to be closely guarded.'

Having said all that, the least I can do is to add that the work done at the Institute for Physical Problems is of very high quality, that its theoreticians are among the best in the world, but also its experimentalists, which in the USSR is rather exceptional. Indeed, in Novosibirsk, where representatives of NMR and ESR were gathered from all parts of the USSR, I was once more struck by the divorce between the extreme sophistication of the theorists and the obsolete character of the equipment at the disposal of their colleagues.

I regret to have to say once more that in Akademgorodok, as in the Institute for Physical problems, my two lectures, because of the added attraction for the audience of being delivered in Russian, had their usual success. I started with a line by Pushkin: 'Gallicisms will be dear to me', my usual gambit, and went so far as to slip in a couple of lines from the *Requiem*, greeted with applause by a large part of the audience.

A man

From the chapter in which I described my impressions of Harvard I extract the following lines: 'As a physicist and a human being, Ed Purcell is perhaps the man I admire the most. I have never met anyone more profoundly authentic, more detached from the wish to appear other than he is. (Correction: since I wrote these lines a year ago, I have met another man like him, but more of this later.)'

Later is now, and the man is Andreï Sakharov.

His name, his brilliant career, his fight for human rights, his shameful treatment at the hands of the Soviet power, his exile to Gorki, are all too well known to be recalled here. He was the man I wanted to see in Moscow, and I did not quite know how to go about it. Not one of the Soviet scientists I knew in Moscow was admitting to seeing him. I was told that he came every week to the Academy of Science, but that was off-limits to me. I also had the faint impression that few of his fellow Academicians had taken a stand on his behalf, and that some, whom I shall not name here, had behaved disgracefully.

Finally at a dinner in tête-à-tête with one of my Moscow scientist friends, I asked him point-blank whether he knew Sakharov's phone number. He said: 'I don't, but I know someone who might.' He went to ring him up, and came back two minutes later saying: 'He is afraid.' The telephone rang immediately, my friend said: 'He is ashamed', went to the telephone and came back with a phone number. I called the number, first getting Sakharov's mother-in-law, whom I met the following day—a marvellous old girl in her late eighties—then his wife, Elena Bonner, whom I had met in Paris, and finally Sakharov himself. I told him who I was, and that I wanted to see him and to give him a book of mine. He gave me his address and told me to come the following day at 9.30 p.m.

The first thing which struck me was the shabbiness of his apartment. He received me in a gloomy sitting room with nondescript furniture. He himself was wearing a shabby dressing-gown and slippers. This was particularly striking considering the importance that all Soviet dignitaries, even the best of them, attach to status symbols, such as the size of their apartment, their furniture, their books, and their pictures. Here was a man who obviously did not care about any of these things, and this, it seemed to me, was the first element of his strength. He could neither be bought with material goods nor threatened with their loss. I gave him the *Reflections of a Physicist* which I had brought for him, and inscribed it (in Russian): 'To Andreï Dmitrievich, great scientist and fearless fighter for human rights'. At that moment Elena Bonner appeared, and cried: 'What are you doing in this awful room? Come to the kitchen; if you haven't dined I can feed you.' I had dined before coming, and so we sat down to drink tea till 1 a.m. Around 11 p.m., a colleague of Sakharov's appeared, bringing with him John Maddox, the editor of *Nature*.

Sakharov's style of speech is remarkable. Unlike most Russians, he pronounces the letter R like the French. Before the Revolution it used to be called the aristocratic Saint-Petersburg accent, which Lenin is reported to have used. Sakharov speaks slowly; when asked a question, he thinks for a while before answering, and he always says very simple things. He did not sound, and did not wish to sound, like the brilliant physicist who has been elected as a full member of the Academy of Science at thirty-two (an all-time record). I asked him whether it was true that he was Gorbachev's adviser. He laughed and said: 'He phoned me once. I told him that we should free all political prisoners and get out of Afghanistan.'

I also asked him about the behaviour of his colleagues at the Academy who sat on their hands, apart those few who wrote unpublished letters on his behalf to the government, and those who, fortunately even fewer, wrote public letters in which they attacked him.

I wanted to know what his colleagues would have risked if they had spoken publicly in his defence. He laughed again and said: 'Very little; perhaps no travel abroad for a couple of years.'

His main scientific interests at present are astrophysics, particle physics, and cosmology. This is what I wanted to say about Andreï Sakharov. I remember what his colleague Artsimovich told me about him long ago: 'He is a saint. He is of the stuff that saints are made of.'

A brief friendship

On the last day of my stay in Moscow, I met another great star of Soviet physics, Yakov Borisovich Zeldovich, who was born in 1914. There are few great physicists with a span of competence comparable to his. He is a chemist, but, unlike Wigner who also held a degree in chemical engineering, he is a working chemist, and, in fact, one of the world's greatest specialists on explosives. But he is also an outstanding nuclear physicist, an astrophysicist, a cosmologist, a plasma physicist, and I am sure that there are quite a few more fields in which he has shone that I have forgotten. The reason why he is less widely known abroad than some lesser Russian physicists is simple. He almost never goes abroad because, as he told me himself: 'I spent thirteen years in our Los Alamos' (he did not name the place). He is at present head of the theoretical division at the Institute for Physical Problems.

From the beginning of the two hours that we spent together, we found a common language (and I do not just mean Russian), and he told me a lot about himself, his career, and his plans for the future—when he hoped to be able at last to travel widely in the West.

During our chat he told me that he was one of the three or four Soviet scientists who have thrice been Hero of the Soviet Union, which entitles him to three golden stars. Sakharov, who was another, was stripped of his stars when he began to misbehave. (Now that the times have changed there is a campaign going on among his friends, to have them restored to him, but the person who probably cares least about it is Sakharov himself.) Zeldovich also told me that a holder of even two stars is entitled to have his statue erected at his place of birth. This makes it a problem for Prokhorov, who was born in Australia, of all places.

I parted with Zeldovich, having agreed to correspond, and hoping to meet in the West soon. It was not to be.

In his first letter to me he said: 'I recollect our meeting in the Institute for Physical Problems with great warmth. The two hours spent with you were unusually interesting from a scientific point of view, but even more important were the friendship and confidence which arose between us—I take the liberty of writing this for both of us . . .'

In my reply at the end of October I wrote: 'My stupid word processor doesn't know any Russian and so I am writing to you in English . . . I am a little sad at the idea that circumstances have only permitted this first meeting between A and Z at a time when neither of us will see three score years and ten again. But better late than never . . .'

His second letter, of 3 December, scribbled by hand, ended with: '. . . I have the impression all the time that our conversation in Moscow is not over, and that we shall have occasion to meet again and to continue it . . .' Together with it came a letter from his secretary saying: 'With deep sorrow I inform you of the untimely death of Yakov Borisovich Zeldovich. He always spoke of you with great warmth and respect. In memory of this remarkable man I am sending you the draft of his letter, written the day before his death.'

Irreversible?

I said that I would not comment on Mr Gorbachev's *perestroika*, but since I stuck my neck out by offering a thermodynamic model of the Soviet regime, I am duty bound to say a few words about the connection between my model and the Gorbachev revolution, or rather, attempt at a revolution. To a physicist, and I apologize to non-physicists for this aside, I would say that thermodynamic predictions are not valid in the presence of a coherent applied RF field (see for instance the Overhauser effect). *Coherent and applied* from above is precisely how Gorbachev's revolution can be described; it is in no way a spontaneous social evolution. Therefore, and I will not go beyond this statement, what is happening at present in the USSR, does not prove my thermodynamic model false.

It is still by no means clear how *perestroika* will end. Sticking my neck out even farther, I am tempted to offer an opinion that nobody is asking for. I see three possible outcomes:

a) Gorbachev succeeds in carrying out a peaceful revolution which will transform the realm of absurdity into a modern and efficient regime.

b) The conservatives, while paying lip service to *perestroika*, will succeed in smothering it and will turn the clock back.

c) The *peaceful revolution* will turn into a violent and possibly bloody one, and chaos will prevail.

It is clear that at present, b) is what the Russians fear most (or hope for, as the case may be).

This is why Gorbachev puts such an emphasis on the crimes of Stalin, and of late, on the corruption of Brezhnev, and on the celebrated *glasnost* (which does not mean 'transparency' but 'open debate'). Most people will not join his side unless they are convinced that the clock will not be turned back, and the clock can only avoid being turned back if the people *are not afraid* to join his side. Gorbachev could tell his followers, like Franklin Roosevelt: 'We have nothing to fear but fear itself'.

Irreversible or not? That is the question that all the Russian *Gamlets*, (which is how they pronounce Hamlet), ask themselves.

In the spring of 1988, our Academy of Sciences had the privilege of welcoming Roald Sagdeev, a brilliant Soviet scientist, who conjured for us a glowing picture of the democratization and rejuvenation of the organization of Science in his country. No more, he implied, should the rulers of science step straight 'from the desk into the grave'. I congratulated him on having proclaimed ideas from the pulpit of our Academy, which, in past years, he had expressed many times in private only. 'Is *perestroika* irreversible?' I asked. 'It has to be; we have tried everything else and it does not work.'

Time will tell.

United States

Since I came back from Harvard in 1953, I have probably been to the US some thirty times.

Bucolic conferences

An occasion to return there every two years is regularly provided by the Gordon Conferences. These conferences, which exist for many branches of science, are a marvellous invention. They assemble, by invitation only, less than a hundred participants, most of whom know each other. There are no written proceedings, this plague of large modern conferences. They take place in boys' boarding schools, which the Americans call academies, in the pleasant rural environment found in several little towns in New Hampshire. The sessions take place from 9 a.m. till noon, and in the evening from seven to nine. The afternoons are free, and devoted to physical exercise: hiking, swimming, sailing, climbing, golf, and tennis, and, for the fanatics, scientific discussions. After the evening session, till midnight, everybody gathers in a rustic snack-bar. All these little towns are dry: the snack-bar provides only ice and soda-water, and each participant brings his own bottle of liquor. As a consequence, one drinks a lot more in these dry towns. Even those, who, like myself, are small drinkers, come with a bottle, in order to be able to join friends at their table without looking like a sponger.

The living quarters, which are those of a boarding school, are rustic. It has only been in more recent times that my advancing years and my growing reputation have entitled me to a private room and shower, which are scarce. On the other hand, food is abundant and wholesome. Naturally no spirits of any kind are served at meals.

The rosy-cheeked waitresses, who are students from the town's girls' school, look healthy and good-natured. Their christian names are embroidered on their aprons, on the left side of their youthful chests. A matron, young but vigilant, watches over the good behaviour of all concerned. My dear friend Solomon asked one of the girls whose christian name, Susan, was proudly displayed: 'And what's the name of the other one?' Susan blushed and giggled, but the matron had heard, and warned him severely to refrain from such un-American behaviour. The Thursday night dinner (all conferences end at noon on Friday), is a sumptuous feast, served in the open, and its high point is a whole Maine lobster per guest. Several times I had the fearsome task of lecturing on a Thursday night to an audience which was stupefied with food, but, alas, stone cold sober and far from receptive.

A group photograph is always taken in the middle of the week, and I have kept seven or eight of them, going from 1959 up to 1985. It is a curious experience to see all these faces changing and getting slightly older every two years. (I also have three group photographs of the professors from the Collège de France, separated from each other by ten years). I gave my last Gordon lecture in 1985, with the title 'Some lecture room experiments', a selection of some of the 'cutest' things done in my lab; it was rewarded by what politicians call 'a standing ovation', which lasted for several minutes and touched me immensely.

At a colloquium talk which I gave at Harvard in October 1978, I had the great honour of being introduced by the great physicist Steven Weinberg, who was a Nobel Prize winner in 1979. This was on the eve of the announcement of the Nobel Prize for physics, and I think that those who know me would have had some difficulty in recognizing me in Weinberg's presentation. His mind was on other things.

The amusing thing is that, if Weinberg had to wait another year for his Nobel, he himself is the main culprit (at least *I* think so). In his admirable little book *The First Three Minutes*, which had appeared a few years before, he makes it wonderfully clear how important Wilson's and Penzias' discovery of 'background radiation' is for our understanding of the universe. Well, they were the winners in 1978.

I was invited once to La Jolla by George Feher, a brilliant specialist in ESR, who one day 'turned his coat' and became a brilliant biologist. La Jolla is the new campus of the University of California, south of San Diego, at which I had been offered a professorship before my election to the Collège de France. George put me up in a motel twenty miles from his lab, which—an important detail for what follows—is right next to the beach, and rented a car for me. On the Sunday morning which followed my arrival I drove to the lab, which was naturally locked, but I had the key; I undressed in the lab, put on my swimming trunks, came down to the completely deserted beach, and had a delightful swim. Coming out of the water, I realized with dismay that I had absentmindedly put the keys to the car and the lab into a pocket in my trunks, and that both were now at the bottom of the ocean. My despair knew no limits. What was to become of me, all alone on this deserted beach on a Sunday morning, wearing swimming trunks, twenty miles from my motel and six thousand miles from home, without a cent and without access to a phone? One can gauge my distress from the fact that I dived several times, in the insensate hope of recovering my keys. An hour went by—at least I think so, for I had no watch. Then a coloured man made his appearance; he turned out to be the janitor. He let me into the lab, where I pulled on my trousers, and felt immediately better. The janitor knew George's phone number, he came to fetch me, and the following day got me another set of keys; but it took me a long time to forget this hour of unreasoned anguish.

I spent the second half of 1975, as so-called 'Battelle Distinguished Professor', at the University of Washington in Seattle—the main city of the state of Washington, in the extreme north-west of the US. There are three great universities in the US which bear the name of Washington. Besides the one I just named, there is the *George Washington University* in Washington DC, and the *Washington University* in St Louis, Missouri; all very confusing for Europeans. A large number of their letters make a triangular voyage before reaching their destination.

*One of the weak points of that stay was that little of the research pursued in the physics department had any bearing on my own. I took an interest in the work of Gregory Dash, who was responsible for my invitation, and who was doing some beautiful surface physics. I also followed the work of Norval Fordson, who was preparing an experiment aimed at the observation of non-conservation of parity in some atomic transitions. This type of experiment had been suggested in the context of the young electro-weak theory, by the French theoretician Claude Bouchiat, who had shown that this effect, although very small, was not as small as was believed, and could perhaps be observed. (Claude Bouchiat had pointed out that the effect went like the cube of the atomic number rather than the square, as was believed before.) I shall come back to this experiment in a moment.

I gave a dozen lectures, I thought about the possible uses of NMR in surface physics, and I talked with Fordson about his chances of observing the effect predicted by Bouchiat. I spent most of my time preparing the course that I was going to give at the Collège from the following January. My project was to describe the theory and the experiences through which the Cornell physicists had two or three years earlier, discovered the superfluidity of ^{3}He, in which NMR had played an important part. It was an enormous piece of work: I read a large number of articles on the subject, which I planned to blend into a coherent ensemble, and I made it the theme of my course for '76 and '77. I devoted a long chapter to it in the monograph *Order and Disorder* which I published with Goldman. It was not clear, however, why I should be doing this ten thousand kilometres from home.*

The strong points of our stay were the beauty of the American north-west, and the climate, which was marvellous in summer, and rainy but mild in winter. From the university campus, which was within walking distance of our apartment, I could see the magnificent Mount Rainier. It is about the same height as the Mont-Blanc, but it rises straight from the sea, which makes it far more impressive. There was, above all, the marvellous kindness of the Americans in that part of the country, without equal anywhere else in America.

In no other American city did I find a courtesy and a patience comparable to that of the inhabitants of Seattle. To discourage automobiles from invading the centre of the city, public transportation was free within a perimeter surrounding the main department stores and administrative buildings. I remember a queue which had formed in front of a bus while the driver was patiently explaining to an old lady the way to another bus stop, and without any display of impatience from the people in the queue. One could have thought oneself in England—the England of yesteryear, I should specify.

We had made the trip from Paris to Seattle in an unconventional manner. In April 1972 Suzanne had a grave heart attack, from which she had recovered, but without having returned in 1975 (nor indeed since) to her former state of health. Since her accident she had not been on a plane, and I was afraid for her of the two flights—first across the Atlantic, and then across the American continent (there was no direct flight from Paris to Seattle). I had been thinking of crossing the Atlantic by boat and the American continent by rail. I abandoned the first part of my project, for the only transatlantic crossings were with the Polish boats which carried immigrants to Canada, but I kept the second. However, I was told that American transcontinental trains were now in a pitiful state, and so we chose to go by plane from Paris to Montreal and by train, with Canadian Pacific, from Montreal to Vancouver. Unlike our trip across America more than twenty years ago, when we had travelled by coach, this time we had a spacious sleeper at our disposal, which was far roomier than those in European trains, and had a private washroom. Over two-thirds of the trip the landscape is very monotonous, and the vast plains of the Manitoba are frankly boring, but the three days of rest did Suzanne a lot of good. After the Rockies the view becomes magnificent. Many travellers fly over two thirds of the trip, from Montreal to Calgary, and go by train over the last third. In Vancouver we were greeted by my former mentor, Maurice Pryce, who for many years had been a professor at the University of British Columbia. I also saw Walter Hardy, who had worked at Saclay on deuterated hydrogen HD, and Volkov, the author of the mysterious Volkov notes which I had been deciphering with Horowitz thirty years before. After three days at Vancouver, a city of great beauty, we went by bus to Seattle, which is just across the Canadian border.

*In the autumn of 1977 I attended a conference on the various experimental aspects of the electro-weak theory, which was taking place at Fermilab, the location of the largest American accelerator. One of the main themes was the discussion of four experimental results from Seattle, Oxford, Novosibirsk, and Paris, following the suggestion by Claude Bouchiat on the possibility of observing non-conservation of parity in some atomic optical transitions. The first three experiments had been carried out on bismuth, and the last, by Marie-Anne Bouchiat, Claude's wife, on caesium. The great advantage of bismuth with respect to caesium was the size of the effect to be expected, which was much larger in a heavier atom. Its weakness, which in my opinion outweighed the advantage of size, was the large number of spurious effects, both experimental and theoretical, which threatened to overshadow the main phenomenon completely.

The reports from the four laboratories were as follows:

Seattle and Oxford reported what amounted to a zero-result, once all the causes of error had been analysed and estimated by their authors. Novosibirsk—which, it should be remembered, operated on the same element, bismuth, with the same methodology—reported a finite result compatible with the predictions of the electro-weak theory. It seemed to me that there was no reason to believe the Anglo-Americans more or less than the Russians. Marie-Anne Bouchiat's results were of a different nature. In her experiment there were no uncertainties of a systematic nature, but, considering the weakness of the effect predicted by theory for caesium, a lighter atom, *statistical* errors far exceeded the magnitude of the expected effect; or, in other words, the signal-to-noise ratio was much smaller than unity. It was necessary to improve this ratio considerably before drawing any conclusions, and she fully intended to devote the coming years to it.

If I am spending so much time on this problem, which is outside my sphere of competence, it is because of some amusing aspects of what followed. There was not much to choose, on the experimental level, between the Russian and the Anglo-American results, but the theoreticians chose to believe the latter—which contradicted the theory—perhaps because it is easier to believe bad news than good news. A wind of pessimism blew over the conference, but not for long. The very next day (!) two theoreticians at least presented versions of the electro-weak theory, which were compatible with the negative results from Seattle and Oxford.

This conference had at least one favourable result for Oxford, or rather for the Oxford physicist responsible for the results: he landed a newly created professorship in Oxford shortly afterwards.

Some time later, an experiment performed at very high energy, on deep inelastic scattering of polarized electrons from a target of liquid deuterium, showed that parity was indeed violated in electro-weak interactions, that the results from Oxford and Seattle were artefacts, and that, at least in my personal opinion, those from Novosibirsk had been no more than a lucky gamble. The only scientifically honest work had been that of Marie-Anne Bouchiat, who, after a few years of hard work, was able unquestionably to demonstrate a violation of parity in an atomic transition of the caesium atom.*

This conference had been dedicated to Ben Lee, a highly talented theorist, who had died in a road accident shortly before it. My only reason for recalling this fact is to sneak in an excellent story about his namesake, T. D. Lee, who, with C. N. Yang, discovered the violation of parity in weak interactions. This is the story.

T. D. Lee is greatly admired by the entire Chinese community of America. An American colleague, fond of Chinese cooking, asked his advice about dishes he should order in Chinese restaurants. 'You would not know how to pronounce its name correctly,' said T. D. Lee. 'Let me write it down for you.' T. D. Lee's friend went to a good Chinese restaurant in New York, and, after showing his piece of paper to the owner, ate a fabulous dish. Some time later, in San Francisco, the same piece of paper produced an equally delicious dish, although quite different in shape and taste. Surprised by this geographical disparity, he showed his piece of paper to a Chinese friend, who translated what the paper said for him: 'This man is my friend; treat him well, signed: T. D. Lee.'

Far East

This story provides me with a transition to the next leg of my voyage into my memory: a journey made in 1964 across the Far East (alas, no China).

This journey had been proposed to me by the Division of Cultural Relations of the Ministry for Foreign Affairs. Its hard core, so to speak, was a stay of a month in Japan, where I was to visit laboratories and to give lectures in several large cities. It originated with an invitation from Professor Ryogo Kubo, the great specialist in statistical mechanics, whose ideas I had incorporated into several chapters of my *Principles*.

An Indian specialist in NMR from Bombay, Professor Dharmatti, whom I had met at various conferences, had also sent an invitation through our Cultural Relations.

Together with them, we built up an itinerary. Its various steps were to be Bombay, New Delhi, Benares, and Calcutta in India; Bangkok in Thailand; Phnom-Penh and Siem Reap, the city of the temples, in Cambodia; Hong Kong, and in Japan Tokyo, which would be the starting-point from which I would visit other Japanese cities. We decided to skip Vietnam in spite of the insistence of one representative of Cultural Relations.

A problem arose before I left: what language should I use for my conferences? I was told: 'Impose our language everywhere.' 'If you mean that I will have to lecture in French, I prefer to stay at home. I know for certain that in Japan, as in India, no audience will be able to follow lectures given in French. However much I would enjoy this beautiful journey, I will give it up rather than spending the taxpayer's money in what would amount to a symbolic gesture.' In the end I only had to promise to seize all reasonable opportunities of expressing myself in French, and to encourage my interlocutors to do the same. I shall tell later of a disastrous attempt in Tokyo.

The reader need not worry: the *Guide Bleu* describes all the touristic marvels of the countries we visited far better than I could do it, and I shall refrain from detailed descriptions.

In Bombay we were met by a representative of the French Consulate, who took us to our hotel. We were seized immediately round the throat by the incredible poverty of the outskirts of the city near the airport, and by the pestilential smell—'the odour of India', said our guide—which emanated from them.

The splendour of the Tata Institute of Physics, where everything was: '*luxe, calme et volupté*', made a striking contrast with the poor devils squatting on their heels, a few steps from the entrance to this citadel of knowledge. The ability of the Indians to remain in that position for long periods is incredible. Sometimes, leaving the hotel in the morning and coming back at night, we found the same characters who had been there in the morning, crouching in the same posture.

We had been warned against eating any food that was not thoroughly cooked, such as salads and fresh fruit, and drinking anything but tea. At a picnic organized by Dharmatti's students, one of them peeled oranges with his long slender fingers and offered us segments, which it would have been churlish to decline. The capacity of the Indians for eating gracefully with their fingers is remarkable. I remember an Indian visitor at the Saclay cafeteria who, out of all that I was offering him, accepted only an oily sardine and a scoop of vanilla ice-cream, and ate both with his fingers, without licking them once. Just try it.

In New Delhi we were met by the French Cultural Attaché whom I found pretentious and unpleasant at first, but who rapidly revealed himself to be a very nice chap. He confessed he had feared that the awaited professor from the Collège de France and his spouse would be pretentious and unpleasant people. He made us visit everything that one visits in New Delhi, and also the Central Physics Laboratory, where I found the building and the equipment equally Victorian.

During one of the tours on which he took us around New Delhi, we found ourselves blocked on a narrow country road by a sacred cow, which grazed peacefully without paying any attention to the blowing of our horn. Our guide got out of the car, looked right and left to make sure that there was nobody around, and vigorously kicked her lank and 'all o'er teemed loins'. I shall never forget the look of surprise and outrage I read on the visage of that cow. Never had she been so insulted.

What struck me most in the Indian crowds that we saw pacing up and down the pavements of Bombay and New Delhi was the extraordinary beauty of children's faces. When they gaze at you intently, their immense eyes literally suck you in.

Unfortunately we did not have time to make a detour to Agra and visit the Taj Mahal, thus remaining forever one down on most visitors to India. It took us a full day to fly the 800 kilometres from New Delhi to the holy city of Benares. At each of the numerous, variously technical, stops of our plane, an old Fokker, teams of mechanics busied themselves around it, replacing some pieces of it by others which looked just as worn out.

In Benares, besides the ritual visit to the temples, we were able to see pilgrims bathing in the sacred river, and a few young men swimming in impeccable crawl style, heads immersed in the water, while a cow was gliding peacefully down the river awaiting her next reincarnation. Our guide had mentioned the custom of the Benares women of leaving their breasts uncovered, a custom which had become obsolete and was observed only by the oldest women—something we were mercifully spared.

Our last city in India was Calcutta, where we spent twenty-four hours: twenty-four too many. It was our fourth stop, but it was the Ninth Circle. In Bombay, people crouched on their heels, and crows whirled over their heads cawing stridently. In Calcutta, people lay full length on the pavement under the watchful eye of vultures, silent and sinister sentries. At our hotel, an enormous Victorian pile of a building, as it was our last evening in India, and to raise our sagging morale, we relaxed our vigilance in food matters a little—a damnable profligacy for which we paid dearly all the way to Hong Kong.

In Bangkok, where our Cultural Relations had reserved a comfortable room for us in a modern hotel, we found a complete change of scenery. The people looked well fed and prosperous, and everywhere sumptuous victuals were spread: fishes of all kinds and colours, known and unknown in Europe, and, above all, marvellous fruit, huge golden pineapples, mangoes, and many others I had never seen before. Alas, for us it was boiled fish, boiled rice, and boiled fruit. Cursed Calcutta!

After India, we found the temples and palaces vulgar with their over-ornate roofs, freshly gilded, and their loud colours; but we loved the innumerable little canals, the floating markets, and, above all, the sight of the little kids returning home from school, each one paddling in his own tiny boat, the size of a nutshell.

We had the privilege of visiting the atomic reactor, which had been donated by the United States for educational purposes. (May I be pardoned for recalling here a delicious misprint which I saw once in a CEA publication. 'The rector of the University of Pennsylvania, cooled with heavy water . . .'.) The director of the Bangkok reactor, who had the rank of Air Marshal, (on the strength of his important charge, not because he was an airman), complained to me that the Americans had omitted to donate, with the reactor, the funds necessary for its functioning. He had to stop the reactor because the funds at his disposal were barely sufficient to remunerate the numerous guards of the machine.

In Cambodia, where everybody spoke French, we spent a day in Phnom Penh, the captial, before flying in a little plane to Siem Reap, which is the starting point for visiting Angkor-Vat and the other temples. Thanks (if I may use that word) to the Khmer Rouge, and then to the Vietnamese invasion, this unfortunate country had been closed to tourists for over twenty years: having been able to visit it, is a high point of one-upmanship, comparable to the Kudos I acquired by a private visit to the Lascaux caves, which are closed to visitors. I was indebted for that favour to a famous prehistorian, who had come to see me when he was a candidate for the Collège de France. I shall be content with saying that Angkor Vat is, like Lascaux, unforgettable, and leave it at that.

In Hong Kong we discovered two sides of Chinese 'civilization', cooking and tailoring. I had indifferent memories of a few meals in the Chinese restaurants of the Latin Quarter when I was a student; and, after the war, Chinese dinners I had in Paris or New York, although somewhat better, were nothing to write home about. The only memorable occasion in a New York Chinese restaurant was the paper I drew from a 'fortune cookie', which proclaimed: 'You have a very special magnetism', which, in view of my trade, brought merriment to my companions.

The Chinese cooking in Hong Kong was a discovery. I say unhesitatingly that not only is it as refined as the best French cooking, but it is far easier to digest—which, considering our barely faded memories of Calcutta, was a double blessing. After two days we boldly ventured into a restaurant, where waitresses circulated between the tables, with enormous trays hanging from belts round their necks, loaded with mysterious-looking little pots, which contained anonymous but devilishly inviting dishes. We tasted at random, ignorant of what we ate, but never once disappointed.

With respect to tailors, Van Vleck had given me the address of his, who had kept his measurements, and for many years had been sending him his suits. I ordered three lightweight suits from him, which cost me the price of one in France, and half-a-dozen shirts. Suzanne was measured for a suit and a skirt. And, unique experience, never to be renewed—we had each a pair of shoes made to measure, which were the same price as ready-made.

Between eating and getting clothed we found the time to make a few excursions in this extraordinary town. The time passed very rapidly. Then came the turn of Japan. My scientific mission was beginning in earnest.

Of Japan I had three different pictures. The first, that of my twenties, was of a fascist, militarist, and conquering country, which thirty years earlier had vanquished the giant Russia of the tsars, and which was in the process of swallowing the giant China. On the commercial side, it was beginning to flood the world with incredibly shoddy goods at incredibly low prices. I remember an exhibition of Japanese goods in Paris, some time in the thirties, and indeed I am not likely to forget it. The goods displayed could be purchased at the end of the exhibition, and I let myself be tempted by a fantastically cheap bicycle—100 francs, instead of the starting price of 600 for French bicycles. It was a bicycle like all bicycles, with two wheels, a frame, handlebars, a chain, two pedals, etc. I rode it home, happy and proud of my purchase, and then some more for a couple of days. On the third day, something incredible happened: the bicycle literally disintegrated, the handlebars remained in my hands, the chain stopped pulling the cog, the front wheel separated from the frame—and where, a minute ago, had been a bicycle, there was a pile of junk. It is sometimes said that a well-designed machine is one in which all the parts begin to wear out at the same time. From that viewpoint my bike had been designed by a genius. Such was my experience of Japan in the thirties.

When I said at the beginning of this chapter, perhaps with some exaggeration, that the Japan of today has become an industrial suburb, I was simply alluding to the overabundant information available to everyone about that country, to which for my part I have nothing to add.

The Japan of 1964, which meanwhile had become a democratic and peace-loving country, was just starting on its fantastic technological and economic take-off. The train which took us from Tokyo to Kyoto at more than 200 kilometres per hour was the fastest and the most modern in the world, but the dream of each Japanese professor for a few years, was still to return from a long stay in the US with an American car.

On our arrival in Tokyo we found lodgings in the *Maison Franco-Japonaise*. A room on the second floor had been reserved for us by the *Relations Culturelles*. It was not a very comfortable lodging, if the word 'understatement' has a meaning. A whole cargo of peach-stones had gone into the stuffing of our pillows and our mattresses, but there was worse. Far worse: our neighbours on the left-hand side were a young couple with a two-year-old child who suffered from nightmares every night. Just as bad were our neighbours on the right-hand side, who had a six-month-old lusty baby, with the healthiest pair of lungs that happy parents might wish for. The worst by far was our window, which opened on to the main Tokyo suburban railway line, through which something like a thousand trains passed between 5 and 8 a.m. I was seriously considering going to an hotel for which I would have to pay out of my own pocket, when the happy moment came to leave for Kyoto.

Our great white train was a marvel, and proud of its speed, which a meter displayed in each carriage. We had the good luck of catching a sight of Fuji-Yama in all its glory, which is wrapped in fog in that season nine times out of ten. At each end of the carriage there was a 'western' toilet and a Japanese one, in which, I own, I never quite understood the posture expected from the user. There was, it is true, a sketch showing this posture, but in the 'Western' toilet only. In Kyoto we spent a delightful week in a traditional Japanese inn, or *ryokkan*, provided fortunately with a 'Western' toilet. We soon got used to sleeping on mattresses laid straight on the floor, and to the fact that our room had no individual existence, so to speak. The walls were mobile; and once, coming home in the middle of the afternoon, we found a group of Japanese drinking their tea in what had become a sitting room. It is also true that after the *Maison Franco-Japanese* we would have felt comfortable anywhere.

As a city, Tokyo is a horror. Imagine an immense ensemble of small nondescript provincial towns, all alike and glued together. Kyoto is very beautiful, but with spots of unbearable ugliness here and there, like their hideous television tower, which murders a charming district. A Japanese colleague explained it to me: 'My compatriots have a feeling for beauty, but they have no feeling for ugliness'.

We also spent a few days in Osaka and Nagoya, which are south of Tokyo, and in Sendai, in the north. Everywhere I gave lectures and visited laboratories. Their equipment was not lavish but in general adequate, and the research workers strongly motivated. My *Principles* had just been translated into Japanese, and my lectures received a kind reception everywhere, except for the jokes, with which I have the deplorable habit of sprinkling my lectures, and which for the first time did not do well.

I keep smarting memories of my first plenary conference in Tokyo, in a packed lecture room. I naturally gave my lecture in English, and, in front of all these attentive but unscrutable faces, I risked one of my customary jokes in the hope of making sure, from a few smiles noticed here and there, that, if not my subject, at least my English was reaching the audience. The faces remained impassive. A second and a third attempt had the same fate. I was beginning to despair when Professor Kubo, who was the chairman, guessed at my distress. He got up and, turning his back on me so as to face the audience, roared with laughter. The whole room burst immediately into laughter, and the ice was broken. Kubo assured me afterwards that my audience had feared to show a lack of respect for me by laughing.

That is as it may be. It is a fear which did not trouble the urchins in the street much, who burst into laughter just from looking at us. It seems that it was the length of our noses which gave rise to their mirth.

I have said nothing about Japanese food, which, become blasé after Hong Kong, we found mediocre. As Suzanne put it: 'They give you very little and so it does not hurt you.'

We dutifully visited the prescribed temples and sanctuaries, for which I refer my reader to his favourite guide-book.

Before leaving Japan, out of a sense of duty, I let myself be talked by the President of the Franco-Japanese Society into giving its members a lecture in French. At the last moment it was explained to me that, in spite of their attachment to our language and our civilization, some of the members feared to be unable to follow my lecture in French, and I was supplied with an interpreter. I pronounced a few phrases in French and then let the interpreter translate them into Japanese. From the expressions of some of the physicists in the audience I gathered that, though my interpreter appeared to speak French fluently, he understood it very poorly, which is a more frequent occurrence than is generally thought. On the other hand, I had occasion to observe that he understood English quite well. In desperation, we adopted the following procedure: I pronounced two or three phrases in French, loud and clear. I then whispered them in English to my interpreter, who then pronounced them in Japanese. The comedy lasted for two hours, but I had done my duty by our language.

We left Japan by the polar route. We had the pleasure of seeing the sun rising twice within an hour, and I saw two white bears.

Geneva: Rocking the boat

In April 1986 I received a letter from Professor Wolfgang Kummer, President of the CERN Council, asking me to serve as chairman of an international Review Committee, which had the task of looking into the organization of CERN, the large European laboratory for high energy physics, with a view, I quote:

to advise the Council how human and material resources, employment conditions, structure, operations and future use and development of facilities might be developed to operate with maximum cost effectiveness and value for money at alternative levels of funding by present Member States, and to assess their consequences for the CERN programmes and for services to Member States.

to assess the possibilities for engaging and enlarging other sources of funds and resources

to report within one year findings and recommendations to the CERN Council and hence to the governments of the Member States.

It is my pleasant duty to acknowledge that Professor Kummer does not normally write like that. The above bears the inimitable mark of having been drafted by a committee, and an international one at that, being part of a resolution of the CERN Council.

Besides me, for I accepted the CERN offer, the following six nationals of member states had also agreed to serve on the Committee:

Dr M. Boyer (Spain; President of the 'Banco Exterior de Espana')

Dr C. De Benedetti (Italy; Managing Director of Olivetti)
Prof. B. F. F. Fender (United Kingdom; Vice-Chancellor of the University
of Keele)
Prof. W. Paul (Fed. Rep. of Germany; Bonn University)
Mr Haakar Sandvold (Norway; Director of Ardal og undal Verk A/S)
Mr J. Vodoz (Switzerland; President Amysa SA Yverdon)

I had been given no indication on how these six personalities, or indeed
I, had been selected for the task by the CERN Council. I had never met
any of them before. Some wag had said that there were plans to sell CERN
to Carlo De Benedetti, which was the reason for his being on the
Committee, but this is most unlikely, considering that his thoughts were
already addressed towards buying Belgium.

In a letter of 6 June to the members of the Committee, I outlined some
of my views about our task.

We come from very different walks of life and our only common trait, unless I
am very much mistaken, is that none of us has any special interest in, or special
knowledge of the field of studies pursued at CERN, namely high energy particle
physics. More than the fear of a vulgar conflict of interest, the reason I see for this
selection, is the wish of the Council for a dispassionate look at CERN from our
Committee, which an excessive interest in these studies might bias. We must also
beware of the opposite bias of scientists working in other fields and competing
with CERN for bigger parts of the cake.

It seems to me that our lack of involvment with CERN carries with it a penalty
which is ignorance. I am speaking for myself and perhaps for some of the other
Members of the Committee. This is why my own attitude and perhaps our
collective attitude should be, at the beginning at least, one of humility: we must
get educated, without becoming converts, before we become judges.

Not unexpectedly, my fellow Commissars turned out to be very busy
people and it was not possible to organize a meeting of the Committee
before 8 September 1986. Later it proved necessary, in the wake of the
Collège de France, to schedule our meetings on Sundays. To save time I
had written in my June letter:

I should be very grateful for any suggestions, that you would care to make in
writing, on the way we should proceed, before our first plenary meeting of
September 8 and 9. Meanwhile and to start the ball rolling I would welcome an
opportunity of an encounter with you either at CERN or in Paris before that date.

I received no written suggestions, and only M. Vodoz came to see me in
Paris. At our first meeting in September I told the Committee how I viewed
our collaboration:

It is a Committee of seven Members with one of them acting as Chairman. It is
not one man in charge (the Chairman), reporting to a Committee whose Members
meet every so often to hear what he has to say. Unless there is agreement within

the Committee on this point, the present Chairman cannot see his way to pursue the task he has begun, not so much because he is unwilling but because he is unable to carry it out.

There was unanimous agreement from the members.

Getting educated, as I had said in my letter, but also getting organized were my most urgent tasks.

I had already had an experience, which I have described in an earlier chapter, of getting educated in the field of particle physics, back in 1965. During the following twenty-odd years, particle physics had moved forwards, while I myself was, I suppose, moving backwards. I found that I could still understand the gist, if not the sophisticated details, of the outstanding problems. What made it easier than I might have feared, was the fact that, thanks to the advances in theory, and also in experiment, of which CERN had recently grabbed the lion's share, the landscape of particle physics was a good deal less confusing in 1986 than in 1965.

I was fortunate in having been able to enlist the assistance of two colleagues, who probably between them did more work than the seven members of the Committee, Chairman included: Professor Pierre Petiau from the Particle Physics Laboratory at the Ecole Polytechnique, and Professor Christopher Llewellyn-Smith from Oxford University. Besides their expertise in the field of particle physics, they both knew their CERN backwards: who did what, why and how.

The CERN management had also put at the disposal of the Committee an experienced secretary, Madame Simone Dubois, who gave yeoman service (or is it yeowoman?) to the Committee.

I discovered what I had already suspected, namely that the directors of CERN, and first and foremost its Director General, Professor Herwig Schopper, were men of the highest calibre, who wholeheartedly gave us the benefit of their competence and assistance. It was only to be expected that they would not see eye to eye with the Committee on all points. It was all very well for the Committee to make proposals about drastic changes in the personnel policy. Once their report had been submitted to the CERN Council, the members of the Committee returned to whatever they were doing; the directors stayed behind and had to live and work with that personnel.

We received the same kind assistance from all levels of the organization. In the course of my work I interviewed many leading physicists from CERN and elsewhere, including CERN's Director-Elect Carlo Rubbia, a most interesting man. He is far too well known to need a description from me. The only thing I can say from personal experience, borrowing a formulation used by Bleaney when speaking of another Nobel winner: 'I found him very easy to talk to; all you have to do is listen.'

Our Committee submitted to the Council, for its meeting of December

1987, a final report of 166 pages. All parts of it had been discussed and approved unanimously by the members of the Committee. In matters of finance and management, the specialized knowledge of M. Vodoz, M. Boyer and M. Mancinelli, who after a couple of meetings had stood in for M. De Benedetti, proved particularly useful.

I do not plan to say anything about the contents of the report. Those who have an interest in CERN have either read it or seen accounts of it in the press, and I do not see why I should inflict it on my other readers.

I do not want to leave Geneva without including two brief excerpts from two documents which were not part of the report. The first is taken from my presentation of it to the Council. It is aimed at Britain whose reluctance to take its full part in CERN expenses had led to the establishment of our Committee in the first place.

At this point I will take the liberty of stepping out of my Chairman's shoes for a brief moment and of addressing myself to the British delegation, speaking as a rank and file physicist. As a physicist who had learnt his trade in Britain, a trade incidentally as far removed as can be from that practised at CERN. A physicist to whom Britain had given the greatest honours of his career and who takes great pride in having his name in the Charter Book of the Royal Society two lines ahead of that of Margaret Thatcher, the Prime Minister of Britain. Britain, this country of Newton, Cavendish, Faraday and Maxwell, 'this happy breed of men, this little world . . . this England.' Nearer to us, I think of the great shadows of Dirac, of Moseley, of J. J. Thomson and Aston, of Rutherford, Chadwick and Cockroft, of C. T. R. Wilson, Blackett and Cecil Powell, and I do not wish to forget John Adams without whom CERN would not be what it is.

All the friends and admirers of Britain and of British science would be as sad as I if this great country were to decide that it could not afford to devote the same proportion of its income as the other European countries are willing to do, to the science that these men created not so long ago.

The second brief excerpt could be entitled: 'How to make friends and influence people.' It is taken from the 'Initial Comments on the final report of the CERN Review Committee' by the CERN Staff Association.

The Association also considers that, throughout the report, there is an attitude of ill-will towards the CERN staff, which comes through in subjective or fallacious arguments, mixed with half-truths, untruths, offensive insinuations, unsubstantiated gossip, misleading associations, and stylistic triviality which are quite astonishing in a document of this kind.

To me, O my reader, *stylistic triviality* was the 'most unkindest cut of all'.

I should have taken leave here of this unforgettable document, but I have never been able to leave well enough alone, and I shall add another brief excerpt from the same source. It is about *'an original and constructive proposal to the Council for reducing the personnel budget immediately . . .*
All this for the price of one yearly cup of tea (in Geneva) per head of

population in the Member States!' Work out for yourself how much money it is, for the Staff Association does not say. And what couldn't one do with a ham sandwich!

The Netherlands

Is there a physicist who does not cherish The Netherlands, this little country, homeland of Huygens and Leuwenhoek, and, nearer to us, of Van der Waals, of the great Lorentz, of Zeeman, Kammerlingh Onnes, of Kramers, Zernike, of Gorter and Casimir?

Is there a European who does not love this country, the most civilized in Europe, its towns where the wind of liberty blows, reflected in their canals, its marvellous painters, Vermeer and Van Gogh, its skies, its cows, its windmills, its quiet determination to survive and prosper below sea level, the calm, the dignity, the courtesy, the good health of its dwellers?

There is, to be sure, the language, but one gets used to it.

In 1950, at that conference where, as I have told before, I celebrated at thirty-five my coming of age as a physicist, I discovered Amsterdam, and then, during successive visits, Leyden, Haarlem, Delft, and Utrecht.

My first stay of some length in Amsterdam took place in 1969. I had been asked to give a dozen lectures to chemists and physical chemists on a subject of my choice. I chose the Jahn–Teller effect. Its definition does not matter here but one should know that its study involves some knowledge of the theory of finite groups, which in those days were not much taught to French physicists. So, chemists, you can imagine! I started cautiously by giving my Dutch audience some smattering of this theory. After my second lecture a small delegation came to let me know that they had known it all for quite some time, and that they would not mind hearing something new.

That year in Amsterdam there was an extraordinary exhibition of Rembrandt paintings. Museums from all over the world had sent their greatest masterpieces. I very much admired a painting of 'Bathsheba expecting David' of which I had never even seen a reproduction. 'Where does it come from?' I asked one of the attendants. 'But from the Louvre, Monsieur.'

My second long stay in The Netherlands was in Leyden in 1980. For four and half months I was the incumbent of the Lorentz Chair, to which a physicist from abroad is invited every year. I gave twenty-four lectures on my little games with nuclear magnetic order to an attentive and competent audience, and I have excellent memories of it. It was the first time, with the exception of my Collège lectures, that I had been able to get to the bottom of the problem, and, thanks to the questions and remarks from my listeners, clarify my own ideas before putting them on paper later, in the monograph *Order and Disorder*.

There is the marvellous, perhaps apocryphal, story of a lecture given at the Lorentz institute by David Hilbert, the great mathematician, in 1927. It seems that for some reason he could only get to Leyden in time by flying to Amsterdam, at a time when many people were shy of going by plane. Hilbert had sent ahead the title of his lecture: 'A demonstration of the Fermat Theorem'. He disappointed his eager audience by lecturing on something quite different. Asked afterwards why he had given that title, he replied: 'If my plane had crashed I would have passed to posterity as the man who had at last proven the Fermat Theorem.'

Israel

This will be short. I have already spoken of my trip to Israel in 1957. I returned there in 1962 for a conference on ESR, in 1968 with Kastler and Friedel for a Franco-Israeli meeting, in 1980 to give the annual lecture in honour of Giulio Racah, a great theoretician whose work is a landmark in atomic and nuclear spectroscopy, and finally in 1986 for an *honoris causa* doctorate from the Haifa Technion.

I do not wish to speak of Israel any further for the following reason. One cannot, at least *I* cannot, speak of Israel without speaking of Jews. It so happens that for various reasons I find it difficult to speak about Jews to non-Jews. Since it is by no means certain, nor indeed desirable, that Jews should be the only readers of this book, I shall not tell any more stories about Israel.

Just one thought perhaps. Before the existence of Israel, it was generally agreed that Jews had the makings of excellent physicians, distinguished scientists, virtuoso pianists and violinists, great financiers, etc. But there was a unanimous agreement, which in my youth I was not far from sharing myself, that never, never, could they become a nation of soldiers and farmers. Let the inherited IQ maniacs chew on that—Nobel winners or not—who swear by nature and scorn nurture, and who explain gravely that coloured people are genetically unfit for intellectual professions.

At one time or another I have found myself in most European countries, including those of Eastern Europe, but all of a sudden I find that I have very little to say about it.

Perhaps I could round off this chapter with a Belgian story and a Bulgarian story. In 1961 I went to Louvain in the company of Kastler, Bleaney, and Halban, to give lectures at the Catholic University in the city. At the closing banquet I happened to be sitting next to Canon Lemaître, who was not only a catholic dignitary but also a distinguished cosmologist, and whose model of the universe was very popular before the Big Bang came along. He turned out to be a gay companion and a hearty trencherman. All of a sudden he asked me a riddle: 'What is the difference between a saint and a martyr?' I confessed my ignorance. 'A saint, you see, never errs, never does anything wrong, sees to it that others do not err either, and, to sum it up, is perfect.' 'Very well, but what's a martyr?' 'A martyr is one who has to live with him.' The riddle owed its spice to the personality of its author. I thought I had guessed who the martyr was, but before I had time to ask him whether he had one particular saint in mind, the *Rector Magnificent* of the university rose to pronounce the closing speech: or rather speeches, for he spoke in English, French, Flemish and, more briefly, Latin. During the dinner I had asked my kind neighbour whether there would be an after-dinner speech. 'Monseigneur will do himself violence, when the time comes,' the good cleric had said.

And now the Bulgarian story. Bulgaria combines socialism and capitalism. In the seaside resort of Varna on the Black Sea, where I had gone with Suzanne for a meeting of the steering committee of the International Union of Physics, the shore is surrounded with a fence which forbids access to the sea, except through a door. A cashier collects a tithe from would-be bathers on behalf of the state. That is the capitalist part. At 4 p.m., his day's work is completed and he leaves; but first locks the door lest the socialist state be robbed. That is the socialist part.

'Why did you come back so soon?' asked Suzanne. 'They have locked up the sea.'

The groves of Academe

I have immortal longings in me
Cleopatra

The customs—The visits—The costumes—Graphite and diamond—
* 'Theory or Experiment'—The Foreign Societies—* Predicting the
past—'Twelve physicists'

An uprooted little Russian schoolboy, a studious *lycéen*, an undergraduate in want of guidance, a postgraduate in search of research, a soldier, firstly 'defeated', lastly 'victorious' on either side of four verdigris years, a late beginner in physics, a mature physicist, a professor and research leader, a director, what else? Academician, what else!

The great cancerologist Antoine Lacassagne, a member of the *Académie des Sciences*, had died on 16 December 1971. It was the news of his death which for the first time, planted in my head, the ludicrous idea of becoming an Academician. Before I explain what it was that attracted me to an Academician's estate, it is not a bad idea to say what the *Académie des Sciences is* exactly, or rather what it *was* in late 1971; for, unlike the Collège de France, it has changed considerably in the last seventeen years. A change that was badly needed, if the truth be told.

I was surprised at the thought that the *Académie*, the 'old lady of the Quai Conti', as it is called, was the Collège's junior by over a century: it seemed so much more ancient.

It was made ancient, to start with, by the age of its members: the oldest member of the Geometry Section, Paul Montel, was ninety-six, followed by Maurice Fréchet, ninety-three, then by my two former examiners, Denjoy and Garnier—who had jointly flunked me thirty-six years ago—respectively eighty-seven and eighty-five. Last came the youngster, Gaston Julia, who was seventy-nine. (There was one vacancy in the section.)

Not all the sections were so aged, but from nearly one hundred members of the *Académie*, three more were over ninety, and quite a few over eighty. The average age was well above seventy. Alfred Kastler had plotted two curves representing, for the last hundred years, the age of the Academicians on entering the Academy and on their death. He found that the two curves were getting closer to each other and would cross before the year 2000.

The rules of the *Académie* also had a distinct flavour of antiquity. Apart from two sections with a special status, which I shall describe soon, the Academicians were grouped in sections of six members, according to their speciality. To be admitted into your section, say, Physics, you had to wait patiently until one of its six members—your colleague, often your friend or teacher—agreed to die and to leave room for you . . . or for another. I called it the 'Rule of the Corpse'.

The names of some of the sections also had the sweet smell of antiquity, such as 'Geography and Navigation' or 'Rural Economy', which were entitled to six members each, as many as Physics.

Two other sections, of fourteen and twelve members respectively, relaxed the rules to some extent by accepting candidates from all fields.

The first was the section of the so-called 'Free Academicians'; the second, the so-called 'Non-Resident Section', was reserved for dwellers in the provinces. It was no easier to get into the 'Free Academicians,' Section, (the 'Non-Residents' did not concern me) than into a specialized section. The vacancies were more frequent, but you faced rivals from all fields, and excellence in your own was no guarantee of success (nor was it in specialized sections). At the time when I put my name down as a candidate for Lacassagne's succession, the *Académie* included six other physicists outside the Physics Section, from these two sections (plus de Broglie, the life Secretary).

A candidate for the *Académie* was expected carefully to compose what is called a *Notice des Titres et Travaux*; a brochure in which as I had explained in my own *Notice*: 'he describes what he thinks are his merits, without irritating by a display of false modesty, or shocking by brazen self-confidence. It is a narrow path.'

The *Notice*, of which at least a hundred copies must be printed (not mimeographed!), is then sent to all the members with a covering *handwritten* letter, which is appropriately respectful, announcing the candidacy and requesting an appointment. The whole operation, production of the *Notice*, and the hundred or so visits (a little less in fact, as a few Academicians were bedridden and did not grant interviews) represented an investment of between three and six months in the life of the candidate; and in the case of failure, God (and God only) knew when the next chance would come.

'Wherefore did I climb on that galley?' The answer is not easy. Thirst for fame? I am not so sure. Later, when I had become a member, and we debated the requirements to be met by a reformed *Académie*, I suggested the following: the impossibility of using French scientists from outside the *Académie* to build a Shadow Academy of greater excellence. I very much doubt that the *Académie* of 1972 could have met that criterion. In mathematics, the following were missing: Henri Cartan, André Weil, Laurent Schwartz, Jean-Pierre Serre; in biology and medicine: Jean Hamburger, Jean Dausset, André Lwoff, Jacques Monod, François Jacob, Boris Ephrussi—a by no means exhaustive list.

And what about physics? Well, in physics, Alfred Kastler, the Nobel

Prize-winner, had narrowly squeaked through on his fourth attempt. In fairness to the *Académie*, it must be recognized that it was not impressed by such foreign toys. It had refused entrance to Marie Curie, to Irène Joliot, and on a first attempt to André Lwoff, who could not be bothered with visits.

My physicist friends from abroad knew the names of de Broglie, Kastler, and Néel of course, but very few had heard of the ten others (unfairly for some, I think). No, indeed, thirst for fame, or to give it its proper name, vanity, was not what drove me onto this galley.

I perceive several other motives to my candidacy.

I have described how, when I was a soldier in 1939, I had landed in the depths of the *France profonde* or 'grass-roots France'—in the midst of peasants, farm workers, butchers and cattle merchants—and had found the experience interesting. With all due respect to the *Académie*, it contained another aspect of the *France profonde* which attracted me.

What could have been more fundamentally, authentically, viscerally French than the *Académie des Sciences* of 1972, with its customs and rites, its *Secrétaires Perpétuels* (Perpetual Secretaries, *not* Life Secretaries—the members of the *Académie* are the immortals!), its *plis cachetés* (sealed envelopes containing 'discoveries' for posterity's eyes only), its archives, its secret committees and open sessions, its *jetons de présence* (tokens of attendance to sessions), its yearly *séances solennelles* under the *coupole*, where Academicians make their entrance to the roll of the drum, wearing the green embroidered coats and the swords of their trade (for those willing to spend a small fortune), its *Comptes-Rendus*, superbly ignorant of, and ignored by, foreign parts, its nonagerians so green, and I do not mean the costumes!

What fun for one who came in from the cold, uprooted and forbearless, to be admitted into this exclusive and muffled world—so deliciously oldfangled.

There was also on the horizon, which sixteen years before had looked so far away, the certainty of keeping links with my brethren, which only illness or death could break. This is what 'Academic Immortality' stands for. When, after my election, the *Secrétaire Perpétuel*, Louis de Broglie, led me into the Sessions Room for the first time, all my new fellow-members (*confrères*, not *collègues*!), stood up. 'I do hope that you appreciate this homage from your *confrères*,' said my neighbour, a very old gentleman. 'They will only stand up for you once more after this.'

Lastly, I thought, it is only from within that one can criticize the Académie, and seek to reform it without being suspected of sour grapes. All these reasons, put end to end—not all very noble perhaps—tilted the scales and made me accept the ordeal of the visits.

This *Académie* is no more. The reform of 1976, which was forced upon it by President Giscard d'Estaing, but was greeted enthusiastically and energetically elaborated on by a majority of Academicians, has kept the appearance but changed the realities. The number of Academicians was brought to one hundred and thirty. The hateful 'Rule of the Corpse' was abolished and replaced by regular triennial elections for the whole *Académie*. I was instrumental in introducing new rules: to rejuvenate the *Académie*, at each election one half of the candidates at least had to be below fifty-five. (These rules were further extended in 1987: a fraction of the candidates must now be younger than fifty. Furthermore, whenever a member reaches eighty, he still keeps all his privileges as a member, but a vacancy is proclaimed. Visits are optional. Even the *Secrétaire Perpétuel* now resigns at seventy-five!)

To increase the foreign readership of the *Comptes-Rendus*, a sizeable summary in English was not only authorized but recommended. To improve their quality, an editorial committee now referees the publications, which before the reform were accepted on the recommendation of one single member, who sometimes might be too indulgent.

Following the reform, the scientific standard of the *Académie* improved considerably. All the scientists I have mentioned are now members, with the exception of Jacques Monod who died too early, as well as many younger scientists of great quality. The Academy of 1988 would completely eclipse any Shadow Academy one might imagine.

But let's return to my own candidacy. I do not want to keep the reader waiting, who, after having made such a long journey with me since my childhood, must surely be on my side. I was defeated, by a couple of votes, in the fourth round of a hotly contested election, but defeated all the same. The winner, Raymond Latarjet, a learned cancerologist (and a great mountaineer to boot) had the advantage over me of being a cancerologist, seeking to succeed another cancerologist; and under the circumstances my close defeat was more than honourable. Let my friendly reader be reassured. A few months later a Free Academician died, the odious 'Rule of the Corpse' came into play, and I was elected by a large majority.

I have bad memories of my Academic visits, for reasons which have nothing to do with the persons I visited. In April 1972, the heart attack of which I spoke before, a massive coronary, struck Suzanne; and from April to June, my visits, like all my activities, were haunted by thoughts of her health. Still, I remember my five nonagenarians with pleasure.

I had met Paul Montel six years earlier, at a party for his ninetieth birthday. He had remained standing for two hours, and had pleasantly attributed all the honours showered on him to his 'incurable longevity'. After six years, at ninety-six, he was less vigorous but still as lively and witty.

At the end of my visit to Maurice Fréchet he asked me, gently: 'Would you kindly remind me of your name and pardon my bad memory; I am old, I am even very old.' What about me, who have started to forget names before the age of seventy!

My third nonagenarian, Albert Caquot, had been a great engineer who at one time had worked for the French air force. Our discussion of aeronautical engineering during the war was confused by a slight misunderstanding: we were not speaking of the same war.

The fourth, Jacques Duclaux, was ninety-five when I visited him, and died at a hundred and one. He had been a professor of general biology at the Collège de France, and explained to me that he had been a very bad lecturer indeed. 'My lectures,' he said, 'only took shape after three years of lecturing, whereas the Collège rules required a new subject every year.'

The fifth was Robert Debré, a great paediatrician (the father of the former Prime Minister Michel Debré). I told him that I had given up medical studies because I could not bear the sight of sick people. He surprised me by saying that it was the same with him, and that he became a paediatrician because children were the only patients he could bear to see.

After my election I received letters from bespoke tailors offering to supply the made-to-measure green costume which I would doubtless wish to wear in the course of my academic duties. One of them went so far as to praise the skill and experience of his embroideresses! Not one of these kindly craftsmen mentioned the cost of the costume in his letter, for fear, I think, of frightening away the new Academician. I did not follow up their offers.

My colleagues, friends, and disciples asked me to name the gift they should offer me, the sword worn with the Academic costume being the usual choice. I declined the sword for lack of a costume to wear it with, but I let it be known that a gold pocket watch with a lid, a perfectly useless object, which I had always dreamed of owning but had never had the extravagance to buy, would give me great pleasure. I was offered one, with a chain and an inscription within the lid.

Yet, in 1980 I became the happy owner, or rather the usufructuary (there *is* such a word) of a superb green costume. This is how. That year the *Secrétaire Perpétuel*, Paul Germain, had asked me to deliver the traditional lecture on a subject of my choice, at the *Séance solennelle* which takes place in December under the *coupole*. I needed a costume for that and I did not have one. Germain informed me on this occasion that some Academicians bequeathed their costumes to the Academy, and that one of those might fit me. Indeed I found one which fitted me very well.

I have never met M. André Mayer, former Professor of Physiology at the Collège de France, which he left long before I entered it; but I know things about him that even his children may not know, namely his chest and waist measurements, because they are exactly the same as mine. Since then, I have worn this costume which fits me so well at every *séance solennelle.* I take good care of it, and it will return in good condition to the Academy when I am unable to wear it.

Once the costume had been found, some minor points remained, such as choosing the subject and writing up the lecture. I decided to speak about fundamental research: hardly a new subject, but one very dear to my heart. I liked this lecture so much myself that I gave it room next to my Cherwell–Simon lecture of 1968 in *Reflections of a Physicist*; and I think that, once again, the audience shared my feelings.

I forgot to say that I was addressing President Giscard d'Estaing, surrounded by three or four ministers. My lecture was already written up when I learned that the President would be present. I was asked to forward a copy to the presidential palace, because, I was told, the President might wish to answer some of the points that I would be raising.

All of a sudden I noticed in my lecture an unfortunate parallel with the effects of slow neutrons on artificial graphite and on diamond. Not so long before the President had been persistently attacked by some satirical journals for accepting a gift of diamonds from an African potentate during a visit to Central Africa. In my lecture these diamonds would have been dynamite, and I hastily replaced diamond by silicon, which, let me remind the purists, has the same crystal structure as diamond.

In 1984 Professor Jean Hamburger organized a series of debates on epistemology. In one of them I was opposed to the eminent mathematician, René Thom, who is widely known for his theory of catastrophes. Our debate was on the relative importance of theory and experiment in the natural sciences.

The title of Thom's contribution was: '*The experimental method: a myth of the epistemologists (and of the scientists?)*' His conclusion was: '*In our era, it is our thinking which must be preserved from the arrogant authority of experiment.*'

I have decided to include here parts of my refutation of his thesis (carefully cleared of any prickles it might have contained), because I think that they may throw some light on a few aspects of the history of contemporary physics, which are imperfectly known or imperfectly understood; and also on the ideas of someone who, after all, is the main character of this book.

* Theory or Experiment (an archaic debate)

> There are more things in heaven and earth, Horatio
> Than are dreamt of in your philosophy

I have always been impervious to philosophy, to its methods and its vocabulary. I have never felt the need for a formal definition, for my own usage or for others, of the concepts of 'theory' or 'experiment', which are

part of my everyday scientific activities. I think that those who have a need
to know these things, know them.

This reminds me of the lady in the London zoo, who points her umbrella
at a hippopotamus and asks the keeper: 'Is it male or female?' 'Madam,'
says the keeper, 'I cannot see who might be interested by the answer to
your question, except another hippotamus; and he *knows*.'

Under pressure, I might say that, for me, experiment is an activity
pursued in the laboratory, and the gist of it is to confirm or invalidate
(*falsify*, says Karl Popper) preconceived ideas, to give rise to new ideas, to
improve its own methods and techniques, and, last but not least, to bring
considerable satisfaction to those who practise it.

'If I translate Zozime,' says *Jerôme Coignard*, an amiable cleric, Anatole
France's favourite hero, 'it is because I find sensuality in the act.' A few
weeks before his death, Albert Michelson was telling Einstein: 'If I have
spent a goodly part of my life improving my interferometer, it is because I
have found it enjoyable.'

My definition of theory would be: putting in a coherent order an
ensemble of ideas which have been, or will be, facing experiment. That
too is enjoyable.

I see that I have slyly introduced the word 'idea' into my definitions:
don't ask me to define it, that would be philosophy. I have been told that
to reject philosophy is also to philosophize, only badly. Be that as it may,
whatever my scientific failures, I prefer to ascribe them to my intellectual
limitations, rather than to my reluctance to philosophize.

I have realized very recently that, without knowing it (like M. Jourdain,
who discovered that he had been speaking in prose all his life), I have been
a follower of Karl Popper, in his claim that a hypothesis which no
experiment could *conceivably* prove wrong is not scientific. M. Thom, my
opponent, claims that Popper's philosophy is 'limited, myopic, devoid of
interest.' So much the worse for me.

An illiterate in matters philosophical, I am inclined to think, wrongly I
am sure, that to 'expostulate why day is day, night night, and time is time'
is a good example of a philosophical debate, and 'were nothing but to
waste night, day, and time.'

In trying to prove, against M. Thom's assertions, that experiment is
essential in science, I shall take examples from the only science of which I
have an inkling, physics. I will not have to go back to Newton and
Gallileo: our own century will suffice.

If we analyse the progress of physics from 1900 till today, we shall find
that theory and experiment are indissolubly linked together. It sometimes
happens that an ensemble of experimental results, which is inexplicable in
the framework of existing theories, literally forces the theorist to cut the
Gordian knot and to formulate a new theory. In 1900, to explain the

spectral shape of blackbody radiation, Max Planck reluctantly formulated the incongruous, bizarre, *ad hoc* hypothesis that the energy emitted by an oscillator may only take discrete values, in quanta $h\nu$ proportional to its frequency ν; and this marked the beginning of the greatest revolution in the scientific thinking of modern times, the birth of quantum theory.

In 1913, it is again experiment which forces Niels Bohr to make a series of postulates every bit as strange and unnatural as the one made by Planck: only a restricted class of electron orbits, circular or elliptical, can exist in an atom. Contrary to the laws of electrodynamics, the electron moves on these orbits without radiating any energy, but a jump of the electron from an orbit of energy E_1 to another of energy E_2 will produce a radiation of frequency: $(E_1-E_2)/h$. It is between 1923 and 1928 that de Broglie, Schrödinger, Heisenberg, Dirac, Pauli, Born, and others build up, from what was a mere collection of miraculous recipes, the grandiose construction of the human mind which is quantum mechanics in its present form. This form is final in the same sense that Newtonian mechanics is final. Just as Newtonian mechanics was *not* dethroned by relativistic mechanics in the range of velocities which are small compared to the velocity of light, and as quantum mechanics *did not* dethrone classical mechanics in a range where all the quantities which have the dimension of an action (that is of energy multiplied by time) are much larger than the Planck constant h, no future theory will dethrone quantum mechanics in the range where innumerable experiments have sealed its validity for ever.

To the development of quantum theory, closely related to experiment, one may be tempted to oppose the advent of special relativity in 1905, born in the brain of a twenty-six-year-old, second class technical expert at the patent office in the city of Bern.

Had he been influenced by the negative result of Michelson's experiment, had he even heard about it? The question is not settled, and Einstein himself keeps silent on this point; but no matter. The weaknesses of the theory of an absolute ether were no doubt his main motivation. When, in 1906, Kaufman's experiments gave results which contradicted the predictions of relativity, Lorentz and Planck were shaken, but Einstein remained unmoved; and better experiments showed him to be right. It would be foolhardy to conclude on this one example of the primacy of theory over experience: *Quod licet Jovi non licet bovi.*

A little known episode of Einstein's career is his collaboration with de Haas, Lorentz's son-in-law, in experimentally demonstrating the relation between the angular moment **J** and the magnetic moment **M** in bulk matter. The principle of the experiment is simple: a vertically suspended iron bar is suddenly magnetized, and starts rotating because of a proportionality relation between **M** and **J**. This relation contains a dimensionless factor g, called the gyromagnetic factor, which, according to classical electrodynamics, is unity. Einstein and de Haas imagined an ingenious resonance method which enabled them to observe the expected rotation and to check the value unity predicted for g, within 10 per cent. Alas, their result was quite, quite false: 100 per cent false. The theoretical value of g is *not* 1, as predicted by the classical theory, but 2. The difference is due, by a supreme irony, to a relativistic effect, first demonstrated rigorously by Dirac. What had happened? Did Einstein and de Haas knowingly cook their data to obtain the result they expected? Not really, but they had been careless. Delighted to have observed the expected rotation, they contented themselves with an estimate rather than a measurement of the magnetizing field and of the magnetization. A first series of experiments yielded a value of 1.02 for g, in miraculous agreement with what they expected. A second value of 1.48 was discarded as abnormal. Did they think that the classical theory was too beautiful to be false? It was de Haas who revealed the facts in 1923; Einstein never said a word.

I would like to cite in contrast the story of two experimentalists, who remained little known in spite of their experimental skill and professional integrity. It is in some way symmetrical of the previous one.

Fritz London had predicted that the magnetic field imprisoned in a superconductor can take discrete values only, multiples of (hc/e) where e is the electron charge. In 1961 two German physicists did observe this flux quantization, but with a value for the flux quantum which was some 40 per cent smaller than the theoretical value. After looking in vain for a calibration error, they resigned themselves to publishing this bizarre result. Almost immediately (in fact in the same issue of *Physical Review Letters*), the theoretician C. N. Yang showed that in the so-called BCS (Bardeen, Cooper, Shrieffer) theory of superconductivity—which predicts that electrons form pairs in a superconductor, the so-called Cooper pairs—the charge which appears in the flux quantum should be $2e$ rather than e; this reduced the quantum by a factor 2 and brought the experimental value of the German authors in agreement with theory, within a margin of experimental errors. Everybody, including myself, seems to have forgotten their names. Most unfair!

Another authentic anecdote in which experimentalists had the last laugh is Otto Stern's measurement in 1923 (more than twenty years before the discovery of NMR) of the magnetic moment of the proton, using the molecular beams method. Learning of Stern's attempt, Pauli commented glibly: 'A useless experiment; what does the *Dummkopf* expect to find, apart from a nuclear Bohr magneton?' The *Dummkopf* found nearly three times as much.

I now wish briefly to recall the main steps in the development of quantum electrodynamics. If I have chosen this example, it is because the close association of theory and experiment seldom emerged as strikingly as in the building of this magnificent cathedral of modern physics (and also because it is a domain to which M. Thom devotes one of his least indulgent comments).

In the late twenties quantum formalism, including the treatment of electromagnetic phenomena, was well established. One knew how to calculate all the processes of energy exchange between radiation and matter. More precisely, one knew how to calculate them to the lowest order of perturbation theory, which most of the time was good enough, for the coupling between matter and radiation is weak: the coupling constant which measures its strength is small: $\alpha \approx (1/137)$.

But whenever one tried to improve the accuracy by calculating higher order terms, one *always* found divergent integrals and infinite results. Over fifteen years a whole army of theoreticians, including Heisenberg, Pauli, Dirac, Born, Weisskopf, Bethe, Heitler, and many others, tried in vain to clear the theory of these cursed divergences. Was there something rotten in the state of quantum electrodynamics?

The deadlock was suddenly resolved in 1947 by an experiment of Willis Lamb's. Using radiofrequency techniques, he found that the first two excited levels of the hydrogen atom, distant from the ground level by some ten electron-volts, which, according to the rigorous Dirac theory, had the same energy, were actually separated from each other by a few microvolts. At almost the same time, another experimentalist, Polycarp Kusch, discovered another departure from the Dirac theory: the gyromagnetic factor of the electron was not 2 exactly, but differed from it by approximately one part in a thousand.

The theoreticians soon realized that at the origin of these departures were the vacuum fluctuations of matter and radiation, which had been considered before, but had always led to infinite results. But now the theoreticians *knew*, thanks to Lamb and Kusch, that these effects were real, that they were measurable, and that they were small, as they should be, because of the smallness of the coupling constant. In less than three years, thanks to the efforts of Schwinger, Feynmann, Tomonaga, and Dyson, a new theory was born, the so-called renormalization theory, which permitted the unambiguous isolation of the divergent parts of the integrals to all orders in α, and their incorporation into a term of mass and a term of charge, singling out a finite part to be compared with experimental results.

A marvellous invention of Richard Feynmann's, the diagram method, which has since been extended to many other fields of physics, completely transformed perturbation theory by making it possible, through a pictorial representation, to write down all the terms of order n immediately. As the order n increases, the number of the terms becomes larger, their magnitude smaller, and their calculation heavier. What justifies the calculation of terms of high n, in spite of their extreme smallness and the great complication involved in their calculation, is the extraordinary accuracy of the experiments and the quasi-miraculous agreement between theory and experiment. This agreement demonstrates both the correctness of the renormalization procedure and the aptness of the theory to provide a correct picture of the physical reality.

There is little doubt that the renormalization theory could easily have been discovered in the thirties. The theoreticians whose names I cited earlier lacked neither the mathematical skill nor the imagination for it. What *was* lacking was the confidence that quantum electrodynamics was fundamentally sound. Experiment alone could and did provide that confidence. Thereafter the treatment was quickly found, and the patient was cured.

I have said that quantum electrodynamics covers all the known facts accurately and completely. The important point is that it does so without a single *adjustable* parameter.

I would like to illustrate it by a counter-example, the little story of Billy Jones.

The action takes place during the Civil War. A recruiting officer from the Union cavalry rides through a village in the west. On each barn door a dozen concentric circles have been drawn in chalk, for shooting practice. In the dead centre of each target there is a single bullet hole. The officer asks a bystander:

'Who's the man who has been practising here? He is good.'
'That's Billy Jones playing with his forty-five.'
'How far from the target does he stand?'
'Thirty yards.'
'Does he take careful aim?'
'Who, Billy? No, he draws and he fires.'
'Say, that's some marksman! The Union cavalry could use a man like that.'
'Begging your pardon, Lieutenant, Billy is not the man for you.'
'You let me decide that. Did you say that these shots are from thirty yards?'
'Oh, thirty, thirty-five, sometimes it's forty.'
'And he does not spend a lot of time aiming?'
'I told you, he draws and he fires.'
'All right, here's a dollar for you; go fetch me this Billy Jones.'
'Here I go, Lieutenant, and many thanks. I'd better tell you, though: Billy shoots first and *then* draws the circles.'

As a last example of close cooperation between theory and experiment, I would like to relate the discovery of non-conservation of parity in weak interactions, which is responsible, among other things, for the β-decay of nuclei. A theory is said to conserve parity when it is impossible to distinguish the events it describes from their image in a looking-glass. It had been known for a long time that parity was conserved with great accuracy in electromagnetic interactions, and in the strong interactions responsible for the nuclear forces, and it had been assumed that it was also conserved in weak interactions. There was no experimental evidence for believing otherwise. Once more an experimental discovery set the ball rolling. Two particles baptized τ and θ had been discovered in cosmic radiation, which within the experimental error margin had the same mass and the same lifetime, but decay modes which corresponded to opposite parities. This remarkable equality of mass and lifetime for two seemingly different particles, was puzzling. Two theoreticians, T. D. Lee and C. N. Yang, dared to ask the question: what if τ and θ were the same particle, capable of decaying through two different modes? (In a famous mystery story one of a pair of twin brothers is a murderer and the other an honest citizen. The detective solves the mystery by showing that the murderer and the honest man are the same person.) Lee and Yang examined all the existing experimental evidence on which the assumption of the conservation of parity was based, and concluded that nothing in it was incompatible with parity violation. Two new experiments, in which a violation of parity would show up if it existed, were imagined and promptly performed. They showed that not only was parity violated, but that the violation was as strong as possible, meaning that the parity violating terms had the same weight as the parity conserving terms.

Thus the loop was completed in three steps: experimental discovery of the two particles τ and θ, theoretical hypothesis of Lee and Yang, experimental proof of parity non-conservation. For the anecdote, let us add that, as for the measurement of the proton magnetic moment by Stern, the great Pauli missed another opportunity of keeping his mouth shut and predicted that the proof would fail.

I may surprise some by saying that theoretical physics is not an exact synonym for mathematical physics. Admittedly, in its final stage a theory must have a mathematical formulation, but this is sometimes an ancillary task once the initial idea has been formulated in ordinary language. Niels Bohr's initial concept of the compound nucleus, which can be expressed in a few sentences, has given food for thought to nuclear physicists for two decades. How much of the shell model of the Nobel prize winner Maria Mayer was contained in this simple question by Fermi in a seminar: 'Have you thought about spin–orbit coupling?' The life work of Louis de Broglie can be summed up in a single idea of genius: the *photon*, which is a wave, is also a particle; why could the *electron*, which is a particle, not also be a wave?

And what more beautiful piece of theoretical physics than the discussion where Einstein imagines a whole sequence of hypothetical (*gedankene*) experiments to demonstrate the inconsistency of quantum mechanics, and where, every time, Bohr detects the flaw in his argument—culminating with Einstein's overlooking of the shift of the light frequency in a gravitation field?*

After my election to the *Académie des Sciences*, several foreign academies beckoned me in. In 1974 I was elected Foreign Honorary Member of the American Academy of Arts and Sciences, and in 1977 Foreign Associate of the US National Academy.

In 1981 I became a member of the Pontifical Academy. The Director of its Chancellery, the charming Father di Rovasenda, had invited me to submit a *Notice de Titres et Travaux*, before the election, not unlike the one our *Académie* used to require. I did not want to compose another *Notice*, and asked him to see a sign of humility in my refusal, rather than pride. 'If my work needs promotion from myself in order to attract your favours, it means to me that it is not worthy of them, and that my place is not among you.' True or false, this 'humility' did not shock the members of the Pontifical Academy too much, for I was elected.

In 1981, I was spending a sabbatical in Oxford, when the Vatican invited me to a plenary session of the Academy, with all expenses paid for Suzanne and for myself. An audience with the Holy Father was on the programme, which filled my catholic Suzanne with emotion.

On the day of our flight the Alitalia air traffic controllers went on strike, making it impossible for us to be in Rome in time for the audience. We spent an anxious afternoon at London airport. Finally, late in the evening, a single direct flight to Palermo was announced. We took it with a heavy heart, for it seemed materially impossible to get back from Palermo to Rome in time for the papal audience. Once aboard, we were informed that the plane was going to Rome instead of Palermo, to the despair of the numerous Sicilians on the plane. A miracle!! We arrived in time for the audience.

In October 1986 the Pontifical Academy celebrated its fiftieth anniversary. A certain number of lectures of a general nature were scheduled. I was asked to offer, in *ten to fifteen minutes*, a talk with the theme: 'Where to, Physics?'—something like '*Quo Vadis Physica?*' It was a nice homage to my quality of '*Horizontal*' physicist. I though it more prudent to 'predict' the past and to answer the question 'Where from, Physics?' instead, somewhat arbitrarily choosing the end of the Second World War in 1945 as a starting point. Here is this 'prediction', which does not overlap too much with what I said earlier about 'theory and experiment'.

*The revolution of quanta and relativity was well behind us, the discovery of the positron had sealed their wedding, the atomic spectra, in which the effects of the nuclear magnetic moments were an infinitesimal detail, appropriately termed 'hyperfine structure', had yielded all their secrets. A theory called quantum electrodynamics gave a satisfactory clue to the calculations of all atomic processes to the first order, whilst exhibiting a deplorable tendency to yield infinite answers to all attempts to go beyond the lowest approximation. Physics of the solid state and statistical mechanics, developed in the framework of quantum theory, had explained electric and thermal conductivity, even if superconductivity remained a mystery. The existing theory of phase transitions was considered adequate, except for what were deemed minor details. Optics had become a classical discipline, meaning dead. Nuclear physics had known its first triumphs, whether sublime or tragic. The neutron and nuclear fission were known, the neutrino hypothesis had restored faith in conservation of energy, Yukawa had explained the origin of nuclear forces through the exchange of a heavy particle between nucleons, which was believed to have been identified in cosmic radiation, and was called a 'mesotron'. The conservation of parity, that is the identity of the universe and of its mirror image, was a dogma. Cyclotrons and betatrons, which seemed gigantic, were able to accelerate protons, deuterons, alpha particles, and electrons to energies which seemed fabulous, of the order of a hundred million electron volts or MeV.

Lastly, gigantic electron calculators born during the war to respond to the needs of weaponry, were capable of performing hundreds of operations per second, with no other limitations to their performance apart from space and cooling requirements, and the increasing frequency of failures in the electronic tubes responsible for their operation.

The landscape was going to change, and fast.

During the following forty years theory and experiment advanced rapidly in all the fields that I have enumerated, stimulating each other, and forging new tools and perfecting the old ones in the process.

In atomic physics, new short-wave technique, inherited from radar, were able to detect an anomaly that was minute but pregnant with meaning, in the fine structure of atomic hydrogen, this crown jewel of the alliance between Relativity and Quanta. Together with a similar anomaly in the magnetic properties of the electron, it harboured the clue to the unexplainable and unbearable divergencies of quantum electrodynamics.

Emboldened by experiment, theoreticians at last dared to subtract two infinities from each other in order to extract finite terms which corresponded to these minute corrections. This gave birth to the theory of renormalization, which was later extended to a large domain of theoretical physics. Diagram methods were invented which made possible the successful completion of otherwise inextricable calculations, sometimes far removed from the field of quantum electrodynamics.

Tiny nuclear magnetic moments, suitably excited by resonance methods, gave rise to signals whose detection—under the name of nuclear magnetic resonance or NMR—yielded one of the most penetrating tools for the probing of matter in bulk, later of biological molecules, and now, through a technique known as NMR imaging, of the hearts and the loins of humans.

The physics of the solid state, and in particular of a type of solids known as semiconductors, had led to what is perhaps the most fantastic revolution of our time, by giving rise to the transistor and from there to integrated circuits, and so-called chips, which have increased the performance of computers by millions (and before long by billions), whilst diminishing their overall size by comparable factors.

The enigma of superconductivity was solved, and simultaneously a new type of superconducting material, whose nature was better understood and whose performance improved, increased the magnitude of the magnetic fields produced in the laboratories by a significant factor, whilst incomparably decreasing the energy consumption.

Quite recently an even newer type of superconductor has been discovered, which works at temperatures well above liquid nitrogen, but whose mechanism baffles the physicists at the time of writing these lines.

Optics was revitalized, firstly by a clever combination of polarized light and radiofrequency fields, but above all by the invention of the laser, which was soon made tunable, and gave rise to a new science—non-linear optics—as well as revolutionizing spectroscopy. The applications of the laser to communications, to holography, to ophthalmology and other fields of medical practice, to industry in all sorts of ways, and, alas, to weapons, are innumerable.

One did discover the Yukawa particle, which turned out to be different from what one thought; one proved that the neutrino was more than a convenient fiction; one discovered that, in the so-called 'weak interactions', parity was violently violated.

The energy of accelerators increased by three orders of magnitude, creating swarms of ephemeral particles which one classified with some difficulty into rational schemes. Time-reversal—something which everyday experience contradicts on our scale, but which on the microscopic scale is another dogma—also turned out to be violated, but only very slightly. Particle theories of great mathematical sophistication were elaborated, which gave up all attempts to describe reality in any detail, but had a physical content which, at least for the layman writing these lines, seemed to reduce in the last resort to the statement: 'all's in all'.

Then, following some beautiful experimental and theoretical discoveries made during the last fifteen years, things took a better shape, at least for the time being. There now exists an ensemble of theories resting on an indisputable set of experimental facts, known as the 'standard model'. In that model there are two types of ultimate constituents of matter: on one side the 'quarks', of which there are three in each nucleon, which experience so-called 'strong interactions', and are described by a theory known as 'quantum chromodynamics'; on the other hand the 'leptons', which interact with each other and also with quarks in the framework of a theory called 'electro-weak', which is a synthesis of quantum electrodynamics and of the theory of weak interactions. The present dream of particle physicists is the reunion of quantum chromodynamics and electro-weak theory in the framework of something called 'grand unification'. They believe that such a theory gave a correct description of reality in the first few instants of an incredibly hot universe just after the Big Bang. To recreate conditions akin to these in the laboratory, they insistently demand ever more powerful accelerators. Beyond the grand unification, there is a further step: Einstein's old dream, the reunion with gravitation.

The physics of matter in bulk did not lag behind. New concepts overturned the theory of phase transitions, showing that, behind the immense variety of physical phenomena, their behaviour in the vicinity of a phase transition was identical. These predictions were checked experimentally with great accuracy. New methods for the study of condensed matter were developed: first and foremost the laser, but also diffraction of slow neutrons and electrons, recoilless gamma spectroscopy, NMR, and many others.

Two-dimensional systems attracted great interest: especially the most important of them, surfaces, for which a new tool, the tunnelling microscope, offers matchless possibilities.

Finally, disordered systems in all their aspects turned out to be of paramount theoretical and experimental importance. A new type of statistical mechanics, which does not imply ergodicity, is exciting great interest. At last simulation methods, or 'computer experiments', where reality is an unwanted guest, are in great favour.

I have come to the end of this inventory, in which every branch of physics may consider itself to be neglected, misunderstood, or plain forgotten. I beg the forgiveness of any colleagues who happen to be working in such fields.

Let me now turn for a moment to our colleagues, the biologists, whose lightning advances are, according to some, liable to make us physicists jealous. Dear colleagues, do not believe it: if we sincerely rejoice in your triumphs, it is because we consider that you belong to our community. You have borrowed some of our equipment and our techniques, which constitute our hardware; this is of little importance. But you have adopted our way of thinking, which is our software, and this is vital.

Fellow physicists of living matter, I greet you.*

In 1983 I was elected a Foreign Member of the Royal Society. It is much harder for a foreigner to be elected to the Royal Society than to either of the two American academies to which I belonged, for two reasons. The Royal Society elects fewer Foreign Members, and, what's more, a prospective Foreign Member of the Royal Society has to compete with American scientists, which naturally does not occur in elections to foreign membership of American academies. This election pleased me immensely because, scientifically, England is my second homeland.

The invitation to the ceremonial dinner of the Royal Society, which I received after my election, insisted on full evening dress. I followed the brilliant suggestion of my good friend Nicholas Kurti, and, instead of a hired tail coat, made my appearance in my green Academic costume. I attracted a lot of good-natured attention.

In October 1986 I gave the second *Claude Bernard* lecture at the Royal Society (the first had been given by François Jacob). The Royal Society was the first to benefit from my freewheeling description of nuclear magnetic order, as given in an earlier chapter. I would hardly have dared deliver it at the Pontifical Academy.

The Royal Academy of The Netherlands did not become my sixth Academy, but it did better by me, much better. In 1982 it awarded me the thirteenth Lorentz Medal—much less well-known than the Nobel, but appreciated by the *connaisseurs*. During a reception presided over by the then Minister of Research, Jean-Pierre Chevènement, I pronounced the following 'lecture', of which I insert an excerpt here, because it contains some little stories about physicists (apocryphal or not), which I have not told before (and also in order to boost myself a little).

Twelve physicists

The Lorentz medal is awarded to a physicist, preferably a theorist, every four years. It was founded around 1925 by the Royal Academy of The Netherlands in honour of the great physicist Antoon Lorentz, who was for many years Professor of Theoretical Physics at the most prestigious Dutch university, Leyden. Apart from a metallic disc bearing the names of Lorentz and of the laureate, it is unlike prizes such as the Nobel, the Fermi, or the Wolff in that it does not carry any material wages of success with it, to alleviate the hardships of everyday life for deserving scientists. To me its value resides entirely in the names of my twelve predecessors.

For those who are not physicists I shall very briefly recall what they did, and to relieve the tedium of such a list I shall tell a few anecdotes about them on the way.

This is what I have heard about Lorentz himself. Whenever he was sent a theoretical paper, he looked at the terms of the problem; and if he found it interesting, he put the paper aside and solved the problem himself. He then compared his solution to that of the author. If they agreed he threw both in the waste paper basket; if they disagreed, he threw away the one he had received and published his own.

The first laureate in 1927 was **Max Planck**, the father of the quanta. Even to non-physicists I hardly need to say more. Everybody remembers that Planck made the revolutionary assumption that light was emitted and absorbed in discrete quanta rather than continuously. Frightened by his own daring, Planck at first tried to restrict his hypothesis to emission: light was emitted in quanta but could be absorbed continuously; which inspired Einstein with the following comment: 'He goes to the bathroom from time to time, but never stops eating.' Speaking in German, Einstein used two very direct verbs.

The second laureate in 1931 was **Wolfgang Pauli**, one of the most profound theoreticians of quantum mechanics, who discovered the exclusion principle which bears his name, and is responsible for the stability of atoms. The countless stories about Pauli all revolve around the fact that meekness and modesty were not his principal virtues. (*But I have already told all my stories about Pauli.*)

The third laureate in 1935 was **Peter Debye**, who created the theory of crystalline vibrations and plasma oscillations, and invented adiabatic demagnetization. According to Kapitza, Schrödinger spoke once in 1925 on de Broglie's new theory of matter waves at Debye's seminar in Zurich. Debye said: 'What kind of waves are these? Where's the wave equation?' Whereupon Schrödinger is supposed to have come back a week later with *his* wave equation.

The fourth in 1939 was **Arnold Sommerfeld**, a great mathematical physicist, the author of important papers on wave propagation and diffraction, and of a relativistic generalization of Schrödinger's equation. Heisenberg and Pauli were two of his most prestigious students.

Professor Hund (of Hund's rule) told me the following story (I give my source because I found it hard to believe): After doing his doctor's thesis under Sommerfeld in Munich, Heisenberg applied for a position in that university but Sommerfeld discouraged him: 'Heisenberg, you are a clever man,' he wrote to him. 'You should be able to understand that Munich is a little too much for you.' Which shows that one can be a remarkable theorist and a bad judge of men.

This is all there were before the war. The first after the war in 1947 was **Hendrik Kramers**, another pioneer of quantum mechanics, and the author (at the same time as Brillouin and Wentzel) of a powerful semi-classical approximation. He is also the author of a famous theorem in magnetism, on which rests the possibility of observing magnetic resonance. No story about him.

In 1953 the laureate was **Fritz London**, author of a phenomenological theory of superconductivity which was very useful, and still is. He and Heitler imagined a quantum theory of chemical valency. No story.

In 1958 the laureate was **Lars Onsager**, a specialist in the dynamics of irreversible processes, who discovered the reciprocity relations which bear his name, and an exact solution of a long range order problem in two dimensions, which revolutionized the theory of phase transitions. He was one of the most profound thinkers of his time and, I can testify to this, one of the worst lecturers who ever existed. Fortunately, at Yale University where he was a professor, he had a colleague named Kirkwood, a very distinguished physical chemist in his own right, who had the double privilege of comprehending Onsager and of being comprehensible to the outside world, thus providing the missing link.

In 1962 the laureate was **Rudolf Peierls**, a polymath, who brought important contributions to quantum field theory, to the theory of condensed matter, and to nuclear physics, where he improved on Bohr's model of the compound nucleus and played an important part in the development of the bomb. He is a charming and likeable man. Some time ago he received the Fermi prize, but he also made a respectable sum of money under somewhat bizarre circumstances as a reward for not being dead.

This is how it happened. There always had been rumours that, besides the Soviet spies, Burgess, Maclean, and Kim Philby who had fled to the USSR, there had been a fourth man, a scientist. A London journalist imagined, God knows why, that Peierls had died, and suggested in a book that he was the fourth man. A settlement out of court on the amount of damages was promptly made between Peierls' solicitors and the publisher's. Peierls had told me that if he had gone to court he would eventually have obtained far more, but by then, he said, he might indeed have been dead.

In 1966 the laureate was **Freeman Dyson** who rigorously demonstrated the equivalence, which was far from obvious, of Schwinger's and Feynman's treatment of quantum electrodynamics, and also the possibility of renormalizing the theory to all orders. He also did important work on disordered systems. A problem solver, he solved quite a few of them 'to order', upon request.

A Cambridge undergraduate during the war, he had been drafted into a group doing operational research on the effects of the strategic bombing of Germany. He displeased the brass by making two suggestions. He recommended doing away with machine guns on the huge Lancaster bombers: there was a large dead angle along which they could not shoot to hit enemy fighter planes, and what was worse, their dead weight slowed down the plane, making it harder to escape these enemy fighters. A second recommendation dealt with the loss of life caused by the opening mechanism of the hatches, which did not leave enough time for the crew to jump out with their parachutes.

Both recommendations were indignantly rejected: there was no question of sending men to combat unarmed, or of encouraging them to abandon ship.

In 1970 the laureate was **George Uhlenbeck**, one of the greatest specialists in statistical mechanics, also widely known for his and Sam Goudsmit's brilliant discovery of the anomalous magnetic moment of the electron spin—which brings us back to our old friend, the great Pauli. After submitting their paper for publication, Goudsmit and Uhlenbeck showed it to Pauli, who, although as young as they, was already famous.

Pauli wasted no time in explaining to them that their paper was worthless and should be withdrawn. They rushed to do it, but woe! or rather hosanna!, it was too late, the paper had come out. Another of their colleagues, also a Dutchman, R. de L. Kronig, was not so lucky: he too had shown a similar result to Pauli but *before* submitting it to a journal, and had received the same advice.

One should not think that Pauli was a monster; he was, well . . . Pauli!

In 1974 the laureate was my friend and teacher **John Van Vleck**, the father of modern magnetism, and responsible for its fruitful marriage with quantum mechanics—a young bride at the time. He was the teacher of several generations of American physicists.

Van Vleck was a *tenth* generation American. His ancestor, Tillman Van Vleeck (with two 'e's), arrived in what was then called New Amsterdam in 1650. His mother was a Raymond: the Raymond family came from England in the seventeenth century and, according to a family tradition, were descended from the French count Raymond VI of Toulouse, who had found refuge with the King of England after his defeat by Simon de Montfort in the Albigensian wars. This makes Van Vleck an honorary Frenchman.

Finally, the last laureate (or rather the last but one) was my colleague **Nicolaas Bloembergen**, one of the pioneers of nuclear relaxation, the inventor of the three levels maser, and the author of some important discoveries in the field of non-linear optics. He told me once that, after Charles Townes had offered his wife a ruby to celebrate the discovery of the ruby laser for which he had got his Nobel prize, Bloembergen's wife reproached him for the lack of a similar gift in honour of his maser, which also used a crystal. 'If you insist, I am willing,' replied Bloembergen. 'But I must warn you, my maser works on cyanide.'

Six of the twelve laureates won a Nobel, all but Planck, *after* their Lorentz medal. This seems to have become an unwritten tradition. Whereas the Nobel prize comes from interest on some capital, the only capital which the Lorentz Foundation possesses, is, or at least was until this year (1982), the list of its laureates. I have grave doubts about the dividend on the thirteenth investment. I am perfectly sincere in saying this. Those who are inclined to doubt my sincerity should remember Jules Renard's saying: 'Even false modesty is a very good thing.'

(I learned with great pleasure that the thirteenth laureate in 1986 was **Gerhardt 'Tooft**, *a valuable investment which enhances the value of the Lorentz 'captial'. He made an 'honest woman' of the electro-weak theory, this synthesis of quantum electrodynamics and the theory of weak inter-actions, by proving its renormalizability. It was a step of the same importance as that accomplished by Freeman Dyson for quantum electrodynamics.*

Just as Dyson had been kept from the Nobel by the rule of 3, that is by

Feynman, Schwinger, and Tomonaga, so was Tooft by the trio Glashow, Salam, and Weinberg. The Nobel Committee would be well advised to associate Dyson and Tooft some time in the future.)

And that's the end.

Epilogue

On the first page of the Introduction I spoke of a poem by Pushkin, *Eugene Onegin*, '. . . which is over five thousand lines long, and which I entered forcibly into my memory, under circumstances I shall perhaps recount.'

These are the circumstances.

After Suzanne's heart attack, there was a period when I was unable to work, to read, to sleep. I got out of it by learning this poem by heart. I have chosen one of the final verses of this poem as a conclusion to my book. A clumsy rhymester, I have translated its contents more or less faithfully, whilst inevitably betraying the poet's magic. May his light shadow be merciful to this unskilful mark of gratitude.

> Whoever you may be, my reader,
> A friend or foe, I'd like to take
> My leave of you as your well-wisher.
> Farewell. Whatever in my wake,
> You looked for in these careless verses,—
> Wild recollections of past courses,
> Relief from labour's heavy yoke,
> Live pictures or some cutting joke,
> Or even grammatical mistakes
> God grant that in this book you find
> Daydream or frolic for your mind,
> And for heart's content or scribblers stakes
> A crumb at least to fit your mood.
> On this let's part. Farewell for good.

Index

Note: 'AA' means 'Anatole Abragam'

Abrikosov, Alexis 206, 305
Académie Française 58, 255
Académie des Sciences
  age of members 342, 345–6
  candidate procedures 343
  Collège de France members in 226
  costume 346–7
  debate on theory vs. experiment 347–57
  lecture by AA 347
  Life Secretaries 58, 344
  motives for candidacy 344
  reform of 344–5
  Rule of the Corpse 343, 345
  rule of 342–3
  visits required of candidates 343, 345–6
Academy of Science (USSR) 320, 321
accelerators 122–4
  design of 165–6, 173–4
  problems encountered 174–5
Adams, John 173
ADRF (adiabatic demagnetization in rotating frame)
    274, 276, 282
AEC (Atomic Energy Commission, USA) 166, 168
Agrégation 30
Agrégation de physique 41, 52, 172
Aigrain, Pierre 178, 264
Akademgorodok (USSR) 320
Akhmatova, Anna 317–18
Aleksey (lodger in Moscow) 9
Algiers uprising (1958) 217
Allais 196
alternating gradients principle 166
Altschuller (Russian physicist) 307
American Academy of Arts and Sciences, Foreign
    Honorary Members 226, 354
Amsterdam
  conference (1950) on radiofrequency spectroscopy
    144, 152, 155
  lectures (1969) 339
Anderson, Philip Warren 199
Anderson, Weston 181
Andronikaschvili, Eleuther 305
Andronikov, Heracles 305
antiferromagnetic ordering 270–1
anti-Semitism
  in France 45
  in Russia 19, 308
Armenia, rivalry with Georgia 310
'Arnie' 177–9
Arnold, Jim 181
Aron, Raymond 260
Arrowsmith (by Sinclair Lewis) 36–7
Arsac/Arzac (farmhand) 72
arsenic-doped silicon, ESR spectrum of 178, 187

artificial radioactivity, discovery of 148, 188
artillery fuses 100
Artsimovich 322
Astier (teacher) 225, 226
Auden, W. H. 303
Auger, Pierre 50, 61, 103, 148
Auger effect 61
Aziz (schoolfriend) 36

Baccalaureat 33
Bacchella, Gian 290
back-of-envelope calculations 116. 142
Bagguley, Desmond 141
Baïssas, Henri 249
Bakuriani (USSR) 305
Bangkok 331–2
Bardeen, John 165, 180, 350
Basov, Nicolas 302
Bataillon, Marcel 224, 229
Batiushkov (Russian poet) 34
Battelle Distiguished Professor 326
Bauer, Edmond 60
BCS (Bardeen, Cooper, Shrieffer) theory of
    superconductivity 180, 350
Bédier, Joseph 229
Belgium 340–1
Bellevue laboratory 104
Belley 99–100
Benares (India) 331
Bérenger (commander) 97, 98
Berkeley (USSR) 167
  Bevatron 166
Berlin, Sir Isaïah 302
Bertaut (crystallographer) 91
Berthelot, André 201, 214, 215, 216, 250–1, 308
Bertin, Mlle (school mistress) 25
Bertrand, Joseph 222
Bethe, Hans 50, 117, 150, 231
Bettelin (school master) 81–2
Biot, Jean-Baptiste 222
Birmingham
  AA's reaction to 124–5
  conference (1947) on theoretical physics 115, 117,
    120
Birtwhistle (author) 53
'black tie' invitations 297, 301
Blackwell, Sir Basil 300–1
Blanc-Lapierre, André 257–8
Blatt, John 150, 151
Bleaney, Brebis 135, 139, 140, 145, 158, 181, 197,
    199, 243, 302, 340
Bloch, Claude 103, 105, 106, 108, 110, 121, 132,
    171, 173, 182, 251, 263
Bloch, Eugène 48, 52, 53, 54
Bloch, Felix 117, 159, 160, 163, 164, 179–82, 191,
    192, 193, 208, 209–10, 215, 284

Bloch, Léon 52
Bloembergen, Nicolaas 161, 164, 199, 361
Blum, Leon 69
Bohr, Niels 116, 119, 124, 133, 182, 206, 349, 353
Boltzmann, Ludwig 267
Bombay 330, 331
Bonner, Elena 321
books
  by AA 197–9; *see also Reflections of a Physicist*
    and *Principles of Nuclear Magnetism*
  childhood 11–12
  collaboration (1970) with Bleaney and others
    243–4, 312, 313
  collaboration (1985) with Goldman 275, 304,
    312, 313
  how not to write 151
  Russian 44, 52, 312–13
Borghini, Michel 195, 196, 235, 245
Born, Max 53, 132–3, 182
Borovick-Romanov (Russian physicist) 305, 318
Bouasse, Henri 52
Bouchiat, Claude 326, 328
Bouchiat, Marie-Anne 328, 329
Bouffard, Vincent 288–9
bourgeois, Russian attitude to 10, 18–19
Bowra, Sir Maurice 131
Boyer, M. 335, 338
Bragg peaks 278
Brattain, Walter 165
Braudel, Fernand 224
Brelot (lecturer at Grenoble) 90
Briand, Aristide 50
Bricout (author) 53
Bridgman, Percy Williams 165
Brillouin, Léon 53, 60, 359
Bristol, conference (1957/1959) on defects in solids
  217–18
British Council 121, 125
Brittany, walking holiday in 65
Broglia family 56–7
Broglie, Louis de 50, 54, 56–9, 248, 344, 353
Broglie, Maurice de 57, 224
Brookhaven (USA) 168
  Cosmotron 166, 171
Brossel, Jean 177, 178, 183, 264
bubble chambers
  accidents with 254
  Mirabelle project 254, 257, 308–11
  Nobel Prize for 235
Budé, Guillaume 221
Buishvilli (Russian physicist) 235
Bulgaria 341
Burgess, Guy 360
Burns, Mrs (landlady) 129

calcium fluoride 276, 277, 280
Calcutta 331
California University 214, 325
Cambodia, visit to 332
Cambridge (UK)
  Faraday Society meeting 181
  research at 135
Cambridge (USA) 159–66
Capra, Frank 1
Capron, Jean-Pierre 113

Caquot, Albert 346
Cartan, Henri 343
Carver (student with Slichter) 164
Casimir, Hendryk 119, 192, 205–6, 299
Casimir, Mme 206
Casimir operators 119
Cavendish Chair (Cambridge) 135
CDI (Differential and Integral Calculus) 46, 47
CEA (Commissariat à l'Energie Atomique)
  AA as Director of Physics 250, 251–2
  AA as Director of Research in physics 264
  AA formally employed by 110
  AA offered High Commissioner's job 263–4
  AA's initial grade 111
  AA's resignation as Director of Physics 263
  AA started work at 105
  administrative structure 112, 250
  Administrators General 112, 113, 248, 262
  associate convention with Collège de France 266
  budget presentation 217
  change (1970) in top management 262
  collective agreement 111–12
  cost of projects 264
  Directors' meeting 253
  dismissal of Joliot as High Commissioner 147,
    149
  early meetings 105–6, 107
  ESR/NMR laboratory proposal 183, 214–15
  formation of 103
  High Commissioners 49, 112, 113, 147, 149, 248,
    262
  internal mobility proposal 262
  lecture course 182–32
  Perrin as High Commissioner 49, 148, 250
  reorganization (1953) 170
  staff grades 112
  staff promotion 217, 252
  unit councils 261, 262
  see also DEP, DPA, DPh, DPNPS, SPM, SPSRM
CERN
  Directors General 151, 179, 225, 337
  Review Committee on 335–8
  Staff Association's reaction to Review Committee
    338–9
  synchrotrons 122, 123, 173
CGT (Confédération Générale du Travail) 149, 153,
  217
Chadwick, James 148
Chamberlain, Owen 235, 236
Chamfort (humorist) 204
Chanet, Father (Louis de Broglie's tutor) 57
chanterelles (berries), picking of 93
Chantre (farmhand) 71–2
Chapellier, Maurice 274, 275, 276, 290
Châteauroux, military training at 69–72
Châtillon 105, 106, 107
Chazy, Jean 42
Cherwell, Lord (Frederick Lindemann) 136–7
Cherwell–Simon lecture (1968) 299, 347
Chevènement, Jean-Pierre 358
childhood
  in France 23–34
  in Russia 5–19
Children's Encyclopaedia 14
Chinese restaurants 329
Christophilos, Nicholas 166

Clarendon Laboratory 125, 135–9, 242
Claude Bernard lecture (1986) 358
Clifton, R. B. 135
Closets, François de 256
CNRS (Centre National de la Recherche Scientifique)
    50, 103, 111, 252
Cohen-Tannoudji, Claude 183, 228
Cohn-Bendit, Daniel 259
Collège de France 220
    AA elected as professor 226
    AA's lectures 230–2, 238
    Académie des Sciences members in 226
    administration of 222, 229–30
    associate convention with CEA 266
    course on tensors 60
    elections 223
    number of professors 221
    physicists in 225, 228–9
    professors' salaries 222
    structure 221–3
Collège de Saint-Raphaël 80–3
collider mode 175
Combrisson, Jean 183, 185, 187, 190, 191, 195,
    216, 244, 251, 261
Communist Party, Joliot's support of 149
Comptes Rendus de l'Académie des Sciences 124,
    272, 344, 345
computerized literature search 293
computers
    comments on 277
    early type 355
Cooper, Leon 180, 350
Cooper pairs 350
Copenhagen interpretation 132
Corps des Mines 41, 110, 113, 121
cosmic ray studies 61, 133
Cotton, Aimé 42, 43
Cotton, Eugène 104, 216
Courant, Ernest 166
Courant, Robert 56
Courrier, Robert 229
Courteline, Georges 70, 255
Coustham (Roubeau's assistant) 234
Couture, Pierre 113, 248
coworkers (listed) 196, 244–7, 288–90
Cox, Steve 289
Cribier, Daniel 207
cricket 130
critical mass calculations 103, 116
Croissy-sur-Seine 43
Croze (lecturer) 42
Cryogenics 243
Curie, Marie 208, 344
cyclotrons 122–4

Daladier, Edouard 69
'Dames' Delight' (Oxford bathing place) 131
Darmois, Eugène 42, 60
Darriulat, Pierre 123
Dash, Gregory 326
Dausset, Jean 343
Dautray, Robert 171
Dautry, Raoul 112, 113
David (AA's uncle) 23, 28, 84
de Bange field gun 73

De Benedetti, Carlo 336
Debiesse, Jean 154, 172–3, 183
Debré, Robert 346
Debye, Peter 359
Decerf, Anatole 32, 33
Decline and Fall (by Evelyn Waugh) 80
Delrieu, Jean-Marc 245–6
Denjoy, Arnaud 46, 342
DEP (Département d'Etudes des Piles, CEA) 170,
    171, 214
Destouches, Jean-Louis 55, 59
Devons, Sam 219
Devoret, Michel 247
Dharmatti (Indian professor) 329
diagram methods 351, 355
Dirac, Paul 54, 55, 117–18, 197, 206, 236, 284
Dirac's delta function 46, 55
Dirac's matrices 54
DNP (dynamic nuclear polarization) 271
    in liquids 188–90
    in solids 193–6
Doctor Lee's Chair of Experimental Philosophy
    (Oxford) 135, 146
Doctor of Philosophy, Oxford University 144–5
Doctor of Science
    Oxford University 299–300
    Paris University 49
Doppler effect 238
Doyle, Sir Arthur Conan 199
DPA (Direction des Piles Atomiques, CEA) 248
DPh (Direction de la Physique, CEA) 248, 249–50,
    251
DPNPS (Département de Physique Nucléaire et de
    Physique du Solide, CEA) 113, 216
Dubna (USSR)
    accelerator 166, 175
    neutron beam studies 286
Dubois, Simone 337
Duclaux, Jacques 346
Dumézil, Georges 224
duMond, Jesse 218
Dupouy, Gaston 159
Dyson, Freeman 151, 360, 361–2

Earth's magnetic field, measurement of 190–1
Ecole des Houches 116, 251
Ecole Normale Supérieure 41, 148, 177, 244
Ecole Normale Supérieure de Saint-Cloud 289
Ecole de Physique et Chimie 148, 185, 274
Ecole Polytechnique (Zurich) 289
Ecole Secondaire de Breteuil 24–8
Ecole Supérieure d'Electricité 101–3, 104–5
Ecole Supérieure des Télécommunications 274
Eddington, Arthur 52, 239
Edinburgh, conference (1949) on nuclear physics
    132–3, 134
Einstein, Albert 52, 57, 58, 120, 138, 182, 239,
    349–50, 353–4, 359
Eisenkramer (technician) 290
El Al airline 218, 219
electromagnetic forces 256
electronic antiferromagnetism 278, 282
electro-weak theory 357, 361
    experimental aspects of 328–9
elementary schools, discipline in 227

Elliott, Sir Roger 144, 145
Energie Nucléaire (periodical) 101
Enseignement du Futur 227
entropy 271–2
Ephrussi, Boris 343
Ertaud, Jacques 106, 110
ESR (electron spin resonance) 139–41
Estéve, Daniel 247
'Eves' (solid-state physicist) 213
experiment
  definition of 348
  theory tested by 14–15, 348–57
Ezratty, José 196, 244, 245

Fabergé jewels 315
Fabry, Charles 42, 43, 53, 60, 106
Far East travel 329–35
father (of AA)
  advice on return to Russia 55
  arrest 85, 86
  arrival in France 48
  background 6–7
  death 85
  internal exile 44
  progress in Russia 43–4
  wartime habits 84
Feher, George 325
Fender, B. F. F. 336
Fermi, Enrico 102, 213, 214
Fermilab
  conference (1977) on electro-weak theory 328
  Tevatron 123, 174
Fermi Prize 360
Fermi statistics 193
Fermon, Claude 289
ferrets 64
Ferretti (Italian theorist) 115
ferromagnetic ordering 269–71
Feynman, Richard 134, 135, 148, 165, 351, 362
FFI (French Forces of the Interior) 95, 96–100
field gun crew 98
Field medallists 226
First Three Minutes (by Steven Weinberg) 325
Fisher, Michael 299
Fock, Vladimir 54, 55
Fond-de-France 91
Fordson, Norval 326
Fouchet, Christian 255
Foundation Bernard Grégory 245
Fountaînebleu, military training at 75–7
Fournier, Gérard 290
France
  arrival in 23
  schooling in 17–18, 24–34
François the First 221
François-Poncet, André 1
Franco-Japanese Society 335
Fréchet, Maurice 342, 345–6
Freeman, Ray 196, 246
French history 26–7
French language 25–6, 31
  papers published in 152
French literature 31–2
Frenkel, Ya. 52, 54
Fréon (Auger's collaborator) 61

Friedel, Jacques 264, 340
Frisch, David 117
Frisch, Otto 116
Froissart, Marcel 228, 229
Fuchs, Klaus 120, 134

Gabor, Dennis 197
Galetti, Simone 65
Gamow, George 117, 208–9
Garnier, René 42, 46, 342
Gaudy (dinner at Jesus College, Oxford) 297, 301
Gaulle, General de 77, 97, 103, 172, 187, 191, 254, 255, 301
Geneva 181–2
geniuses 59–60
Gennes, Pierre-Gilles de 198, 199, 207, 228
Gentner (German physicist) 103
Georgia, rivalry with Armenia 310
Georgian toasts 306
German language 33, 51
Gif-sur-Yvette 170
Giraud, André 113, 253, 262, 263
Giscard d'Estaing, Valéry 227, 344, 347
Giulio Racah Lecture 340
Glaser, Donald 235
Glashow, Sheldon 123, 362
Glättli, Hans 246, 289
Glikman, M. and Mme 88, 91, 101
Godard, Jean-Luc 2
Goldhaber, Maurice 168
Goldman, Maurice 196, 199, 235, 244, 266, 274, 275, 276, 283, 312
Goldschmidt, Bertrand 109, 110, 253
Goldzahl (particle physicist) 252
Gorbachev, Mikhail 318, 319, 323
Gordon Conferences 324–5
Gordy, Walter 218
Gorter, Cornelius 142, 144, 159, 177
Gosse, René 91
Goudsmit, Sam 168, 360–1
Goursat, Edouard 46
Grand Ecoles 36
Grand Prix de la Recherche Scientifique 191
grand unification theory 357
grass, walking on 301
Greek language 30–1, 83
Gregg, John 289–90
Grégory, Bernard 225, 226
Grenoble
  University 90, 91, 94
  wartime stay 88–90
Griffith, James 141
Griffith, John 138, 299–300
Grimaud (Préfect de Police) 260
Grosjean (school principal) 83, 85
Grosser, Alfred 86
group theory 55, 119
Groves, General Leslie 207
Gudule (hen) 93
Guéron, Jules 109, 110, 183
Guéron, Maurice 245
Guillaumat, Pierre 112, 113, 250, 253
Guillermond, Antoine 39
Gumilev (Russian poet) 317

Haas, Arthur de 349–50
Hahn, Erwin 167, 170, 297
Hahn and Hartman method 277–8, 283
Halban, Hans 103, 148, 223, 224–5, 340
Hamburger, Jean 343, 347
Hansen, William 159, 167
Hardy, Walter 246
HART (Heavy Artillery on Rail Tracks) 69, 73
Hartree 54, 145
Hartree—Fock wave functions 54, 145
Harvard College
    colloquium talk (1978) 325
    fellowship (1952–3) 152
    lectureship (1953–4) 212
Hegel 229
Heisenberg, Werner 117, 132, 141, 182, 359
Heitler, Walter 359
Hermitage (Leningrad) 315, 317
Herpin, André 182, 215, 216, 251
Hewish, Anthony 197
high-resolution NMR 267–8
Hilbert, David 56, 340
Hirsch, Robert 113, 249, 253–4, 255, 262, 309, 310
Hodgkin, Dorothy 303
Hofman (schoolboy) 33–4
Holweck Prize 196–7, 275
Holweck pump 104
Hong Kong, visit to 332
Hood (school principal) 80–1, 82, 83
Horeau, Alain 230, 266
Horeau, Mme 230
horoscopes 254
Horowitz, Jules 103, 105, 106, 110, 120, 124, 144, 150, 152, 155, 170, 171, 248, 251, 253, 254
horses, AA's dislike of 75
'Hot Horse Herbie' approach 287
Hund, Friedrich 359
Hutchison, Clyde 158
hydrogen, accidents with 254, 298
hyperfine structure 140, 142–3, 354
Hyppolite, Jean 229

ILL (Institut Langevin—von Laue) 241
Imbert, Pierre 239
India, visit to 330–1
Indians' eating habits 330
Institute of Nuclear Physics (Algiers) 257–8
Institute for Physical Problems (Moscow) 204, 207, 308, 318, 320
Institute for Theoretical Physics (Moscow) 307
Institut Henri Poincaré 50, 51, 55, 117, 197
interdisciplinary research 280–1
interpreters 210–11, 308
intestinal blockage (1982) 302
Israel, visits to 218–19, 340
Israeli girl friend 45–6
Ivanenko (Russian professor) 207–8, 209

Jacob, François 343, 358
Jacquinot, Jacques-François 289
Jacrot 207
Janoczy (Hungarian physicist) 134
Japan, visit to 332–5

Japanese bicycle 333
Japanese food 334
Jeffries, Carson 167, 235, 242–3
Jerme, Denis 245
Jesus College (Oxford)
    AA as Honorary Fellow 300, 301
    AA as student 127–9
Jeunesse Patriote 39, 45
Jews
    attitudes to 19, 45, 308, 340
    status declaration (France, 1940) 79, 80
Jèze, Gaston 45
Joe (AA's uncle) 6
Joliot, Frédéric 61–2, 103, 107–8, 113, 147–9, 201, 222, 223
Joliot-Curie, Irène 103, 148, 344
Josephson, Brian 197, 240
Journal de Physique 124, 152
Julia, Gaston 46, 342
Julien, Charles-André 33
Jupiter accelerator proposal 257–8

Kalinga Prize 209
Kapitza, Piotr 204, 207, 308, 359
Kastler, Alfred 89, 153, 177, 178, 183, 220, 260, 340, 342, 343–4
Kaufmann, Walter 349
Kazan (USSR), conference (1969) on ESR 307–8
Kelvin, Lord (William Thomson) 136
Kent University, Doctor *honoris causa* 303
Khâgne 35, 36
Khalatnikov, Isaac 305
Khalatnikova, Mrs 306, 307
Khrushchev, Nikita 202, 203
Kiev (USSR) 210
King Solomon method 195, 277
Kipling, Rudyard 271, 288
Kirkwood (physical chemist) 359–60
Klein, Eva 65
Klim (butler) 82
Kohn, Walter 199, 214
Kolka (childhood friend) 10–11
Kosygin (Russian premier) 255
Kowarski, Lew 103, 106–7, 108–9, 110, 125, 147, 148, 152, 153–4, 250, 264
Kramers, Hendrik 359
Kremlin, visit (1972) to 315
Kronig, R. de L. 361
Kubo, Ryogo 329, 334
Kuhn, Heinrich 137
Kummer, Wolfgang 335
Kurti, Nicholas 136, 137, 197, 297, 298, 302
Kusch, Polycarp 161, 165, 351
Kyoto (Japan) 334

Lacassagne, Antoine 342
ladies' fashions, childhood viewpiont 13
La Ferrière d'Allevard 91–2, 94, 96
Lagarrique, André 225, 226
La Jolla (USA) 214, 325–6
Lamb, Willis 124, 165, 238, 351
Lamb shift 238
Landau, Lev 117, 205–6, 207, 209
Landesman, André 196, 199, 244, 245
Langevin, Paul 58, 60, 208

Laporte, Yves 230
Latarjet, Raymond 345
Latin 25
Laue, Max von 51
Laval, Pierre 69
Lebedev Institute (USSR) 304
Le Burdin 93
Lee, Ben 329
Lee, T. D. 208, 329, 353
Lehmann, Pierre 164
Lelong (lecturer at Grenoble) 90
Lemaître, G. (cosmologist) 340–1
Lenin, Vladimir Ilyich 17
Leningrad
   official visit (1956) 210
   tourist trips to 314–15, 317
LEP (Large Electron–Positron) collider 123
Leprince-Ringuet, Louis 134, 153, 224, 225–6
leptons 356
Lequesme, Susanne 85; *see also* wife (of AA)
Les Houches 116, 251
level-crossing (NMR technique) 292–3
Lévêque, Antoine 164
Levy-Mandel, Robert 251
Lewis, Sinclair 36
Leyden University 226, 289, 291, 339, 358
Liberté (trans-Atlantic ship) 156
Licence (university degree) 41–3, 47
Lifschitz/Livshits, Eugene 205, 313
Lindemann, Frederick (Lord Cherwell) 136–7
Lindemann (aircraft) spin manoeuvre 136–7
linear electron accelerators 124, 256
lithium fluoride 195, 276, 281
lithium hydride 281, 282
Little (English girl) 65
Livingston, Stanley 166
Llewellyn-Smith, Christopher 337
Lobachevski 307
Lomonosov University (Moscow) 207
London, Fritz 60, 350, 359
Lorentz, Hendrik Antoon 57, 349, 358
Lorentz Chair (Leyden) 226, 339
Lorentz Institute 340
Lorentz Medal 358
   winners listed 358–61
Los Angeles 167
Louvain Catholic University 340
Luchikov, Slava 247
Lwoff, André 343, 344
Lycée Buffon 24, 28
Lycée Janson de Sailly 28–37
Lyon-la Doua 97, 98
Lysenko, Trofim 203

McCarthyism, effects of 116, 153
Maclean, Donald 360
Macmillan, Harold 296, 300(footnote)
Maddox, John 321
magic crystal 242–3
magnetohydrodynamics research 261
magnetometers 190–1
Malinovski, Alexandre 247
Mancinelli (CERN Review Committee member) 338
maquis 94
Mariani (Brillouin's assistant) 60

Marina, Princess (Duchess of Kent) 303
marine zoology 64–5
marriage (of AA) 85, 97
Marshall, Walter 239, 240
Maryland, conference (1952) on magnetism 157, 158–9
Massain, Robert 32
Math. Elem. 37
mathematicians, attitude to weapons 90
mathematics 15, 32, 46–7
Mathématiques Générales course 40
Maurice (cook at Hood's school) 81
Maurras, Charles 69
Maxwell, James Clerk 135, 197
Mayer, André 346
Mayer-Goeppert, Maria 353
Mécanique Rationelle course 42
medicine, as career 36–7, 40
Mendelssohn, Kurt 137, 243
Mériel, Pierre 290
Merton College (Oxford)
   AA as Honorary Fellow 300
   dining at High Table 295–7
   private party (1983) 302
mesotron 355
Messiah, Albert 121–2, 171, 182, 204, 219, 251, 263
Meyer, Philippe 121
Michel, Louis 132
Michelson, Albert 348
microscopic probes 277–8, 283
Migdal, Arcady 305, 315
Mikes, George 130
military training 70–8, 98
Minder, Robert 224
Mirabelle project 254, 257, 308–11
Mitterand, François 227
Moch, Jules 114
Molière (quoted) 96, 343
Molotov, Viatcheslav 207, 208
Monod, Jacques 89, 260, 343, 345
Monroe, Marilyn 199
Montel, Paul 342, 345
Moon, Philip 237, 238
Moroccan soldiers 99
Moroccan workmen 28
Moscow
   childhood house 9, 204, 306–7
   childhood in 5–19
   tourist trip (1972) 315–16
   visit (1956) to 203–4, 207, 210
Mössbauer, Rudolf 119, 237, 240, 241
Mössbauer effect 237, 238, 241
mother (of AA)
   appearance 8 9
   backround 7
   education 7–8
   on medicine as career 37
   wartime experiences 86, 88, 91, 93
motion narrowing 163
Mott, Sir Nevill *Preface* 217
Mott and Massey 197
Mulhouse 99
muon 292
muonium 292
μSR (muon spin resonance) 291–3

National Academy of Sciences (USA), Foreign Associates 58, 226, 354
National Yosemite Park (USA) 167–8
Nature 321
Néel, Louis 191, 205, 277, 278, 305
negative spin temperature concept 162
negative temperature
  characteristics of system at 311
  Soviet regime viewed as system at 311–12
Nemours
  living conditions at 74
  military training at 72–5
Netherlands, visits to 144, 152, 155, 339–40
Neumann, John von 90, 109
neutrino 134
neutron, discovery of 148
Nevsky Prospekt (Leningrad) 317
New Delhi 330–1
New Quantum Theory 53
News and Mosaics 13
Newton, Sir Isaac 161
Niagara Falls 168
Nierenberg, W. 161
Nimrod accelerator 174
NMO (nuclear magnetic order) 269–71, 275–6
NMR (nuclear magnetic resonance)
  discovery of 159, 355
  high-resolution NMR 267–8
NMR imaging 176, 268, 355
Nobel Prize
  comments about 166, 361
  effect on young winners 240, 241
  refusal of 236
  winners 58, 132, 133, 134, 148, 160, 161, 165, 177, 180, 205, 240, 304
  Collège de France members 226
Nomenklatura 87
Nora (daughter of family doctor) 80, 82
Normaliens 148, 149, 228, 250, 289, 290
Novosibirsk (USSR) 320
Nozières, Philippe 228–9
nuclear antiferromagnetism 278–80, 282
nuclear β-decay 352
nuclear electrons 102
nuclear ferromagnetism 269, 271
nuclear fission, discovery of 148
nuclear forces 256
Nuclear Magnetism, Order and Disorder (by AA and Goldman) 275, 304, 312, 313, 326
nuclear polarization 176
nuclear pseudomagnetism 284–6, 288
nuclear reactor design 108
Nyura (childhood friend) 307

Oak Ridge (Tennessee, USA) 218
Odehnal, Milan 247
Old Quantum Theory 53
ONC (Office of Naval Research, USA) 168
onomastics 12
Onsager, Lars 359–60
Oppenheimer, Robert 2, 207, 213
optical pumping 177
Orbit Group 171–2, 173, 251
order, external and internal 269–71

Order and Disorder, see Nuclear Magnetism, Order and Disorder
ordered rotating phases 283–4
Orlov, Yuri 307, 312
Orme des Merisiers 244, 256, 257, 288
Orwell, George 12, 313
Overhauser, Albert 164, 189, 193
Overhauser effect 164, 177, 188, 189, 194
Overhauser shift 245
Oxford
  AA's reaction to 125
  house rented in 297–8
Oxford University
  AA as student 127–46
  AA as Visiting Fellow 294–303
  background information 127–31
  doctor *honoris causa* 299–300
  Honorary Fellows 300–1
  thesis (1950) examination 144
Oxford University Press 55, 197–9, 244, 275

Packard (co-discoverer of NMR) 159, 167, 184
Pahlia (lodger in Oxford) 130
Panier (civil servant) 258
Panier commission 258
paramagnetic electron spin resonance 141–3
paramagnetic impurities, method of producing 291
Paris
  arrival in 23
  conference (1950) on theoretical physics 134
parity non-conservation 352–3
Parker, Dorothy 176
'Parson's Pleasure' (Oxford bathing place), 130–1
particle physics, introductory course 251
Pasquette (technician) 290
Paul, W. 336
Pauli, Wolfgang 117, 119–20, 124, 151–2, 180, 206, 350, 359, 360–1
PCN (Physics, Chemistry, and Natural Science) course 38–40
Pecker (astrophysicist) 91
Pecqueur, Michel 113, 266
Peierls, Lady Genia 117
Peierls, Sir Rudolf 115–17, 124, 153, 238, 302, 360
Peierls instability 116
Pellerin, Jean 1, 204, 249, 252, 308, 311
Pennsylvania, University of 214, 220
Penrose, R. P. 142–3
perestroika 323–4
Pernot (CEA official) 121
Perrichet 30, 32
Perrin, Francis 47, 49–51, 53, 59, 103, 107, 113, 148, 149, 154, 183, 214, 215, 220, 223, 224, 226, 248, 249, 250, 253, 258, 262, 264–5
Perrin, Jean 47, 50, 61
perturbed angular correlations 162–4
Petiau, Pierre 337
Petit, Claudine 65
Petrosyants, Andronik 309, 310
Peychès, Ivan 60
Peyrefitte, Alain 255, 309
Peyrou, Charles 225
Philby, Kim 360
philosophers, writings by 62
Physical Review 50, 143, 163, 168, 180, 181, 272

Physical Review Letters 178, 238, 240
Physique Générale course 42, 43, 63
Pinot, Marcel 290
Pioneers 18
pions 134, 256
Pisarev (Russian journalist) 37
Planck, Max 349, 358–9, 361
Poincaré, Henri 57
Poincaré, Raymond 50
Poitiers, military training at 77
Poitrenaud, Jacqueline 245, 246
polarized beams 233–4, 280
polarized targets 234–6, 280
Polonski, M. and Mme 91, 92, 93
Polytechniciens 106, 228, 250, 253
Pomerantchuk (Russian physicist) 205
Pompidou, Georges 191
Pont-de-Claix 98
Ponte, Maurice 53
Pontecorvo, Bruno 134, 306
Pontifical Academy 365
'Popov' (Russian physicist) 304
Popper, Karl 238, 348
popularist books 56, 208
Porneuf, Madeleine 293
positron, discovery of 148
Pouillet (administrative assistant) 216
Pound, Robert 159, 161–2, 163, 168, 186, 192, 212, 239
Pound box 162
Powell, Cecil 133, 134
Pré, du (Dutch physicist) 192
Prentki, Jacques 170, 201
Press contacts 255–6
Prigogin 208
Principles of Nuclear Magnetism (by AA) 55, 161, 163, 181, 186, 188, 194, 197–9, 220
  Japanese translation 334
  misunderstanding of topic 268
  Russian translation 312, 313
private schools, teaching in during war 80–3, 85–6
Proca, Alexandre 109, 115, 132
Proceedings of the Royal Society 143
Proctor, Warren 192, 195, 196, 246
Proctor's Walk 144
Prokhorov, Alexandre 304, 322
proton synchroton 123, 173
Provotorov (Russian physicist) 235, 304
proximity fuse 100
Prugne, Pierre 308, 309
Pryce, Maurice 108, 118, 120, 125, 128, 132, 139, 141–2, 143, 145, 152, 197, 327
pseudomagnetic moments 279
pseudonuclear magnetism 287–8
pumpkin dishes 81
Pupils' Committee 16, 18
Purcell, E. M. 44, 144, 155, 159, 160, 164, 180, 192, 193, 269, 320
Pushkin, Aleksandr 1, 2, 11, 135, 313, 320, 364
puttees 70, 75

quantum chromodynamics 356
quantum electrodynamics 350–2, 354
  divergencies of 118, 355
  renormalization of 134, 351, 352, 355

quantum theory
  books on 51, 53, 109, 121
  experimental basis of 349
quarantaine, meaning of word 74
quarks 356
Queen Elizabeth the First 128, 129

rabbit shooting 63–4
Rabi, Isidore 160, 164, 165, 187
Racah, Giulio 340
radioelectricity course (at *Supelec*) 101–2
Raissa (AA's aunt) 84
Ramsey, Norman 144, 160–1, 164, 213, 285
Raphael (AA's uncle) 8
Rayleigh, Lord 135
recoilless nuclei 236–9
Redfield, Alfred 163, 198
red shift 239–40
Reflections of a Physicist (by AA) 152, 159, 165, 180, 188, 228, 256, 262, 321, 347
Rehovot (Israel), conference on nuclear physics 218
relativity
  books on 51
  Bouasse's reaction to 52
Rémy, miniature firing range 75–6
Renard, Jules (quoted) 1, 109–10, 118, 361
Renon, Gérard 113
renormalization theory 134, 351, 352, 355
research students, treatment of 61–2
resonance condition (in cyclotrons) 122
'Richard' 83
Richards, Sir Rex 296, 300(footnote), 302
Robert, Claude 245
Robert, Jacques 253, 254
Robert, Louis 224
Robinson, Nevile 242
Rocard, Yves 53
Roinel, Yves 288–9
Romanovich, Sergey 7
Rome 365
Roosevelt, Franklin 323
Roscoff (Brittany) 64–5
Rose, Morris 177
Rosenblum, Szolem 104, 210
Rosenfeld, Léon, 110, 124, 133, 150–1
Rossi, Lieutenant 96
rotating crystal method 243
rotating-frame concept 272–4
Roubeau, Pierre 234, 235, 290
Royal Academy of The Netherlands 358
Royal Society (UK), Foreign Members 58, 226, 357–8
royalties
  Oxford University Press 298
  Russian translations 313
Rubbia, Carlo 123, 235, 337
Rubinstein, Mlle 82, 83
Runyon, Damon 287
Russia
  AA's boycott of regime 307
  childhood in 5–19
  departure from 5–6
  schooling in 16–19
  thermodynamic model of regime 311–12

Russia (*cont.*)
 tourist trip (1972) 313–16
 tourist trip (1986) 316–17
 visit (1956) to 201–11
 visit (1961) to 303–4
 visit (1965) to 308–10
 visit (1968) to 305–7
 visit (1969) to 307–8
 visit (1987) to 318–22
Russian press 319
Russian publishing systems 44, 52, 312–13
Russian theorists 286
Rutherford, Lord 236, 268
Ryle, Martin 197
Ryter, Charles 196, 235, 245

Saclay (CEA HQ) 170
Sagdeev, Roald 324
Saint Basil's Church (Moscow) 5
Saint-Cyr, military training at 77–8
Saint-Raphaël 80–3, 85–6, 87–8, 89–90
Sakharov, Andrei 259, 307, 312, 318, 320–2
Salam, Abdus 123, 362
Samuel (Brelot's assistant) 90
Sandvold, Haakar 336
San Francisco 167
Sartre, Jean-Paul 89, 236, 260
Saturne synchrotron 174, 251
Schlumberger, Marcel 62–3
Schmidt (professor at Leyden) 291
schooling
 in France 17–18, 24–34
 in Russia 16–19
Schopper, Herwig 337
Schrieffer, Robert 180, 350
Schrödinger, Erwin 359
Schwartz, Laurent 37, 55, 89, 260, 343
Schweinerei 187, 188
Schwinger, Julian 134, 165, 208, 214, 362
sconce 128–9
s-configuration 143
SCS (Super Synchrotron Collider) 174, 175–6
Scythian treasure 315, 317
Seattle, conference (1956) 208, 209–10
Seattle (Washington, USA) 326–7
semiconductors 356
Serpukhov (USSR), accelerator 308–10
Serre, Jean-Pierre 221, 343
75mm field guns 73, 76, 98
Shakespearian actors 12
Shaw, George Bernard 12
Shockley, William 165
Siberian Ulcer 8
Simon, Sir Francis 137, 146, 298
Sir Henry Savile Fellowship 301
Slater, J. C. 158
Slichter, Charles 56, 164
Smyth report 108
Snyder, Hartland 166
Solomon, Ionel 171, 177, 183, 184, 185, 190, 191, 235, 239, 244, 325
Solvay Conferences 57, 208
Sommerfeld, Arnold 117, 359
Sorbonne courses 41–3
Soviet . . . , *see* Russian . . .

SPA (Service de Physique Appliquée, CEA) 261
SPCN course 41–2
spin–lattice relaxation 188
spin temperature concept 182, 191–3, 271
SPM (Service de Physique Mathematique, CEA) 170–1
SPSRM (Service de Physique du Solide et de Resonance Magnétique, CEA) 215, 216
SPS (Super Proton Synchrotron) 173
SRO (Student Reserve Officer) 72, 75, 76, 77
Stalin, Joseph 84–5, 202, 311
Stanford (USA) 167
status-of-Jews declaration 79, 80
Stefan (lodger in Moscow) 9
Stern, Otto 350
Stevens, Ken 144, 145
Stoner, E. C. 158
STO (Service du Travail Obligatoire) 88, 94
strategic bombing, Lindemann's approach 137–8
Strauss, Admiral 2
strong focusing 165–6
 savings due to 174
strong interactions 356
student riots (1968) 230, 259–60
Sullivan, Neil 246–7
Supelec 101–3, 104–5, 288
superconductivity, theory of 180, 350
superconductors 356
Superstant 256, 258–9
synchrotron radiation, theory of 123–4

tapirs (private pupils), taught by AA 44–5, 63, 86
Tata Institute of Physics 330
Tatyana, (AA's aunt) 6
τ particles 353
Taupe 35, 36
taupins 36
taxicab syndrome 173–4
Tbilisi (USSR) 306
Teillac, Jean 113
Terray, Lionel (quoted) 267
Thailand, visit to 331–2
theory
 definition of 348
 experimental testing of 14–15, 348–57
θ particles 353
Thirion, Jacques 216, 233
Thom, René 347, 348
Thomson, Sir Joseph J. 135
Thomson, William (Lord Kelvin) 136
thulium phosphate 287
Tokamak machine 259
Tokyo 333, 334
Tolman, Richard 197
Tolstoy, Aleksey 11
Tolstoy, Leo 11, 12
Tomonaga, Sin-itiro 134, 165, 208, 362
'Tooft, Gerhardt 361–2
Torrey, Henry 159
Townes, Charles 177, 304, 361
TP (*travaux pratiques*) 39
translation (of AA's books) 312, 313
Trocadero theatre (Paris) 31
Trocheris, Michel 103, 105, 106, 108, 110, 170, 171, 182, 197, 251

Trotsky, Leon 17
truncated dipolar interaction 273
tunnelling mechanism 208
Tutton salts 142, 144–5
TV filming 183
two-lattices model (of antiferromagnetism) 205, 277, 278

Uhlenbeck, George 168, 360–1
Ulam, Stanislaw 90
ultrarelativistic accelerators 175
'Underhauser' 189–90
Underhauser effect 189, 191, 194
UNESCO, Scientific Director 61
unit councils (CEA) 261, 262
uranium fission 103, 116
Urbina, Christian 289
USA
    fellowship (1952–3) 154, 156–69
    immigration procedure 157
    tour (1955) of resonance laboratories 184–5
    visa application 153–4
    visits to 324–9
USSR—see Russia

Valbreuze, de (Director of *Superelec*) 100
Val-Richer (estate in Normandy) 63
Vancouver, University of British Columbia 145, 327
Van de Graaff, Robert 58, 164
Van der Meer, Simon 123
Van Vleck, John 141, 144, 152, 158, 159–60, 197, 214, 299, 361
Varenna conference centre 218
Varian instruments 183, 184, 191
Varna (Bulgaria) 341
'Vera Semyonovna' 16, 17
Viansson-Ponté, Pierre (journalist) 259
Vichy *Milice* 88, 91
Vodoz, J. 336
Vögeli, Miss 82
Volkov, George 108, 327
vortices theory 206–7
Vu-Hoang-Chau 276

Waller, Ivar 240
wall newspapers 16–17, 18
Ward, John 145
wartime rations 87
war
    declaration of 69
    end of 100
Washington University (Seattle, USA) 326

Watteau, Antoine 51
Waugh, Evelyn 80, 201
wave mechanics 59
    probabilistic interpretation of 132
weak focusing 174
weak interactions 356
Weil, André 343
Weinberg, Steven 123, 299, 325, 362
Weiss, Pierre 141
Weiss field 283
Weisskopf, Victor 109, 150, 151, 152, 298
Weiss mean field theory 276
Wenckebach, Tom 289, 291
Wentzel, Gregor 119, 359
Westinghouse 212–13
Whittaker and Watson 56
wife (of AA)
    in Cambridge (UK) 118
    in Far East 332
    first meeting 85
    heart attack 327, 345, 364
    marriage 85, 97
    met Fermi 214
    in Oxford 131, 297
    papal audience 354
    in Russia 313–16
    in USA 154m 156–69
Wigner, Eugène 208, 322
Wigner–Kowarski formula 108–9
Wigner–Weisskopf theory 151
Williams, F. I. B. 245, 256
Wilson, Sir Harold 301–2
Winchester College 138
Winter, Jacques 183, 196, 244–5, 274
Winter, Stanislas 251
Wolff, Etienne 230
Wolff Prize 151
Wykeham Chair of Theoretical Physics (Oxford) 139, 144

Yang, C. N. 208, 329, 350, 353
Yukawa, Hideki 133, 208
Yukawa particles 133–4, 356
Yvon, Jacques 105, 113, 149–50, 152, 154, 170, 171, 183, 214, 215, 216, 248, 262

Zagorsk monastery (USSR) 315
Zavoysky (Russian physicist) 141, 307
Zeeman effect 140
Zeeman order 269, 271, 272
Zener, Clarence 212
Ziman, John 145
Zinoviev 8